ENCYCLOPEDIA

of

SOCIAL ISSUES

ENCYCLOPEDIA
of
SOCIAL ISSUES

Volume 2

Chronic Fatigue Syndrome – Esalin Institute

Editor
JOHN K. ROTH

Marshall Cavendish
New York • London • Toronto

OUACHITA TECHNICAL COLLEGE

Project Editor: Robert McClenaghan
Research Supervisor: Jeffry Jensen
Acquisitions Editor: Mark Rehn
Photograph Editor: Valerie Krein
Production Editor: Cynthia Breslin Beres
Proofreading Supervisor: Yasmine A. Cordoba
Layout: James Hutson

Published By
Marshall Cavendish Corporation
99 White Plains Road
Tarrytown, New York 10591-9001
United States of America

Library of Congress Cataloging-in-Publication Data

Encyclopedia of social issues / editor, John K. Roth
    p. cm.
   Includes bibliographical references and index.
   1. United States—Social conditions—Encyclopedias. 2. United States—Economic conditions—Encyclopedias. 3. United States—Politics and government—Encyclopedias. 4. Canada—Social conditions—Encyclopedias. 5. Canada—Economic conditions—Encyclopedias.—6. Canada—Politics and government—Encyclopedias.—I. Roth, John K.
HN57.E59 1997
306′.0973—dc20   96-38361
ISBN 0-7614-0568-2 (set)   CIP
ISBN 0-7614-0570-4 (volume 2)

First Printing

PRINTED IN THE UNITED STATES OF AMERICA

Contents

CONTENTS

ENCYCLOPEDIA

of

SOCIAL ISSUES

Chronic Fatigue Syndrome (CFS): Medical condition in which patients experience prolonged, intense fatigue and other symptoms, including painful bones and joints, loss of memory and the ability to concentrate, and difficulty in sleeping. The syndrome gained attention during the mid-1980's, when numerous cases were reported around Lake Tahoe, California. Names that became associated with the condition included fibromylagia, chronic mononucleosis, Epstein-Barr virus, and the "yuppie flu." By the mid-1990's, however, many patients and physicians had decided that the term "chronic fatigue immune dysfunction syndrome (CFIDS)" best conveyed the complexity and origins of the condition.

Although some estimates have claimed that as many as five million Americans suffer from CFS, a precise diagnostic test has not been developed to determine if the syndrome exists in an individual patient. The cause has also eluded researchers. Theories about its origins range from genetic weaknesses in the immune system, the presence of undetected viruses, impairment of muscles, and the effects of environmental toxins that create chemical sensitivities and weaken the immune system. Medical skeptics assert that CFS might be psychological in origin, and medical associations question whether the syndrome really exists. Such skeptics often lump CFS with other psychological disorders such as the nineteenth century condition called neurasthenia.

For patients with the array of specific symptoms that accompany CFS, there exists little doubt of the reality of the illness. The CENTERS FOR DISEASE CONTROL AND PREVENTION (CDC) has established a group of symptoms that serve as a basis for identification and diagnosis. They include extreme fatigue for six months or more, low-grade fever, swollen lymph nodes, headaches, muscle soreness, loss of memory or concentration, and sore throat. The syndrome occurs more frequently among women than men. Patients often find themselves immobilized, unable to hold a job or even work at home. Treatments include prolonged rest, a regimen of antibiotics, and intravenous infusion of blood products to bolster a flagging immune system. Sometimes the syndrome clears up after a few months or years; in some patients, however, it persists for years without tangible relief.

To publicize the syndrome and raise national awareness of those impaired by its effects, patient groups have created a number of lobbying and informational bodies, including the National Chronic Fatigue Syndrome and Fibromylagia Association of Kansas City and the Chronic Fatigue and Immune Dysfunction Syndrome Association of Charlotte, North Carolina. The work of these groups has led to government-funded research on CFS at the Centers for Disease Control and Prevention and the NATIONAL INSTITUTES OF HEALTH (NIH). Efforts to define a cause for the syndrome, to identify effective treatments, and to determine the prevalence of CFS among patients in the United States and other countries are ongoing. Research on the workings of the immune system and the ways in which it can be disabled or severely damaged may offer important clues about the future treatment of this baffling condition.

SUGGESTED READINGS: Jesse Λ. Stoff and Charles R. Pellegrino's *Chronic Fatigue Syndrome: The Hidden Epidemic* (New York: Random House, 1988) and David S. Bell's *The Disease of a Thousand Names: CFIDS: Chronic Fatigue/Immune Dysfunction Syndrome* (Lyndonville, N.Y.: Pollard Publications, 1991) are good introductions to the medical and public health issues surrounding CFS.

Chy Lung v. Freeman (1875): U.S. Supreme Court Case. *Chy Lung v. Freeman* arose from a California statute that required a bond for paupers, convicted criminals, and "lewd and debauched women" entering the state. The Court, reviewing an instance of twenty women who had been detained, ruled that the statute violated constitutional principles of federalism, because regulations concerning the admission of foreign subjects into the country belongs exclusively to Congress and not to the states. The Court emphasized that the California statute could enable a state to embroil the United States in a conflict with a foreign country.

Circumcision, female. *See* **Clitoridectomy**

Circumcision, male: Removal of the foreskin of the penis. In many cultures, including the United States, circumcision is a routine, but controversial procedure performed early in infancy.

The foreskin is the richly innervated and sensitive tissue that sheaths the shaft of the penis. While its intact presence can add to the tactile pleasure of sexual stimulation, its actual function is unknown. Removal of the foreskin reduces the amount of penile sensation but in no other way interferes with sexual or reproductive function. (Circumcision should not be confused with castration, which is a totally different procedure that removes the testes, resulting in reduced hormone production, impotence, and infertility.)

In many cultures, circumcision is done as a religious or other social ritual. In some non-Western, especially tribal, cultures, circumcision is done as a puberty ritual by cutting off the foreskin without using anesthesia; when a boy is ready to show that he can endure the painful procedure without complaint, he is initiated into manhood. In cultures with a Judeo-Christian heritage, including the United States and Canada, circumcision is done in early infancy as a religious ritual (more often by burning rather than by cutting off the tissue, but in either case without anesthesia).

In the West, what began as a Jewish tradition has evolved into a standard medical procedure. Most Western doctors routinely recommend circumcision of newborn boys regardless of the parents' religious background. In fact, many people have never seen an uncircumcised penis, and many circumcised individuals do not even know that they have been circumcised. The rationale for circumcision as a medical procedure is that bacterial infections of the penis, as well as some SEXUALLY TRANSMITTED DISEASES, are more frequent in cultures where individuals remain uncircumcised than in cultures that practice circumcision; this effect has been attributed to the fact that smegma (a combination of semen, dirt, and bacteria) can accumulate in the folds of the foreskin if it is not washed thoroughly and frequently. This supposed health benefit of circumcision is debatable, however, as some argue that the important factor is not whether a culture practices circumcision but whether people have access to clean water and are educated about personal hygiene.

Whether to circumcise a newborn baby is, for many, an ethical issue: The newborn has no say in whether or not to undergo the painful procedure, and the health benefits are minimal at best. Other concerns include the fact that the procedure is irreversible and the fact that any surgical procedure has risks of its own (the risk of removing too much tissue and creating a serious deformity, the risk of excessive blood loss, and the risks of anesthesia). As a result of this debate, if changing practices in Western health care lead to a reduction of "unnecessary" surgeries, circumcision may again become a religious ritual for those who choose it rather than a routine procedure recommended to everyone.

Shannon Faulkner becomes the first woman to attend the Citadel military academy. (Reuters/Corbis-Bettmann)

Citadel case (1995): Sexual discrimination and harassment controversy. Shannon Faulkner, a female high-school student, brought a class-action suit against the Citadel, an all-male, state-supported, military college. The Citadel's male-only admissions policy was found to be illegal under the EQUAL-PROTECTION clause of the Fourteenth Amendment, and the school was given three options by the court: to admit women, to become a private institution, or to devise a plan that would provide equal opportunity for women. Faulkner was admitted to the school in 1995 amid much public scrutiny, but she dropped out shortly after entering, claiming severe SEXUAL HARASSMENT and incidents of hazing. Nevertheless, she and others proclaimed her actions as representing a victory for women's rights.

Citizen's Clearinghouse for Hazardous Waste (CCHW): Environmental advocacy group founded in 1981. CCHW was founded by Lois Gibbs and other residents of Love Canal, a community outside Buffalo, New York, who successfully fought for relocation for local families living in homes that had been built over

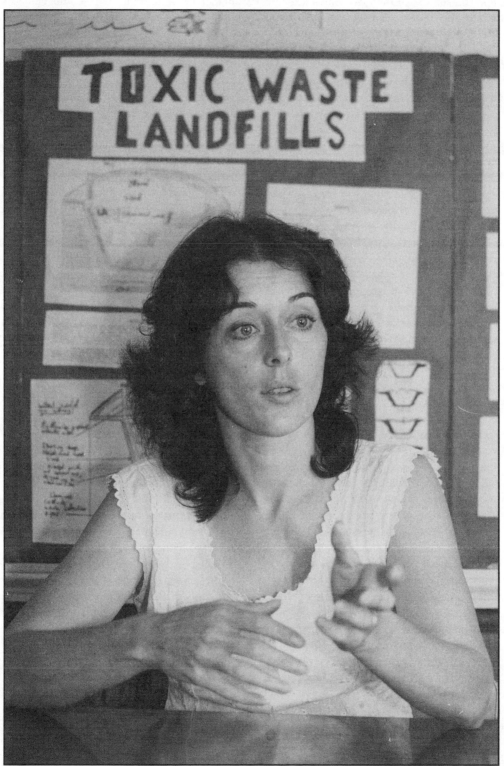

Citizen's Clearinghouse for Hazardous Waste founder Lois Gibbs addresses reporters. (AP/Wide World Photos)

a toxic dump. The success of the Love Canal struggle helped initiate the federal SUPERFUND program. CCHW has been assisting people struggling for environmental justice since 1981. Through organizing, leadership development, research, and technical assistance, CCHW provides skills and information to start local environmental groups, strengthen existing groups, and develop networks crossing class and race lines to protect public health and the environment.

Citizenship, Canadian: Canada was created by waves of immigration, beginning with English and French settlers who were attracted to the natural resources and vastness of North America. Previous to this, North and South America were populated by divergent tribes; in contemporary terminology, these peoples are sometimes referred to as the First Nations, Aboriginal Peoples, or Native Indians. The history of Canadian settlement involved intermarriage between native women and European settlers, with the women providing survival skills in the harsh climate, the protection of their tribes, and continuity born from conjugal relationships.

Background. The long-term struggle between English and French colonial powers is the backdrop from which to understand the eventual emergence of the Dominion of Canada under the control of the British Crown. As time progressed, however, more and more European immigrants came to settle in the area, first along the St. Lawrence seaway and the easterly parts of the country, then moving westward through southern Ontario and into the prairie provinces. The peak year of Canadian IMMIGRATION was 1912, when 400,000 men and women arrived at Canadian shores. Immigration from non-European countries was selective; men who were potential laborers for the railway were permitted access to the country, but they could not be accompanied by their families. Chinese laborers were forced to pay a head tax in order to enter the country.

In 1976, the Canadian Parliament passed an immigration act that changed Canada's immigration laws. From this point onward, fundamental principles of nondiscrimination, family reunion, and humanitarian concern for refugees and the promotion of Canada's social, economic, demographic, and cultural goals would direct Canada's immigration policies.

Starting in 1990, the government of Canada announced a five-year plan determining the absolute number of immigrants who could enter the country each year. On an annual basis, this number is reassessed and adjusted. In order to understand Canadian citizenship and immigration procedures and policies, its legal, social, and demographic components must be understood.

Legal Issues. Canadian citizenship can be acquired in three ways: by birth in the country, by Canadian parentage, and by application. Canadian citizens have an absolute right to come into or remain in the country, to seek political office, and to vote in federal, provincial, and municipal elections.

While not Canadian citizens, another group of persons who have the right to come into and remain in the country (if certain conditions are met) are referred to as "permanent residents," a status acquired through the Canadian immigration process. Permanent residents of Canada can apply, after having met specific criteria, to become Canadian citizens.

A number of legal options are available for a person wishing to immigrate to Canada. The three major immigration categories are family class, refugees, and independent immigrants. Family-class immigrants are sponsored by a Canadian citizen or a permanent resident nineteen years-of-age or older. Family-class applicants, including but not limited to wife or husband, dependent child, and parents, are not assessed under Canada's immigration point system but must meet the basic criteria of good health and character. In these cases, the sponsoring relative has to assume responsibility for the basic needs of the applicant for up to ten years. Since the 1970's, immigrants entering Canada with the status of family class have steadily increased, but current economic and political pressures are now de-emphasizing this category of immigrants.

Refugees entering Canada have their status defined by the United Nations Convention and Protocols on the Status of Refugees. Central to the definition of a refugee is the individual's well-founded fear of persecution for reasons of race, religion, nationality, or membership in a particular social or political group.

Independent immigrants, unlike family-class immigrants and refugees, include entrepreneurs, investors, assisted relatives (who do not qualify under the family-class specifications), and self-employed individuals. They are judged on various characteristics for determining suitability for life in Canada. From a maximum of 136 possible points, independent immigrants are assessed on education, vocational training, employment experience, the demand in Canada for their occupa-

Many recent Canadian immigrants have come from Asian countries. (Dick Hemingway)

tion, arranged employment, location of choice, age, knowledge of English or French, and personal suitability. There is a separate bonus for assisted relatives and for immigrants who are self-employed. Depending on which immigrant category one qualifies for, the minimum points required for entry into Canada vary; twenty-five points are required for an entrepreneur or investor, while a minimum of seventy points are needed for the category self-employed, skilled worker, or assisted relative.

Immigration patterns have changed substantially in recent decades. Until the 1960's, most immigrants came from Western European backgrounds. More recent immigrants come largely from Asia, the Caribbean, Africa, and South Africa. Hence, Canada is more culturally and ethnically diverse than in the past.

Social Issues. From a social perspective, there are two distinct cultural ideologies that can be identified to explain the integration of divergent racial, cultural, and ethnic groups into a host society: "melting pot" and "multiculturalism." Within the MELTING-POT ideology, immigrants are expected to assimilate into the host culture. MULTICULTURALISM, on the other hand, encourages immigrants to retain their ethnic and cultural distinctiveness. Canada has officially adopted the multicultural model. From the 1960's onward, Canada has attempted to support and celebrate the divergent racial, cultural, and ethnic backgrounds of all its people.

The generations of immigrants who have arrived in Canada have come with high expectations: dreams of freedom, employment opportunities, and a better life for their children. The transition into Canadian society is not always an easy one. IMMIGRATION and resettlement are major upheavals in people's lives. Friends and family are left behind. For some, simple day-to-day activities such as grocery shopping or seeking health care and other social services may seem complicated and unfamiliar. The laws, languages, customs, religions, and educational backgrounds of the immigrants may be different from those that dominate Canadian society. This may create difficulties. For example, employment and related educational credentials may not be recognized by Canadian employers or educational institutions. In addition, visible minority immigrants may encounter RACISM and DISCRIMINATION.

The process of immigration continues to be a gendered experience. For women, particularly those whose lives are centered around the domestic sphere, immigration can be an isolating and lonely experience. While one's husband and children are getting exposed to the new culture and language (through employment and schooling), the woman may remain alone at home without a support network. Stress related to settlement in a new country can occur on several levels. Traditional role patterns in the family may change, particularly if children are cast into the role of interpreters, or if women who have never before been in the labor force are working for pay.

In Canada, immigrants may face a number of barriers that hinder their integration in society: the inability of some new immigrants to speak either English or French; the difficulty of getting education credentials, degrees, diplomas, and work experience accredited; and selected hostility by some Canadians to newcomers.

Demographic Issues. Each year since World War II, the average level of immigration to Canada has been between 200,000 and 250,000 people. The majority of immigrants settle in Canada's large urban centers, notably Montreal, Toronto, and Vancouver. Two reasons why immigrants are drawn to the larger urban areas are the increased opportunities for employment and the ability to connect with the established immigrant communities in those locations. Many services in urban centers are provided to immigrants in a familiar cultural context and their language of origin. Referred to as "Little Italy," "Chinatown," or "Little Bombay," these closely knit cultural enclaves insulate members of distinct ethnic, cultural, or racial groups from contact with mainstream society, thus providing both advantages and disadvantages to group members. For women and seniors with limited English or French language skills, life in such a community appears safe and familiar. One obvious disadvantage to these small, cultural communities is that contact with mainstream society becomes highly problematic, creating increased vulnerability for individual immigrants.

Immigrants contribute to Canadian society in a number of ways. Consistently, IMMIGRATION systems favor highly educated groups of people. Seen in this light, the immigration process offers the country a net educational gain. They bring a variety of diverse cultural backgrounds and experiences, thus enriching the multicultural fabric of Canadian society. Additionally, they facilitate trade linkages with their countries of origin. Immigrants also fulfill specific needs of the labor market, attracting workers in occupations underrepresented by Canadian nationals. Finally, with an aging population and low fertility rates among Canadians, immigration attempts to redress the work force imbalance.

—*Nancy Nason-Clark*

SUGGESTED READING: Employment and Immigration Canada's publication *Canada's Immigration Law* (Ottawa, Canada: Public Enquiries Centre, 1993) is a thorough overview of Canadian immigration laws and citizenship requirements.

Citizenship, U.S.: Every nation claims the right to determine its own criteria concerning the acquisition and loss of citizenship. Under international law, countries can award citizenship to anyone they please. Individuals who qualify as citizens, in turn, possess certain rights and responsibilities that are determined by the law of their country. The United States is no exception to these principles and practices.

U.S. Criteria. The Fourteenth Amendment to the U.S. CONSTITUTION provides that "all persons born or naturalized in the United States, and subject to the jurisdiction thereof, are citizens of the United States." In the United States, therefore, the main criterion for the acquisition of citizenship is the *jus soli* principle, which asserts that all those born on the soil or within the territorial jurisdiction of a country are its citizens. Other countries emphasize the principle of *jus sanguinis*, or the law of blood ties, which asserts that children follow the nationality of their parents, regardless of the place of their birth. The United States recognizes this principle in a qualified way, primarily in connection with children born to U.S. citizens abroad, provided proper notification of the birth with the U.S. government is undertaken. In addition to these two principles, the United States acknowledges by law that persons born in such territorial possessions as Puerto Rico, the Virgin Islands, and Guam are U.S. citizens. Other exceptions for the attainment of citizenship at birth are acknowledged in the law.

Birth on American soil may automatically confer citizenship on a child, but if the child's parents are not U.S. citizens, the fact that they had a child on U.S. soil neither confers citizenship on them nor protects them from deportation if their residence in the United States is illegal. Indeed, a child born under these circumstances is likely to have dual nationality. Under U.S. law, such a child would be required at the age of eighteen to accept U.S. citizenship formally. Children born in the United States to parents who are diplomats representing foreign countries are not considered U.S. citizens.

U.S. citizenship can also be obtained through NATURALIZATION, a process by which an alien applies for

A 1986 mass swearing-in ceremony for more than fourteen thousand new U.S. citizens in Miami. (UPI/Bettmann)

Marchers in New York City call for the granting of U.S. citizenship to newly arrived Third World immigrants. (Impact Visuals, Arvind Garg)

citizenship and undergoes a period of residency and education prior to taking an oath of citizenship. Persons seeking citizenship through naturalization must demonstrate proficiency in English and a knowledge of the fundamentals of the history, principles, and form of government of the United States. Children under the age of eighteen whose parents acquire U.S. citizenship also acquire citizenship derivatively.

U.S. law prohibits individuals who actively advocate or teach the violent overthrow of the government, who are current members of subversive parties advocating such policies, or who have actively participated in SEDITION, sabotage, or attacks on the officials of the government from becoming citizens. Those seeking naturalization must also show that they entered the United States legally. Petitioners for naturalization are investigated by the IMMIGRATION AND NATURALIZATION SERVICE (INS). Following a positive determination of the petitioner's application and a favorable hearing in open court, petitioners take an oath of renunciation and allegiance, renouncing allegiance to any other foreign power and swearing allegiance to the United States.

Former citizens of the United States who have renounced their citizenship or who served in the armed forces of the enemies of the United States during World War II and who later wish to resume U.S. citizenship must apply for naturalization and successfully complete the naturalization process.

Rights and Privileges. Citizens of the United States are entitled to the protections of the CONSTITUTION in regard to their individual liberties and civil rights. Section 1 of the Fourteenth Amendment to the Constitution provides that: "No State shall make or enforce any law which shall abridge the privileges or immunities of citizens of the United States; nor shall any State deprive any person of life, liberty, or property without due process of law; nor deny to any person within its jurisdiction the equal protection of the laws." The individual liberties, which are granted to aliens as well as citizens, include the freedoms of religion and speech, the right of association and assembly, the right to a fair and speedy trial by jury, the right to confront one's accusers, the freedom from unreasonable searches, seizures, and detention, and the right of DUE PROCESS and EQUAL PROTECTION of the law. All of these rights are qualified rights; none is absolute. Speech or assembly that is dangerous to public safety is not protected, nor are religious practices that threaten public safety or health.

Apart from the individual freedoms that U.S. citizens enjoy, they also have civil rights that are not bestowed on aliens. These include the rights to vote, to run for, and to hold office. Under the Fifteenth Amendment to the Constitution, neither the U.S. government nor state governments may abridge the right to vote on account of race. In addition, U.S. citizens may not be discriminated against for purposes of employment, housing, or public benefits.

Although citizens may claim certain rights, they also have certain responsibilities or duties. These include the duty to pay taxes, to obey the laws and Constitution of the United States, and to serve, when called upon, in the defense of the nation in time of war or national emergency. If citizens fail to perform these duties, they may be tried and punished to the full extent of the law. In the United States, citizens are not obliged to participate in politics or to vote nor are they required to support governmental policies, which they may seek to change through the political process. This right cannot be denied, as it is fundamental to the U.S. system of government.

Immigration and Refugees. The United States has long been a favored destination of peoples living under politically repressive governments or in economically depressed nations. The first European inhabitants were religious dissenters from England. Later waves of IMMIGRATION from Ireland, Southern Europe, Germany, Eastern Europe, and Russia swelled the U.S. population in the late 1800's and early 1900's. The Chinese sought work in the mines and on the railroads of the American West. Mexicans sought employment in Texas during World War II, when labor was needed. After World War II, numerous refugees from COMMUNISM sought haven and citizenship in the United States.

In the 1990's, immigration continued at a high level, and debate continued to rage about who and how many should gain admittance. During times of economic expansion, such issues are not so problematical; during times of economic RECESSION, however, citizens typically grow protective of their jobs and seek to limit immigration. A certain number of immigration slots have been allocated to refugees who need asylum from persecution, but even these are subject to reduction under political pressures, as are the number of slots allocated to regular legal immigration. The pressures are even greater during periods of substantial illegal IMMIGRATION. Voters in California expressed frustration with illegal immigration in passing PROPOSITION

City of Richmond v. J. A. Croson Company

187 in November, 1994. Lying behind that initiative was resentment toward the U.S. federal government, which legally required public assistance programs for immigrants but failed to fund them, forcing the states to pay and thus placing disproportional tax burdens on immigration-affected states such as California, Texas, and Florida. Critics of Proposition 187 claim, however, that the initiative had racist overtones. Regardless, the legislation's passage illustrates how citizens can be galvanized to protect their interests when they perceive them as threatened by uncontrolled immigration.

Summary. Every government has a right to determine who its citizens will be. However, in an age of global communication and transportation, disparities of development among countries, and numerous regional civil wars, people have both the opportunity and the incentive to seek better lives elsewhere than in their countries of origin. Thus, pressures for emigration grow, even as developed countries try to control their borders and prevent illegal immigration. For a country such as the United States, whose history is one of immigration and whose population is one of immigrants, these new pressures are particularly problematical. How open should the doors be? To what extent should the interests of existing citizens be favored in contrast with the desires of the millions of prospective immigrants who seek a share of the American Dream? Such questions will perhaps never be fully resolved.

—*Robert F. Gorman*

SUGGESTED READINGS: For a good history of the idea of citizenship, see Peter Reisenberg's *Citizenship in the Western Tradition* (Chapel Hill: University of North Carolina Press, 1992). For those interested in the kinds of books citizens seeking to be naturalized read in preparation for citizenship, see Solomon Wiener's *Questions and Answers on American Citizenship* (New York: Regents, 1970) and Carolyn Bain's *It's Easy to Become a Citizen: The Complete, Simple Guide to American Citizenship* (New York: Hawthorn Books, 1968). In *U.S. Immigration and Refugee Policy: Global and Domestic Issues* (Lexington, Mass.: Lexington Books, 1983), editor Mary M. Kritz brings together numerous informative articles concerning the role of immigration and refugee issues in the American political arena and economic system.

City of Richmond v. J. A. Croson Company

(1989): U.S. SUPREME COURT case. The *Richmond* decision made it much more difficult for cities and states to establish race-conscious affirmative action programs. In 1983, the Richmond, Virginia, city council had adopted a "set-aside" program for city contracting under which 30 percent of all city construction subcontracts were to be granted to minority-owned business enterprises. The J. A. Croson Company, a contracting firm which had been the low bidder on a city project, sued the city when its bid was rejected in favor of a higher bid submitted by a minority-owned firm. By a six-to-three vote, the Court ruled that the set-aside program violated the EQUAL-PROTECTION clause of the Fourteenth Amendment by establishing a racial classification. The decision cast doubt on the future of race-conscious programs designed to remedy past discrimination.

Civil disobedience:

Civil disobedience: Deliberate, open, and nonviolent breaking of the law to preserve some moral principle or to achieve some goal of social policy. Civil disobedience can take place in authoritarian states, where it may have limited aims or be intended to overthrow the regime. In democracies, it is a form of protest with limited aims. In cases in which disobedients do not accept the political structure, there is an attempt to establish a moral community with those enforcing the law.

Central elements of civil disobedience define its traditional meaning. It is called "civil" because, although it involves breaking the law of the civil (the state's) order, it is peaceable and therefore "civilized." In democracies, civil disobedience is thus limited in its means as well as its ends. Democratic states tacitly acknowledge this fact in the mild punishments typically meted out to disobedients. Acceptance of the state's punishment is likewise essential to the meaning of civil disobedience in democracies.

Civil disobedience always involves protest against some public policy. It can be direct or indirect. It is direct if the laws broken are themselves believed to be morally wrong, as when segregation laws in the American South were broken by civil rights protesters in the 1950's and 1960's; it is indirect when the laws broken are accepted as legitimate, as when trespassing laws were violated during antiwar protests in the 1960's.

Civil disobedience has been used throughout the world but is a creation of Western civilization, where it has deep roots. In ancient Greece, Sophocles' drama *Antigone* presented the idea of a higher law to which

Antigone appeals in disobeying the state. Socrates refused to obey the state, accepting a death sentence rather than defy the law by fleeing. Early Christianity was replete with refusals to obey the Roman state. Later, the Protestant Reformation gave rise to forms of nonviolent resistance to authority, as Protestant sects such as the Quakers refused obedience to laws they considered morally wrong.

Nineteenth century writings of American Henry David Thoreau and Russian Leo Tolstoy influenced Mohandas K. Gandhi's nonviolent movement against British rule of India from the 1920's to the 1940's. In the United States, there is a rich tradition of civil dis-

obedience, from eighteenth century Quakers to Martin Luther KING, Jr.'s nonviolent resistance to racial SEG-REGATION of the 1950's and 1960's, protests against the Vietnam War, and more recent examples such as the ANTINUCLEAR and antiabortion movements.

Several controversies concerning civil disobedience stand out. Some critics feel that legitimation of disobedience strikes at the rule of law, the heart of a free society. Other commentators note that some disobedients no longer believe that they must accept punishment, since they believe their aims to be just. Still others allege that the belief in nonviolence appears to be breaking down, especially among younger disobedi-

Madalyn Murray O'Hair, a prominent atheist and advocate of separation of church and state, is arrested for disrupting a Texas city council prayer service in a 1977 act of civil disobedience. (UPI/Corbis-Bettmann)

ents. Finally, some observers have pointed to anti-democratic tendencies in some civil disobedients, as some lawbreakers insist that their goals be implemented regardless of the majority's will. Constitutional democracy, however, places limits on the majority as well as on the minorities, and civil disobedients typically argue that majority policy violates conscience. However controversial, civil disobedience seems destined to continue to play a role in the politics of free societies.

Civil procedure: Rules governing how a civil (non-criminal) lawsuit is conducted, including pretrial matters, trial proceedings, and post-trial issues. Procedural rules create the process that is to be followed, the documents that are to be presented, and the general conduct of the trial.

An overriding concern is the constitutional requirement of DUE PROCESS of law contained in the Fourteenth Amendment: adequate and proper notice of the pendency of a suit and an opportunity to appear to present evidence before a neutral and detached tribunal. Procedural due-process rules help ensure fairness and reasonableness in the decision-making process.

All states and the federal government have extensive rules governing litigation, but certain steps are common to all. A suit is generally commenced when an attorney (on behalf of the plaintiff) drafts a document called a complaint and a writ of summons, which are served on the opposing party (the defendant) in accordance with state law. The complaint explains the plaintiff's claims and requested relief. The summons notifies the defendant of the need to file an answer or response to the complaint, or set forth any legal defects. If the defendant fails to respond within the appointed time, a default judgment is entered.

After the complaint has been served and filed with the court, the discovery phase begins, where the parties attempt to learn as much as possible about the case. Commonly used tools are interrogatories (written questions to be answered under oath addressed to the parties), oral depositions (examination of a witness or party under oath outside of court before a court reporter who transcribes the testimony for later use at trial), and requests for production of documents or inspection of other items in possession of the opposing party (to prevent surprise at trial).

Throughout the discovery phase, the parties communicate with the court through motions (formal requests for rulings by the court on matters of law) of various types, often to cure defects, narrow the issues, or compel compliance with prior rulings. Prior to trial, a pretrial conference (also called a settlement conference or conciliation) may be convened by a judge in order to discuss the issues, evaluate the case, and attempt to reach an out-of-court settlement.

Procedural rules help to guide the parties in gathering their evidence and presenting it at trial. The first stage of trial is the voir dire, or jury selection, in which potential jurors are questioned about any bias that would adversely influence their decision-making role. After a jury is selected and sworn in, the plaintiff's attorney makes an opening statement outlining the case to the jury. The defendant's attorney has the option of making an opening statement at this time or waiting until presentation of their evidence. The standard burden of proof in a civil case is proof by a preponderance of the evidence (establishing that the facts alleged in the complaint are more likely than not true). Through examination of witnesses, the evidence brought at trial must be sufficient to establish each of the facts in the complaint and support the legal claims (a "*prima facie* case").

At the conclusion of the plaintiff's case, the defendant presents evidence in response to that of the plaintiff to cast doubt on the plaintiff's version of the facts. Often the plaintiff may offer additional testimony in rebuttal at the conclusion of the defendant's case. After both parties have concluded the presentation of evidence, each attorney makes a closing argument (or summation) in which each attempts to persuade the jury of the most plausible version of the case and to convince the jury to decide in their client's favor.

The judge then instructs the jury on the law to be applied in the case, the jury deliberates, and returns a verdict. A dissatisfied party may choose to request post-trial relief or appeal the decision.

Civil religion: A set of beliefs that sees a nation, its institutions, history, and cultural practices as sacred and designed to further some ultimate divine plan. The idea was first developed by Jean-Jacques Rousseau (1712-1778), who defined civil religion as a set of simple dogmas established by a sovereign to help promote social cohesion among citizens. The American civil religion, according to sociologist Robert Bellah, is a mixture of Protestantism and nationalism that casts national symbols, heroes, holidays, and political rituals

Televangelist Billy Graham is applauded by congressional leaders after his 1996 acceptance of the Congressional Gold Medal. (Archive Photos, Pool, Reuters)

in a religious light. While many view civil religion as desirable because of its contributions to national unity, others see it as having the potential to promote intolerance toward those who disagree with the majority.

Civil rights: A broad concept that covers all attempts to promote political, social, and legal equality for groups and individuals that have in one way or another historically been denied equal treatment. The concept is most closely associated with the struggle by African Americans for equality; in the United States and Canada, the concept has broadened to include efforts to promote equality for all ethnic and racial groups, the struggle against gender inequality, and the protection of rights of workers, children, homosexuals, and people with disabilities.

While wide agreement exists on both the moral necessity and legal command that all individuals be treated equally, there is still sharp disagreement on the degree of government action necessary to promote and protect equality. Many conservatives argue that only individuals should be protected against acts of discrimination, that the legal procedures established since the 1960's are adequate to protect individuals against discrimination, and that certain groups, especially those defined by perceived "voluntary" behavior such as gays and lesbians, deserve no special protection against discrimination. Others argue that discrimination against groups in society is still pervasive. They point to the continuing economic and social inequality between English-speaking whites and other groups, such as Native Americans, African Americans, and Latinos, and argue that society must continue programs, such as AFFIRMATIVE ACTION programs, to promote equality for these groups. For other groups, such as women, children, people with disabilities, workers, and gays and lesbians, the struggle for equality has often become one not for blind legal equality but for the protection of difference within a broader society.

Background. The concept of civil rights emerged in the eighteenth century as a subset of natural rights.

CONSTITUTIONAL LOCATIONS OF IMPORTANT CIVIL RIGHTS

Right	Amendments to the U.S. Constitution													
	1	2	3	4	5	6	7	8	9	10	14	19	24	26
Freedom of religion	✔										*			
Freedom of speech	✔										*			
Freedom of the press	✔										*			
Freedom of assembly/petition	✔										*			
Right to bear arms		✔												
No unlawful quartering			✔								*			
No unreasonable searches or seizures				✔							✔			
Right to due process					✔						*			
Speedy trial by jury						✔								
Jury trial in civil cases							✔							
No excessive bail or cruel and unusual punishments								✔						
Recognition of unnamed rights									✔		*			
Powers reserved to states and to the people										✔	*			
Equal protection of the law											✔			
Voting rights												✔	✔	✔

Source: From William C. Lowe, *Blessings of Liberty: Safeguarding Civil Rights.* Human Rights series, Vero Beach, Fla.: Rourke Corp., 1992.
*Rights that have been incorporated into the Fourteenth Amendment by Supreme Court decisions.

Civil rights were seen as complementary to other sets of rights such as political and PROPERTY RIGHTS. Civil rights included the rights of legal equality before the courts, the right to make and enforce contracts, and the right to get and keep property. In the debate over the addition of the BILL OF RIGHTS to the U.S. Constitution, James Madison noted that one of the goals was to ensure that the "civil rights of none shall be abridged on account of religious belief or worship" and that equal rights of conscience not be "in any manner, or on any pretext, infringed."

The Nineteenth Century. Equal civil rights did not imply equal political rights in the nineteen century, and not until after the Civil War did the concept extend across racial lines. In 1857 chief justice of the U.S. Supreme Court Roger Taney, in the case *Scott v. Sandford* (the "Dred Scott decision"), gave the clearest statement of the limits of civil equality in the United States when he wrote that African Americans had "for more than a century been regarded as beings of an inferior order . . . so far inferior that they had no rights which the white man was bound to respect; and that the negro might justly and lawfully be reduced to slavery for his benefit."

Early struggles for civil rights in the United States centered on three issues: the right of all white men to be treated equally; the rights of women; and the rights of African Americans before and after the end of slavery. In Canada during the nineteenth century, the struggle for equal treatment by the French-speaking people, generally centered in Québec, dominated the early struggles for equality. The 1830's and 1840's saw the intensification of the struggle for the end of slavery in the United States. The abolitionist movement became closely connected with efforts to promote more rights for women. With the Civil War, sparked in part by the refusal of one part of Northern opinion to accept the interpretation of the Constitution put forward by Taney

The partition of public transportation facilities into "separate but equal" sections for whites and blacks was validated by the 1896 *Plessy v. Ferguson* decision. (UPI/Corbis-Bettmann)

in the *Dred Scott* case, the debate shifted to the extent of the civil and political rights that African Americans would have after the end of slavery.

The U.S. Congress passed the first Civil Rights Act in 1866; it was designed to promote basic civil equality for African Americans. In 1868 the states ratified the Fourteenth Amendment to the Constitution, which granted citizenship to "all persons born or naturalized in the United States" and ordered that all receive "equal protection of the law." In 1870 the states ratified the Fifteenth Amendment, which guaranteed the right to vote to all men regardless of "race, color, or previous condition of servitude." Despite the seemingly ironclad nature of these guarantees—and of those found in later Civil Rights Acts passed during Reconstruction—after 1876 especially African Americans had to defend these rights themselves against hostile whites in both the South and North and in the face of general indifference from the federal government. In PLESSY V. FERGUSON (1896), the Supreme Court sanctioned the doctrine of "SEPARATE BUT EQUAL," which allowed racial segregation in almost all facets of life as long as treatment was equal; in practice, in both North and South, separate was never equal. In 1898 the Court allowed states to use a number of legal contrivances, such as literacy tests and poll taxes, to prevent African Americans from voting as long as these acts made no mention of race.

The retreat from the promotion of civil rights for African Americans after 1876 was mirrored by the treatment of other groups within American society. Throughout the antebellum era, the movement for the abolition of slavery had been fairly closely connected with the movement for greater rights for women. This movement had emphasized the rights of married women to control property independently of their husbands and to have greater access to divorce. The movement had achieved gains in property rights for women but failed to link SUFFRAGE for African Americans with suffrage for women. Although several organizations kept up the fight after 1876, only a few new states in the West granted women the right to vote before 1900.

As courts in the United States had undercut the protection of civil rights for African Americans, they also undercut protection for workers. As industrialization proceeded in the late nineteenth century and the United States went from a nation mostly of farmers to a nation mostly of urban workers, workers increasingly sought to organize unions to negotiate with employers over wages and working conditions. Culminating in the case *Lochner v. New York* (1905), which struck down a state law limiting working hours to ten a day, courts ruled generally that neither state governments, the federal government, nor even negotiated contracts between unions and employers had sanction of law since they violated a perceived freedom of contract. Indeed, the first antitrust laws, designed to curb the growth of monopoly in industry, were initially most effectively used to declare much union activity illegal restraints of trade.

The late nineteenth century saw a great wave of immigration into the United States and Canada from Europe, Asia, and Latin America. European immigrants came increasingly not from the homelands of earlier immigrants in northern and western Europe, but from southern and eastern Europe. Immigrants from China and Japan came to the rapidly growing West Coast of North America. Immigrants from Latin America, especially Mexico, swelled the already existing communities of Hispanics that had lived in the American Southwest since the United states had defeated Mexico and annexed the region in 1845. All these groups faced varying degrees of discrimination. Many of the "new immigrants" from Europe were Catholic or Jewish and faced prejudice on account of religion. Generally, the dominant white Anglo society emphasized assimilation for European immigrants. For Asians, predominantly Chinese and Japanese, however, attempts were made by state governments to proscribe their rights. In 1882 Congress passed the Chinese Exclusion Act, which barred further Chinese immigration, and in 1924 the Japanese became the only group officially barred from naturalization to citizenship. Mexican immigration to the United States increased dramatically after the beginning of the twentieth century, mostly to California, Arizona, New Mexico, Texas, and Colorado. These immigrants generally lived in segregated rural settlements or *barrios* in cities.

The Twentieth Century. The twentieth century saw the beginnings of the long struggles by a variety of groups within American and Canadian society to gain equality. Perhaps the most important early successes came in the women's SUFFRAGE MOVEMENT. After more than fifty years of intensive campaigning by women's rights groups, campaigning that eventually included women chaining themselves in regular shifts to the gates to the White House, the Nineteenth Amendment to the U.S. Constitution, ratified in 1920, extended the right to vote to women. The coalition of

President Lyndon B. Johnson confers with Civil Rights movement leaders at the White House in 1968. (Archive Photos)

women of many different political beliefs with Progressives and other reformers quickly fell apart, however; a proposed equal rights amendment was never ratified. Likewise, advocates for birth control or other extensions of rights for women made little headway between 1920 and the end of World War II.

The NEW DEAL brought social reform in the aftermath of the Great Depression, and the Depression itself helped spark a rapid growth in union activity. The Wagner Act (NATIONAL LABOR RELATIONS ACT) of 1935 declared that "employees shall have the right to self-organization, to form, join, or assist labor organizations, to bargain collectively through representatives of their own choosing, and to engage in concerted activities, for the purpose of collective bargaining or other mutual aid or protection." Although the labor movement long consisted of competing factions (the AMERICAN FEDERATION OF LABOR organized craft workers, while the more militant Congress of Industrial Organizations organized workers throughout individual industries), the labor movement remained strong through the 1970's.

After World War II, African Americans began to organize and agitate more directly for their civil rights. Thurgood Marshall led the NATIONAL ASSOCIATION FOR THE ADVANCEMENT OF COLORED PEOPLE (NAACP) in a series of court cases that culminated in the 1954 BROWN V. BOARD OF EDUCATION OF TOPEKA, KANSAS case, in which the Supreme Court declared SEGREGATION in public schooling to be inherently unconstitutional. At roughly the same time, the Reverend Martin Luther KING, Jr., led the MONTGOMERY BUS BOYCOTT to protest segregation on public transportation and quickly transformed that movement into the Southern Christian Leadership Council, which spearheaded direct efforts to attack segregation throughout the South. The movement for greater rights for African Americans divided between those who fought for integration like King and the NAACP and advocates of BLACK POWER, such as the STUDENT NONVIOLENT COORDINATING COMMITTEE, Stokely Carmichael, and MALCOLM X until his assassination in 1965. The movement reached its peak in the mid-1960's, when Congress passed the CIVIL RIGHTS ACT OF 1964,

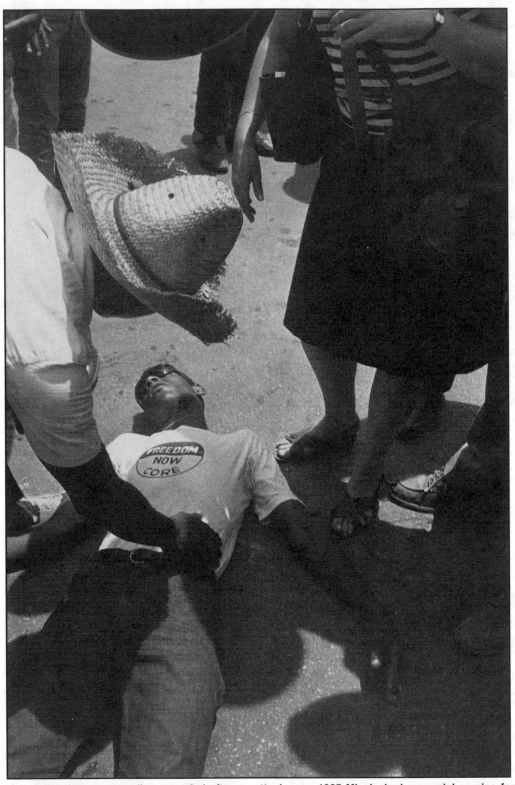

A civil rights demonstrator lies wounded after an attack on a 1965 Mississippi memorial service for slain civil rights workers. (UPI/Corbis-Bettmann)

which outlawed most forms of public discrimination on the basis of race, religion, and gender, and the VOTING RIGHTS ACT of 1965, which authorized the federal government to oversee elections and voter registration in states and regions where African Americans had previously not been able to vote in numbers proportional to their part of the population.

In part inspired by the CIVIL RIGHTS MOVEMENT, other ethnic and racial minorities in the United States and Canada began to organize and agitate for their rights and for greater political representation. Several organizations emerged among Hispanic Americans; perhaps the most notable was the UNITED FARM WORKERS union led by César CHÁVEZ. Chávez's success in organizing mostly Mexican American farmworkers inspired movements that led to greater political power and cultural consciousness among Mexican Americans.

Agitation for greater equality for women also increased throughout the 1960's and 1970's, fueled in part by a rapidly increasing proportion of women in the workplace. Betty Friedan became the most visible leader of a movement that sought workplace and social equality. Women used the Civil Rights Act of 1964, which outlawed most forms of discrimination on the basis of gender, to get the courts to order equal pay and affirmative action programs for women. The women's rights movement, however, met great opposition from cultural conservatives. In addition to those who believed gender equality violated natural or religious mandates, many charged that the feminist movement undermined family stability.

In Canada, language rights and self-determination for the French-speaking majority of Québec have long proved contentious. While both French and English have long been recognized as official languages in Canada, the rights of French speakers outside Québec and of English speakers in Québec have sometimes been overridden in attempts to promote cultural unity. During the 1960's, Réné Lévesque organized the PARTI QUÉBÉCOIS to lead the struggle for independence for Québec. Although a referendum for independence in association with the rest of Canada failed after his party gained control of the provincial government in the 1970's, the party did pass Bill 101, which in essence required the use only of French in public places. The bill galvanized opposition among non-French speakers in the province and throughout Canada and helped lead to an ongoing crisis over the relations of Québec with the rest of Canada.

Likewise, during the 1960's, Native Americans began to organize to gain both better treatment from American society and greater autonomy and self determination. Gradually, Native American nations began to win court cases that forced federal and state governments to live up to the often violated letter of treaties. The AMERICAN INDIAN MOVEMENT, founded in 1968, took more direct means of dramatizing the plight of Native Americans. The movement occupied both Alcatraz Island in San Francisco Bay and the village of Wounded Knee in South Dakota. While Native Americans nations gained more autonomy, reservations remained generally poverty-stricken. In Canada, a 1969 government report that called for full assimilation of aboriginal peoples into Canadian society and the ending of reservations sparked a protest movement that eventually led to the recognition by the federal government of a general right to self-government.

Current Debates. While the vast majority of people in the United States and Canada seem committed to civil equality for all people, the nature of that equality is the subject of contentious debate. Conservatives tend to define civil rights in negative terms as the absence of discrimination. Liberals on the other hand, generally hold a broader definition of civil rights that includes positive action to promote equality. In some cases this position leads to support for group rights that range from a special status for members of a group to self-determination.

Negative Constructions of Civil Rights. According to many critics of positive action, the struggle for civil rights by minorities in the United States and Canada has been won, and programs such as affirmative action programs are a form of "reverse" discrimination against whites and males. Critics of positive attempts to promote equality have several important concerns. Many argue that positive action to protect civil rights is now unnecessary. They point out that discrimination on almost any grounds is illegal. When incidents of discrimination occur, the individual concerned has the ability to seek legal redress. Indeed some members of groups that have received special protections have begun to argue that those protections (notably affirmative action) stigmatize successful minority members.

A growing number of influential individuals have begun to argue that positive attempts to promote equality in fact promote public fragmentation. In the United States, some point to the ongoing crisis over Québec as a worst-case example of where emphasis on so-called group rights can lead. They particularly point to the growing use of Spanish in the United States and to bilingual education as harbingers of the same type of discord. Likewise, others charge that the greater emphasis on civil rights has created a culture of victimization that in fact inhibits success by minority members.

Many believe that continuing efforts to promote equality for members of previously discriminated against groups results in reverse discrimination. In the United States many whites and males see affirmative action as allowing lesser-qualified minority group members to take slots in schools, be hired for jobs, benefit from minority set-aside programs in government contracting, and be promoted. In Canada, efforts to protect the French language, especially in Québec, are seen by some as discrimination against English speakers. Efforts in the United States to increase African American and Hispanic political representation through redistricting plans that try to concentrate minority voters in particular districts have been successfully challenged.

Many conservatives still challenge, essentially on moral grounds, granting civil equality to gays and lesbians. Some still favor measures to suppress homosexuality. A greater number oppose efforts to identify gays and lesbians as minorities deserving of special protection. A few states and localities, most notably the state of Colorado and the city of Cincinnati, have attempted through law or referendum to prohibit protection of the rights of gays and lesbians as gays and lesbians.

In the 1980's and 1990's, conservatives made great gains in rolling back positive efforts to promote equality by arguing that their necessity is past. Under Ronald Reagan and George Bush, conservative appointments to the judiciary began to question the scope of such programs. In 1995, the Supreme Court imposed much tighter standards on when and how race, ethnicity, or gender may be used in consideration of efforts to remedy past discrimination. In ADARAND CONSTRUCTORS V. PEÑA (1995), which put severe limits on the ability of the federal government to "set aside" contracts for minority-owned businesses, the Court put it succinctly: The Constitution protects "persons, not groups."

Positive Constructions of Civil Rights. Supporters of continuing efforts to promote equality, on the other hand, argue that such measures are still necessary given the continuing inequality in American and Canadian society. They charge that legal change has not brought true civil rights. Many argue that legal equality can never be enough, but that some groups need special protection or status in multicultural societies. Some go so far as to argue for some form of self-determination for minority groups.

In the United States, African Americans still earn less than the rest of the population. Women and other minorities hold many fewer managerial positions than white males. In 1994 voters in the state of California approved PROPOSITION 187, which sought to deny access to public services to illegal aliens. Although implementation of the measure was suspended by the courts, it seemed to many observers to be indicative of a growing hostility to Spanish-speaking peoples.

Minorities are also still the victims of threats and violence, and Asian and Latino immigrants often face overt and covert discrimination. Gays and lesbians are the targets of some groups. Many progressives argue that efforts to prevent aliens (legal and illegal) from using social services, to require the use of English in all public functions, and to prohibit protection for the rights of gays and lesbians show the need for continuing efforts to promote equality actively.

Such efforts have led to progress toward a more equal society in both Canada and the United States; the passage of the AMERICANS WITH DISABILITIES ACT in 1991 in the United States, for example, has widened access to the mainstream to millions of Americans. Critical debates remain, however, both about the degree of action required to give everyone equal access to the mainstream and about the necessity of promoting the concept that there is only one mainstream.

—*Gregory H. Maddox*

SUGGESTED READINGS: A comprehensive discussion of the history and philosophy of civil rights in the United States can be found in James MacGregor Burns and Stewart Burns's *A People's Charter: The Pursuit of Rights in America* (New York: Vintage Books, 1993). Howard Zinn in *A People's History of the United States* (New York: Harper & Row, 1980) gives an older and more radical view of many of the same debates. Cornel West has become perhaps the foremost defender of the need for continuing action to promote equality; see *Race Matters* (Boston: Beacon Press, 1993). See also John Edgar Wideman's *Fatheralong: A Meditation on Fathers and Sons, Race and Society* (New York: Pantheon Books, 1994) for a more personal view.

Shelby Steele has become the most well-known black critic of traditional civil rights tactics; see his *The Content of Our Character: A New Vision of Race in America* (New York: St. Martin's Press, 1990). For the struggle for gender equality and its critics, see Susan Faludi's *Backlash: The Undeclared War Against American Women* (New York: Crown, 1991). On the Chicano movement, see Carlos Munoz, Jr.'s *Youth, Identity, Power: The Chicano Movement* (New York: Verso, 1989). For civil rights struggles in Canada, see Evelyn Kallen's *Ethnicity and Human Rights in Canada*, 2d ed. (Toronto: Oxford University Press, 1995), and *Label Me Human: Minority Rights of Stigmatized Canadians* (Toronto: University of Toronto Press, 1989).

Civil Rights Act of 1964: Federal civil rights legislation enacted to remedy racially discriminatory practices in the United States. The act was later amended by the Civil Rights Act of 1991.

The struggle for civil rights for African Americans reached a peak in 1963, when activists such as Martin Luther KING, Jr., organized protests in Birmingham, Alabama, and throughout the South. Though most such demonstrations were themselves nonviolent, several protests resulted in reactive violence against children and adults. With concern for the unrest in the nation, and at the urging of U.S. attorney general Robert Kennedy, President John F. Kennedy presented a civil rights bill to Congress. The bill contained eight provisions and was assigned the working number H.B. 7152. This bill was to become the historic Civil Rights Act of 1964. Though several civil rights bills had been passed in prior years, this was the first bill to be passed with the original content largely intact; moreover, its sweeping provisions made it the most significant legislation to address the civil rights of African Americans and other minority groups.

The bill moved slowly through the legislative process, enduring long debate and a lengthy Senate filibuster. After President Kennedy's assassination, however,

President Lyndon B. Johnson signs the Civil Rights Act of 1964 into law. (Archive Photos, D.P.A.)

and with the strong support of the new president, Lyndon B. Johnson, the bill was passed and was signed into law on July 2, 1964.

The act is broken into separate titles. The major provisions include a VOTING RIGHTS provision, a prohibition against discrimination in public accommodations and discrimination in federally financed programs, and orders requiring DESEGREGATION in schools and in public facilities. The act also extended the life of the COMMISSION ON CIVIL RIGHTS through 1969 and authorized the commission to serve as a national clearinghouse for civil rights information and to investigate voting-fraud charges. Another provision dealing with voting rights directed the Bureau of the Census to collect statistical data based on race, color, and national origin in certain districts. The act also created the five-member EQUAL EMPLOYMENT OPPORTUNITY COMMISSION (EEOC) to investigate employment discrimination charges. Laws were also enacted prohibiting employment discrimination on the basis of race, color, religion, and sex. Though the act was primarily developed to deal with racial discrimination, the inclusion of gender references effectively provided legal remedies for female victims of discrimination as well.

The act has been updated and amended by the passage of the Civil Rights Act of 1991. These amendments were enacted to strengthen existing federal civil rights laws and to counter Supreme Court decisions that had weakened the scope and effectiveness of earlier federal civil rights protections. Significant provisions of the 1991 amendments provide for the awarding of damages in cases of intentional employment discrimination and unlawful harassment.

SUGGESTED READING: A thorough discussion of the history and development of the Civil Rights Act of 1964 can be found in *The Longest Debate: A Legislative History of the 1964 Civil Rights Act* (Washington, D.C.: Seven Locks Press), by Charles and Barbara Whalen.

Civil rights legislation: Civil rights legislation in the United States stems from attempts to guarantee to its citizens the provisions of the Thirteenth and Fourteenth Amendments to the U.S. CONSTITUTION.

Historical Background. Upon completion of the Civil War and with the ratification of the Thirteenth Amendment (1865), Congress passed a Civil Rights Act in 1866 that defined citizenship to include the recently emancipated slaves and protected all citizens against arbitrary individual actions depriving them of equal benefits of the laws. In addition, the Fourteenth Amendment (1868) protected United States citizens against any state action that would abridge any citizen's privileges or immunities, or deprive any citizen of DUE PROCESS of the law, or deny any citizen the EQUAL PROTECTION of the law. Following a Supreme Court decision in 1873 narrowly defining federal citizenship and placing protection of most CIVIL RIGHTS in state governments, Congress passed the Civil Rights Act of 1875, which guaranteed equal rights in places of public accommodation and forbade the exclusion of African Americans from jury duty.

Two subsequent Supreme Court decisions further limited protection of the rights outlined in the Fourteenth Amendment and in the 1875 Civil Rights Act. The Civil Rights Cases (1883) stated that discriminatory actions by individuals were constitutional, and *PLESSY V. FERGUSON* (1896) ruled that state laws supporting SEGREGATION of races were constitutional as long as an equality of accommodation existed.

Thus, by the end of the nineteenth century, the protection of the civil rights of federal citizens of the United States had been considerably limited. No new federal civil rights law was passed until 1957.

Contemporary Developments in the United States. Following the *BROWN V. BOARD OF EDUCATION OF TOPEKA, KANSAS* (1954) ruling of the Supreme Court and the success of the MONTGOMERY BUS BOYCOTT (1956) under the leadership of Martin Luther KING, Jr., an attempt was made in Congress to pass a civil rights act. Carefully guided through the Senate by its majority leader, Lyndon B. Johnson, the Civil Rights Act of 1957 provided a psychological but not a political boost to the hopes of African Americans. The act created a Civil Rights Division in the Justice Department headed by an assistant attorney general and permitted federal attorneys to obtain court injunctions against any interference with the right to vote. The act also established a Civil Rights Commission, which had the power to investigate discriminatory practices concerning voting and the denial of the equal protection of the law. The commission was also given the authority to issue reports, findings, and recommendations to the president and Congress.

Three years later, Congress passed the Civil Rights Act of 1960. This act made it illegal to attempt to avoid prosecution either for bombing offenses or for interference with courts' orders pertaining to the INTEGRATION of schools. Federal judges were also given the author-

A Nation Gone Wild!   A Nation's Leaders Gone Berserk!

While They Try To Impose A So-Called

"Civil Rights" Law!

10% Civil Rights - - 90% More Federal Power

A National "Fair Employment Practice" Law
To Be Enforced by the U. S. Attorney General and the Federal
Courts, Despite the Fact That It Covers a State Situation.

The Bill Has Passed The House

And Will Soon Be Filibustered In The Senate

 The Nation is being disarmed gradually making it defenseless while its Departments of State carries on disgracefully . . . . . a Disastrous Foreign Policy.

There is serious trouble in Viet Nam, Cuba, Panama, Cypres and the Congo . . . Potential Trouble in Malaysia and countries all around the world . . . Needless Sacrificing of Our Sons! AND ALL THE TIME the Nation is Bankrupt and going Further in Debt.

 The National Debt Is Over $315 Billion.

 The Proposed Budget Is $99 Billion.

The cover of a pamphlet assailing the Civil Rights Act of 1964.

ity to appoint referees to hear claims that state election officials had illegally denied the right to register and vote, but the law was difficult to enforce because the burden of proof rested upon the ability of the Justice Department to provide specific cases of the denial of the vote based on race or color.

The landmark Civil Rights Act came in 1964. Beginning with the SIT-INS in 1960 and culminating with the MARCH ON WASHINGTON and the assassination of John F. Kennedy in 1963, increasing pressure was applied to the members of Congress to pass a stronger civil rights law.

Composed by the remnants of the Kennedy Administration and conducted by President Lyndon B. Johnson, the CIVIL RIGHTS ACT OF 1964 was the most encompassing action to protect and promote the civil rights of federal citizens since the ratification of the Fourteenth Amendment. Of the eleven sections of the act, the most important were the following: Title I forbade the unequal application of voting registration requirements, required that all literacy tests be in writing and be available for review, established a sixth-grade education as presumptive of literacy, and gave the attorney general the power to file suits if it were believed that a pattern of voter discrimination existed; Title II barred DISCRIMINATION in places of public accommodation (such as concert halls, sports arenas, and large hotels or lodging establishments), and permitted individuals as well as the attorney general to seek relief through civil injunction; Title III authorized the DESEGREGATION of all state or locally owned public facilities; Title IV provided for technical and financial assistance to be provided by the Office of Education to local school districts seeking desegregation; Title VI barred discrimination in any federally assisted program and permitted the cessation of federal assistance if discrimination were discovered; and Title VII prohibited several different categories of employment discrimination (including religious and sex discrimination) and created the EQUAL EMPLOYMENT OPPORTUNITY COMMISSION (EEOC), which had the power to investigate charges brought by wronged parties and could assist the attorney general in civil action suits.

The next major civil rights laws passed were the Civil Rights Act of 1968, Title IX of the 1972 EDUCATION AMENDMENTS ACT, the REHABILITATION ACT of 1973, and the 1975 AGE DISCRIMINATION IN EMPLOYMENT ACT. The 1968 act provided federal protection to civil rights workers and prohibited discrimination in either the rental or sale of housing. Title IX of the 1972 Education Amendments Act extended protection against discrimination based on sex, while the 1973 act barred discrimination against the handicapped.

Beginning with the Supreme Court decision in *Grove City College v. Bell* (1984), in which the court narrowed the coverage of Title IX of the 1972 Education Amendments Act, and several Ronald REAGAN Administration actions that were seen by civil rights proponents as curtailments of the gains made in civil rights legislation in the twenty previous years, efforts began in Congress to restore the rights that were perceived to have been lost. The result was the Restoration Act of 1988, passed over President Reagan's veto. The act restored the broad coverage of Title IX of the 1972 Education Amendments Act, reinstituted Title VI of the 1964 Civil Rights Act, and restored several aspects of the Rehabilitation Act of 1973 and the Age Discrimination in Employment Act of 1975. The act also made it clear that if one agency in an institution received federal funding, the entire institution had to abide by the federal antidiscrimination laws.

Two years after the passage of the Restoration Act, Congress failed for the first time in twenty-five years in an attempt to pass a civil rights law. The civil rights bill, introduced in its 1988-1989 term, attempted to amend Title VII of the 1964 Civil Rights Act to permit financial awards for pain and suffering and punitive damages in intentional-discrimination cases. The bill also intended to overturn or modify seven Supreme Court cases involving civil rights in the following ways: make on-the-job discrimination subject to suits by the Justice Department; place the burden on the employer to prove that its action was necessary to the business; and make employers liable for intentional discrimination even if the same decision would have been made for nondiscriminatory reasons. President George BUSH vetoed the bill, and neither the Senate nor the House could garner the necessary two-thirds vote to override the veto.

In the 1991-1992 term of Congress, civil rights proponents were able to push through a civil rights bill that was a result of a compromise between the Bush Administration and the lawmakers. Two events perhaps influenced the Bush Administration's desire for a compromise: The first was the controversy that arose in the Supreme Court confirmation of Clarence THOMAS; the second was the primary election performance in the Louisiana governor race of David DUKE, a former leader in the KU KLUX KLAN who ran

President George Bush signs the 1991 Civil Rights Act. (Reuters/Corbis-Bettmann)

as a Republican. Civil rights supporters also agreed to several key compromises. The Civil Rights Act of 1991 made it easier for workers to file suit and win job discrimination lawsuits; it allowed workers to receive limited money payments as victims of harassment and discrimination; and, overturning a 1989 Supreme Court decision, it required that employers had to show that hiring and promotion requirements were directly related to job performances.

Until 1995, Congress had been exempt from eleven civil rights laws (including the 1964 Civil Rights Act), but that exemption was ended on January 23, 1995, when President Bill CLINTON signed into law the Congressional Accountability Act.

Canadian Civil Rights Legislation. For the first time in Canadian history, in the CONSTITUTION ACT of 1982, the civil rights of Canadian citizens were provided in one written document. Prior to that time, citizens were protected against arbitrary executive action, but the courts did not have the power of judicial review of the legislative action. Since the full implementation in 1987 of the Constitution Act, Canada has labored to provide full protection of civil rights to all its various ethnic and cultural minorities. —*Robert L. Patterson*

SUGGESTED READINGS: Good introductions to basic civil rights legislation can be found in *Federal Civil Rights Laws: A Sourcebook* (Washington, D.C.: Government Printing Office, 1984) and Kenneth L. Karst's *Law's Promise, Law's Expression: Visions of Power in the Politics of Race, Gender, and Religion* (New Haven, Conn.: Yale University Press, 1993). Charles W. Whalen and Barbara Whalen's *The Longest Debate: A Legislative History of the 1964 Civil Rights Act* (New York: New American Library, 1985) provides a complete history of the 1964 act. In *We Overcame: The Story of Civil Rights for Disabled People* (Falls Church, Va.: Regal Direct, 1993), Richard Bryant Treanor gives a most thorough story of civil rights legislation related to physically disabled Americans.

Civil Rights movement: Modern struggle to end legal SEGREGATION. The movement reversed JIM CROW LAWS mandating segregation through CIVIL DISOBEDIENCE tactics and legal actions, and it inspired other movements for social change.

Scholars may disagree over the dates of the modern Civil Rights movement, but it is generally agreed that the 1954 BROWN V. BOARD OF EDUCATION OF TOPEKA, KANSAS (1954) Supreme Court ruling set the stage. The *Brown* decision declared that "SEPARATE BUT EQUAL" public schools were inherently unequal. More than fifty years of segregated education was reversed, although the ruling was met with massive resistance and was not immediately implemented in the Deep South. Segregationists resisted the law by cutting off tax money for desegregated schools and even closing some schools to avoid integration. Nevertheless, the Supreme Court ruling inspired hope for change among African Americans, and concerted efforts were soon made to reverse Jim Crow segregation in other areas of life. Civil rights protests were nothing new in the United States, but the movement that occurred after 1954 was different in scope and intensity as well as results. Segregation on every level was attacked—from hotels and restaurants to rest rooms and water fountains.

World War II and After. African American leaders such as Frederick Douglass, Booker T. Washington, and W. E. B. Du BOIS had long before fought for equal rights for blacks. Their efforts and those of others were inspirational to the leaders of the modern Civil Rights movement. That long struggle for justice was brought to a head after World War II. Blacks had served their country with distinction in both the armed services and the defense industries during two world wars only to be rewarded with second-class citizenship. The GREAT DEPRESSION had been the "great leveler" of American society in terms of creating a much more even economic status for large numbers of blacks and whites. The prosperity that followed World War II inspired African Americans to seek a greater share of the American Dream than had been available in the past.

World War II also brought the end of colonialism in areas such as Africa. Independence for African countries inspired blacks in America to seek their freedom and presented a dilemma for the United States in the Cold War struggle with the Soviet Union. African dignitaries were embarrassed by the segregated public facilities they encountered in the United States, and this made excellent propaganda for the Soviets. The tragedy of the Nazi Holocaust against the Jews had a profound impact on race relations in the United States. The event raised disturbing questions about the possible end results of RACISM in America if tensions continued to escalate. These and other factors indicated that the time was ripe in the late 1950's for a civil rights struggle.

Early Developments. The modern movement for social change in the area of race relations began in 1955,

The Reverend Martin Luther King, Jr., and other leaders of the Civil Rights movement begin the final leg of the 1965 Selma-to-Montgomery march. (UPI/Corbis-Bettmann)

soon after the *Brown* decision. A teenage African American named Emmett Till was brutally murdered for allegedly flirting with a white woman. He was visiting Mississippi relatives and had been raised in the North, away from the race codes of the South. The event was an international disgrace for the United States, and it inspired demands for change.

That same year, Rosa PARKS was arrested in Montgomery, Alabama, for refusing to give up her seat to a white person on the city bus. Hers was not the first segregation incident of this nature, but she became the inspiration for the first major civil rights protest of the modern era. She was the secretary for the local branch of the NATIONAL ASSOCIATION FOR THE ADVANCEMENT OF COLORED PEOPLE (NAACP) and a model citizen in the community. Within days thousands of African Americans in Montgomery joined in a boycott of the city transportation system. It took more than a

year, but the buses were finally desegregated, and the movement had its first major success.

The event brought to the forefront of the struggle a young preacher who had just begun his ministry in Montgomery, the Reverend Martin Luther KING, Jr. King was well-educated, a powerful speaker, and a disciple of nonviolent CIVIL DISOBEDIENCE. Two years later, he would bring together like-minded individuals to form the SOUTHERN CHRISTIAN LEADERSHIP CONFERENCE (SCLC) to coordinate civil rights activity. The main strategy endorsed was borrowed from Henry David Thoreau and Mohandas K. Gandhi, with a liberal dose of Christian love added. Loving the enemy and refusing to retaliate in kind when attacked by racists would win the hearts and minds of most Americans to the ideals of human equality. Nonviolent civil disobedience moved the conscience of the nation as no other force for social change ever had in the past. In

A teenage girl holding a Confederate flag taunts civil rights marchers in Mississippi. (Archive Photos, Express Newspapers)

the end, the abandonment of that commitment to nonviolence would be the single greatest factor in bringing on the end of the Civil Rights movement.

After Montgomery, the next major development in the civil rights struggle was the LITTLE ROCK CRISIS. In 1957, nine black students tried to desegregate Central High School in Little Rock, Arkansas. Governor Orval Faubus called out the National Guard to prevent the children from entering the school. Television cameras showed whites yelling at a fifteen-year-old black girl, "Lynch her!" Eventually, President Dwight D. Eisenhower sent in National Guard troops, and the law of the land was implemented.

Sit-ins and Freedom Rides. In February, 1960, four black students from the local Greensboro, North Carolina, Agricultural and Technical College sat down at a Woolworth's lunch counter to be served. African Americans could be served everywhere else in the store, but Jim Crow laws drew the line at whites and blacks eating together. A new strategy was introduced to the struggle: SIT-INS. In the following days, hundreds of students joined in, and eventually downtown department stores in Greensboro were desegregated. Within the coming year, some seventy thousand people participated in sit-ins throughout the South, and more than three thousand were arrested. Some activists were brutalized by white segregationists. The sit-ins inspired the formation of the STUDENT NONVIOLENT COORDINATING COMMITTEE (SNCC) and brought young people to the forefront of the struggle.

The next strategy resurrected from the past, which also proved to be more successful than ever before, was the freedom ride. The Supreme Court had outlawed segregation in bus terminals and interstate transportation, so in May, 1961, a group of blacks and some whites decided to test the ruling. They were members of another important civil rights organization, the CONGRESS OF RACIAL EQUALITY (CORE). A white mob attacked the activists in Anniston, Alabama, with pipes, bricks, and knives. A firebomb was eventually tossed into a bus, and another busload of freedom riders was attacked near Anniston. One person's injuries were so bad that he was confined to a wheelchair for life.

Another bus was attacked in Birmingham, with police allowing the mob to beat up the activists with impunity. Members of the SNCC and the SCLC quickly joined in the FREEDOM RIDES, but King had more reservations about this strategy than any other; freedom riders were often brutalized. The John F. Kennedy Ad-

ministration also had strong opposition to the Freedom Rides because of the violence and the lack of state or local law enforcement. When John Siegenthaler, the federal official who was sent to negotiate with the governor of Alabama, tried to intervene on behalf of activists being beaten in Montgomery, he, too, was knocked unconscious by the mob. Federal marshals were eventually sent, and only their intervention prevented disaster when whites charged the First Baptist Church where King and other leaders were gathered to encourage the activists.

In regard to another freedom ride, the Kennedy Administration made a deal with the local authorities in Alabama: If they prevented mob violence, they could arrest the riders. By the end of the summer, more than a thousand activists had participated in Freedom Rides, with most being young Southern blacks. The results were mixed. On the one hand, the Interstate Commerce Commission (ICC) banned bus companies from using segregated terminals. On the other hand, the KU KLUX KLAN (KKK) grew in size and Governor George Wallace of Alabama became a nationally prominent figure who would play a major role in the next two presidential elections.

The Movement Expands. Wallace won national notoriety trying to keep the University of Alabama segregated; the year before, a crisis occurred at the University of Mississippi. In 1962, Governor Ross Barnett blocked the admission of James Meredith, the grandson of a slave and a military veteran. Even though two African Americans had been admitted to the University of Georgia the previous year (including future Public Broadcasting Service newscaster Charlayne Hunter-Gault), it was the confrontation at "Ole Miss" that seemed to signal the end of segregated higher education in the Deep South. The Kennedy Administration sent several hundred federal marshals to assure the admission and safety of Meredith. A riot broke out in which two people were killed and some 375 injured; Meredith was nevertheless admitted, and he went on to become a lawyer. Governor Wallace tried a similar stand the following year at the doors of the University of Alabama, declaring, "Segregation now; segregation tomorrow; segregation forever," but Alabama was desegregated without major incident.

The next important event in the civil rights struggle occurred in Birmingham, Alabama, in 1963. "Bombingham," as it was known to African Americans, was considered to be the most segregated city in the South. White supremists had bombed some sixty homes and

African American youths are sprayed with a firehose in Birmingham, Alabama, in 1964. (UPI/Corbis-Bettmann)

churches during the previous two decades with no arrests. Police Commissioner Eugene "Bull" Connor was notorious throughout the South for having one of the most brutal police departments in the country. As Connor and his policemen became more and more brutal, newspaper and television cameras showed the world the depths of racial hatred in the Deep South. Most Americans were unaware of just how inhumane Jim Crow laws were, but views changed. People were confronted with scenes of police beating children and women and saw firehoses (which could shred the bark from a tree) turned on nonviolent demonstrators. Police dogs were also used against activists, and some law-enforcement officials in the South resorted to the use of cattle prods. People who had straddled the fence on civil rights issues now came out in support for the end of Jim Crow.

Reverend King was arrested for the thirteenth time in the civil rights struggle and placed in Connor's overcrowded jail. When local white ministers urged patience, the SCLC leader wrote perhaps the most powerful modern statement in favor of CIVIL DISOBEDIENCE, his "Letter from a Birmingham Jail." He insisted that "freedom is never voluntarily given by the oppressor." When the jails were filled with adult activists, thousands of children took to the streets, some as young as six years old. They met the firehoses and police dogs head-on and changed the course of history. The Kennedy Administration sent in federal mediators, and the president delivered the strongest civil rights speech since Abraham Lincoln. He declared, "the time has come for this nation to fulfill its promise" to African Americans. Kennedy submitted to Congress what was to become the most sweeping civil rights legislation since Reconstruction: the CIVIL RIGHTS ACT OF 1964.

Soon after Kennedy's speech, Medgar Evers, Mississippi state secretary of the NAACP, was assassinated in front of his home. (His wife, MYRLIE EVERS-WILLIAMS, would go on to become head of that national organization, and his brother would become the first black mayor of a Deep Southern city since Reconstruction). Despite the assassination, the Civil Rights movement triumphed in Birmingham as business leaders agreed to desegregate local public facilities and to hire more blacks.

In August of 1963, some quarter of a million activists gathered at the Lincoln Memorial to show support for the civil rights bill. Tensions flared between young and old leaders of the movement concerning how militant the protest should be. Ultimately, however, it marked the high point of the movement as differences were put aside, and Martin Luther KING, Jr., delivered one of the most memorable speeches in modern history, the "I Have a Dream" speech. He declared that he dreamed of the day when "all God's children . . . will be able to join hands and sing in the words of the old Negro spiritual, 'Free at last.'"

Two weeks later, four black Sunday-school children were killed in a dynamite explosion at Birmingham's Sixteenth Street Baptist Church. Riots that ensued took the lives of two more young African Americans. Congress went on to pass the 1964 Civil Rights Act, which dismantled Jim Crow. A Southern legislator tried to kill the bill by amending it to outlaw discrimination in hiring on the basis not only of race but also sex. The ploy backfired, and women had their first taste of equal treatment under the law as the Civil Rights Act was signed by Lyndon B. Johnson with four major provisions: It outlawed discrimination in hiring, required equal access to all public accommodations, empowered the Justice Department to bring lawsuits against segregated public schools, and cut off federal funds to state and local programs found to be practicing DISCRIMINATION. It failed to resolve the issue of voting, which remained the last phase of the Civil Rights movement.

Voter Registration. In the Deep South during the 1950's, more than 90 percent of eligible black voters were not registered to vote. In several areas of the South, blacks outnumbered whites, and voting was believed to be the key to empowerment. Voting, however, was a dangerous activity, because traditionally the KKK and other such groups had terrorized potential black voters, and some African Americans had paid with their lives for trying to exercise their constitutional rights. Activists decided to target Mississippi in a concerted voter drive in 1964.

Mississippi had the nation's lowest rate of voter registration among blacks (in 1960, less than 2 percent of eligible blacks were registered) and was the poorest state in the country. Bob Moses (also known as Bob Parris) was one of the key leaders in the voter campaign. In 1961, he left Harlem for Mississippi and found an uphill battle in the voting drive. He and other activists came up with the idea that a thousand, primarily white, college students should be recruited during the "freedom summer" of 1964 to help in voter registration. It proved to be a pivotal experience in the history of the Civil Rights movement because it occurred

Civil Rights movement

right at the time Black Power ideas were surfacing. Tensions between blacks and whites would further the black nationalism of the decade. Workers tried to put their differences aside and formed the Council of Federated Organizations (COFO) to coordinate the voting activities. The country had largely ignored the trials and tribulations of black activists; with whites entering the South in large numbers, it was believed, things would change in a hurry with the attendant publicity.

Three of the workers, two of them white, were killed at the very beginning of the summer—Michael Schwerner, Andrew Goodman, and James Chaney. Before it was over, thirty-seven black churches and thirty homes had been burned or bombed, and at least eighty civil rights workers had been beaten. But optimism was high, and by the fall of 1964, activists had formed the Mississippi Freedom Democratic Party to send a biracial delegation to the Democratic National Convention. It claimed to represent the entire population of the state rather than the traditional, all-white delegation representing the state's segregationists. When they tried to unseat the regular delegation, however, they were offered only two token representatives, and they decided to walk out of the convention. Many of the activists were disillusioned and bitter about the possibility of working within the system to bring about social change. Many young blacks also charged white activists with assuming positions of leadership and stealing publicity from black leaders in the movement.

Most of the more moderate leaders of the Civil Rights movement continued to work for voter registration. After the freedom summer, the focus of the voting drive changed from working at the state level to putting pressure on the federal government for action. In 1965, King and other leaders decided on a march from Selma, Alabama, to the state capitol in order to express their concern for voting rights.

One more time, the violence of white racists would bring much-needed sympathy to the cause of civil rights. Two marches were attempted before the third

A civil rights protester injured at a 1965 demonstration in Alabama. (Archive Photos)

was successful. Police attacked the first marchers, and James Reeb, a Northern white minister, was killed by a white mob. Although a black man, Jimmy Lee Jackson, had recently been fatally shot by a state trooper in a nearby voter protest, Reeb's death brought a national outcry. King turned the second march around to avoid police attack, but the third march included thousands from all over the country and was escorted by a federalized National Guard. The event did not end without tragedy, however: Viola Liuzzo, a Chicago mother of five children, was murdered as she drove activists in her car. Congress passed the VOTING RIGHTS ACT of 1965, the last major achievement of the Civil Rights movement. The law removed obstacles to voting and authorized federal agents to assure fair voting practices.

What some considered victory was not enough for others. The struggle for voting rights persuaded SNCC leader Stokely Carmichael and others to create the Lowndes County Freedom Organization; its symbol was a black panther. A new phase of the struggle was emerging: BLACK NATIONALISM. Although some scholars conclude that the BLACK POWER MOVEMENT was separate and distinct from the more moderate struggle known as the Civil Rights movement, it can be argued that both were part of the same attempt to attain justice.

Aftermath and Black Power. The social and political atmosphere of the United States dramatically changed in the mid-1960's. Civil disturbances swept through urban America at the very time the war in Vietnam escalated with U.S. bombing and ground troops. The Civil Rights movement entered into a more cynical and militant phase. With change coming slowly, black power advocates came to drown out more moderate voices in the late 1960's. Two major groups that shaped the Black Power movement were the Black Muslims (NATION OF ISLAM) and the Black Panthers. The Black Muslims are a religious organization that had its origins in the 1930's. It was founded by Elijah MUHAMMED, but by the 1960's, a young rival, MALCOLM X (Malcolm Little), had emerged as the group's most compelling spokesman.

The other major black power organization was the BLACK PANTHER PARTY. Founded in 1966 in Oakland, California, by Bobby Seale and Huey Newton, the Panthers began as a self-defense organization directed against POLICE BRUTALITY. The shift away from nonviolence brought on white backlash. The same white Americans who had supported the Civil Rights Act and Voting Rights Act opposed black nationalism.

Conclusion. Civil rights activity continued into the late 1960's with the federal government's War on Poverty program and King's Poor People's Campaign, which he never lived to see materialize. The only significant achievement of the movement after 1965, however, was an open-housing ordinance in 1968, which was ultimately so watered down as to be ineffective. King's assassination that year removed the most important civil rights leader in modern times. Nevertheless, the Civil Rights movement transformed America. It led to the Civil Rights Act and the Voting Rights Act and legally brought an end to SEGREGATION. It also inspired other social protests. With all its achievements, however, it left much to be done in the struggle for racial justice.   —*Benjamin T. Harrison*

SUGGESTED READINGS: The most authoritative work on the Civil Rights movement is Taylor Branchs' *Parting the Waters: America in the King Years, 1954-1963* (New York: Simon & Schuster, 1988). A well researched account of the SNCC can be found in Clayborne Carson's *In Struggle: SNCC and the Black Awakening of the 1960's* (Cambridge, Mass.: Harvard University Press, 1981). William H. Chafe has written a brilliant analysis of all sides of the conflict on a local level, *Civilities and Civil Rights: Greensboro, North Carolina, and the Black Struggle for Freedom* (Oxford, England: Oxford University Press, 1980).

David Garrow wrote the standard biography of King in *Bearing the Cross: Martin Luther King, Jr., and the Southern Christian Leadership Conference* (New York: Random House, 1986). Malcolm X and Alex Haley's *The Autobiography of Malcolm X* (New York: Ballantine Books, 1964) is a powerful statement on black power. A well-researched account of CORE can be found in August Meier and Elliot Rudwick's *CORE: A Study in the Civil Rights Movement, 1942-1968* (New York: Oxford University Press, 1973). Howard Sitkoff's *The Struggle for Black Equality, 1954-1980* (New York: Hill and Wang, 1981) is a concise and balanced survey of the movement.

Class: Categorization of people in a society in a hierarchical fashion according to degree of power and prestige. Those with the most prestige and power are placed at the top of the pyramid, those with the least of these fall toward the bottom, and all other members of society are variously arranged between these two extremes. This pyramidal model makes clear that those with the most are fewest in number and those with the least are greatest in number.

A worker examines a luxury car during a party for automobile industry executives. (Jim West)

A stratification system is said to exist in all known societies. The most ancient means of categorization was on the basis of age and gender, with male elders most often holding the greatest prestige and power.

In Western societies, social class is determined by a combination of factors that include level of income, EDUCATION, occupation, WEALTH, and lifestyle. In turn, these factors determine one's place on the social ladder and the degree of prestige and power one is given by other members of the society.

In most Western cultures, the higher one's income, the greater the opportunities available to one. In capitalistic societies, financial success is deemed highly desirable and commendable. Further, it is generally understood that an individual's educational level affects one's social ranking; the higher one's education, the greater the respect and deference one is generally given. Income and education frequently correlate, with higher salaries being paid to occupations requiring extensive education and long training. A good example of this would be the education needed to become a physician, a profession that is both highly esteemed in the United States and maintains a higher income than other less education-intensive jobs.

Wealth involves more than the salary that is made each year. It is the sum total of the accumulated money and assets, such as real estate or stocks and bonds, that is acquired. Wealth is related to ownership—of a home, a company, a factory—and through ownership, the ability to influence others is increased; that is, power is manipulated.

These interrelated factors determine an individual's lifestyle. A person's relative ability to purchase a home, a car, and a wardrobe and to provide not only for the necessities of life but also for recreation, quality purchases (such as "name-brand" items or high-priced homes, cars, and clothes) and to accumulate an economic surplus all contribute to the categorization of social class and the acquisition of prestige and power.

An alternative view of social class was developed by Karl Marx in the mid-nineteenth century. He defined a person's class position by one's relationship to the means of production. In other words, one either owned the equipment and means of making a product (in which case one was a member of the class Marx called the "bourgeoisie") or sold one's labor to the owner in exchange for a wage (in which case one was a member of the "proletariat"). Marx predicted the eventual overthrow of the bourgeoisie by the proletariat in an attempt to escape oppression, an event that has not occurred on the scale that Marx envisioned.

Clean Air Act Amendments (1970, 1990): Amendments to the 1963 Clean Air Act. The 1970 amendments created the Environmental Protection Agency (EPA), set national standards for air quality, and strengthened existing limits on automobile emissions. The air-quality and auto-emission standards of the 1970 legislation were to be achieved by 1975 but had not been met by the late 1980's. The 1990 amendments set revised deadlines for meeting air-quality and auto-emission standards. A timetable for the reduction in sulfur dioxide and nitrogen oxide emissions from coal

combustion and guidelines for a gradual phaseout in the manufacture of CHLOROFLUOROCARBONS (CFCs) and other ozone-depleting chemicals were also established.

Clean Water Act (1972): U.S. federal legislation. The Clean Water Act was enacted in 1972 on the premise that prevention is a fundamental part of environmental quality. The act set a national goal of creating or preserving fishable and swimmable surface water and provided for the establishment of water-quality standards and effluent limitations; its major targets were point-source polluters. Periodic reenactment of the legislation changed its emphasis to control of non-point-source pollution. The 1992 reen-

President George Bush signs 1990 amendments to the Clean Air Act. (Archive Photos, Reuters, Gary Cameron)

actment of the legislation incorporated new components dealing with storm water and pretreatment; it also gave states slightly more flexibility in setting minimum contaminant levels for a variety of toxic chemicals.

Clear and present danger: Legal standard used in regulating the FREEDOM OF SPEECH granted by the First Amendment to the U.S. Constitution. The doctrine was first articulated by Supreme Court chief justice Oliver Wendell Holmes in *SCHENCK V. UNITED STATES* (1919), which concerned the right of the government to regulate speech in time of war. The court ruled that freedom of speech may be restricted if it creates "a clear and present danger" or brings about "substantive evils." The doctrine was upheld in several subsequent cases until a 1969 Supreme Court decision overturned it.

Clinical death: Phase in the death process when heartbeat and respiration cease. Clinical death is distinguished from BRAIN DEATH, in which event the brain stem ceases to function, and from cellular death, in which all cellular activity stops. Normally, clinical death occurs first, followed quickly by brain death; when medical intervention occurs, however, the heart and lungs may be kept operative past brain death. Controversy has swirled around such issues as whether brain-dead people should be kept clinically alive and whether brain-dead persons must be allowed to undergo clinical death before organs are removed for transplanting to other people.

Clinton, Bill (William Jefferson Blythe IV, b. Aug. 19, 1946, Hope, Ark.): Forty-second president of the United States. His inauguration on January 20, 1993, fulfilled a lifelong ambition to influence public policy and attain the highest office in the land.

William Jefferson Blythe IV was born three months after his father died in an automobile accident. When his mother married Roger Clinton, the boy adopted his stepfather's last name. In 1963, as a delegate to the Boy's Nation program in Washington, D.C., he met President John F. KENNEDY and decided to make politics his career. After graduating from Georgetown University in 1968, he spent two years as a Rhodes Scholar at Oxford University before entering Yale University Law School. While at Yale, he met fellow student Hillary Rodham, whom he married on October 11, 1975. Their only child, Chelsea Victoria, was born on February 27, 1980.

After graduating from Yale in 1973, Clinton returned to Arkansas to practice law and teach at the University of Arkansas School of Law, but he soon ran for public office. In 1976, he was elected state attorney general; two years later, at the age of thirty-two, he became the youngest governor in the nation. His policy of raising gasoline taxes and automobile license fees to finance an ambitious highway-improvement program proved unpopular, and he was defeated when he ran for reelection in 1980. Clinton returned to office in 1982, beginning a ten-year span in which he reformed Arkansas' educational, welfare, and health-care systems, winning a reputation as the most effective governor in the nation.

Most observers did not believe that President George BUSH could be defeated in 1992 after his successful leadership during the Persian GULF WAR. Many leading Democrats declined to run, but Clinton entered the presidential primaries and received his party's nomination despite many personal attacks on his character. When ROSS PEROT mounted an independent candidacy for the presidency, the contest became a three-way race that Clinton won with 43 percent of the vote to Bush's 39 percent and Perot's 19 percent.

Clinton's first two years in office were marked by both successes and failures. The nation recovered from a business recession. Congress passed a budget that reduced the deficit, agreed to a sweeping anticrime program, including a ban on the sale of some ASSAULT WEAPONS, and established a national-service program to employ young adults in community service. Clinton appointed many women and minorities to prominent government positions. Passage of the NORTH AMERICAN FREE TRADE AGREEMENT (NAFTA) and the GENERAL AGREEMENT ON TARIFFS AND TRADE (GATT) began a process intended to open the whole world to the benefits of free trade. A wide-ranging health-care reform proposal, for which his wife was a major spokesperson, proved too complex and failed passage. Controversial appointments and scandals involving members of his administration led to widespread criticism, as did his uncertain leadership of U.S. foreign policy. In the 1994 Congressional elections, Republicans took over the majority of both houses of Congress for the first time since 1954 and threatened to reverse the social policies, advanced by Democratic presidents

President-elect Bill Clinton in December, 1992. (Reuters/Corbis-Bettmann)

First Lady Hillary Rodham Clinton testifies before the Senate Finance Committee on Health Care in 1993. (Reuters/Corbis-Bettmann)

from Franklin D. Roosevelt to Jimmy CARTER, that Clinton favored.

Clinton, Hillary Rodham (b. Oct. 26, 1947, Chicago, Ill.): First Lady of the United States. Hillary Rodham grew up in a middle-class neighborhood in Park Ridge, Illinois. She won academic honors while completing her undergraduate degree at Wellesley College and in 1973 was graduated from Yale University Law School. At Yale, she met fellow law student Bill Clinton, who shared her idealism and commitment to public service. They married on October 11, 1975; in 1980, their daughter Chelsea was born.

Even as a young girl, Hillary had been interested in politics and current events. Early in life, she decided to combine private legal practice with public service. In 1968, she worked for the House Republican Conference, and in 1974 she joined the staff of the House Judiciary Committee during the Watergate investigation that eventually led to President Richard M. NIXON's resignation.

After she moved to Bill Clinton's home state of Arkansas, she taught law at the University of Arkansas. In 1977, she became a partner in a major Little Rock law firm and continued to work there while Bill served four terms as governor of Arkansas. She helped to shape public policy by serving on several major reform commissions, and she headed the Arkansas Education Standards Committee, which overhauled the entire state educational system. She was twice named as one of the "One Hundred Most Influential Lawyers in America."

Hillary Rodham Clinton and Bill Clinton presented themselves as a team in the harsh 1992 presidential campaign against Republican incumbent George BUSH. She confronted accusations that her husband had been unfaithful, and she came under scathing attack from some critics because she broke traditional stereotypes that required candidates' wives to play low-key roles in campaigns. In 1993, Bill Clinton named his wife director of a task force with a mission to plan a massive overhaul of the nation's HEALTH-CARE SYSTEM, which she found to be a costly, inadequate structure that did not provide insurance coverage for thirty-seven million Americans. Her proposed reform plan included health-care cost controls and provided medical insurance coverage for all Americans. In 1994, Congress rejected her plan. Critics charged that it was too complicated, required too much government involvement, and would lead to tax increases. Business organizations fought it because it required employers to pay employee health benefits. Many experts, however, believed that continuing problems in the health-care system would eventually force the nation to accept some such plan.

After defeat of the health-care plan, Hillary reduced her visibility as First Lady. She immersed herself in work with voluntary organizations that helped children and women. In 1995, she conducted a successful tour of South Asia, promoting worldwide improvement in education and health care for females. As First Lady, she was often compared to Eleanor Roosevelt. Both received criticism as they challenged stereotypes, but both left a lasting mark on history.

Clitoridectomy: Excision or surgical removal of a woman's clitoris, also known as clitorectomy or "female circumcision." The operation is practiced routinely in many countries of West and East Africa and parts of the Middle East, and occasionally in other areas of the world.

Several types of clitoridectomy have been recognized. Some writers distinguish only between the removal of the clitoris (or part thereof), with or without the labia minora, and the far more drastic infibulation, which includes the removal of the labia and the sewing up of the entire vulva; this practice is also known as pharaonic circumcision (technically, infibulation may take place without the removal of the clitoris). Others, including novelist Alice Walker, a well-known critic of the practice, make finer distinctions depending on the degree of severity of the operation.

The operation, and the primitive circumstances in which it is often performed, can cause serious medical complications. The operation is usually performed with little regard for hygiene, mostly by women in rural areas who claim special skills. The death rate among women who have undergone that operation, especially infibulation, may be as high as 6 percent as a result of complications. Moreover, women who have undergone the procedure generally have difficulty experiencing physical pleasure in sexual intercourse, since these sensations are largely dependent on the clitoris.

Clitoridectomy has been performed on an estimated 75 million women and female children in the countries of East Africa (Djibouti, Kenya, Somalia, Sudan, Tanzania, Uganda), the countries of West Africa (Benin, Burkina Faso, Chad, the Gambia, Ghana, Guinea,

Cloning

Ivory Coast, Liberia, Mali, Mauritania, Niger, Nigeria, Senegal, Sierra Leone, Togo) and, to a lesser extent, in other parts of Africa, including Egypt, Ethiopia, Cameroon, the Central African Republic, and Zaire. Other countries around the world where clitoridectomy is practiced include the United Arab Emirates, Oman, Bahrain, Yemen, Saudi Arabia, Indonesia, and Malaysia. Incidents of clitoridectomy have been reported in the United States, Great Britain (where it has been outlawed), India, Pakistan, and France.

In many of these countries, there are associations that have dedicated themselves to eradicating the practice. The struggle against clitoridectomy, however, has to confront tradition. The reasons given for the operation include arguments based on religion, even though the practice is not mentioned in the Koran (many of the countries where clitoridectomy is practiced are predominantly Muslim) nor advocated in the Bible. Folk traditions also contribute to the practice's persistence. Some members of the African Dogon people, for example, believe that boys and girls are born androgynous and that the distinction between the sexes must be made by surgical intervention. In the case of infibulation, an emphasis on virginity or—when sowing is renewed after childbirth—enhancing a man's pleasure in sexual intercourse contributes to the decision to perform the operation. In addition, some defenders of the practice argue that clitoridectomy is an integral and legitimate part of many cultures; Kenyan politician and anthropologist Jomo Kenyatta, for example, defended clitoridectomy as a cultural tradition and commented that the attempts to curb the practice represented, with respect to African nations, efforts to "disintegrate their social order and thereby hasten their Europeanization." The crusade against clitoridectomy is thus viewed in some cultures as Western interference, yet another obnoxious manifestation of European imperialism.

American attention has been brought to the issue largely by the work of novelist Alice Walker, whose 1992 novel *Possessing the Secret of Joy* concerns the lifelong agony of a victim of clitoridectomy. Walker and Pratibha Parmar have also produced the nonfiction work *Warrior Marks: Female Genital Mutilation and the Sexual Blinding of Women* (1993), which gave rise to a documentary film.

Cloning: Isolation and production of multiple copies of genetic material, deoxyribonucleic acid (DNA). The process is generally carried out to isolate specific genes, with the goal of sequencing their structure or inserting the genes into another cell. Such a process is called "GENETIC ENGINEERING." Most often, cloning is used to study the function of a specific gene or to attempt correction of a defective gene. Some observers, however, have expressed concern that through gene cloning and attendant genetic engineering, altered or dangerous life forms might be created.

Coattails: Political term referring to a popular presidential candidate's ability to bring votes to other candidates of the same party. Voters attracted to a presidential candidate might also vote for members of the candidate's party whom they would otherwise ignore; the congressmen who thus owe their victories to the president generally offer their support for the president's programs. A president who brings in many new congressmen from his party would be said to have "long coattails." While presidential coattails once offered a measure of a president's power, many political scientists now claim that coattail voting is declining and rarely determines an election.

Cobain, Kurt (Feb. 20, 1967, Aberdeen, Wash.—April 5, 1994, Seattle, Wash.): Lead singer, guitarist, and songwriter for the band Nirvana, the most critically successful GRUNGE rock band. His SUICIDE consecrated his popular image as the representative figure of his forlorn and futureless generation, sometimes referred to as GENERATION X. Because his suicide was followed by several copycat suicides, it has raised questions about the dangers of celebrity role models.

Born in Aberdeen, Washington, a bleak logging town approximately two hours southwest of Seattle, Cobain grew up in a broken home; his father, an auto mechanic, and his mother, a secretary, were divorced when he was eight. He spent much of his childhood and adolescence being shifted from one relative's house to another's, passing occasional nights under the local bridge. In 1987, he formed the band Nirvana with bassist Chris Novoselic. (They were joined by drummer David Grohl in 1990.) Nirvana's first album, *Bleach* (1988), attracted little attention outside of Seattle—where, however, the band had quickly developed a large following in the thriving local music scene.

Nirvana's breakthrough came with their 1991 album *Nevermind*, which sold nearly ten million copies. The

Kurt Cobain during a 1993 performance. (AP/Wide World Photos)

Cocaine and crack cocaine

album was buoyed by the single "Smells Like Teen Spirit," an MTV hit that quickly became a grunge anthem. Its refrain, "Here we are now, entertain us/ I feel stupid and contagious," articulated the way many youths felt about the inanity of much popular culture—and, perhaps, their own lives.

Nirvana's music helped define the raw nature of rock and roll in the 1990's. The anger and frustration expressed in Cobain's lyrics and voice, however, were the band's most distinguishing features. While some took these lyrics to express the frustrations of a generation, others saw them simply as expressing the anguish of a tortured soul.

Cobain's suicide deeply saddened thousands, if not millions, yet it was not a surprise. Just weeks earlier, in Rome, he had attempted a drug-and-alcohol suicide and had briefly lapsed into a coma. While trying to overcome heroin addiction, Cobain was also coping with extreme stomach pains, from which he suffered

his whole life; according to friends, he was also having increasing trouble dealing with his sudden, meteoric success and his status as idol to millions. In his suicide note, he suggested that he no longer believed in himself as a rock star, claiming that "the worst crime is faking it." Cobain was survived by wife, Courtney Love, a controversial former model who fronted her own successful band, Hole, and their daughter, Frances Bean.

Critics of Cobain complained that his cynical attitude toward life and "cowardly" suicide had a disastrous influence on countless impressionable young people. Cobain's defenders, on the other hand, argued that his musical talent lifted people up, perhaps ultimately saving lives.

Cocaine and crack cocaine: Powerful stimulants derived from the South American coca plant. Cocaine, a white powder that is typically snorted or injected by

A pipe used to smoke crack cocaine. (UPI/Corbis-Bettmann)

users, was prescribed for medical purposes in the nineteenth century, and private cocaine use was legal in the United States until the 1930's. Cocaine use declined when amphetamines were introduced, but the drug again became fashionable in the 1960's, although high prices limited its popularity.

In the 1980's, crack cocaine, a mixture of cocaine and other chemicals that produces smokable "rocks," began to appear in American cities. Because crack is far cheaper than pure cocaine, its production made the drug available to millions of impoverished inner-city users, and crack use soon became a major urban social problem. Both cocaine and crack can have serious medical side effects and are extremely psychologically addictive.

Codependency: Learned pattern of maladaptive responses to relationships and relationship problems characterized by overconcern with and desire to control the behavior of others. These responses can be psychological, emotional, and behavioral. Often, codependency is experienced as a constricted ability to express needs and concerns related to interpersonal problems; unspoken rules or expectations are often an obstacle. This response pattern is frequently observed in individuals who have problems with addictive behaviors (such as SUBSTANCE ABUSE, EATING DISORDERS, GAMBLING, or compulsive sexual behavior) or other mental disorders, as well as in their partners, spouses, or other family members.

Cold War, end of: Reduction of U.S.-Soviet rivalry, brought about by fundamental changes in the hostile and confrontational relationship between the two superpowers.

Background (1945-1985). The Cold War between the Western democracies and the communist world dominated international affairs in the decades following World War II. Mutual suspicion after 1945 divided the world into two armed camps, characterized by opposing military alliances and large military budgets. The United States undertook a "containment" policy, resisting extension of communist influence and Soviet power. A massive arms race, including development of destructive NUCLEAR WEAPONS, jeopardized world peace in the postwar era.

Competition between the two SUPERPOWERS, while not leading to direct conflict, shaped the atmosphere of the period. This deeply rooted rivalry existed in Europe, Africa, the Middle East, and Asia. Occasionally, regional disputes erupted into conflict, as in the Middle East or Southeast Asia, with the superpowers supporting opposite sides. The United States and Soviet Union portrayed each other as dangerous, aggressive, and expansionist.

The arms buildup and ideological competition continued into the early years of President Ronald REAGAN's administration. In a famous 1983 speech, he called the Soviet Union the "evil empire" and promised to keep America militarily stronger than its rival. The development of improved nuclear weapons during this period created more tensions, and even terminated U.S.-Soviet arms-control negotiations.

Ending the Cold War (1985-1991). Changes in this long-time antagonism emerged after Mikhail GORBACHEV came to power in the Soviet Union in 1985. He and Reagan consulted at several high-level summit meetings. George BUSH succeeded Reagan as president in 1989 and continued negotiations with Russian leaders to resolve existing tensions and potential dangers. Serious and sustained efforts during these years eventually resulted in agreements that greatly lessened the danger of a third world war. Treaties eventually eliminated intermediate-range nuclear missile systems, reduced military forces and weapons in Europe, and removed many long-range strategic nuclear missiles.

Such significant achievements helped end the Cold War. In addition, communist governments in Eastern European states fell from power in 1989. The infamous Berlin Wall, dividing the historic city into democratic and communist sections, came down in late 1989 and the two German nations united in 1990. The Warsaw Pact, the main alliance of the Soviet Union and its East European allies, was abolished in 1991.

The cooperation between Gorbachev, Reagan, and Bush between 1985 and 1991 significantly changed the Cold War era. Gorbachev received the Nobel Peace Prize in 1990 for his contributions. The United States supported the beginnings of democratic reform in the Soviet Union in 1989 and 1990, as its totalitarian system began to weaken. Serious political and economic problems there had gotten worse for several years, however, and the nation disintegrated in late 1991. The fifteen republics of the former Soviet Union now existed as separate states, most of which joined the new COMMONWEALTH OF INDEPENDENT STATES (CIS).

The Relationship in the Post-Soviet Period (after 1991). The post-Soviet period initially promised posi-

Russian president Boris Yeltsin and U.S. president George Bush celebrate the end of the Cold War in 1992. (AP/Wide World Photos)

tive Russian-American relations. President Boris YELTSIN, the new Russian leader, visited the United States in early 1992. He and President Bush signed a "Statement of Principles" declaring the end of the Cold War. The agreement also broadly defined the future relationship between Russia and the West, emphasizing cooperative behavior.

Additional negotiations led to more arms-control agreements, including the second Strategic Arms Reduction Talks (START II) to expand the reduction of strategic nuclear weapons of the two superpowers. Bush and Yeltsin signed this treaty in Moscow. Beginning in 1993, Presidents Bill CLINTON and Yeltsin met periodically and both governments sought a framework for cooperation between the two nations.

The breakup of the Soviet Union in 1991, however, did not mean that Cold War suspicions and potential dangers had disappeared totally. Four of the CIS republics (including Russia) still possessed powerful nuclear weapons capable of potential use against Europe and the United States. Boris Yeltsin, a former leading official of the Communist Party, now portrayed himself as a proponent of democracy. His use of military force to overthrow the Russian Parliament in Moscow in October, 1993, raised serious questions about his democratic commitment. Russia's foreign policy also appeared threatening to several adjacent European nations. Large numbers of Russian troops and other military forces of the former Soviet Union remained in Eastern Europe, although negotiations eventually led to their withdrawal in 1994.

Time would tell how words of friendship could be translated into reality. Russia and the West understandably continued to hold different national interests and sometimes conflicting strategic objectives. The superpowers, still possessing NUCLEAR WEAPONS, remained influential and powerful nations. Reductions of armed forces and nuclear weapons systems generally followed the treaty schedules, a trend that significantly lowered the potential danger of major conflict. Yet the former adversaries occasionally found it difficult to strengthen their cooperation in the new era. Tough negotiations and controversial proposals slowed consensus and agreement. The potential danger of destabilizing the political and military balance in Europe never fully disappeared. Neither side eliminated all of their nuclear arsenals, nor ever promised to do so.

Beyond confronting military questions, differences over economic issues also undercut the positive atmosphere that initially existed in the aftermath of the Soviet Union's demise in 1991. Yeltsin's plans for economic reforms as well as his promised support of democratic values and political systems in Russia quickly became tangled in serious economic problems and other domestic disputes. Russia felt the West provided insufficient amounts of long-term economic assistance. Nor did democratic reform evolve smoothly in Russia, and Yeltsin's forceful ouster of the Russian Parliament by military action in late 1993 shook Western confidence in his leadership.

America's favorable attitude toward Russia eroded further in late 1994 when Russian forces began a major offensive against the independence movement in Chechnya (a region attempting to secede from Russia). This small but intense civil war, continuing for many months without achieving a decisive victory, caused massive civilian as well as military casualties. Western governments, including the United States, criticized the Russian leadership for its deadly attacks against the Chechen population.

Conditions in Southeast Europe also revealed differences between Russia and the West. After the disintegration of Yugoslavia in 1991-1992, civil war erupted between competing regions and groups. Russia and the West occasionally disagreed over possible solutions to end the civil war, especially in Bosnia-Herzegovina, leading to more criticism and coolness.

Another reason for East-West disagreement arose when several states of Eastern Europe sought membership in the NORTH ATLANTIC TREATY ORGANIZATION (NATO). Russia vigorously accused the United States and the West of anti-Russian hostility and an effort to create instability in Eastern Europe by bringing NATO closer to Russian territory. Although the West gave assurances that admitting more states to NATO did not indicate an anti-Russian policy, Moscow continued its opposition. Thus, differences and problems continued to exist in the East-West relationship even after the Soviet Union's collapse in 1991.

Implications for the Future. RUSSIA AND THE UNITED STATES have shown that they can successfully negotiate significant reductions of their opposing military forces (especially nuclear missiles) and establish a basis for cooperation. The level of competition and danger of the Cold War has greatly declined. Future relations between the two SUPERPOWERS will depend primarily on international issues on which they can agree. American financial assistance to Russia in the post-Cold War period seems certain to continue. Russia's need for outside help provides limited Western leverage in influencing government policies. It appears probable, however, that the future relationship between Russia and the United States will undergo occasional and sometimes serious disputes. The two superpowers are likely to disagree on substantial issues, for the Cold War heritage is difficult to erase completely. Each side will press for its own advantage, and the possibility of expanded military weapons systems and defense budgets is both logical and probably inevitable. Future Russian and American leaders will determine the direction of the relationship, based on their nation's objectives. Overall, the relationship is far more positive than in prior decades. *—Taylor Stults*

Colorado Constitution Ballot Amendment 2

SUGGESTED READINGS: *NATO After Forty Years* (Wilmington, Del.: SR Books, 1990), edited by Lawrence S. Kaplan, provides a broad analysis of NATO's significance. Richard Crockatt's *The Fifty Years War: The United States and the Soviet Union in World Politics, 1941-1991* (New York: Routledge, 1995) illustrates the long period of confrontation. Don Oberdorfer, *The Turn: From the Cold War to a New Era: The United States and the Soviet Union, 1983-1990* (New York: Poseidon Press, 1991) traces the Reagan-Gorbachev period.

Michael R. Beschloss and Strobe Talbott's *At the Highest Levels: The Inside Story of the End of the Cold War* (Boston: Little, Brown, 1993) deals with major leaders and events between 1989 and 1991. John L. Gaddis, a leading scholar of the Cold War, broadly interprets the subject in *The United States and the End of the Cold War: Implications, Reconsiderations, Provocations* (New York: Oxford University Press, 1992). Boris Yeltsin's *The Struggle for Russia* (New York: Random House, 1994) gives a Russian perspective on the end of the Cold War.

Colorado Constitution Ballot Amendment 2: Antigay legislation. Arguing that the state of Colorado was "under siege by the radical and intrusive homosexual lobby," activist Kevin Tebedo formed Colorado for Family Values (CFV) in 1990 with help from national religious organizations. At the top of CFV's agenda was an initiative petition forbidding the state of Colorado, or any local government in the state, to enact CIVIL RIGHTS LEGISLATION aimed at protecting gays and lesbians from discrimination and repealing any such ordinances already in existence. Placed on the November, 1992, Colorado ballot as Amendment 2, the measure passed. Gay rights proponents quickly organized a Colorado boycott in retaliation, and the AMERICAN CIVIL LIBERTIES UNION (ACLU) and other groups joined in challenging Amendment 2 in the courts.

Coming out: Process of revealing to others that one is homosexual; gay men and lesbians often describe this as "coming out of the closet." As a minority group often condemned and not understood, most homosexuals in Europe and the United States live "in the closet"—pretending they are heterosexual—in order to live without censure. In recent decades, however, increasing numbers have begun coming out rather than hiding their sexual orientation and relationships. Many gays support coming out as a way to educate the public about gay people and bring about greater toleration of homosexuals.

Commander in chief, U.S.: Role of the president established by Article II, section 2 of the U.S. Constitution. Suspicious of executive powers, the Constitution's framers specifically divided responsibilities for national defense; the president was named as the commander of the military, but Congress was given the power to declare war. The ensuing "invitation to struggle" between Congress and the president over the conduct of military policy has been one of the U.S. government's most contentious issues. In the wake of the Civil War and for much of the twentieth century, presidential control over foreign policy and war making was not regularly challenged by Congress. In the aftermath of the Vietnam War, however, the 1973 War Powers Resolution attempted to reassert Congress' role in military and war-making policy.

Commission on Civil Rights, U.S.: Government agency created by the Civil Rights Act of 1957 and reestablished by a similar act in 1983. The commission collects and studies information on DISCRIMINATION or denials of EQUAL PROTECTION of the law because of race, color, religion, age, sex, handicap, or national origin. It further investigates the administration of justice in such areas as VOTING RIGHTS, enforcement of federal CIVIL RIGHTS laws, and equality of opportunity in education, employment, and housing. Although the commission does not have enforcement authority, it submits reports to the president and to Congress, which often result in action through statutes, regulations, or executive orders.

Commission on Human Rights, U.N. (UNCHR): Human rights organization established by the United Nations Economic and Social Council (ECOSOC) in 1946. Its original mandate called for the submission of proposals for an international bill of rights and international conventions on specific rights. The UNCHR was also to make recommendations regarding the status of women, the protection of minorities, and the prevention of discrimination. The commission has pre-

A French delegate to a 1947 meeting of the U.N. Commission on Human Rights chats with U.S. representative Eleanor Roosevelt. (UPI/Corbis-Bettmann)

pared many international declarations and conventions, the most notable of which is the UNIVERSAL DECLARATION OF HUMAN RIGHTS. The forty-three members of the Commission, who represent an equitable geographical distribution, are elected for three-year terms and meet each year to discuss reports on human rights violations throughout the world.

Commodification: Medical and ethical term. Commodification, in the realm of REPRODUCTIVE ISSUES, refers to economic transactions involving human reproductive tissue. Reproductive cells—sperm, eggs, or zygotes—become commodities to be bought and sold. Payments also could be viewed as being compensation for the inconvenience of providing the tissue or as compensation for surrendering rights to the tissue, rather than as being in exchange for the tissues themselves. Commodification also has been used to refer to employment of a surrogate gestator, a woman who agrees to become pregnant with and carry to term a baby that she will give up to someone else. This agreement, if it is to be called commodification, involves a payment to the gestator in excess of actual costs related to the pregnancy. Those opposed to this practice often refer to it by the less neutral, more negative term "baby selling."

Common Cause (CC): Nonprofit, nonpartisan citizens' lobby founded by John Gardner in 1970. Common Cause seeks to improve the way government works, through the activities of its 250,000 members, most of whom participate in determining priorities and policies through an annual issues poll. Working at both the state and national levels, CC members advocate for open, honest, and accountable government through LOBBYING campaigns, public speaking, and letter-writing. Some of the group's most successful reforms have been in the areas of campaign financing, open meetings, lobby disclosure, civil rights, and the federal budget process.

Common good: Idea that social interests override individual interests. The use of the phrase in English has been traced back to the fourteenth century; originally, it referred to the public property of a community or corporation. Later, the phrase came to mean the good of the society that supersedes the interests of

individuals. The concept also implies that there exists a single supreme value from which all other values are derived. Great political philosophers of the seventeenth and eighteenth centuries such as John Locke and Jean-Jacques Rousseau elaborated on this notion as the cornerstone of civil society and responsible government, although they typically used such alternative phrases as "common weal," "public good," and "general will" rather than "common good."

Far from being of mere historical interest, however, the concept of common good enjoys wide currency in contemporary debates concerning public policy, democracy, and the function of government. One of the contemporary uses of the concept is in the search for a proper balance between private interests and the public well-being in societies based on liberal democracy and free enterprise. The discussion centers on how to persuade—or else compel—individuals to restrain the impulse to achieve selfish ends at the public's expense. For example, although everyone benefits from a clean environment, some members of the community who count on others to keep the environment clean may engage in littering or polluting; this is sometimes called the "free rider problem." It is clear how the "common good" would be compromised if enough people operated in this manner.

Larger contemporary social problems encompass not only the conflict of individual and public interests but also the conflict of the policies of corporations, and sometimes even governments, with the present and future welfare of society. The debate involves the impact of new technologies and procedures in the areas of production (commercial innovations), reproduction (genetic engineering), and control (military and police action) on the quality of life and freedom for all. Other arenas of controversy include the limits of economic development and the sustainable use of natural resources.

The concept of the common good has thus not withered away under the pressures of economic, military, political, and technological competition. It has, rather, expanded to include the universal interests of the global human community over the course of many generations on the one hand, and the complex interests of large self-interested parties such as corporations and governments on the other.

Common law: A term that describes a variety of circumstances that act as guideposts for judicial decisions. These include established principles of law, precedent cases, and the values, attitudes, norms, and principles of ethical behavior held by a given community. Common law becomes law as a result of judicial decisions; it is not passed by legislative bodies, nor does it appear in statute form. For example, definitions of obscenity vary widely from one location to another, and laws regulating obscenity are thus often dependent on common-law definitions.

Commonwealth of Independent States (CIS): Association of nations that emerged from the breakup of the SOVIET UNION. In late 1991, as the result of severe internal problems, the Soviet Union disintegrated into fifteen independent countries. Three of these regions established the CIS in December, and nine additional states eventually joined the group. Russia is the largest CIS member in both territory and population, followed by the Ukraine. Differences among CIS members have involved questions of political authority and leadership in the CIS, trade and economic problems, rights of ethnic minorities in member states, foreign-policy objectives, border disputes, and military issues.

Communism: Political ideology originally based on the idea of members of a community living together and sharing goods and resources. In the mid-nineteenth century, the term came to connote the most radical concept of economic egalitarianism.

In 1847, on behalf of the League of Communists, a European international association, Karl Marx and Friedrich Engels prepared a statement of policies and principles. Published in 1848 as *The Communist Manifesto*, it presented their theory of societal evolution based on the dialectal philosophy of Georg Hegel and the materialism of Ludwig Feuerbach. According to Marx and Engels, societies passed through four stages of development—slavery, feudalism, capitalism, and socialism—in which economic classes contended with one another, thereby producing the next stage. The proletariat, or working class, would be the only class remaining when a socialist society was attained; the stage of communism, when the institutions of the state would wither away, would come about without violence. A new, moral human being would emerge, and all would give "according to their means" and receive "according to their needs."

Marx maintained that the nineteenth century was the age of CAPITALISM, in which the wealthy bourgeoisie owned the means of production, principally factories. The proletariat, he wrote, would grow in numbers as the bourgeoisie grew in wealth, which would be concentrated in fewer and fewer hands. The lower class would then rise in revolt and establish the "dictatorship of the proletariat"—the rule of the working class—and build socialist society.

In the twentieth century, many Marxists advocated nonrevolutionary roads to socialist society. After the victory of the Bolshevik forces led by Vladimir I. Lenin in the Russian Revolution of 1917, a distinction was made between the nonrevolutionary reformers, who became known as socialists or social democrats, and those who advocated revolution, who became known as communists. Lenin emphasized this characterization by changing his party's name to the Communist Party; his followers became known as both communists and Marxist-Leninists.

After World War II, the Soviet Union imposed communist regimes on the nations of Eastern Europe; around the world, a number of other countries, notably China, fell under the control of communist governments based to varying degrees on the Leninist model. Although the communist countries claimed to be only in Marx's socialist stage of development, outsiders generally characterized their one-party dictatorial regimes as constituting true communism. In capitalist countries, socialists continued to seek power through electoral processes.

Communism had been controversial even before Marx and Engels published their theories. In most Western societies in the nineteenth and early twentieth centuries, communists were generally viewed as dangerous radicals, and communism remained a fringe movement. The strains of World War I brought communists to power in the Soviet Union; in the West, the economic pressures of the GREAT DEPRESSION of the 1930's helped spread the ideology's popularity. The prestige accruing to the SOVIET UNION as a result of its vital contribution to the defeat of Nazi Germany in World War II did much to enhance the standing of communist parties in the West. Yet communism also aroused strong opposition. The repressive and often brutal nature of the Soviet regime and its satellites earned them international condemnation; in some societies, "communism" became a virtual synonym for "totalitarianism." In the United States, the House Committee on Un-American Activities (HUAC) ag-

A Soviet tank driver helps to remove a Communist Party statue from a Moscow street in 1991.
(Reuters/Corbis-Bettmann)

gressively pursued suspected domestic communists; though HUAC's tactics eventually brought it into disrepute, anticommunist rhetoric remained a staple of American political life throughout the Cold War era.

In the early 1990's, the Soviet Union, torn by internal strife and economic pressures, collapsed, and parliamentary republics based on democratic principles emerged in most of its former states, including Russia. Communist regimes in Eastern Europe had begun to disintegrate in the late 1980's, as the Soviets allowed greater independence to their satellites; there, too, parliamentary governments became the rule. Although communist regimes remained in power in China, Cuba, North Korea, and Vietnam, anticommunists gleefully pronounced the "death of communism" and claimed that Marxist theories had been proven a total failure in practice. Defenders of Marxist ideology replied that the Soviet Bloc's experiments in socialism had been tainted by the totalitarian nature of its regimes and that true communism had not been achieved, let alone tested, in the former Soviet empire.

Communitarianism:
Political theory that rejects the idea that the state should be indifferent to the personal choices and values of its citizens. Communitarians believe that people's very conceptions of themselves, as well as of the rights that they ought to enjoy, are products of their social environment. Since the community is a necessary element in an individual's identity, the community may make demands on the individual not only to support the community but even to take the community into account when making personal decisions about such things as sexual or economic behavior.

Community policing:
Philosophy of police service that emphasizes CRIME PREVENTION and the restoration of closer community ties.

"Community policing" lacks a concrete definition, though it is generally agreed that the term originated in 1986 to describe crime-reduction programs started in Houston, Newark, Santa Ana, San Diego, Baltimore, and Toronto. There are literally hundreds of activities that fall under the heading of community policing, from victim recontacting to graffiti removal to newsletters. All of the activities share the idea that a community's problems are best defined by its citizens. This notion of adapting to local circumstances is also called problem-oriented policing. Whatever name they are given, such programs all have in common a hope for friendly, two-way communication between police and citizens. Preventing problems before they lead to crime by involving citizens in what they and the police can do together best describes community policing or the synonymous term, neighborhood-oriented policing.

One sign of community policing is foot patrol. Police on foot have more immediate contact with people, talking with them about neighborhood problems, the kinds of services the police provide, and listening to the needs and wants of a community's citizens. Foot patrols encourage the sharing of information on criminal activity, but community policing is directed less at serious crime than at problems of disorder such as vandalism, noise, abandoned lots, troublesome bars, sites for open drug dealing, and homelessness. Police become generalists who can offer direct assistance, organize volunteer help, or obtain city services on behalf of someone in the community.

Another sign of community policing is decentralization. Officers no longer respond to radio calls outside of their geographic area. Additionally, community policing tries to provide all of the services that a police headquarters would provide, often utilizing an empty storefront for a local office. Officers do their own record keeping and scheduling. Management does not evaluate the community police officer by traditional standards, but by the appropriateness and creativity of their projects.

Critics suggest that community policing is meaningless and unworkable and that its goals are unclear. No one really knows what it means to restore a sense of community or if reducing fear of crime truly means a better quality of life. Some communities may have deteriorated too far and would benefit more from get-tough strategies. Even if community policing were to work, some critics question whether it intrudes into private matters too much.

Critics also contend that the idea that friendly conversation accomplishes anything is naïve. Close contact offers the possibility of corruption or misuse of services for political reasons. It is unfair that some neighborhoods receive better quality services and depend on the skills of the individual officer. Recruitment and training of police is not done with community policing in mind.

Management, it is argued, cannot implement a philosophy. Without complete commitment on everyone's

Foot patrols by uniformed officers are an essential part of community policing. (James L. Shaffer)

part, community policing will remain an add-on program, used by administrators as a buzzword to sound progressive, rather than seriously facing the problems within each community.

Comparable worth: Payment of equal wages for jobs, including those dissimilar in nature, deemed to be of comparable value. Comparable worth is a workplace issue that provides for a nonmarket alternative to determine wage structures to equalize compensation in different types of occupations.

Wage rates would be determined by breaking down jobs according to their worth as measured by knowl-

edge, skills, effort, responsibilities, working conditions, and other important job requirements and characteristics. Such an assessment of job worth would be done by assigning numerical points to these characteristics. For example, if their total points added up to be equal, a nurse's aide would be paid the same as a tree-trimmer.

The purpose of comparable worth is to close the wage gap that exists between the sexes in the United States. This gap continues to exist even after the implementation of the EQUAL PAY ACT of 1963, which mandated equal pay for the same job in a workplace, and Title VII of the CIVIL RIGHTS ACT OF 1964, which outlawed discrimination of various kinds in hiring and

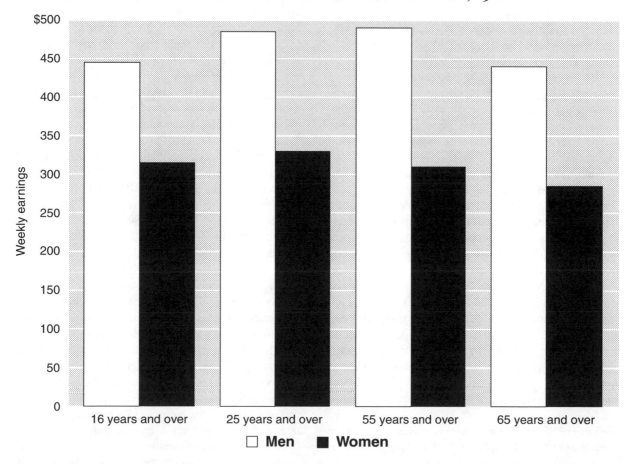

THE MALE-FEMALE WAGE GAP:
AVERAGE U.S. FULL-TIME EARNINGS BY GENDER, 1988

Source: From Shirley Ann Wagner, *Equality Now: Safeguarding Women's Rights.* Human Rights series, p. 54. Vero Beach, Fla.: Rourke Corp., 1992.

Computer bulletin boards

firing. The wage gap of about one-third or more that has remained between average male and female earnings could not be accounted for exclusively by gender discrimination and was traced to the fact that male white- and blue-collar occupations historically paid better than pink-collar ones—such as waitressing, teaching kindergarten, clerking, and retail selling—held mostly by women. Accordingly, by the 1980's, the feminist movement and unions catering to female memberships spearheaded the comparable worth movement to close the continuing wage gap between the sexes.

Those opposed to the concept refer to the fact that job breakdowns according to points are necessarily subjective in their evaluation, raising the question of "worth to whom?" Opponents also state that women's choices are often made freely, in order to avoid dangerous, onerous, dirty, or other undesirable work. Such critics also believe that a woman's desire to be a homemaker or to follow her spouse's career while interrupting her own often account for wage differentials. In addition, critics of comparable worth are troubled by the effects that the resulting pay scales may have on the female aggregate or specific employment levels. Also, using comparable worth instead of the market forces of demand and supply for wage determination would tend to make the latter unresponsive to changing market conditions.

Authorities expected to apply the concept—government agencies and the courts, primarily—have also been ambivalent in implementing comparable worth because of the ideological (it runs against free enterprise), constitutional (due process considerations), administrative (the criteria to establish job worth), and economic problems (the possible lowering of employment levels) that it raises. Thus, while a few states and municipalities have passed comparable worth laws applying to women in the public sector, there has been little movement in the private sector. The U.S. EQUAL EMPLOYMENT OPPORTUNITY COMMISSION (EEOC) and most court cases in which women have tried to achieve equal pay on a comparable worth basis have been inconclusive, though the wage disparity remains.

Computer bulletin boards: Electronic announcements posted on on-line computer networks. Performing essentially the same function served by messages on cork bulletin boards in grocery stores or in advertising, computer bulletin boards alert community members to upcoming events, important neighborhood news, items for sale, and the formation of common interest groups. In these ways, they may encourage community interaction, stimulate business, and provide a way for individuals who ordinarily might not have an opportunity to meet to become acquainted.

Commonly referred to as a "BBS," short for "bulletin-board service," computer bulletin boards may be seen as specialized libraries and meeting places. Individual bulletin board owners set up a computer that contains libraries (or databases) and meeting places (or electronic communication facilities). These databases and communication facilities may then be accessed by outside parties. Such access is generally accomplished via the use of a home computer, a modem, an electronic communication software program, and a common telephone line. These components allow the outside party, or home-computer user, to contact the computer maintaining the BBS. The outside party uses a computer that is attached to a modem, which in turn is hooked to a phone line. Once an electronic software package is operating, it allows the home computer to send information through the modem and the phone line to allow communication with the BBS computer. Alternatively, electronic bulletin boards may be accessed via the INTERNET if the BBS is connected to the Internet. This involves the same types of procedures—one computer communicating with another—but is accomplished over a larger network of computers, rather than just between one home user and a BBS computer.

Computer bulletin boards have several advantages and disadvantages. In terms of advantages, they allow individuals from virtually any location to read the information contained on the bulletin board at any time of the day or night. To accomplish this, all an outside user needs to know is the phone number or Internet path to access the BBS. Additionally, electronic bulletin boards have the capability of being very large as a result of the ability of computers to store information digitally. Thus, a BBS allows for communication on a great variety of topics in considerably more detail than any cork board or piece of printed advertising.

Controversy and some disadvantages, however, are also present. First, the purpose of any bulletin board is determined and regulated by the individual owner. Thus, some bulletin boards may focus on topics of debatable moral and social value. In this way, the questions of what can be posted and who should be allowed to have access to such services have become controversial. Additionally, the accuracy of information posted by any BBS is only as good as the preparer has made the information. As a result, misinformation may be spread widely if it is posted on a BBS and accessed by a large community of electronic users. Thus, though computer bulletin boards offer some unique benefits, they must be used with caution and evaluated on an individual basis. Further, the value of any BBS will vary by individual, depending on their reasons for accessing it.

Computer crime: Illegal acts involving COMPUTERS or computer technology. Born in the information age, computer crime became a serious problem by the early 1990's, as computers began to be used in all facets of modern society. Common computer crimes include theft, fraudulent or unauthorized use of computers or computer files, data modification, and espionage.

Definition and Categories. In the latter half of the twentieth century, the world began to recognize that not all crime was violent or personal. "WHITE-COLLAR CRIME" committed by persons who were far from the typical "street thugs" was identified as a serious threat to property. White-collar criminals were, typically, respectable, hard-working members of their communities; they were also taking advantage of their employment to commit crimes.

By the 1970's, white-collar crime had taken on a new venue: computer-related crime. The proliferation of computers in business operations created a situation in which the computers could be stolen for profit or could be used in other illegal ways.

There are two main categories of computer crimes: those in which a computer is a target and those in which a computer is an instrument. When computers are the targets, the most common computer crimes are theft or destruction of computers or software, illicit use of software, and viruses that destroy data. Using a computer as an instrument is typically exhibited in "hacking" or the more serious crime of ESPIONAGE. There are also crimes related to computer use, the most common of these being the fraudulent use of automatic-teller machines.

The most basic crimes involving computers are those in which the computer itself is the target. The size of personal computers and components makes them easy targets for theft. Furthermore, the standardization of computer parts, combined with ease of removal and installation, makes computers one of the easiest of all consumer goods to "strip" for parts,

which can be resold with little chance that police will be able to trace their origins. Computers may also be the object of sabotage. Disgruntled employees or former employees often destroy computer equipment or data in an effort to exact revenge on employers.

Viruses. Viruses are the "street crime" of computer crimes. Like street crimes, they are unpredictable—even those who create and spread such viruses do not know the extent of the damage they may cause or who will be affected; like street crimes, moreover, computer viruses often affect those who are least able to pay for the damage. Because of these factors, viruses are the computer crime most feared by individual computer users. Notices on INTERNET groups about new viruses send shock waves among users, and several national organizations have been developed with the sole purpose of providing security against viruses.

A virus is a program developed to operate within other programs in a computer. Computers operate through "executable programs," or series of commands that allow the computer to perform certain functions. Viruses cause the computer to function in ways other than those that the operator desires. Viruses spread when programs in which the virus is embedded are copied from computer to computer.

Not all viruses are destructive. Because part of the lure of viruses to those who make them is to see how far they will spread and how much notoriety they can gain, some viruses do nothing more than alert the user that the virus has struck. Other viruses, however, may cause all information contained in a computer to be destroyed.

Hackers. Hacking is the archetypal computer crime. It may come in the form of unauthorized use of a computer (browsing), fraudulent alteration of information (adding false claims or deleting unfavorable information), data modification, or destruction of data. It may also include theft by a computer often via banking transactions.

While hacking may be perpetrated by the stereotypical computer whiz breaking into a company's computer to explore or cause damage, hacking is more often an effort to steal money, services, or other goods of value. Financial institutions are thus more likely targets of pure hacking than other companies.

Computer Espionage. Hacking in which information in the computer is the target is considered computer espionage. As companies increasingly rely on computers in their operations, it becomes easier to gain information about a company or its products by tap-

Robert Morris, Jr., leaves court following his 1990 conviction on charges of having created a destructive computer virus. (AP/Wide World Photos)

ping into its computers. Individuals, other companies, and foreign entities have resorted to computer espionage in efforts to gather information, trade secrets, and intelligence from companies around the world.

Although hacking into a company's computer by foreign entities or other companies is a serious problem, most computer espionage occurs at the hands of a company's own employees. They may use the information themselves (in order to run a business on the side, for example), or they may sell the information to others.

Computer Criminals. Most computer crimes are committed by someone who takes advantage of access to a computer or information. The typical computer criminal is an employee in a position of trust with no prior record of criminal activity. Yet computer criminals also include organized-crime figures who use computers in their business and common street criminals who find ways to ply their trade by using computers.

Internet. The interconnectivity and the public access to the Internet has greatly increased the potential for computer-related criminal activity. For example, criminals have attempted to use the Internet to gain access to computers of the Department of Defense and the National Aeronautics and Space Administration (NASA). Other Internet uses have been added to the list of computer crimes. For example, housing and transmitting information that is considered pornography has come under legal scrutiny; in a celebrated 1995 case, a man was arrested for posting to an Internet news service a graphic story about the rape and murder of an acquaintance.

Costs and Investigations of Computer Crimes. It is estimated that as little as 10 percent of all computer crimes are actually reported. As a result, there are no precise figures concerning the actual costs of computer crime. Estimates place the annual loss to computer crimes at between $100 billion and $300 billion, but the National Computer Security Agency cautions that the true figure could be much higher.

Most of the general abuse of computers is detected by accident or discovery, like other criminal victimizations. As such, computer-crime investigations are conducted like those of other crimes. Because computers are structured, logical machines, computer criminals must follow patterns, practices, and courses of action that assist in the detection and investigation of computer crimes. For example, a computer that is accessible by modem is susceptible to hacking from outsiders,

while information taken from a computer that has no outside links but that is protected by passwords points to someone who has access to such information as a part of their employment.

Likewise, computer-crime detectives do not have to be computer geniuses, although sophisticated computer users are generally incorporated into computer-crime teams. Many computer crimes are solved by examining information other than the computer. For example, key information can often be obtained by focusing on employees who could commit a crime without detection, determining whether any employees have a grudge against the company, or discovering whether any employees have computer skills beyond those called for by their jobs.

The Future. Many futurists predict that the world will soon become a cashless society in which all transactions will take place through the transfer of electronic funds. Should this occur, the use of computers to steal, redirect, and alter electronic funds could well become the world's number one crime, far outpacing any threat of theft or embezzlement that currently exists. It can safely be said that when the world gets to the twenty-first century, computer criminals will be waiting there. —*Jeffrey T. Walker*

SUGGESTED READINGS: One of the earliest treatments of computer crime is *Computer Crime* by August Bequai (Lexington, Mass.: D.C. Heath, 1978). A thorough discussion of computer criminals from a variety of perspectives may be found in *Computers in Criminal Justice: Issues and Applications*, edited by Frank Schmalleger (Bristol, Ind.: Wyndham Hall Press, 1990). Security and investigation techniques are covered in the government publication *National Conference on Criminal Justice Bulletin Board Systems* (Washington, D.C.: Bureau of Justice Statistics, 1994). The "future" of computer crime (much of which is here already) is explored in *Crimewarps: The Future of Crime in America*, by Georgette Bennett (Garden City, N.Y.: Anchor Books, 1987).

Computer dating: Facilitation of new acquaintances and relationships between people with similar interests via computers. Individuals may record their social and romantic interests in computer databases. Such databases are maintained by services specializing in introducing people, for example, in-person dating services and ON-LINE computer bulletin boards. Individuals wishing to meet others locate these types

A New York couple who met through a computer dating service celebrate their engagement. (UPI/Corbis-Bettmann)

of services, sometimes pay a fee, provide information, and are then matched, via a computing process, to individuals with similar likes and dislikes. The services provide a new way for people to meet individuals they ordinarily might not encounter in their everyday lives, but they have also been criticized for their commercial aspects and their screening processes, which have sometimes been alleged to provide insufficient security for subscribers.

Computer viruses: Computer programs designed to damage computer software. Computer viruses affect only software (programs and files); viruses do not damage computer hardware.

Computer viruses spread when an infected computer file or program is introduced to a computer. Viruses work by attaching copies of themselves to other files. When activated, viruses disrupt the normal functioning of a computer by ruining programs, deleting files, or even erasing the contents of the computer's memory. Some viruses have been programmed to activate themselves after a period of months or even years; the

notorious "Michelangelo" virus, for example, attacks computers each year on May 6, the anniversary of the artist's birth. Most government and business computers and other sophisticated computer users employ antivirus programs to detect and eradicate viruses.

Computers: Machines capable of manipulating and storing information. The growth of computer-based information management has affected almost every aspect of life in the late twentieth century.

Issues associated with computers include the loss of jobs following automation, the depersonalization of relationships between individuals, and the potential invasion of privacy by governments and business. On the positive side, computers eliminate tedious mental labor and computer networks allow nearly instantaneous communication between individuals as well as make available to them the treasures of the world's libraries, universities, and museums.

Historical Overview. Electronic computers were developed during World War II for use in designing complex weapons. In the immediate postwar years, heavy industry, banks, insurance companies, and government agencies purchased computers to save labor costs by automating processes that were otherwise labor intensive. Assembly lines became populated by industrial robots, telephone operators were replaced by automatic switching networks, and the number of clerks needed to manage the finances of companies and governments diminished greatly. Perhaps the greatest early impact of computers was on consumer finances. As the human effort required to send out bills and keep track of debts and purchases diminished, banks and merchants found it profitable to allow purchases of even low-cost items on a time-payment basis, and charge accounts and credit cards became widely available. This greatly increased the immediate buying power of individuals with moderate incomes and stimulated the development of retail businesses.

A unique feature of the evolution of computer technology has been a continuing decrease in size and cost, while the speed and information storage capacity have increased markedly. The first computers were large, slow, and so expensive that only governments and the largest corporations could afford to build them. In the 1950's and 1960's, advances in semiconductor technology and the development of computer languages that could be used by businessmen and engineers who were not computer specialists made it possible, and then necessary, for any large company or government agency to purchase a mainframe computer to maintain its financial, production, and personnel records. The 1970's saw the development of personal computers, which could display information on rapidly spinning magnetic disks. Computers began to appear in individual households at this time and were used for both computer games and information storage. The 1980's saw the extensive development of applications software, which allowed individuals with no technical knowledge of computer operation to perform specific

ENIAC, a massive early computer. (UPI/Bettmann)

tasks. Key to this development were increases in computer memory capacity and the development of the computer "mouse," which made it possible to directly manipulate objects on a computer screen. Among the most important of these developments are the word processor, which allows a document to be written and revised many times before a printed copy is made, spreadsheets, which allow the easy storage and manipulation of numerical information, databases, which allow items of information to be stored in a manner that can then be searched for items meeting a particular requirement, and communications packages, which allow computers to exchange information with other computers. The 1990's have been marked by the emergence of the INTERNET, a family of computer networks around the world that allow the rapid exchange of information among computers, and the appearance of commercial networks, which allow access to the Internet to anyone with a home computer and telephone line.

Computers and Privacy. The immense information storage capacity of computers and the ease with which computers can search through databases pose a potential threat to individual privacy. Schools maintain computer records of student grades and disciplinary actions. Government agencies maintain records of the taxable income, employment history, and military service of individual citizens. Courts and police departments maintain records of criminal charges brought against individuals. Insurance companies maintain records of medical treatments received by their subscribers. Credit bureaus maintain records of debts and payments. With most financial transactions taking place by check and credit card, and businesses likewise using computer database technology to maintain inventory records, it is, in principle, possible for anyone with broad computer access to develop a very accurate profile of the spending habits of any individual. In database marketing, sellers of various commodities can purchase the customer records of other sellers and target their sales approaches to individuals who are their best prospects. While this development provides some advantages in allowing sellers and buyers to find each other, it also means targeted mailings, phone calls, and other forms of sales pressure on the individual. The most frightening possibility connected with the growth of computer databases is the possibility that a government official or unauthorized person could acquire information that could be used to coerce subsequent behavior or to destroy the reputation or career of an individual. Lawmakers have been sensitive to the possibility of computerized invasions of privacy and have passed legislation to prevent improper access to information.

Computers and Work. The implementation of computer technology in factories and businesses displaced many skilled workers from their jobs while creating a limited number of more highly skilled jobs and a larger number of jobs requiring lesser skills. Thus, a plant that employed hundreds of skilled workers to operate an assembly line might come to require only a few engineers to monitor the activity of the industrial robots that replaced them. Computer technology and the accompanying advances in high-speed communications have largely eliminated the need for managers, accountants, and clerks to work physically near the production facility or one another. Many companies have moved their management and financial operations from cities to suburban or rural settings more appealing to workers. A substantial number of office workers no longer travel to any workplace but rather "TELECOMMUTE" from their homes, making connection with their employer's computer system to receive and send documents electronically. Computer technology has also played a role in the deindustrialization of the United States, Canada, and other economically developed nations, with the establishment of production facilities in foreign countries with lower labor costs.

Computers and Creativity. In many American families, interest in computers first developed in children of school age and then spread to their parents. Many school systems now require that some sort of computer use be taught in all schools, beginning with the elementary grades. Computer bulletin boards allow the subscribers to share their opinions with like-minded individuals. Electronic mail allows the nearly instantaneous exchange of information between computer users. The World Wide Web is a network of computers that makes available large quantities of information that other users can access at their leisure.

The accessibility of computerized information is greatly enhanced by the development of hypermedia and compact disc read-only memory (CD-ROM) technology. Hypermedia are combinations of text, sound, and still and moving pictures that are interlinked by symbols on the computer screen. CD-ROMs are information storage devices that can contain far greater amounts of information than portable magnetic media. A moderately lengthy encyclopedia can be encoded, including hypermedia links to animation sequences

Personal computers continue to be made smaller and more portable. (Reuters/Corbis-Bettmann)

and short sound excerpts, on a single CD-ROM. The World Wide Web provides hypermedia links to resources around the world.

The motion-picture industry has been quick to utilize computer-graphics technology to develop new special effects. Motion-picture images can be manipulated in digital form, extensive artificial elements can be combined into images involving human actors, and computer animations can be combined with conventional photography in a most convincing manner.

—*Donald R. Franceschetti*

SUGGESTED READINGS: The case that information technology is forcing a radical transformation of industrialized societies is stated with some force in Daniel Bell's *The Coming of Post-Industrial Society: A Venture in Social Forecasting* (New York: Basic Books, 1973). An optimistic view of the changes that information technology has made possible in the lives of individuals is found in Stewart Brand's *The Media Lab: Inventing the Future at M.I.T.* (New York: Viking, 1987). The notion that computers are changing the way individuals view themselves is explored by Sherry Turkle in *Second Self: Computers and the Human Spirit* (New York: Simon & Schuster, 1984).

An important early statement of the potential role of computers in the education of children can be found in Seymour Papert's *Mindstorms: Children, Computers, and Powerful Ideas* (New York: Basic Books, 1980). An outline of the privacy issues associated with widespread computer use and networking can be found in Warren Freedman's *The Right of Privacy in the Computer Age* (New York: Quorum Books, 1987). A glimpse into the fast-paced culture of the designers and marketers of personal computers can be found in Tracy Kidder's Pulitzer Prize-winning *The Soul of a New Machine* (Boston: Little, Brown, 1981).

Condoms: Contraceptive sheaths that fit over the penis to prevent conception. Also known as prophylactics, condoms are usually made of latex rubber, although some are made of other materials, such as the intestines of sheep. Latex condoms also provide protection against sexually transmitted diseases such as

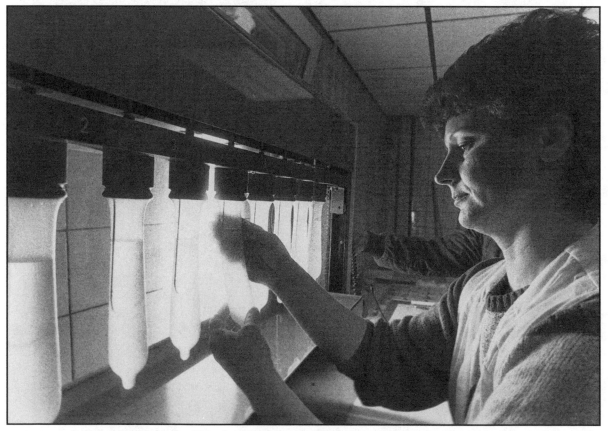

A technician at a manufacturing plant tests condoms for reliability. (UPI/Corbis Bettmann)

syphilis, gonorrhea, and AIDS. Condoms are widely available in grocery stores, convenience markets, pharmacies, department stores, and can be obtained through the mail. Almost half of all condoms purchased are bought by women.

When stored and used according to the manufacturer's directions, condoms are quite reliable at preventing pregnancy and the transmission of disease. Most failures are the result of either infrequent usage or improper application. Manufacturing standards used in the United States specify that every condom be individually tested at pressures greatly exceeding those encountered in normal usage.

Medical experts suggest that using a spermicide with a condom will adequately control both pregnancy and the spread of SEXUALLY TRANSMITTED DISEASES, including HIV infection. A common spermicide is nonoxynol-9, which is available in a jelly-based product. The spermicide can be spread to the inside of a condom or applied within the vagina. The only way to guarantee that both diseases and pregnancies are prevented, however, is to abstain from sexual relations and intimate contact.

Condoms vary in price from a few cents to several dollars; price variations reflect the materials used and the quantities purchased. Less-expensive condoms are made of thicker latex rubber that provides a better barrier than that found in more expensive models, which have thinner walls and thus are advertised as having superior sensitivity. Thinner walls, however, can withstand less pressure before they break. As a result, thinner condoms are more likely to fail and lead to disease transmission or pregnancy.

Controversy has arisen over both the dissemination and advertising of condoms as effective ways to combat the spread of AIDS and other sexually transmitted diseases. Both government and private commercial efforts to promote condom use on television and radio broadcasts have met stiff resistance from conservative groups that claim such messages promote promiscuity. Similar criticism has been directed at condom-distribution programs at universities and public schools. Advocates of condom use reply that such programs are sensible, necessary reactions to a severe threat to public health.

Conference of Catholic Bishops, U.S. (USCCB): Religious organization headquartered in Washington, D.C. Formed in 1966 at the behest of the VATICAN II

conference, the USCCB, an all-male organization of members of the Roman Catholic hierarchy, studies and makes policies on topics that relate to Church sacraments, the English liturgy, religious education, and Church discipline. In conjunction with the United States Catholic Conference, with which it shares affiliation, the USCCB examines national issues that affect the general public. Its activities are administered by a general secretary and a staff of both religious and lay persons.

Confidentiality: Information about a person that cannot be released to a third party without that person's consent. Only certain mental-health professionals, lawyers, and clergy are authorized to maintain truly confidential information.

While most attorneys and clergy can avoid releasing private information, few doctors are able to, despite office policies against releasing information. Laws pertaining to confidentiality were predominately written to allow mental-health treatment that would be ineffective if the patient were afraid to reveal personal problems. Therefore, psychiatrists and psychologists can protect patients' confidentiality. Some states also afford confidentiality to patients seen by other mental-health professionals or by medical doctors treating substance-abuse disorders.

Under laws germane to confidentiality, the client is the one who determines what information may or may not be released, and to whom (family, friends, or employers). The client also determines how long such information may be released. When confidentiality applies and a subpoena is received to provide protected information, an attorney files a "motion to quash," which essentially quashes the attempt to obtain records. However, if the person claims insanity as a legal defense, the person is consenting to the release of information to substantiate the claim. Further, if a person is court-ordered to receive treatment, the therapist is obliged to report the client's status.

A person seeking treatment should be aware of several limitations of confidentiality. Laws are designed to protect vulnerable minors and the elderly from harm, and the responsibility of the therapist to report abuse and neglect is clear. When a therapist has reason to believe a child or elderly person is being abused or neglected, the therapist is bound by law to report the situation. Likewise, if a client discloses abuse or neglect to a minor or elderly person by their own hands,

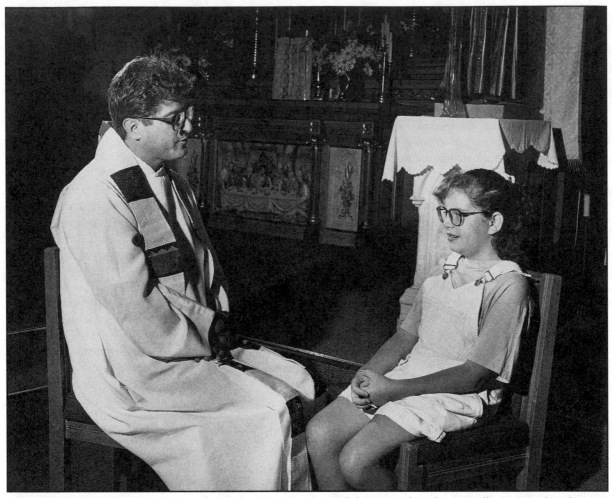

Information given to clergy members in confessions or other religious practices is generally protected under confidentiality laws. (James L. Shaffer)

by a spouse, or any other person, the therapist is legally compelled to report the information.

Not all patients have the exclusive right to confidentiality. Age is a factor. Usually a person gains the right to confidentiality in adolescence, which permits mental health professionals to withhold information from parents and guardians. The specific age requirement varies from state to state. This is a controversial issue, especially since suicidal thoughts and plans may be reported to the therapist. Moreover, once confidentiality is granted, parents and guardians do not have access to confidential information, even if they are paying for the treatment.

Another limitation involves physical disease. If an appropriate professional identifies that the client has a contagious disease of the magnitude of hepatitis, AC-QUIRED IMMUNE DEFICIENCY SYNDROME (AIDS), or a

SEXUALLY TRANSMITTED DISEASE, the professional is required by law to report this to the designated institutions, for example, the CENTERS FOR DISEASE CONTROL AND PREVENTION (CDC) or the health department.

The final exception to confidentiality involves threatening harm either to oneself or someone else. If the mental health professional believes that the threat is serious, he or she must take any action necessary to protect the client or the intended victim. Such actions include notifying law enforcement, obtaining a court order for involuntary commitment, and warning the intended victim.

Conflict of interest: Clash between ethical obligations and personal (mainly financial) interests. In a democracy, it is incumbent on all officeholders to avoid any situations in which the public may perceive them to be in a conflict of interest, thus jeopardizing their integrity. Political figures, civil servants, lawyers, accountants, and numerous other professionals may find themselves caught between their professional responsibilities and their private financial affairs. Many countries have legislation and detailed regulations making it illegal for any civil servant or politician to utilize his position for private financial advantage. Politicians and civil servants in particular are obliged at all times to further the public interest and to govern as impartially and as fairly as possible. When they fail to do so, it is often because of the existence of some conflict of interest that has influenced their judgment.

In some jurisdictions, even the appearance, if not the fact, of a conflict of interest, is disallowed by the law. For example, a civil servant in a government department that awards contracts to private enterprises would be in a clear conflict of interest if the individual operates a private business that receives any such contract. Even if the firm is not awarded a contract, the appearance of a potential conflict of interest would exist.

As a solution to an actual or potential conflict of interest, governments often ask politicians to divest private financial interests likely to conflict with their public organizations. A civil servant in a conflict may be transferred to a different department, asked to cease the offending tasks, and temporarily or permanently be removed from any duties that generate the conflict of interest. Rules of disclosure require employees to inform the government about any outside activities that may cause a conflict of interest.

Conflict-of-interest legislation attempts to prevent public figures from indulging in corrupt practices to enrich themselves at the expense of the taxpayer. It aims to run government on the basis of impartiality, fiscal responsibility, and a commitment to ethical obligations to serve the public, not individual private interests. A conflict of interest may cause any government employee or politician to serve individual interests over those of the people. Sarah Williams comments in *Conflict of Interest: The Ethical Dilemma in Politics* (1985) that conflicts of interest arise not only when there is a clash between public and private interest, but also when the two converge. The potential for conflicts of interest doubly challenges the individual's integrity.

Conflicts of interest can also affect the private sector, particularly where an employee's outside activities adversely affect and compromise the employer's business interests. Conflicts of interest can be perceived to exist when an employee gains unfair private advantage at the expense of the employer's legitimate business interests. Of current interest is the problem likely to be caused when any employee uses information acquired in a professional setting to further personal gain. Such an individual would be considered to be in a clear conflict of interest.

Congress, U.S.: Legislative body of the U.S. federal government. Congress consists of two separate houses, the Senate and the House of Representatives. In the Senate, each state is represented by two senators who serve for six-year terms. The size of the House is set by law at 435 members, who are proportionally divided among the states according to population. Representatives serve for two-year terms. Generally, Congress functions in the dual capacity of people's representative and national legislator. As representatives, members are expected to reflect the interests and needs of their local constituency while serving as intermedi-

PUBLIC OPINION, 1994: HOW HIGH ARE THE ETHICAL STANDARDS OF U.S. CONGRESSMEN?

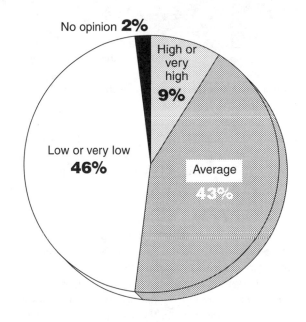

Source: George Gallup, Jr., ed., *The Gallup Poll: Public Opinion, 1994* (Wilmington, Del.: Scholarly Resources, 1995).

A 1993 meeting of the House Rules Committee. (AP/Wide World Photos)

aries between government institutions and the folks back home. As legislators, members of Congress also have the responsibility to write laws for the entire country. Frequently these responsibilities compete with one another when members seek to protect narrow constituent interests (such as keeping open a military base) and national interests (such as reducing the federal debt by closing unnecessary bases).

Leadership. Each house elects leaders to administer the chamber. Their duties include presiding over debate, referring bills to the appropriate committees, and appointment to key committee assignments. The Speaker, along with the majority and minority leaders of both parties, oversees the day-to-day operations of the House. In the Senate, the vice president is technically the presiding officer. In practice, however, this rarely happens, leaving Senate governance to the majority leader in consultation with the minority leader.

In addition, both houses employ a "whip system" for conveying information between party leaders and rank-and-file members. "Whips" are individual members of Congress whose functions typically include disseminating instructions from their party's leadership, counting potential supporters for major bills prior to a key vote, and keeping the leadership apprised of the general disposition of the party caucus.

The Legislative Process. Initially, all prospective legislation (known as bills) is submitted on the floor of the member's chamber. In accordance with each body's rules and procedures, a bill is referred to the appropriate subcommittee with policy jurisdiction. At the subcommittee stage, bills go through a three-step process of hearings, mark-up, and committee report. During the course of hearings, committee members call witnesses to testify as to the relative merits or weaknesses of the proposed legislation. Interest groups, celebrities, academics, and other members of Congress frequently take part in this first stage of committee work. Hearings are also an excellent opportunity to begin setting the terms and boundaries of a public policy debate. Once testimony is concluded, the committee proceeds to settle on the exact wording of the bill. Under the chairman's leadership, the committee reviews each bill line by line. If members disagree as to the precise wording a bill should take, there is opportunity to debate the matter, with the final decision being reached as a matter of majority vote.

If the bill passes the subcommittee, the committee staff (nonpartisan employees of the committee who assist in legislative analysis) then authors a report outlining the pros and cons of the bill and the subcommittee's rationale for final adoption. The bill and report are then referred to the full committee for a second round of review. It is important to note that because of the high number of bills submitted to Congress each session, the legislature must delegate most of the responsibility for writing legislation to its subcommittees. Having made this delegation, Congress is disin-

clined to overrule subcommittee decisions except in rare circumstances. This makes the subcommittee stage the most crucial in an already precarious legislative process. In fact, most bills die at the subcommittee level, often without hearings.

Critics of this decentralized system believe that it creates a series of independent fiefdoms that place too much power in the hands of too few. Upon referral to the full committee, bill consideration takes on a faster pace. On rare occasions, there may be additional hearings. More commonly, the full committee is inclined to defer to the judgment of the subcommittee, particularly if the bill found overwhelming support. The bill may be amended in the full committee, though the pressure at this point is clearly to drop those bills that have no hope of passage, in the full house and to put forward only those bills with a reasonable chance of passage. Knowing this, the subcommittees usually anticipate the concerns of the full committee before they report out a bill.

If approved by the full committee, the measure moves to the floor of the chamber. At this point, the

President Bill Clinton addresses a joint session of Congress in 1993. (Reuters/Corbis-Bettmann)

procedures of the House and Senate differ significantly. In the House, all but the most innocuous legislation is referred temporarily to the Rules Committee. This committee does not pass judgment on the merits of the bill but rather determines under what restrictions the bill will be considered on the floor. A "rule" is adopted by the committee that determines how much, if any, debate will be allowed on the bill and the date of the final vote. Likewise, the rule determines what, if any, amendments will be permitted from the floor. If the rule is adopted by the House, consideration of the bill proceeds in accordance with the time constraints and restrictions of the rule. With 435 members in the House and the time pressures of a heavy workload, debate is often an abbreviated affair, with members giving "speeches" that often last as little as a minute or less.

In contrast, the Senate has nothing comparable to the House Rules Committee. Technically, there are no time limits on Senate debate. Some legislation is dealt with expeditiously through unanimous consent agreements (similar to rules approved by the House), but senators always have the option of unlimited debate on the floor. Senators commonly use this provision to conduct FILIBUSTERS, instances in which a single senator or a group of senators attempts to block the passage of legislation by refusing to relinquish the floor in debate. Apart from unanimous consent, debate can be ended only by the passage of a "cloture" motion, when three-fifths of the senators present vote to conclude the debate. While a single individual cannot block consideration, a dedicated minority of forty-one or more members can hold the chamber hostage.

Once legislation has been adopted by the full chamber, the proposal is sent to the other house for consideration and possible adoption. The more important bills are commonly introduced simultaneously in both houses to speed consideration. In the end, legislation must pass in identical form in each chamber. Mindful of this requirement, committees are pragmatic in their attempts to anticipate the priorities and concerns of the opposite chamber; otherwise, Congress could conceivably spend most of its time reconciling even the most trivial legislation. When each house insists on different forms of the same bill, a temporary committee, called a conference committee, is created to reconcile the two versions. Committee membership is drawn from both houses and consists of individuals who are appointed by their chamber's leadership. These "conferees" are given broad instructions from their houses to fashion a compromise version acceptable to a majority of both houses. Once such a compromise is negotiated, the committee dissolves and the legislation returns to the floor of each house for a final vote. If approved by both houses, the legislation is sent to the president.

The president has several options at this point. If signed, the bill becomes law. If left unsigned, the bill becomes law in ten days provided Congress remains in session. If the legislation adjourns within ten days of a bill's passage, the bill dies unless signed by the president. This is known as a "pocket veto." The last option available to the president is to formally veto a bill and return the measure to Congress with objections. The legislature may then reconsider and amend the bill or override the president's veto with a two-thirds vote in each house in which case it becomes law without the president's signature.   —*Bruce Turner Hall*

SUGGESTED READINGS: An excellent general survey of Congress can be found in Roger Davidson and Walter Oleszek's *Congress and Its Members*, 4th ed. (Washington, D.C.: Congressional Quarterly, 1994). For a detailed and lively account of the history and evolution of Congress, see Alvin Josephy's *On the Hill: A History of the American Congress* (New York: Simon & Schuster, 1979). Congressional relations with the president are considered in George Edwards' *At the Margins: Presidential Leadership of Congress* (New Haven, Conn.: Yale University Press, 1989).

The seminal texts on congressional structure and procedures are Walter Oleszek's *Congressional Procedures and the Policy Process*, 3d ed. (Washington, D.C.: Congressional Quarterly Press, 1989) and Steven Smith's *Call to Order: Floor Politics in the House and Senate*, (Washington, D.C.: Brookings Institution, 1989). Of particular interest to students of congressional campaigns will be Gary Jacobson's *The Politics of Congressional Elections*, 3d ed. (New York: HarperCollins, 1992) and Burdett Loomis' *The New American Politician* (New York: Basic Books, 1988). Herbert Alexander provides an exhaustive review of the history of campaign financing in his *Financing Politics: Money, Elections, and Political Reform*, 4th ed. (Washington, D.C.: Congressional Quarterly Press, 1992).

Congress of Racial Equality (CORE): CIVIL RIGHTS group founded 1942 in Chicago, Illinois. CORE played a key role in directing much of the strategy of the CIVIL RIGHTS MOVEMENT of the 1960's. By 1963, CORE

A Congress of Racial Equality demonstrator is arrested at a 1963 Long Island, New York, protest. (UPI/Corbis-Bettmann)

Congressional Black Caucus

claimed seventy thousand members and an annual budget of $700,000. Led by James Farmer and other activists, CORE organized SIT-INS, voter-registration drives, and FREEDOM RIDES throughout the South in the early in middle 1960's. In the latter part of the decade, CORE increasingly aligned itself with the BLACK POWER MOVEMENT in the struggle for racial equality.

Congressional Black Caucus: Legislative service organization founded to increase the effectiveness of African American representation in Congress. As the power of the CIVIL RIGHTS MOVEMENT waned in the late 1960's, African American congressmen began meeting informally to ensure that the needs of the nation's African Americans were not ignored. Officially organized in 1971, the members of the caucus

envisioned themselves as representatives for all African Americans, not merely those from their individual congressional districts.

Reacting to the conservative domestic programs of President Richard M. NIXON, the caucus drafted sixty recommendations, including the withdrawal of troops from Vietnam and the enforcement of civil rights laws. The presentation of these recommendations to Nixon at a 1971 meeting earned the caucus a leadership role in the African American community.

Because the caucus had been unable to define how it could represent all African Americans, caucus leaders changed the group's strategies in 1972. The small number of members prevented the caucus from significantly influencing legislation, prompting the caucus to dedicate itself instead to advancing the careers of black representatives in Congress. Returning members would

Congressional Black Caucus leader Kweisi Mfume urges the United Nations to strengthen its blockade of Haiti in 1993. (Reuters/Corbis-Bettmann)

gain seniority and receive committee chairmanships, thus increasing their power to influence legislation.

Throughout the 1970's and 1980's, the caucus founded several successful programs and helped pass many significant pieces of legislation. Designed to increase the power of black voters in the South, the Black Voter's Participation Network enrolled more than fifty thousand members. National organizations, called "braintrusts," met to discuss African American business, health, and education concerns. The caucus allied with other minority representation groups in Congress to help pass several employment acts and the bill that made the Reverend Martin Luther KING, Jr.'s birthday a national holiday. The caucus also helped President Bill CLINTON pass a major crime bill in 1994 and advised the president on events in Haiti that year.

Designated a legislative service organization (LSO), the caucus received funding, staffing, and office space from the congressional budget. The Republican victory in the 1994 congressional midterm elections raised concerns about the future of LSOs, including the Congressional Black Caucus. Dedicated to drastically cutting the federal budget, the Republican majority announced that funding to all LSOs would be terminated. Minority groups claimed that the cuts were intended to limit their effectiveness in Congress. Attempts to prevent the funding cuts failed, and funding to LSOs was eliminated in early 1995.

The loss of funding was a significant blow to the caucus, but far more troubling was the loss of three committee chairmanships and seventeen subcommittee chairmanships to the victorious Republicans. Control of committees was an important source of caucus power. New Jersey congressman Donald Payne, newly elected chairman of the caucus, announced that the caucus would seek new sources of funding. Acknowledging that the caucus no longer had the power to support the passage of major legislation, Payne saw the new role of the caucus as preventing the passage of legislation that would hurt the nation's poor and middle classes. —*Thomas Clarkin*

SUGGESTED READING: William L. Clay offers a personal account of the Congressional Black Caucus in *Just Permanent Interests: Black Americans in Congress, 1870-1991* (New York: Amistad Press, 1992).

Conscience: An internalized set of personal rules and values that determine the moral "rightness" or "wrongness" of an act. Debates over conscience have entered into discussions of such social issues as CRIME, punitive justice, honor codes, and ethics in the workplace.

Conscience is often described as a "little voice" emanating from somewhere in the back of one's mind telling one what specific behavior is morally "right" and what is morally "wrong." Indulging in the morally "wrong" action is often said to produce feelings of guilt or "pangs of conscience" in the individual. Honor codes in both academic institutions and the workplace are based, at least partially, on the presumption that conscience will act as a sort of insurance that vows of honesty will be upheld.

There is no consensus as to whether conscience exists or, if it exists, from whence it originates. Psychology, under the influence of Sigmund Freud, generally holds that what is commonly referred to as "conscience" is nothing more than the internalized voice of parental authority. This "superego," as Freud called it, echoes the prohibitions and moral instruction embedded in the unconscious from years of parental correction. Having become totally internalized, it continues to warn, censure, and punish people when these instructions are not heeded.

Psychological determinists follow a similar line of thought, holding that humans have been conditioned to respond to situations in certain approved ways. When one acts in ways that violate these approved standards, one must struggle with the inner conflict that arises when one tries to overcome the learned resistance to breaking with these social mores.

Much theology, on the other hand, maintains that this "inner voice" is in fact the voice of God embedded in each person to aid one in distinguishing the morally "right" from "wrong." Since it has been endowed on one by God, conscience must be seen as the supreme judge of morality and must be obeyed at all costs. With this gift of conscience, however, comes the obligation to form it properly, lest it fall prey to error by means of rationalization, ignorance, or self-deception.

This possibility of "erroneous conscience" came to worldwide attention during the Nuremberg Trials of alleged war criminals in the wake of World War II. During the trials, several Nazi doctors accused of putting to death thousands of prisoners used the defense that they were following their consciences in doing so. Although these doctors were sentenced to death, their cases highlighted the use of conscience as a legal defense or, at least, as a consideration in the lessening of guilt.

On the other hand, it is often the case that harsher

Some defendants at the Nuremberg war crimes trials claimed to have been following their consciences. (Corbis-Bettmann)

penalties are meted out to those found guilty of violent crimes who show no remorse for their actions. This apparent "demise of conscience" in perpetrators of violent crimes has been the focus of much speculation by sociologists, psychologists, and theologians. There is virtual agreement by representatives of all these disciplines that conscience can lose its effectiveness if one habitually violates its dictates.

Conscientious objection: Act of opposing participation in combat for moral or religious reasons. In the United States, a person may legally be considered a conscientious objector for opposing participation in all war because of religious, sociological, political, or philosophical convictions.

Since colonial times, there have been individuals in the United States who, because of their personal beliefs, have refused to participate in military activities. Throughout most of U.S. history, conscientious objec-

tors were usually members of pacifist religious sects, such as Quakers or Mennonites, who opposed war in any form.

New questions about conscientious objection were raised during the Mexican-American War (1846-1848). Many Americans opposed the war for nonreligious reasons, believing that President James K. Polk had deliberately begun the war to expand slavery into former Mexican territories. The most famous document relating to this period is Henry David Thoreau's 1849 essay "Civil Disobedience." Thoreau was jailed for refusing to pay his poll taxes, which he believed would be used to further the war effort. Thoreau advocated active disobedience to any law that violated a citizen's personal moral convictions, whether such convictions were religious or not.

During the Civil War (1861-1865), large-scale military conscription was used for the first time in the United States. The draft laws of the time permitted the purchase of individual exemptions and also gave conscientious objectors the option of performing alternative service in hospitals.

By the time the United States entered World War I in 1917, there were many more members of pacifist sects as the result of recent massive immigration. Universal conscription was enacted, but no provision was made for conscientious objection. The result was the widespread arrest and detention and frequent mistreatment of members of traditional pacifist sects, socialists, and others who objected to American participation in the war.

The mistreatment of conscientious objectors by some military authorities during World War I led to more generous provision for objection to service in the conscription acts of World War II. Conscientious objectors could serve in civilian hospitals or enter the service as noncombatants. Similar provisions were made during the Korean War.

New questions were raised about conscientious objection during the VIETNAM WAR. Many young people objected to the war on political, social, and moral grounds rather than for religious reasons. Several important Supreme Court cases during this period helped further to define conscientious-objector status by establishing that one must object to all war rather than a particular war and must base that objection on belief in a supreme being.

More recent Supreme Court decisions have upheld the constitutionality of a male-only draft but have removed the requirements for belief in a supreme being as the basis for objection. Some authorities believe that liberalization of the rules regarding conscientious objection has reduced the potential pool of draftees by up to one-half and that future combat readiness may be severely impaired. Others believe that military conscription is inconsistent with the principles of a free society and that the most liberal interpretation of what constitutes conscientious objection must be allowed.

Conservation: Deliberately limited use of natural resources in order to extend the existence of such resources into the future. Such limited use typically represents a compromise between unlimited utilization, which is often advocated by commercial interests, and full PRESERVATION, which is often advocated by environmental groups. The conservation of natural resources can benefit and sustain the natural world while permitting needed levels of productivity. Yet pro-use critics argue that conservation policies restrict jobs, raise the cost of products made from natural resources, and place burdens on individuals and communities that own private property containing the natural resources, while preservationists argue that

Members of the Civilian Conservation Corps, an early federal conservation program, in 1933. (UPI/Corbis-Bettmann)

conservation fails to prevent irreparable damage to the natural world.

Conservation Council of Ontario (CCO): Canadian conservation group founded in 1951. The CCO is a Toronto-based nonprofit organization of groups and individuals who work for the conservation of natural resources and protection of the environment in the province of Ontario. With members from organized labor, professional groups, industry, and volunteer organizations, the council brings together a diverse coalition of people sharing a common vision. Through a research program, support for community action, and its many special projects, the CCO attempts to foster a social transition from practices of consumption to policies of responsible conservation.

Conservatism: Set of beliefs about the role of government and the rights and responsibilities of the individual. In the last two decades of the twentieth century, conservatism within the United States has become more complex, with two major versions of conservative thought: economic conservatism and social conservatism.

Economic Conservatism. Economic conservatives are convinced that government is too large and that reductions in government programs and regulations are needed. Ronald REAGAN was the major proponent of this viewpoint during the 1970's and 1980's, expressing the opinion that government was the cause of many social and economic problems. During Reagan's presidency, his ideas became the dominant theme of conservatism.

Economic conservatives support market-based solutions to social problems. Although they recognize that the market cannot solve all societal problems, admitting that poverty will remain a problem even in the most productive society, they nonetheless believe that the best way to deal with social problems is through an expanding job and economic base. According to economic conservatives, an expanding economy should be the main objective of government with tax cuts representing the key to prosperity. Government should lower individual and corporate tax rates, thereby returning purchasing power to the individual and business. In 1981, the Reagan Administration proposed the largest tax cut in American history. The economic expansion of the 1980's is cited by economic conserva-

tives as an example of what lower tax rates can accomplish for the nation's job and economic base. Critics, however, respond that the economic expansion of the 1980's did not create high-paying jobs and merely transferred wealth from the lower classes to the wealthy.

When Reagan made his proposal for a tax cut he also called for deep reductions in domestic spending programs. Some programs were cut, while other programs were spared from cuts by congressional action. Despite his call for cuts in government social programs, however, Reagan was unwilling to return to the days when government provided no assistance to the poor. Indeed, Reagan said that government would continue to provide a "SAFETY NET" for the poor and disadvantaged.

Economic conservatives assert that churches, community groups, and private charities are better able to provide assistance to the poor than is the government. President George BUSH adopted this point of view when he said that in the United States a "thousand points of light" exist to care for the poor; by this remark, Bush meant that there were a multitude of private groups ready to lend assistance.

Although economic conservatives are not enthusiastic supporters of government social programs, some economic conservatives are willing to use government activism to help the poor. Jack Kemp, housing secretary under President Bush, developed several ideas for using the powers of government activism to assist the poor. Kemp's ideas were based on the enterprise-zone concept. Enterprise zones are low-income areas of cities and towns designated by government to receive special tax breaks. These tax incentives are then made available to private businesses that relocate in the enterprise zone. According to Kemp, this approach is an effective way to create new investment and jobs in low-income areas. Nevertheless, Kemp's views produced controversy among economic conservatives, with many critical of Kemp's ideas to use government to fight poverty.

The reluctance of economic conservatives to support government activism is related to their belief in individualism. According to the economic conservative, the ability of the individual to make choices is the highest value in a political system. Anything that restrains the choice of the individual is viewed with suspicion. It is for this reason that some economic conservatives have adopted a laissez-faire, or hands-off, approach to life-style questions. Some economic con-

The presidencies of Ronald Reagan and George Bush helped to redefine American conservatism. (UPI/Corbis-Bettmann)

servatives are PRO-CHOICE on the ABORTION issue and supportive of the equality of rights for gay citizens. According to this perspective, government should not make value judgments that the individual is able to make. While this perspective is not the majority view among economic conservatives, it nonetheless is an important component of the economic conservative viewpoint. Governor William Weld of Massachusetts is an economic conservative who is also pro-choice and a supporter of gay rights. At the 1992 Republican Convention, Weld delivered an address in which he called for a government that stayed out of the "corporate boardroom" and the "couple's bedroom."

Social Conservatism. The social conservative viewpoint is based on a religious interpretation of American history. Social conservatives maintain that the American Founders were influenced by Christianity, and conclude that the Constitution has a religious component. Social conservatives seek to restore religion to a central place in American life and politics.

In the 1970's, social conservatives became increasingly active in political affairs. The primary reason for the heightened political activism of social conservatives during this time was their conviction that the family and traditional moral values were under attack. The development of FEMINISM and the struggle for ratification of the EQUAL RIGHTS AMENDMENT (ERA) were important factors leading to the political activities of social conservatives. Social conservatives were also concerned about the development of a GAY RIGHTS MOVEMENT in the United States. The Supreme Court decision in *ENGLE V. VITALE* (1962), which prohibited classroom prayer in the public schools, and *ROE V. WADE* (1973), which legalized abortion services, motivated many individuals to become active in political affairs.

Social conservatives advocate several measures to uphold their version of traditional moral values. They support an amendment to the Constitution to allow prayer in the public-school classroom. In addition, they support the teaching of the biblical account of

The political power of the Christian Coalition has posed problems for some economic conservatives who do not endorse extreme social conservatism. (AP/Wide World Photos)

creation in public schools. Social conservatives call for overturning the Supreme Court's decision in *Roe v. Wade* through a human-life amendment to the Constitution. Because social conservatives emphasize traditional values, they express hostility toward gay rights. Many social conservatives have been active in proposing antigay ballot initiatives in Oregon and Colorado. When President Bill CLINTON proposed lifting the ban on gays in the military, social conservatives were active in opposing the proposal.

Controversy. The development of economic and social conservatism has produced some significant tensions. Many economic conservatives are uncomfortable with the political ideas of social conservatism. According to the economic conservative viewpoint, the development of a large government is the primary problem confronting American society. Therefore, economic conservatives support a reduction of government activity in all areas of American life. Social conservatives, however, concerned that their version of traditional values is under attack, favor the use of

government to support the maintenance of traditional values. In the last decade of the twentieth century, the division among American conservatives became increasingly evident. The CHRISTIAN COALITION, a special-interest group representing the views of social conservatives, became more assertive in Republican party politics, calling for an unambiguous Republican stand against legalized abortion. Many economic conservatives, however, are pro-choice and would like to see less of an emphasis on the abortion issue and other social issues. The Christian Coalition's position, therefore, has placed many economic conservatives in an awkward position.

During the last fifteen years of the twentieth century, the issue of whether or not the disagreement between economic and social conservatives has become too large to be solved has developed into one of the most relevant questions in American politics. Former Arizona senator Barry Goldwater, an economic conservative and the REPUBLICAN PARTY's 1964 candidate for president, is pro-choice and is supportive of gay rights. Goldwater supported President Clinton's proposal to end the military's ban on gays. During the national discussion of the gays in the military question, Goldwater was critical of social conservatives. He said that the model of conservatism espoused by social conservatives was not the model that he discussed during the 1964 campaign for president. How the division between economic and social conservatives is handled will determine the direction of conservative thought in the twenty-first century.   —*Michael E. Meagher*

SUGGESTED READINGS: For a discussion of economic conservatism and social conservatism, see Vernon Van Dyke's *Ideology and Political Choice: The Search for Freedom, Justice, and Virtue* (Chatham, N.J.: Chatham House, 1995). For a discussion of the economic policies of the Reagan Administration, see David A. Stockman's *The Triumph of Politics: How the Reagan Revolution Failed* (New York: Harper & Row, 1986). For a discussion of Goldwater's involvement in the development of conservatism see Barry M. Goldwater's *With No Apologies* (New York: William Morrow, 1979). The social conservative view of politics is contained in Russell Kirk's *The American Cause* (Chicago: Henry Regnery, 1957). For a statement on social conservatism made during the Reagan presidency, see Jerry Falwell's *Strength for the Journey: An Autobiography* (New York: Simon & Schuster, 1987).

Constitution, U.S.: Supreme law of the United States, defining the fundamental legal and political framework wherein all major U.S. social issues are decided.

In its Preamble, its seven Articles, and its first ten Amendments (the BILL OF RIGHTS) the Constitution briefly sets forth the political principles and outlines the basic structure upon which the nation's republican government is founded. Although it was only designed to form a national government, it subsequently became the model closely adhered to by most of the nation's fifty states, each assured a republican form of government by Article IV. Accordingly, every state is governed by its own constitution, voluntarily and almost without exception embodying the republican principles and the structure laid down in the federal document. Each state constitution also includes a bill of rights almost identical to the Constitution's first ten amendments.

Origins and Background. The Constitution replaced the Articles of Confederation, upon which rested such national government as newly independent Americans experienced between 1777 and 1788. The Articles' weaknesses were manifest to nearly all influential Revolutionary War leaders. States remained sovereign. The central government—CONGRESS—often wielded less power than individual states and was restricted largely to persuading state governments to act. The central government also depended upon states for its revenues and exercised no authority over citizens of the states. Congressional efforts to finance the war also proved routinely ineffectual. The conduct of a national diplomacy, given state attempts to deal with foreign chancelleries, was made awkward, and because the new nation was surrounded by hostile powers, its very existence was jeopardized. Interstate commerce was seriously hampered by tolls, TARIFFS, and differing monetary standards raised by states against one another. Excesses of democracy led to excessive state borrowing and spending. Not least, the specter of rebellion loomed in the backcountry. These, among other deficiencies, gave impetus to meetings that led to the Constitutional Convention in Philadelphia in 1787 and the efforts to provide a stronger and more stable national government.

The Framers' Intent. Abandoning the Articles of Confederation, the framers of the Constitution sought to establish a national government that would secure both the "public good" and private rights, and above all maximize and safeguard liberty. The spirit as well as the forms of popular government were to be ensured. They were also to be shielded against the dangers of an overbearing or tyrannical majority. What the framers intended to found was a republican government devoted to the preservation of liberty: a representative government in which the best men winnowed and then acted upon the soundest manifestations of the popular will. "Democracy" was not yet a highly valued or entirely acceptable political concept, for the framers' understanding of the concept came from classical Greek and Roman writings—or later European interpretations of them—in which democracy generally was equated with tyranny by majorities or by mob rule. The framers' own perception of rule by majority was emphasized by their belief in governance by the "best and the brightest" men: governance by qualitative majority rule, though always protective of minority rights.

Distinguishing Features. The Constitution in its eighteenth century context contained both radical and conservative features. Then, as now, its radicalism lay

Visitors to the National Archives in Washington, D.C., examine the U.S. Constitution and the Declaration of Independence. (Reuters/Corbis-Bettmann)

in lodging sovereignty, or supreme authority, not with monarchs, potentates, a deity, or even with the national government, but with "We, the people," the phrase that opens the Constitution's Preamble. While creating a popular national republican government that preserved liberty and advanced the common good was the framers' major objective, they were simultaneously anxious to avoid the democratic tyranny and democratic incompetence they witnessed under the Articles. In short, they were obliged to devise means by which a representative government could control the governed, and then further control itself.

To escape these pitfalls, the framers provided for a SEPARATION OF POWERS. Instead of lodging legislative, executive, and judicial power in the hands of one person or one group, they set up three separate branches of government. Article I of the Constitution established the legislative branch centered on the Congress; Article II the executive branch centered on the president; and Article III the judicial branch centered upon the SUPREME COURT. Accordingly, each of these coordinate and equal branches was endowed with separate and distinctive powers.

The framers further contrived a series of checks between the three branches so that each branch might balance the others. Consequently while most legislative power was given to the legislative branch, most executive power to the executive branch, and most of the judicial power to the judicial branch, the framers attempted to "divide and arrange" remaining powers as checks by the three branches upon one another. The creation of a bicameral Congress divided into a differently chosen Senate and House of Representatives, each of which must agree before legislation can be enacted, is one example of this.

There are many other checks. The president, for instance, was made commander-in-chief of the nation's armed forces. While he might lead the country into an armed struggle, as Harry S Truman did in Korea and John F. KENNEDY and Lyndon B. Johnson did in Vietnam, Congress, which alone is charged with the power to spend and borrow (to pay the bills for the other branches), must decide whether to pay for war and whether to limit U.S. participation in such struggles. Furthermore, only Congress can formally declare war. Similarly, the Supreme Court may rule that it is unconstitutional for a president to take a certain action, but the Court cannot enforce this ruling if the president disagrees, for only the president can execute the law. Again, while the president is solely charged with the

conduct of foreign policy, the Senate must approve his choice of ambassadors and must ratify all TREATIES to render them effective. The Congress must also approve presidential executive and judicial appointments, and as it tried to in the instances of Presidents Andrew Johnson and Richard M. NIXON, it can impeach and remove presidents from office. Even terms of office were staggered—representatives serving for two years, senators for six years, presidents for four years, and Supreme Court justices for life—to prevent government by tenacious political elites.

Not only did the SEPARATION OF POWERS and a system of CHECKS AND BALANCES emphasize the framers' belief that power must be shared and controlled, so too did their creation of a federal system. Most modern governments, like Great Britain's, for example, are unitary: Political authority originates with and is concentrated in a national government that in turn creates all lesser units of government and endows them with their powers. However, because the United States comprised a vast territory of almost 900,000 square miles in 1787, it was politically and administratively impossible at that time to bring this huge area under the authority of a central government alone. In addition, with a tiny but diverse population of less than 3.7 million—about 4.5 people per square mile, nearly all living in rural or frontier conditions and accustomed to self-government—a federal system was almost an inevitability given the framers' desire for a government that possessed both strength and a commitment to liberty.

The Constitution consequently provided for a federal system in which power is shared between the national government and the states. To this end, the Tenth Amendment delegates certain exclusive powers to the national government that the states cannot exercise: the power to declare war, to conduct foreign policy, to establish a currency, or to have jurisdiction over the seat of government. The Constitution, however, also provides for concurrent powers, powers whose delegation to the national government does not restrict the states from also exercising them. For example, both national and state governments have the power to tax, spend, and borrow, and both are endowed with power to oversee the general welfare, the so-called police power giving them authority to safeguard the health, safety, welfare, and morals of their citizens.

There are still other powers remaining that the Constitution delegates to the national government, powers that are neither altogether exclusive to it nor are exercised concurrently by both the federal government and

The Supreme Court is the head of the federal judiciary, one of three branches of government provided for in the U.S. Constitution. (McCrea Adams)

the states. These are powers, as the framers believed, which if fully and exclusively employed by the federal government would fatally weaken the states; or conversely, which is exercised fully by the states would debilitate the federal government. Perhaps the most important example is the power to regulate commerce. The Constitution indeed grants CONGRESS power to regulate interstate commerce, just as states may regulate intrastate commerce. There are instances, however, in which the states in their own interests may also regulate interstate commerce, albeit within strict limits defined by decisions of the U.S. SUPREME COURT.

Under Article VI of the Constitution, the supremacy clause, when the states' exercise of concurrent or other powers impinges upon the authority of the federal government, the will of the federal government must prevail. That is, the Constitution, laws, and treaties are deemed supreme and—regardless of state constitutions and laws—must be obeyed. Nevertheless, from 1798 and issuance of the Kentucky and the Virginia Resolutions through the Nullification Crisis of 1832 and the secession of eleven rebellious states in 1861, various states-rights doctrines disputed the supremacy of the Constitution and of federal laws.

The issue of federal supremacy was finally decided on the battlefields of the Civil War by the Union victory in 1865 and settled in constitutional terms by the Supreme Court in *Texas v. White* in 1869. Since the Progressive Era of the early twentieth century, still more pronouncedly after President Franklin D. Roosevelt's NEW DEAL (1933-1938), World War II, and then a half century of the Cold War (1946-1989), federal authority expanded into all reaches of American life to influence social issues far more rapidly than have the still-growing powers of the states.

The Constitution's Durability. Despite having been devised for a predominantly rural eighteenth century society, the Constitution has endured for several reasons. It was, first of all, philosophically based on persisting views of American, indeed, of human character: namely, that people generally are motivated primarily by self-interest and by passions such as ambition, greed, lust, and a longing for power, all unpleasantly but widely perceived to be the emotional foundations for a liberty-loving, individualistic commercial republic, and all needing political mechanisms, such as the Constitution provides, that are designed to control them.

Through every generation, the country's best minds and its major political and judicial leaders, not to men-

tion its innumerable INTEREST GROUPS, have divided over whether to construe the document loosely or strictly, depending on their convictions about broad social issues. Conflicts over diverse interpretations of the Constitution have infused it with fresh meanings and have kept it flexible enough to adapt to changes in people's lives and the nation's circumstances. Because the Constitution is brief and spare in its details, controversies involving vital questions have raged continuously over interpretations of the document and over what its framers intended. Since its ratification, there have been those who, like Alexander Hamilton, John Adams, and John Marshall, believed that the Constitution was properly susceptible to "loose construction." On the other hand, like Thomas Jefferson, whose views about the desirable destiny of the Republic differed substantially from those of Hamilton and Marshall, there have always been "strict constructionists" who insisted that nothing was to be implied from the Constitution's language: It meant just and only what was written.

Judicial Review. As the ultimate decision maker about constitutional questions, the SUPREME COURT has played a seminal role in determining what the Constitution means and in ensuring its longevity. A great American jurist, Charles Evans Hughes, once asserted that in reality the Constitution is what the Court says it is. Power to wield such authority is attributable solely to Chief Justice John Marshall, who dominated the Court from 1801 to 1835. Marshall was a Federalist, a powerful advocate of a strong national government, and although on many issues he was a strict constructionist, he believed nonetheless that the Constitution ought to be an expansible document. He demonstrated this by his landmark decisions on the sanctity of contract and property rights, and on interstate commerce. But it was most significantly evidenced by Marshall's initiation of JUDICIAL REVIEW; the authority of the Court, when cases are appealed to it, to determine the constitutionality of federal, state, and other governmental actions.

Since Marshall's decision in *Marbury v. Madison* (1803), the power of judicial review has distinguished the Supreme Court from high courts in other countries and has made it the ultimate authority in interpreting the Constitution and in resolving litigated constitutional issues. Regardless of differing philosophical outlooks that have marked the Supreme Court over the years, every Court has exercised restraint and discretion in utilizing judicial review. Therefore, although the Court

BAINBRIDGE COLBY,

Secretary of State of the United States of America.

TO ALL TO WHOM THESE PRESENTS SHALL COME, GREETING:

KNOW YE, That the Congress of the United States at the first session, sixty-sixth Congress begun at Washington on the nineteenth day of May in the year one thousand nine hundred and nineteen, passed a Resolution as follows: to wit-

JOINT RESOLUTION

Proposing an amendment to the Constitution extending the right of suffrage to women.

Resolved by the Senate and House of Representatives of the United States of America in Congress assembled (two-thirds of each House concurring therein), That the following article is proposed as an amendment to the Constitution, which shall be valid to all intents and purposes as part of the Constitution when ratified by the legislatures of three-fourths of the several States.

"ARTICLE __.

"The right of citizens of the United States to vote shall not be denied or abridged by the United States or by any State on account of sex.

"Congress shall have power to enforce this article by appropriate legislation."

And, further, that it appears from official documents on file in the Department of State that the Amend-

The official proclamation of the ratification of the Nineteenth Amendment to the U.S. Constitution. (UPI/Corbis-Bettmann)

has declared many state and local laws unconstitutional, it has rarely done so with federal legislation. After *Marbury*, it was not until 1858, in *Dred Scott v. Sanford*, that another act of Congress was declared unconstitutional; after that, not until the mid-1930's did a few of President Franklin D. Roosevelt's New Deal acts share the same fate. Again, not until 1995 was a federal law involving interstate commerce deemed unconstitutional by the Court in *United States v. Lopez*.

The Supreme Court's predominant outlook has alternated many times since 1803 between liberal and conservative tendencies, each Court lending its own twists to constitutional interpretation and thereby ultimately readjusting these interpretations better to suit new times and circumstances.

The Role of Parties. No less than judicial review, another American innovation, continuously operative political parties, has also contributed to the Constitution's durability and adaptability. Popular republican government, a federal system, and increasing democratization generated a great number of elective positions throughout a nation rapidly growing in population and geographical size. Professionalized political parties, which the framers never envisioned, rapidly evolved to slake the need for suitable candidates. Parties subsequently have often championed major social issues through their nationally prominent candidates as well as by means of their propaganda and party platforms. In so doing, they often elevate social questions to constitutionally relevant levels, while helping at once to sanctify and to change popular perceptions of the Constitution's limits and potentialities.

The Growth of Federal Power. Broadened twentieth century interpretations of the Constitution that emerged from the interplay of executive initiatives, congressional legislation, party politics, and Supreme Court decisions have immensely augmented federal power. Critical to the federal government's intimate involvement in regulating the economy—hence its social-economic involvement in labor relations, with wages and hours, with nondiscriminatory hirings, housing, equal-opportunity programs, AFFIRMATIVE ACTION, and WELFARE—have been the "commerce clause," the "general welfare clause," and the "necessary and proper clause" (a source of "implied powers"), all stipulated in sections of Article I. Loose construction of these clauses has also justified passage of much of the nation's social legislation during the 1930's and again during the 1950's through the 1970's.

Amendments and Federal Power. Constitutional amendments have also significantly enhanced the document's viability. The amending process, described in Article V, can be initiated either by two-thirds of the Congress or by application by two-thirds of the states, whereupon Congress calls a convention to consider proposals. Thereafter proposed amendments must gain approval either by three-fourths of the states' legislatures or by conventions in three-fourths of the states before ratification. Amending is slow and difficult. Nonetheless, there are twenty-seven Amendments, seventeen ratified since the first ten amendments, the Bill of Rights, were ratified in 1789. The BILL OF RIGHTS is a guarantor of personal liberties, ensuring people's freedom of speech, press, and religion as well as rights of assembly; to be secure in their lives and properties; not to be deprived of life, liberty, or property without due process of law; to petition government for redress of grievances; to keep and bear arms; and to bar troops from being quartered in their homes, along with a host of defendants' rights. These add to other personal and civil rights, such as the right of prisoners to a writ of *Habeas Corpus* and to BAIL bond, located elsewhere in the Constitution. Collectively, such rights constitute a code of law.

Of the last seventeen Amendments, four have been especially significant in justifying legislation and judicial decisions that have clarified and extended CIVIL RIGHTS. The Thirteenth Amendment abolished SLAVERY and involuntary servitude; the Fourteenth Amendment, as interpreted by the Supreme Court since the 1960's, applies federal procedural and substantive rights embodied in the concepts of "DUE PROCESS" and "EQUAL PROTECTION under the law" against state violations of those rights. The Fifteenth Amendment, also with civil-rights implications, prevents denial of the vote on the basis of race, color, or previous condition of servitude, while the Nineteenth Amendment prohibited denial on the basis of sex. In addition, the Fourteenth and Sixteenth Amendments have played important roles in national economic life: the Fourteenth Amendment in treating corporations as "persons" entitled to due process and equal protection thereby promoting their dominant role in the economy; and the Sixteenth, the income tax amendment, by furnishing the federal government with revenues that facilitated its expansion after the 1930's.

Criticisms. Many feminist, gay and lesbian, pro- and anti-abortion groups into the 1990's found existing interpretations of the Constitution inadequate. Into the 1990's, controversy swirled over the Supreme Court's

1973 decision in *ROE V. WADE*, a ruling that overturned state laws restricting abortions and launched numerous campaigns to alter constitutional provisions. Since the 1970's, leaders of women's movements have struggled, unsuccessfully, for an EQUAL RIGHTS AMENDMENT (ERA). Homosexuals have battled for their own equal rights in public institutions, the armed forces, and businesses; anti-abortion groups have fought to prevent access to abortion clinics and to pro-life literature, looking to the Supreme Court for constitutional support, as have black, Hispanic, and other minority leaders to sustain desegregation and federal affirmative-action laws. Other groups have fought over meanings of the Second Amendment's right to keep and bear arms. Local, state, and national advocates of a balanced federal budget likewise have sought a constitutional amendment to embed their views i the law of the land. Not least, during the twentieth century, particularly since the 1940's, astute political commentators have urged major constitutional changes. In the Progressive Era, Woodrow Wilson argued for a shift to parliamentary government, and many similar observers have criticized the Constitution as unsuited to modern urban, post-industrial life, summarizing its deficiencies as productive of "government by gridlock": government so snarled by separate powers and checks that it has become incapable of positive action.

Nevertheless, the Constitution has acquired a durable aura of popular sanctity, partly because of two centuries of viability and its positive role in shaping a national identity. Amid incessant political conflict over social and economic issues, the document continued at the end of the twentieth century to define the lawful channels and boundaries of political discourse and of American political life. Well aware of the people's predilection for political experiments and fads and of their frequent impatience for change, the framers designed a supreme law that makes fundamental alterations in America's constitutional foundations subject to a set of cautious deliberative processes. The framers expected these processes to require both wisdom and patience in order eventually to produce changes that were both acceptable and sensible. —*Mary E. Virginia*

SUGGESTED READINGS: Through his thirty-five years as a Supreme Court Justice, Hugo Black carried a copy of the Constitution in his pocket, suggesting that the best introduction to the document is the document itself. Conveniently, nearly every U.S. history text reprints it. Catherine D. Bowen's popularly written *Miracle at Philadelphia* (Boston: Little, Brown, 1986) dramatizes daily events. James Collier and Christopher Collier cover the same ground in more scholarly fashion in *Decision in Philadelphia* (New York: Random House, 1986). William P. Haas concentrates on evolution of political themes in *A Constitutional Convention* (Milwaukee, Wisc.: Savant, 1987).

Although scholars have found many of its conclusions inaccurate, Charles Beard's *An Economic Interpretation of the Constitution* (New York: Free Press, 1986) remains a provocative look at the framers' economic motivations, which Forrest McDonald's *Novus Ordo Seclorum* (Lawrence: University Press of Kansas, 1985) reexamines and corrects in light of the intellectual origins of the Constitution. Edward S. Corwin's *The Constitution and What It Means Today*, 13th ed. (Princeton, N.J.: Princeton University Press, 1974) and his *Understanding the Constitution* (New York: Sloane Associates, 1949) are classic expositions of the Constitution at work. John Ferguson and Dean McHenry's *One Nation, So Many Governments* (New York: McGraw-Hill, 1977) explores effects of the Constitution on state and local governments. Paul Eidelberg provides an insightful reinterpretation of the framers and their work in *The Philosophy of the American Constitution* (New York: Free Press, 1968).

Constitution Act, Canadian (1982): Canadian political document. The Constitution Act of 1982 brought the Canadian constitution home from Great Britain, a process known as "patriation." Previously, although Canada had full national independence, its only written constitution had been contained in the 1931 Statute of Westminster, an act of the British Parliament. The Constitution Act fully redefined the legal basis for the nation's existence.

Internal Divisions. In 1982, Canadian prime minister Pierre TRUDEAU asked the British Parliament to pass legislation giving Canada full control over its own constitution. The British complied, enabling the Canadians for the first time to draft a document that deliberately defined Canada as a nation and a commonwealth. This procedure was simply a formality, inasmuch as Canada had long been independent of Great Britain. The true importance of the document was symbolic: to show that Canada was its own master, that there was no question of its being ruled from elsewhere. The opposition faced by Trudeau came not from the British but from opposing forces within Canada. The fragility of Canadian national unity had been

Canada's provincial premiers were divided in their support of the Constitution Act. (Reuters/Corbis-Bettmann)

exposed in May, 1980, when a referendum on sovereignty for the French-speaking province of Québec was held. Although the Québec electorate voted by a 60 percent-to-40 percent margin against having their province seek sovereignty, the election was close and hard-fought, and it left Trudeau convinced that divisions within Canada had to be healed by a permanent constitution. The fact that the separatist PARTI QUÉBÉCOIS was re-elected in the Québec provincial elections in 1981 despite the defeat of its position in the referendum heightened Trudeau's conviction that a fundamental constitutional redefinition was warranted and, indeed, required.

The ten provincial premiers, allotted considerable independence in the Canadian system of government, were far less certain of this. Naturally, René LÉVESQUE, the separatist premier of Québec, was fiercely opposed to the Constitution Act. In addition, however, seven English-speaking provinces refused to give consent to the process, for reasons having largely to do with a desire to maintain as much autonomy as possible and to avoid surrendering any rights to a newly empowered federal government. Only New

Brunswick and Ontario were fully in support. Trudeau, though, using his famous political savvy, managed to outwit his opponents by demonstrating, by virtue of a decision by the SUPREME COURT OF CANADA, that he had the legal right to ask Great Britain to patriate the constitution without the formal consent of the provincial premiers. Having made this show of strength, Trudeau found it easy to get the *pro forma* approval of the leaders of the nine English-speaking provinces.

Tradition and Innovation. The constitution that Trudeau asked the British to patriate was, unlike the U.S. CONSTITUTION of 1787, not drawn from scratch. It incorporated several earlier documents in Canadian legal and political history, including the 1931 Statute of Westminster, which had given Canada full autonomy, as well as the even earlier British North America Act of 1867, which had first set out the terms of a self-governing Dominion of Canada. These documents were superseded or amended by other elements in the constitution, but their inclusion in the document demonstrated a respect and a concern for the continuity of Canadian history and tradition. This stress on tradition was important; although the Canadian constitution for-

Former prime minister Pierre Trudeau, the architect of the Constitution Act, in 1993. (Reuters/Corbis-Bettmann)

malized the democratic practices long predominant in Canada's Britain-derived political culture, the British legal tradition was noticeably antithetical to a written constitution. For centuries, English law had based itself not on any formally encoded statutes but on legal tradition, based on the slow accumulation of previous legal decisions and the consensus of a self-governing people as to what was legally acceptable and what was not. The more abstract liberalism produced by the French and American revolutions favored written legal codes that clearly spelled out the rights and obligations of the general public and their elected representatives. The combination of a written constitution and the retention of the previous documents amalgamated the key tenants of British and American constitutional theory. Most French-speaking Canadians opposed the very idea of a Canadian constitution for fear it would solidify the entrenched existence of a "Canada" the continued desirability of which was still seen to be very much in question. Yet there was even a "French" element in the constitution: the Code Napoléon, an elaborately codified set of legal statutes which was law in Québec as well as in France. The code provided a crucial precedent for Canada's adoption of a national legal document clearly spelling out the terms of the governing process.

Rights and Freedoms. In one respect, the Canadian constitution was very similar to the United States one: It eventually included, at the insistence of a majority of the general populace, a supplemental enumeration of inalienable rights possessed by every citizen. The Canadian equivalent to the U.S. BILL OF RIGHTS was the CHARTER OF RIGHTS AND FREEDOMS, which specifically enumerated thirty-four rights possessed by every Canadian, including religious freedom, tolerance for minority groups, a right to practice cultural diversity, and many other political freedoms. Reflecting the changed political climate, the Canadian BILL OF RIGHTS was less individualistic than the American one, more concerned with the existence of certain social or cultural groupings that were independent of formal political authority; perhaps acquired differences between the two nations came into play as well. Yet the spirits of the American and Canadian constitutions are similar. Both are concerned with saying that certain spheres of life are subject not to governmental interference but rather to the freely exercised choice and responsibility of each individual.

One aspect of the Charter of Rights and Freedoms reflects a difference from the U.S. CONSTITUTION. It

was early established in American constitutional history that the Constitution was subject to JUDICIAL REVIEW; in other words, although the Congress had enacted the laws, the final arbiter of their meaning was the Supreme Court. The Canadian constitution, on the other hand, included a "notwithstanding clause" that gave the federal Parliament and the provincial legislatures powers to override certain clauses of the Charter with regard to very specific contexts and situations where the abstract principles of the Charter may not precisely apply. Thus the Canadian constitution is permeated throughout by a fruitful dialogue between the principles of law and of custom. The Canadian people have largely supported the principles embodied in their new constitution and are often quite proud of the comprehensiveness, precision, and principles shown to lie in the document.

Formal Enactment. The hard work of the Canadian Constitution Act was in the preliminaries; its actual passage was quite easy, and indeed was merely a formality. On March 25, 1982, the British Parliament took what may quite possibly have been its last legal action ever to affect Canada by passing the Canada Act, which contained the full text of the Canadian Constitution Act as drafted by Trudeau and his advisers. Three weeks later, on April 17, 1982, Queen Elizabeth II signed the bill into law, marking yet another formal commemoration of the end of Britain's empire; ironically, the event took place as British soldiers were fighting to regain one of the empire's few last vestiges in the Falkland Islands. Canada was, at last, an independent country, in law as it had long been in fact. Canada retained its membership in the British Commonwealth and the British queen as its sovereign; but from now on Canada alone was to make the nation's laws.

Trudeau envisioned a hard-fought struggle to get Québec to accept the constitution. He was overly optimistic, though, for as of the mid-1990's, Québec had not ratified the document, nor did it seem likely to in the near future. Twice, in the Meech Lake Accords of 1987 and the Charlottetown Accord of 1992, Trudeau's successor, Brian MULRONEY, tried to reach a compromise that would formally enshrine Québec's wish to have its French culture defined as a "distinct society." Both times, however, the accords failed, sunk equally by Québécois who believed that the accords had not gone far enough and by English-speaking Canadians who believed that they had gone much too far. Thus, as the twenty-first century approached, Canada had a constitution, but it still did not have a consensus on what "Canada" meant. —*Nicholas Birns*

SUGGESTED READINGS: Daniel Latouche's *Canada and Québec, Past and Future: An Essay* (Toronto: University of Toronto Press, 1986) is a provocative discussion of the 1982 constitution from a French-Canadian perspective. Edward McWhinney's *Canada and the Constitution, 1979-1982: Patriation and the Charter of Rights* (Toronto: University of Toronto Press, 1982) is a clear and effective exposition of the content of the constitution and the charter. David Milne's *The New Canadian Constitution* (Toronto: J. Lorimer, 1982) provides a good survey, though the book's efforts to seem of contemporary political relevance have made it somewhat dated. Robert Charles Vipond's *Liberty and Community: Canadian Federalism and the Failure of the Constitution* (Albany: State University of New York Press, 1991) gives a look at the bitter aftermath of the euphoria of constitutional patriation, with stress on Québec's position as well as on the hypocrisy and gamesmanship inherent in Canadian federal-provincial relations. Jeremy H. A. Webber's *Reimagining Canada: Language, Culture, Community, and the Canadian Constitution* (Montreal: McGill-Queen's University Press, 1993) examines the cultural context and meaning of Canadian constitutional debates.

Consumer Price Index (CPI): Economic indicator. The CPI is a statistical measurement to show the changes in the average prices of goods and services purchased by the majority of people in the United States. The Bureau of Labor Statistics prepares the CPI, which compares the present cost of certain goods and services with their cost at a previous time. A base of 100 is used, so that an index of 120 means that the average price level now is 20 percent higher than the average price level at the base time period. Information is gathered from more than eighty thousand sources on prices of such items as food, clothing, housing, medical care, transportation, and entertainment. The goods and services on which prices are compared are changed periodically to reflect changes in consumer behavior.

Consumer Product Safety Act (1972): U.S. federal consumer-protection legislation. The Consumer Product Safety Act established the Washington, D.C.-based Consumer Product Safety Commission to enforce federal laws regulating a wide variety of products. The commission, however, has been the subject of criticism from consumer advocates for its often slow responses to consumer concerns.

Consumer rights: Uninformed consumers are easy targets for deception by sellers of products or services and often are the victims of defective workmanship and difficult to detect safety hazards. Consumers have certain ethical, as well as legal, rights regarding protection from harm, standards of quality of products and services, and conduct of business practices.

Definition of Consumer Rights. A consumer is a person of a decision-making age who determines his or her personal wants or needs, uses the proper medium of exchange (money) to buy a product or service, and uses the product or service. There is an assumption by the consumer that when the product or service is purchased, it will meet the needs of the consumer as indicated by its marketing material and labeling. Another assumption by the consumer is that when the product or service is used as specified, it will not be hazardous to the personal welfare and safety of the consumer. Finally, consumers expect full compensation and consideration from manufacturers and providers if the previous assumptions are not met. These assumptions are the established standards and rights of consumers.

On March 15, 1962, President John F. KENNEDY, in a publication to Congress entitled *Special Message on Protecting the Consumer Interest*, stated that there are certain basic principles and rights of consumers. These include the right to safety, protecting against the sale of products hazardous to one's health or life; the right to be informed against fraud, grossly misleading information, faulty labeling, and marketing deception; the right to choose among numerous types and varieties of products and services in a competitive environment; and the right to be heard by manufacturers, providers, government agencies, and legislative councils regarding legal action if purchased products or services are not as expected or promised. This document reinforced the importance of consumer rights in the United States and set a precedence for consumer protection, expectations, and legislation.

The Consumers' Association of Canada (CAC) provides information to and advocates on behalf of Canadian consumers. The CAC strives to secure the consumer rights listed above as well as trying to obtain compensation from suppliers to consumers for any loss

A Consumer Product Safety Commission representative displays a potentially dangerous toy at a 1986 press conference. (UPI/Corbis-Bettmann)

or damage resulting from faulty information, products, or performance and providing consumer education.

Limits of Consumer Rights. Consumers' rights have certain limits. The right to safety guarantees that precautions are taken in product safety, yet it is not absolute: Reason and common sense must be applied. There are many products and services that potentially may be dangerous to a consumer. For example, electric irons may burn skin and materials if left unattended or misused; gasoline used in automobiles and lawnmowers may explode if misused or stored incorrectly; knives, forks, pencils, and pens may impale eyes when used incorrectly; tanning booths are legal services, yet there may be a correlation between tanning booths and skin cancer; and some persons are highly allergic and suffer toxic reactions to numerous products such as cosmetics, foods, detergents, paint or paint removers, and new furniture or rugs. Although these dangers are real, principles of consumer rights do not suggest that these products and services should be removed from the marketplace. Consumers need only be informed of potential harms.

The right to be informed guarantees that facts about a product or service be available for intelligent choices, but it does not dismiss the consumer from his or her responsibility to ask questions and be aware of marketplace procedures and techniques. For example, the person selling a product is under no obligation to tell potential customers where they could purchase it at a lower price, that the consumer does not need the particular product to satisfy a particular need or desire, that the color or style of the clothing offered for sale is not suitable for a particular customer, or that the admired actor or celebrity demonstrating the product does not actually use the product. It is up to the consumer to shop around for the best price for the product or service available and to choose products that will satisfy desires and need.

The right to choose guarantees that a sufficient range of products and services is available for the consumer, but it does not specify how many choices or brands must be accessible. That is, the government has an obligation to protect consumers from monopolistic businesses. This right is limited: Not all possible

Consumer Product SAFETY ALERT

FROM THE U.S. CONSUMER PRODUCT SAFETY COMMISSION, WASHINGTON, D.C. 20207

August 1989

SAFETY WARNING — BUNK BEDS

Falling mattresses or foundations can cause injury or even kill a small child. Mattresses and/or foundations resting only on ledges need cross wires, or other means of support to help prevent dislodgement, even when beds are not stacked.

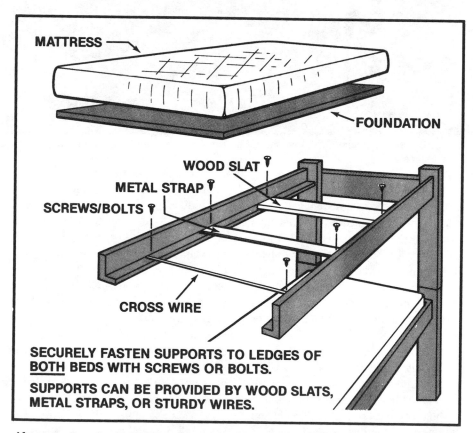

MATTRESS

FOUNDATION

WOOD SLAT

METAL STRAP

SCREWS/BOLTS

CROSS WIRE

SECURELY FASTEN SUPPORTS TO LEDGES OF BOTH BEDS WITH SCREWS OR BOLTS.

SUPPORTS CAN BE PROVIDED BY WOOD SLATS, METAL STRAPS, OR STURDY WIRES.

If mattresses or foundations on either bunk bed rely on side rail ledges as the only means of support, consumers should write to: Bunk Bed Kit, P.O. Box 2436, High Point, NC 27261, and ask for a free cross wire support kit.

A safety warning issued by the Consumer Product Safety Commission. (Consumer Product Safety Commission)

choices can or will be offered in the marketplace. How well this particular right is satisfied is difficult to assess. In general terms, the right and issues of consumer choice are understood, but it is impossible to provide everything for everyone.

The right to be heard guarantees the consumer the right to question and assist in creating consumer legislation and policy. It does not specify the outcome and resolution of policy issues concerning the fair treatment of consumers, product manufacturers, or service providers. For example, it encourages social consumer action, but it cannot force governmental agencies and organizations to grant consumers complete satisfaction or restitution for every case presented.

Costs of Consumer Rights. Providing safe, readily available, quality products and services for consumers involves numerous costs. These costs are associated with creating the idea for a product, experimenting with any prototypes and the actual product, production and assembly, ADVERTISING and promotion, packaging, delivery, putting the product or service on display, selling the product, and satisfying maintenance and warranty agreements. The consumer incurs costs in the time spent shopping and comparing advertisements, transportation to locations of different sellers, and the purchase price of the product. Psychological costs of possible product dissatisfaction also might be incurred.

The question of the value of safety, quality, and information to a consumer is difficult to answer. Consumers deserve available, safe, quality products and services, but in order to identify them—by gathering, investigating, and processing product information—numerous resources must be expended by some person, a consumer interest group or agency, or some type of governmental organization. Only then can the appropriate decision-making process for available products and services be initiated. The consumer alone cannot afford to spend the time and money for extensive research into the quality and safety of all the possible products and services available in order to make an informed choice; choices are made on the basis of limited information. Often, governmental departments and consumer committees, organizations, groups, or agencies are designated to maintain, as much as possible, standards for quality and safety. Consumers are ensured of receiving products that meet some minimum standards.

Government's Role in Protecting Consumers. When there are physical, psychological, or monetary costs associated with deciding on the best product or service available, it often is in the consumer's best interest to allow others to investigate various products and services to discover the safest and most appropriate choices. Government safety regulation of consumer products is performed for this purpose. The government has the resources to thoroughly compare and analyze numerous products and services in a manner that the average consumer could never afford. Once the government has performed its tests and analyses, this information is available to all consumers, so the cost per consumer might be very low even for an expensive set of tests.

Various official agencies and organizations exist to protect consumer rights. The Office of Consumer Affairs was created in 1971 as part of the Executive Office of the President of the United States. This office helps develop information of interest to consumers and government agencies. The FOOD AND DRUG ADMINISTRATION (FDA) is part of the U.S. Public Health Service and produces the *FDA Consumer*, a monthly publication that provides educational articles and summaries of regulatory actions. The FDA was created to ensure the safety of foods and food products as well as the safety and effectiveness of drugs, cosmetics, and medical devices and equipment. The FDA has jurisdiction over labeling of foods, cosmetics, and prescription drugs; requesting manufacturers to recall products; taking legal action against those in violation of the law; and the regulations and safety of all products sold in interstate commerce.

The U.S. Environmental Protection Agency (EPA) has regulatory powers over environmental matters. Its jurisdiction includes but is not limited to standards for indoor and outdoor AIR POLLUTION, water quality, chemical wastes, PESTICIDES, radon gas, radiation, NUCLEAR WASTE products, and noise pollution. The FEDERAL TRADE COMMISSION (FTC), established in 1914, is an independent federal agency organized to protect consumers through the Bureau of Consumer Protection (which keeps the marketplace free from unfair, deceptive, and false advertising), the Bureau of Competition (the antitrust section that stops business practices that reduce competition), and the Bureau of Economics (which provides economic analysis and support for consumer protection activities). The FTC has the authority to investigate and decide if a company's advertising is false and deceptive. If it is, and if the company will not stop its false or deceptive practices voluntarily, the FTC can obtain a court order to stop the advertising.

Consumer rights

The U.S. Postal Service (USPS) is responsible for protecting consumers from mail fraud and advertising deception. It has jurisdiction over vendors who use the United States mail to advertise worthless products and services or who receive money through the mail for such products and services. The DEPARTMENT OF HEALTH AND HUMAN SERVICES is the umbrella department for numerous smaller investigative departments such as the U.S. Department of Agriculture (USDA), which conducts nutrition research and enforces standards for meat and poultry products, including processing and packaging; the United States CENTERS FOR DISEASE CONTROL AND PREVENTION (CDC), which studies environmental and population-based health problems, administers national programs for disease prevention or curtailment, and publishes epidemiological data in the *Morbidity and Mortality Weekly Report*; and the NATIONAL INSTITUTES OF HEALTH (NIH), the federal government's lead agency for conducting and monetarily supporting biomedical research and training of personnel.

The Consumers' Association of Canada (CAC), is an independent, nonprofit, volunteer organization that represents and informs consumers and advocates on their behalf. The CAC publishes a bimonthly magazine, *The Manitoba Consumer*, that provides unbiased information on housing, health, energy, finance, food, and transportation. It offers results of independent testing, purchasing tips, how-to articles, and information on current consumer issues. It is similar to the magazine *Consumer Reports* in the United States.

Important Legislation. Numerous consumer protection laws have been enacted since the beginning of the twentieth century. One of the first and most important acts of consumer rights legislation passed in the United States is the Pure Food and Drug Act of 1906. It regulated food, drinks, and drugs provided through interstate commerce, prohibiting mislabeling and adulteration. The act was updated to become the Federal Food, Drug, and Cosmetic Act in 1936; regulation of cosmetics and medical equipment was added. The Sherley Amendment to the Pure Food and Drug Act was formulated in 1912 to prohibit the labeling of medicines with false therapeutic claims intended to defraud consumers.

The Federal Trade Commission Act of 1914 was passed with the intent of allowing competition in industry by preventing large business monopolies from taking over the marketplace. The Wheeler-Lea Amendment of 1938 gave the Federal Trade Commission the authority to prosecute manufacturers for deceptive advertising or sales practices. The Public Health Service Act of 1944 covers the safety, purity, and strength of biological products, such as blood and vaccines, offered for interstate sale, in addition to the safety of pasteurized milk and the sanitation of food, water, and facilities for travelers.

The Durham-Humphrey Amendment of 1951 stated the distinction between over-the-counter drugs and prescription DRUGS. If a drug could not be taken safely without a doctor's advice, then the FDA had the right to require that drug to be dispensed only by a licensed

MAJOR U.S. CONSUMER-PROTECTION LEGISLATION

Date	Legislation	Major provisions
1906	Pure Food and Drug Act	Regulated adulteration of food and drugs
1914	Federal Trade Commission Act	Banned deceptive food, drug, and cosmetic advertising
1938	Food, Drug and Cosmetics Act	Regulated drug safety
1958	Food, Drug and Cosmetics Act amendments	Regulated safety of food additives; banned carcinogenic additives
1962	Food, Drug and Cosmetics Act amendments	Regulated effectiveness of drugs
1966	Fair Packaging and Labeling Act	Banned deceptive packaging and labeling
1966	National Traffic and Motor Vehicle Safety Act	Set safety standards for tires and motor vehicles
1968	Truth in Lending Act	Required lenders to inform consumers of total loan costs
1970	Highway Safety Act	Created National Highway Traffic Safety Administration
1972	Consumer Product Safety Act	Created Consumer Product Safety Commission

Leading consumer-rights activist Ralph Nader. (UPI/Bettmann)

Congress has acted. The next step is yours.

Caution: Cigarette smoking may be hazardous to your health

american cancer society

Consumer advocates and health professionals successfully lobbied for the addition of warning labels to cigarette packages in the 1960's. (AP/Wide World Photos)

doctor. The Delaney Amendment of 1958 gave the FDA the authority to ban any food additive that could cause CANCER in humans or animals. The Federal Hazardous Substances Labeling Act of 1960 required manufacturers to display prominent warnings on the labels of household products containing hazardous chemicals. The Magnuson-Moss Warranty Act of 1975 required warranties to be written in simple terms easily understood by consumers. The Toxic Substance Control Act of 1976 regulates commerce and industry for protecting consumer health and the environment by requiring testing and restriction on use of specific chemical substances.

The Mail Order Consumer Protection Amendment of 1983, as part of the U.S. Postal Service legislation, requires companies that violate the False Representation Order (FRO) to pay up to ten thousand dollars a day for each violation. An FRO is issued by the U.S. Postal Service to stop companies from receiving money sent through the mail in response to misleading ads. The Nutrition Labeling and Education Act of 1990 mandated that labeling on most food products have standardized portion sizes and a more exact disclosure of the type of fat grams and cholesterol content. Labels became easier for the consumer to read and understand.

Consumer Rights Cases. Consumers have the right to sue those associated with the production or sale of products that cause injury. Such lawsuits have provided the incentive for companies to recall faulty products and fix them, or to interrupt production until a way is found to manufacture products so that they will be safe. Noteworthy examples of recalled products include the Dalkon Shield intrauterine device, the Ford Pinto (with a rear-mounted gas tank), and the flammable "Flannelette" material used in manufacturing clothes for babies.

The FDA investigates more than twenty thousand companies each year. The two cases described below are examples of FDA action.

Potentials Unlimited, Inc., of Grand Rapids, Michigan, marketed cassette tapes, to be played while the user slept. The company claimed that exposure to the tape would cure or reduce allergies, tooth and gum problems, high blood pressure, facial tics, and many other health problems. The FDA took the company to court and obtained a ruling that the tapes were devices and were being marketed with illegal and unsubstantiated therapeutic claims. The company was ordered to systematically erase all the tapes.

Swanson Health Products of Fargo, North Dakota, promoted oil of evening primrose capsules as being effective for controlling high blood pressure. After investigation and testing by the FDA, the capsules were ordered destroyed because they contained an unapproved and questionable food additive called gamma linolenic acid.

When the FEDERAL TRADE COMMISSION (FTC) investigates a claim and finds that a law has been violated, it attempts to gain the company's voluntary, consensual compliance to stop unlawful advertising practices. If the company does not comply, the FTC will seek a court order or injunction to stop the company. The FTC prosecutes only approximately ten cases a year involving unfair business practices and false ADVERTISING. Following are three cases in which the FTC stopped false and misleading advertising.

In 1981, American Home Products Corporation claimed that its products contained a special substance that was often recommended by doctors as an effective pain reliever. Upon investigation, the FTC found that substance to be plain aspirin and ordered the corporation to stop making its advertising claim. In 1983, two Florida chiropractors were stopped from claiming that their expensive laser face-lifts were highly effective for life. Upon investigation, the FTC found the claims to be unsubstantiated. Not only were the chiropractors not qualified to perform face-lift surgery, but surgical face-lifts last no more than twelve years. Kraft, Inc. was investigated for its false and misleading written and television advertisements concerning a slice of "Kraft Singles." Kraft claimed that each cheese slice single had the same amount of calcium as found in five ounces of milk. This was proved to be inaccurate and misleading by the FDA and the FTC. Kraft was prohibited from falsely representing the comparison in future advertisements.

The U.S. Postal Service has postal inspectors who look for misleading advertisements in magazines, in newspapers, and on the radio and television. They look for ads that solicit money for products or services through the mail. Following are three cases of mail-order health schemes that were taken to court by the U.S. Postal Service.

In 1981, the Robertson-Taylor Company marketed several different health products claimed to be effective for reducing fat, stopping arthritis, removing wrinkles, dissolving cellulite, and stopping baldness. The company ignored False Representation Orders issued in 1983 and 1984 to stop mail orders for the products. In 1985, at the request of the FDA and the U.S. Postal Service, Florida authorities shut down the company

Consumer activists in California endorse 1996 legislation to limit lawyers' fees. (AP/Wide World Photos)

and seized its mailing lists and products. The company president was charged with forty-two counts of criminal fraud.

Two executives of Encore House, Inc., pleaded guilty in 1985 to criminal mail fraud and received prison sentences for falsely promoting their Figure-Tron II product. This device was advertised as being able to provide tiny microelectric impulses to tone muscles five hundred times a minute; its use was claimed to be equivalent to doing three thousand sit-ups without moving an inch. After an investigation and the subsequent court proceedings, the company signed an agreement with the U.S. Postal Service and the FTC to pay a $100,000 fine and provide a $250,000 restitution fund for consumers who had purchased the product and wanted their money refunded.

In 1990, postal officials filed a false representation complaint against Puritan's Pride, also known as Nature's Bounty, Inc., for selling nutritional products through a catalog. These products were called Cholesto-Flush (to reduce cholesterol), Prostex (to alleviate problems of painful urination in men), Kidney Flush (to reduce water retention), and Memory Booster (to increase short-term memory). The company admitted no wrongdoing but agreed to stop making questionable claims and to substantiate all future claims for its products.

In Canada, by representing consumers, the CAC has forced businesses to comply with safety regulations by initiating and winning legal battles. For example, as a result of its efforts, manufacturers must use the hazardous product symbol on all appropriate labels, and businesses must install smoke alarms in buildings containing sleeping accommodations. The CAC has worked to improve the inspection of meat products, ban the use of DDT and certain other pesticides, and improve wording in warranties to facilitate consumer understanding.

Consumer Organizations. Prior to the 1960's, the concept "let the buyer beware" (*caveat emptor*) rarely was challenged. *Caveat emptor* was interpreted to mean that businesses could sell products to consumers with little care for their efficacy or safety. Services could be provided without regulation or inspection. Consumers were on their own to determine the quality of products and services, and they were responsible for the results of use.

The elderly and less educated people often were harmed by irresponsible sellers and unscrupulous service practitioners. The consumer movement grew from an escalating public demand for value, justice, and fairness in the public marketplace. The movement had a strong impact on initiating new consumer protection agencies and organizations, and it helped to promote a change in the policies and laws in existence.

The consumer movement succeeded as a result of the efforts of many staunch citizen advocates such as Ralph NADER, Betty Furness, David Caplovitz, Bess Myerson, and Sidney Wolfe. Along with many others, they accepted the challenge of attempting to increase public awareness of the rights of consumers and the necessity of being informed about the marketplace and their role in it. Voluntary, nonprofit agencies were created to monitor the media, advise and educate consumers of their rights regarding possible fraud and quackery, introduce new legislation, modify old legislation, and keep informed about legislation that would affect consumers.

Consumer organizations include statewide consumer leagues, labor organizations, consumer cooperatives, and credit unions. In addition, the Consumer Union (which produces *Consumer Reports*, a magazine that aggressively fights product misrepresentation and myths through scientific testing and analysis of products and services), the Consumer Product Safety Commission (which distributes educational information and redirects complaints about product safety), specialty elderly groups such as the AMERICAN ASSOCIATION OF RETIRED PERSONS (AARP), and business organizations such as the Council of BETTER BUSINESS BUREAUS (BBB, which operates through self-regulation), attempt to ensure that fair and reputable business practices are maintained.   —*Kathleen J. Hunter*

SUGGESTED READINGS: Betty Mushak discusses problems and those willing to fight to solve them in "Environmental Equity: A New Coalition for Justice" (*Environmental Health Perspectives*, November, 1993). Laurence E. Drivon's *The Civil War on Consumer Rights* (Berkeley, Calif: Conari Press, 1990) concerns the civil justice system as it relates to consumers. Upton Sinclair's novel *The Jungle* (New York: Doubleday, Page, 1906) depicts the working conditions in Chicago's meatpacking plants; it alerted consumers as to what might be in the meat they purchased. Charles A. Willard's *The Rights of Consumers: A Basic Overview on the Question of Consumer Product Safety* (Skokie, Ill.: National Textbook Company, 1980) thoroughly discusses how consumer product safety is linked to advertising and issues of mass persuasion.

Ralph M. Gaedeke's "The Movement for Consumer Protection: A Century of Mixed Accomplishments"

Automobile manufacturers perform crash tests to improve consumer safety. (UPI/Bettmann)

(*University of Washington Business Review*, Spring, 1970) gives a good review of the origin and development of the modern consumer movement. W. Kip Viscusi's "Market Incentives for Safety" (*Harvard Business Review*, July/August, 1985) reviews the importance of attention to product safety and consumer well-being in a healthy business interaction. C. Glenn Walters and Blaise J. Bergiel's *Consumer Behavior* (Cincinnati, Ohio: South-Western, 1989) discusses the philosophy of market-driven behavior and consumer decisions. Steven Kelman's "Regulation and Paternalism," a chapter in Tibor R. Machan and M. Bruce Johnson's *Rights and Regulation: Ethical, Political, and Economic Issues* (San Francisco: Pacific Institute for Public Policy Research, 1983), examines the costs involved in consumer product research.

Case Studies in Regulation: Revolution and Reform (Boston: Little, Brown, 1981), edited by Leonard W.

Weiss and Michael W. Klass is a good discussion and review of governmental regulations, including OSHA, and reform. John A. Carlson and Robert J. Gieseke's "Price Search in a Product Market" (*Journal of Consumer Research*, March, 1983) discusses the difference between product costs and convenience costs, both of which affect purchasing decisions.

Consumers Federation of America (CFA): Consumers' rights group. Organized after consumer activism in the 1960's and 1970's revealed that the general public was often the victim of unscrupulous and dangerous products, the CFA seeks to investigate consumer issues and act as advocate on the behalf of consumers to legislators and in the courts. In addition to its legal advocacy, the CFA publishes and disseminates consumer information on many issues that affect consumers. Information on credit, communications products, the environment, food, food processing, health, housing, insurance, political action, transportation and other issues are the subject of CFA involvement.

Contempt of court: Any act or failure to act that directly or indirectly blocks or hinders a court from completing its necessary functions or that takes away from the authority or respectability of the court. Contempts are divided into two general categories, civil and criminal. Civil contempt is the failure of a person to obey a court order that affects or benefits another individual. Criminal contempt occurs when an individual disrespects or defies a court itself. Contempt is punishable by fines and indefinite jail terms at a court's discretion.

Contraceptive devices: Devices used to ensure that heterosexual vaginal intercourse does not result in conception or pregnancy. True contraceptive devices include barrier methods such as male and female CONDOMS, diaphragms, cervical caps, and vaginal sponges, which physically block sperm from reaching eggs, and chemical methods, such as birth-control pills, implants, and spermicides. Birth-control pills and implants prevent women from ovulating, so that no egg is present to be fertilized. Spermicides literally kill sperm inside the vagina and uterus.

When taken as directed, birth-control pills are extremely effective. Barrier methods and spermicides are not very effective when used alone, so it is generally recommended that they be used together. Even in combination, however, barrier methods with spermicides are still much less effective than birth-control pills; barrier methods are more likely to fail and are much more likely to be used incorrectly or to be used only occasionally, resulting in more unwanted pregnancies.

While barrier methods are not as effective as chemical methods for preventing conception, condoms, the most common form of barrier contraceptives, are quite effective at preventing disease transmission during sexual activity. (Chemical contraceptives have no effect at all on disease transmission.) Condoms are thus recommended for disease prevention even when pregnancy is not a worry, for example, during oral or anal sex between heterosexual or homosexual partners, for older couples who are no longer fertile, or when an otherwise fertile female is menstruating.

In addition to devices that prevent conception, there are also mechanical and chemical devices that prevent pregnancy after conception has occurred. While the technical term for these devices is "contragestives," they are almost always included in the category of contraceptives. Mechanical contragestives, or intrauterine devices (IUDs) are specially designed wire or plastic forms that a physician inserts into a woman's uterus to prevent any fertilized egg from implanting into the uterine wall. Some common types of birth-control pills also act as contragestives, preventing pregnancy by manipulating hormones to prevent implantation.

"Abortifacients" disrupt a pregnancy that has already begun; these, too, include both mechanical and chemical methods. Abortifacients are generally not referred to as contraceptives.

Surgical STERILIZATION procedures may or may not be included in the category of contraception devices. While such procedures are the most effective techniques for preventing conception and pregnancy, there are no devices involved. Surgical sterilization involves either cutting the tube that carries sperm into the urethra (vasectomy) or cutting the tubes that carry eggs to

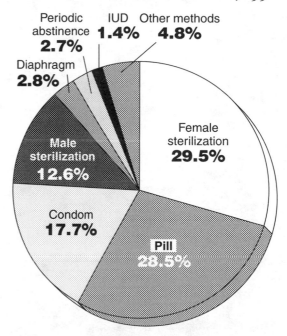

U.S. BIRTH-CONTROL METHODS, 1990

Periodic abstinence **2.7%**
IUD **1.4%**
Other methods **4.8%**
Diaphragm **2.8%**
Male sterilization **12.6%**
Female sterilization **29.5%**
Condom **17.7%**
Pill **28.5%**

Source: Newsweek, March 13, 1995. Primary source: National Center for Health Statistics.

the uterus (tubal ligation). Both procedures are effective, but both are generally considered to be irreversible, so they tend to be used by individuals who do not wish ever to have children.

Contract with America: Legislative agenda designed by Republican House of Representatives members to be enacted if a REPUBLICAN majority were elected in the fall of 1994. This program for legislative action was presented as a rallying point for voters frustrated by years of congressional gridlock on major social and economic questions. Strategists for the party hoped voters would cast their ballots based on the party's promised reforms. Chief among its proponents was its co-author Newt GINGRICH, Republican Whip in the 103d CONGRESS and future Speaker of the House.

Provisions. The Contract consisted of eleven key provisions for legislative action. The first element amended labor and civil rights laws to apply to Congress as well as the private sector. Congress had often exempted itself from such federal laws in part to main-

tain the SEPARATION OF POWERS between the executive and legislative branches. Enforcement of this legislation would have put the legislature in a subordinate position. Additional reforms reduced the number of House committees and supporting staff. The Contract's second component was a BALANCED-BUDGET amendment and a LINE-ITEM VETO. The balanced-budget amendment demanded a balanced federal budget by 2002 but allowed a three-fifths vote of Congress to waive this deadline. The line-item veto permitted the president to rescind all or part of an appropriations bill instead of approving or rejecting the bill in its entirety. The third element consisted of several separate bills designed to fight CRIME. These included measures for victim restitution, revision of the exclusionary rule to permit wider use of evidence seized through warrantless searches, deportation of criminal aliens, more prison construction, and limited the number of death row appeals.

The Contract's fourth element focused on WELFARE reform and required a reduced federal role in administering such programs and favored giving the states increased discretion in running their own programs. The

Newt Gingrich poses with a poster-size copy of the Contract with America. (Archive Photos, Reuters, Win McNamee)

proposal called for the forty-four individual federal programs to be combined into five block grants that would allow wide discretion by states in designing their own welfare system. Some federal restrictions would apply, namely prohibiting the use of federal assistance to anyone on welfare more than five years, to mothers already on welfare, and to children of unwed mothers under eighteen. The fifth element of the Contract would have permitted tax breaks for ADOPTION, and lowered the CAPITAL GAINS TAX. The sixth element sought a tax credit of five hundred dollars per child for families earning under $200,000 a year and higher tax-free contributions to INDIVIDUAL RETIREMENT ACCOUNTS (IRAs). The seventh component focused on national security concerns and demanded a reduction in U.S. contributions to the United Nations (U.N.), blocked the use of DEFENSE SPENDING cuts to pay for social programs, and prevented the placement of U.S. troops under U.N. command without the consent of Congress.

The Contract's eighth element sought to raise the level of yearly income seniors could enjoy without losing any Social Security benefits. Also, the Contract called for the repeal of the previous Congress' move expanding the number of Social Security benefits subject to INCOME TAX. The ninth element, aimed at lowering the capital gains tax, prohibiting unfunded mandates, and establishing a new cost-benefits analysis on any new regulations, placed a moratorium on any new regulations until the passage of the overhaul bill, and a minor bill to reduce legislative paperwork. Unfunded mandates are federal requirements that states provide certain services but without the benefit of federal funding.

The tenth element of the Contract encompassed three initiatives, including revision of product-liability laws limiting the financial responsibility of manufacturers, the creation of "loser pays" provisions for civil suits, and limits on the amount shareholders can claim against companies who have misrepresented the earning potential of their stocks. The final element of the Contract was the constitutional amendment to limit the length of terms of senators and representatives to twelve years each. By the end of the first hundred days of the new Congress, all of these measures had been passed by the House with the exception of the TERM-LIMITS initiative, which was defeated. In contrast to the breakneck pace of the House in passing the Contract, the Senate took several months before considering these initiatives.

Controversy. The two constitutional amendments proved to be the most controversial portions of the Contract. Balancing the federal budget had been a talisman for fiscal conservatives since well before the advent of Ronald REAGAN. The measure easily won the required two-thirds majority in the House but failed by one vote in its first visit to the Senate. Likewise, term limits had become a popular movement nationwide and was touted by many outside of Congress as a means to shake up a legislature dominated by incumbents. Such a measure was particularly attractive to House Republicans who had been the minority party for close to forty years. While most members of Congress were on record as supporting term limitations, they differed widely as to what form the limits should take. Some preferred a twelve-year limitation for all members of CONGRESS. Others supported a twelve-year limit for the Senate and a six-year limit for the House. Congress was also divided as to whether the limits should apply only to consecutive years served or impose a lifetime cap. No single proposal could muster the necessary three-fourths majority for passage.

Voter Reaction. For their part, voters showed a surprising lack of interest in the Contract. Despite the extensive coverage given the Contract by the press, the public remained largely ignorant of the proposal in general, let alone its specific provisions. Public opinion surveys indicated that even after the Republican landslide in November, almost half of the electorate claimed never to have heard of the Contract. More surprising is the fact that during the first hundred days of the new Republican majority, the similar polls showed only a modest rise in voter awareness of the Contract. Even the most optimistic poll indicated little awareness of the specific provisions of the Contract.

Such data demand a more moderate assessment of the Contract than most of its proponents would prefer. The argument that the new Republican Congress was elected with a mandate to enact the Contract is questionable, given the limited public knowledge of the proposal. When voters were questioned about the factors that influenced their choice for Congress, very few cited the Contract as a significant consideration. The two groups who did seem to find the Contract of major significance were the press and Republican pundits. The press saw a new innovation for the normally dull midterm elections and granted it coverage owing to its novelty. After the fall election victory, Republicans were quick to claim the Contract as their key to success.

A 1995 Philadelphia protest against the Contract with America. (Impact Visuals, Harvey Finkle)

Some political commentators believe that the Contract represents a resurgent sense of party identification among voters, that they may have begun to vote increasingly on the basis of a party program and less upon the individual qualities of particular nominees. During the previous twenty years, political scientists noted that voters relied less on a candidate's party affiliation in casting their ballots and expected less from the major parties by way of broadly based programmatic initiatives. Proponents of the Contract claim the 1994 congressional election was a watershed year in which voters became not only more partisan in their voting but also more REPUBLICAN as well.

While the Contract represented an interesting innovation, only time will tell whether voters or the DEMOCRATIC PARTY will adopt such platforms as standard elements of congressional campaigns. The impact may be chiefly electoral. If the Democratic Party produces its own version of the Contract, such platforms could become commonplace. In the wake of the tremendous Republican victory in 1994, Democratic leaders may be willing to copy anything that seemed to work for the Republicans. Of greater significance is the potential of such platforms on governance and accountability. Rather than receiving isolated individual promises by candidates for legislative action, voters may expect the majority party to enact its agenda or be held collectively accountable if they fail. It is still too new to judge such an instrument's popularity with the public. More problematic is the lack of empirical support for such observation. What is known is that since its inception, the public has found the Contract to be only a vague and imprecise symbol of a resurgent Republican Congress.   —*Bruce Turner Hall*

SUGGESTED READINGS: *Contract With America: The Bold Plan by Rep. Newt Gingrich, Rep. Dick Armey, and the House Republicans to Change the Nation* (New York: Times Books, 1994), edited by Ed Gillespie and Bob Schellas, is a pro-Contract overview. For a skeptical critique of the Contract, see Louis Fisher's "The 'Contract with America': What It Really Means" (*The New York Review of Books*, June 22, 1995). A nonpartisan analysis and legislative history can be found in the *Congressional Quarterly Almanac 1995* (Washington, D.C.: Congressional Quarterly, 1996).

Copyright infringement: Violation of the rights of a copyright holder. Because of the increasing number of new technologies making copying and distribution of media ever more easy, copyright infringement has become an increasingly serious problem.

Background. The first U.S. copyright law dates from 1790. There have been four major revisions since, with current law based on the 1976 revision of the 1909 law, effective in 1978. Because new technologies are constantly developing and altering the medium for creative works, the 1976 Copyright Act asserts that "copyright protection subsists . . . in original works of authorship in any tangible medium of expression, now known or later developed, from which they can be perceived, reproduced, or otherwise communicated, either directly or with the aid of a machine or device." Ideas and facts themselves are not copyrightable; however, the unique, tangible form in which the creation is fixed is copyrightable.

A copyright holder reserves the right to copy or reproduce the work, prepare derivative works, distribute copies to the public, and display or perform the work publicly. Works created after January 1, 1978, reserve copyright for the lifetime of the author plus fifty years. Prior to this, copyrights not declared in the public domain lasted for twenty-eight, forty-two, fifty-six, or seventy-five years from their original publication, if renewed.

The United States joined the Berne Convention as of March 1, 1989, providing authors with copyright protection as if they were a citizen of any signatory country. From this time onward, a copyright notice was not required nor must a work have been registered with the Copyright Office. Registration in the United States, however, is still an advantage before claiming copyright infringement. Even if a work is not registered, an author may affix the copyright symbol, a "c" inside a circle (©) along with the first year of publication and the owner's name.

Fair Use. The purpose of the copyright act is "to promote the progress of Science and Useful Arts." The concept of "FAIR USE" has been refined by a series of cases and was further codified in the Copyright Revision Act. The four major factors in fair use involve: the purpose and character of the use; the nature of the copyrighted work; the portion used; and the effect of the use upon the market for the work. Generally, nonprofit, educational agencies that use small portions of a reference work without impacting the market for the work would be well within fair use. Use of excerpts in schoolwork and the publishing of excerpts in reviews are firmly established within fair use. Any usage that erodes the market for the work, however, is usually not fair use; this commercial criterion is considered to have the most weight.

Photocopying. Nothing prohibits a person from selling a legally produced book as a used book. The production of new copies, however, is one of the rights reserved by the copyright holder. A single photocopying of print material is legal by libraries for patrons. While most such use is for excerpts for academic research purposes, an entire work may be copied if a reasonable search fails to locate a legal copy available at a fair price. The system of interlibrary loan of journals also allows copying for patrons as long as the copying is not systematic or intended to substitute for subscribing to the journal. Requests for more than five copies of a given work are used as the benchmark indicating that the library should purchase the book or subscribe for classroom use if the copies are short and do not replace the need for an available workbook.

Multiple copying of journal articles in a corporate setting was not upheld as legal in *American Geophysical Union v. Texaco Inc.* (1992). Because this eroded the market for the journals of five publishers and was conducted by a for-profit company, this case gave legitimacy to the Copyright Clearance Center, an agency set up to allow ready payment by users who wish to remain legal but copy journal articles in a timely manner.

Some college professors had traditionally ordered course packs consisting of collections of different readings, essentially an anthology, copied as the textbook materials for their courses. In *Basic Books Incorporated v. Kinko's Graphics Corporation* (1991), however, a court ruled that Kinko's could not use fair use or the classroom multiple-copy rule, although the court did not rule on the anthology issue directly.

Fax-machine transmissions may be treated similar to photocopying in interlibrary loans, but the copy made to send the fax must be destroyed or it violates the one-copy rule. Scanning print into a database constitutes systematic copying beforehand as well as violating the copyright holder's right to make the derivative electronic work.

Other Media. Licenses from the copyright owner, or more likely the designated agent, are required for public performances and broadcasts. This is especially true if admission is charged, if it is a dramatic performance, or if the performance is not contained solely within a classroom. Broadcast over a standard radio placed in a public area, however, does not require a license, as ruled in *Twentieth Century Music Corpora-*

tion v. Aiken (1975), although certain requirements are specified.

The U.S. Supreme Court decision in *Sony Corporation of America v. Universal Studios, Incorporated* (1984) rejected the producer's contention that the only legitimate use of videocassette recorders would be for production of what would be illegal videotapes. This ruling made in-home use for time shifting of broadcast programs clearly legal but only if restricted to a close circle of family and friends. In 1979, the Kastenmeier guidelines clarified the status of fair use of off-air taping for teachers allowing the classroom playing of such videotapes for a set number of days after broadcast, but only in a "face-to-face" teaching situation.

Fiber-optic and satellite technologies have expanded the ability of one teacher to "reach" a larger audience with a limited amount of interactivity. Because of the broadcast nature of such courses, however, the use of many media, which would be legal in a face-to-face setting, may violate copyright laws. Likewise, course and research materials that may have been legal excerpts of copyrighted materials for personal and private use, may become linked to the IN-

Copyright registration protects the property rights of artists and inventors. (Yasmine Cordoba)

TERNET via home pages, thus widely distributing the work without the copyright holder's permission.

Databases and Digitized Works. The 1991 Supreme Court decision *Feist v. Rural Telephone Services* found that the white-page listings of telephone numbers lacked the creativity or originality required of a copyrighted work. Yet such facts, if arranged in tables or other more useful formats, would be protected. The development of scanning equipment that can digitize pictorial images and then convert the images back into characters usually constitutes infringement of the copyright holder's right to reproduce, distribute, make derivative works, or display those works. In *Playboy Enterprises Inc. v. Frena* (1993), the Court ruled that a photograph owned by Playboy Enterprises had been circulated on an electronic bulletin board in violation of the publisher's distribution rights. While such emergent technology creates new dilemmas in the application of laws originally written to address copyright of print and film, case law eventually clarifies the ambiguity. The ongoing observation that technology has surpassed the copyright code merely indicates that proponents in the new electronics marketplace have not yet contested the issues.

"Pirating" of Books, Videotapes, Cassettes, and Computer Programs. Not all cultures share the heritage of intellectual property rights and copyright protection. In the face of increasingly economical copying technologies, part of the legitimacy of copyright laws depends upon a substantially affluent middle class able to afford legally made copies of educational, cultural, and entertainment materials. In addition, Asian cultures, in particular India and China, often consider imitation to be a sincere compliment, with a resultant reduction in value for intellectual property rights. What Westerners would call plagiarism, lack of appropriate attribution, and copyright infringement may be seen as a legitimate economical means to disseminate the arts and sciences. This remains a serious issue of contention between Western and Asian countries.

—*John Richard Schrock*

SUGGESTED READINGS: Janis H. Bruwelheide's *The Copyright Primer for Librarians and Educators*, 2d ed. (Chicago: American Library Association, 1995) provides a concise summary of print and video copyright for these audiences. *A Guide to Copyright Law in Higher Education*, by Thomas Hemnes, Alexander Pyle, and Laurie McTeague (Washington, D.C.: National Association of College and University Attorneys, 1994) describes copyright law in university applications, where high technology developments are often first applied. *U.S. Copyright Documents: An Annotated Collection for Use by Educators and Librarians*, by Jerome Miller (Littleton, Colo.: Libraries Unlimited, 1981) provides documentation for major copyright law up to 1980.

Corporate culture: Rules and beliefs that influence behavior within a company and the company's image with the general public. Theories of corporate culture as an explanation for a business's success or failure gained acceptance after studies of General Motors revealed how its conservative corporate culture contributed to its slow response times to market changes. Industry analysts believe that corporate culture can determine everything from what is acceptable clothing for the workplace to how receptive management is toward new ideas. In the 1990's, many U.S. companies instituted "dress-down" Fridays in an attempt to promote more open corporate cultures and indirectly encourage innovation.

Corporate responsibility: Social theories of responsibility see obligations to others as morally primary: The primary responsibility of individuals is not to achieve their own interests but instead to advance the interests of other members of society and the society as a whole. Advocates of such theories might argue, for example, that individuals exist to serve the greatest happiness of the greatest number, or the least advantaged members of society, or society as a whole. Theories of corporate responsibility sometimes see businesses as "individuals" with the same sorts of responsibilities. In addition, corporate managers, as individuals, hold the day-to-day executive power of a corporation. Debates over corporate responsibility focus on how managers should exercise their power: To whom should they see themselves as primarily responsible?

The Stockholder Theory. The stockholder theory emphasizes the individual rights of liberty and property, and it analyzes corporations in terms of the rights and responsibilities of the individuals within them. A corporation begins as a voluntary association of investors (the stockholders) who desire to earn a profit. They pool their capital and form a new business enterprise, each believing that it is to his or her advantage to do so. The stockholders appoint directors, who hire managers to use the corporation's capital productively. Managers, therefore, have the responsibility to do what they agreed to when taking the job: to use their skills to manage the corporation's assets in the interests of the stockholders.

The managers will deal with customers, suppliers (of labor, raw materials, and other goods and services), and governments. In each case, the primary responsibility of the corporation's managers is to act in a way that best advances the long-term financial interests of the stockholders. The corporation, as a voluntary association of individuals, operates within the broad framework of respect for each individual's rights to life, liberty, and property, and it operates on the principle that all those with whom it deals are self-responsible agents. The managers will negotiate with customers and suppliers and attempt to form contractual agreements that advance the goals of the stockholders, just as the customers and suppliers will negotiate with the corporation's managers and attempt to form agreements that advance their own goals. If mutually agreeable terms are found, a deal is made; if not, the parties go their separate ways.

The Stakeholder Theory. The stakeholder theory applies the social theory of responsibility to the corporation. It asks managers to see themselves as primarily responsible not to the stockholders but to the entire group of parties who have an interest in the corporation's assets. Parties who have an interest in the corporation's assets are called stakeholders. The stakeholder theory perceives managers as responsible for using the corporation's assets in a way that is best for all the stakeholders, or perhaps for the greatest number of stakeholders or those stakeholders whose needs are the greatest. Stockholders, accordingly, are only one among many groups of stakeholders, and their needs are not seen, in principle, as having special priority.

The stakeholder theory implies that managers may sometimes be called on to act against the stockholders' best interests if so acting would advance the interests of other stakeholders, or at least some especially needy subgroup of stakeholders. The facts that the stockholders provided the capital for the corporation and hired the managers to act in their interests are seen by the stakeholder theory as of secondary importance.

An Example. Debates over the appropriateness of plant relocations provide a clear example of the difference between the two theories. Suppose that a corporation could increase profits by relocating from Delaware to Idaho. Perhaps labor costs or taxes are lower in Idaho, or perhaps Idaho is closer to suppliers or customers, allowing reductions in the cost of transporting supplies or goods.

Although stockholders would benefit from the move, some parties would lose. Current Delaware employees might lose their jobs, current suppliers might lose the corporation as a customer, and the current local and state governments would lose tax revenues. Each of these groups with a stake in the decision might attempt to convince managers not to make the move. On what principle should the managers decide whether to move?

According to the stakeholder theory, two types of considerations might appropriately lead to a decision that it would be wrong for the corporation to relocate. It might be that the gains to the stockholders would be outweighed by the collective losses to the employees, suppliers, and local and state governments; if so, the greatest happiness for the greatest number would require that the corporation sacrifice its more profitable opportunities in Idaho. It might also be that although the gains to the stockholders would be enormous, one particular group of stakeholders, such as the current employees, would be so devastated by the loss of their jobs that preventing harm to these least advantaged stakeholders should override the potential gains to the more advantaged stockholders.

According to the stockholder theory, by contrast, the move would be the moral managerial decision. The corporation belongs to the stockholders, and the managers have a responsibility to manage its assets to obtain the largest profits possible. Delaware employees, suppliers, and governments will lose out if the corporation moves (as potential Idaho employees, suppliers, and governments will lose out if the corporation does not move), but these losses are not the primary responsibility of the corporation.

Other Issues. As the twentieth century drew to a close, public interest groups increasingly made stakeholder claims against the business community. That trend was enhanced by government budget cutting that left social programs with insufficient funding. Corporations were called on to donate to local charities, fund programs to beautify the environment (in positive ways such as building parks or as responses to negative elements such as graffiti), and assist in providing education and skills to local residents. All of these have at least a tangential relationship to the corporation, but it is unlikely that spending money in any of these areas will provide a positive rate of financial return.

Stakeholder groups argue that every business has

Demonstrators call for increased corporate responsibility and government regulation during the Great Depression. (UPI/Corbis-Bettmann)

responsibilities to its community and that because businesses benefit financially from the community, they should make contributions back to it. These groups attempt to insinuate themselves into the corporate morality; they are not clear stakeholders with a claim to corporate resources as strong as that of stockholders, employees, or the government.

More traditional stakeholder groups also have increased their claims. Trends toward corporate downsizing and movement of production to countries with lower labor costs brought cries of protest from labor unions and other employee groups. These groups claimed that business was reneging on its responsibility to provide stable employment at good wages; loyal workers were being sacrificed to enhance business profitability. It did not help the case for business that relocations sometimes occurred at times of high profit-

ability; this made it even easier to claim that corporate greed was overwhelming social responsibility.

—Stephen R. C. Hicks

SUGGESTED READINGS: Peter A. French and others discuss issues of responsibility in *Corporations in the Moral Community* (Fort Worth, Tex.: Harcourt Brace Jovanovich, 1992). Robert Hessen defends the stockholder position in *In Defense of the Corporation* (Stanford, Calif.: Hoover Institution, 1979). The political maneuvering involved in corporate responsibility is discussed in Charles E. Lindblom's *Politics and Markets* (New York: Basic Books, 1977).

Corporate restructuring: Altering the organizational structure, management style and practices, goals, focus, asset base, or capital structure of the corporation in an effort to more efficiently operate the business, reduce costs, and improve profits. Corporate restructurings can be divided into two broadly defined groups: financial restructurings designed to obtain a more suitable system of capital funding for the corporation, and management restructurings intended to use the human resources of the corporation more effectively.

The dramatic decline in interest rates during the 1980's spurred a barrage of notable financial restructurings, such as LEVERAGED BUYOUTS (LBOs), MERGERS, acquisitions, divestitures, and spin-offs—all designed to create value for shareholders by capitalizing on supposed imperfections in the financial markets or inconsistencies in the corporate tax code.

In the early 1990's, management restructurings became extremely popular, taking many forms, including DOWNSIZING, OUTSOURCING, and reengineering. Downsizing involves mass layoffs of personnel, usually at the corporate staff level, to reduce corporate payroll expenses and remove unnecessary layers of middle management. Two prominent U.S. corporations—International Business Machines (IBM) and General Motors (GM)—attempted to alleviate their multibillion dollar annual losses in the early 1990's by downsizing their corporate staffs. Proponents of downsizing contend that American industrial corporations have become excessively bureaucratic in their organizational structure and lack the ability to quickly counteract moves by their foreign competitors. Critics of downsizing argue that it is shortsighted; corporate employees laid off during an economic downturn must be rehired when conditions improve.

Outsourcing is another popular means of restructuring. Industrial components previously manufactured by a large, diversified company may be outsourced to separate, often smaller, companies; thus, the capital invested in producing the components is freed and can be put to use elsewhere. During an economic recession, outsourcing can prevent the need to downsize, because the risks of production have been transferred to another company. In essence, outsourcing is the conversion of fixed costs—investment in property, plant, equipment, inventory, and manpower—to variable costs, which fluctuate with economic activity. The virtual company is one that relies completely on outsourcing for all of its production activities; this revolutionary approach is relatively new but has enjoyed tremendous popularity among start-up ventures lacking the capital to invest in proprietary production capacity.

Reengineering requires a company to jettison its traditional organizational structure and practices. Generally accepted management ideas regarding the division of labor, the need for elaborate controls, and the hierarchical management structure are abandoned in favor of a process orientation.

SUGGESTED READINGS: Michael Hammer's popular book *Reengineering the Corporation* (New York: Harper Business, 1993) describes in detail the concept of reengineering. *Liberation Management* (New York: Alfred A. Knopf, 1992), written by noted business author Thomas J. Peters, portrays a "new economy" in which most business activity will be organized in semipermanent networks of small, project-oriented teams. In their *Transforming the Organization* (New York: McGraw-Hill, 1995) Francis J. Gouillart and James N. Kelly outline a holistic approach to business transformation that focuses on reframing corporate direction, restructuring the company, revitalizing the enterprise, and renewing people.

Corporation for Public Broadcasting (CPB): Federally sponsored communications organization. Encompassing the PUBLIC BROADCASTING SERVICE (PBS) and NATIONAL PUBLIC RADIO (NPR), the CPB was chartered by Congress in the Public Broadcasting Act of 1967. Its mission was to link, promote, and develop the nation's "educational" television and radio stations to provide an alternative to commercial broadcasting. The CPB was largely the work of Democrats; charges of "elitist" leftist bias quickly came from Republicans. In 1972, amid heated controversy, President Richard Nixon vetoed the CPB's budget legislation. While public broadcasting survived, it increasingly became subject to conservative pressure. When Republicans gained control of Congress in 1994, many pressed for the privatization of PBS and NPR. Because the popularity of programs ranging from *Sesame Street* to *Frontline* guaranteed public support, however, the CPB and its 351 community stations escaped with serious but not fatal reductions of its $300 million budget.

Council of Energy Resource Tribes (CERT): Native American advisory group formed in 1975. CERT's members consist of representatives of several dozen Native American tribes who work together to control the development of mineral resources (such as oil, coal, and gas) on tribal lands. The goal of the council is to ensure that tribes, not corporations, profit from the exploitation of tribally owned resources. Members advise tribes on the management of resources and assist in contract negotiations with developers. Although sometimes criticized for endorsing environmental destruction, CERT has been successful in improving tribal control over resources and increasing tribal income.

Courtroom media: Presence of the press in trials and courtroom proceedings. In democratic societies, accused persons have the right to receive fair and impartial trials. In such societies, however, the public and the press also typically have a common-law right to be informed of judicial activities such as trials and pretrial hearings. Conflict can thus arise when the media publishes or broadcasts material that makes it difficult, if not impossible, for accused persons to receive fair trials. Sometimes the press will, in effect, find a defendant "guilty" before any evidence has been presented at trial and before the defendant has had the

opportunity to respond to that evidence. In other cases, pressure may be placed on a jury following publication of members' names and addresses. Prosecutors and judges, too, can be affected by media coverage; in combination, such factors can on occasion deform the legal process, leading to a "trial by media" rather than a trial by peers.

The 1994-1995 O. J. SIMPSON murder trial was only one of many courtroom proceedings to have attracted enormous media and public attention. The Lindbergh baby kidnapping trial of the 1930's, the Sheppard murder trials of the 1950's and 1960's, and the Patty Hearst case of the 1970's, for example, all attracted sensational publicity. These and other such celebrated cases have prompted debate over whether media coverage should be restricted, typically through the issuance of court orders known as "GAG rules," in the interest of ensuring fair trials, or whether concern for free-speech rights should take precedence over such considerations.

While there is a long tradition of common-law protection for press coverage of trials in the United States, the Supreme Court did not consider the question of

Media coverage of the O.J. Simpson trial provoked widespread criticism. (Reuters/Corbis-Bettmann)

constitutional protection of courtroom media until the Sheppard trials. In 1954, Sam Sheppard was convicted of killing his wife in a brutal beating. Although he proclaimed innocence and blamed the murder on an intruder who had knocked him unconscious, his story was widely disbelieved by the press. Editorials were written calling for Sheppard's execution; photographers roamed the courtroom, and newspapers ran front-page pictures of jurors. Sheppard was convicted, but he was acquitted in a 1966 retrial after the Supreme Court ruled that the first trial had been tainted by the surrounding publicity's effects on jurors and other parties to the proceedings. The Court declared that the press did have the right to cover trials; however, the justices also issued a list of remedies that trial courts could use to offset the effects of potentially prejudicial publicity. Chief among these is the voir dire examination process, in which attorneys interview prospective jurors to ensure that they are not prejudiced. Courts can also delay the time of a trial, move a trial to another location, bring in jurors from other communities, and—in extreme cases—sequester jurors to prevent influence from the media or other outside sources.

Broadcast and photographic coverage of trials is allowed in most states, although some states require camera operators to obtain permission from the judge or the other parties involved. Many states have provisions governing the number and placement of courtroom cameras; the American Bar Association Code recommends that television cameras be used for instructional and administrative purposes only at the discretion of a judge.

Coyotes: Slang term for paid guides who smuggle aliens across the U.S. border with Mexico. The term connotes the cleverness of the guides, who are reputed to know the best routes and the safest methods of entering the United States while avoiding border patrols. It also, however, alludes to the untrustworthiness of some guides; many have misled their clients after relieving them of cash, while others have abandoned

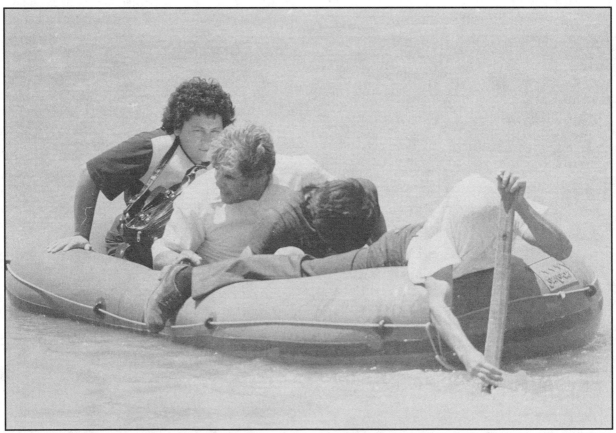

A coyote (shown with his face covered) ferries illegal immigrants across a river at the U.S.-Mexico border. (AP/Wide World Photos)

their clients without transportation in the desert areas of the Southwest.

Crack cocaine. *See* **Cocaine and crack cocaine**

Creationism and evolution teaching: Public school controversy. Creationism, the belief that the biblical description of the beginnings of life on earth is literally true, has contributed to conflict in U.S. school systems for much of the twentieth century. Creationism directly contradicts one of the fundamental tenets of modern biology, evolution, which theorizes that different forms of life, including humankind, developed gradually over millions of years.

History. Evolutionary theory is based on the work of Charles Darwin and Alfred Wallace. Darwin served as naturalist on the HMS *Beagle*, a survey ship, for five years in the 1830's, collecting specimens and keeping meticulous records. When he returned to England, he began working through ideas regarding transformation of species. He had devoted almost twenty years to assembling evidence to support his theory when Alfred Wallace, a naturalist working independently of Darwin, came to similar conclusions to explain variations and changes in animals.

In 1858, Wallace sent Darwin a copy of his essay "On the Tendency of Varieties to Depart Indefinitely from the Original Type." On July 1, 1858, both Wallace's essay and extracts from a paper by Darwin were presented to the Linnean Society of London. Darwin planned a massive work but instead condensed his argument into only 490 pages, published in November, 1859, as *The Origin of Species by Means of Natural Selection, or, The Preservation of Favored Races in the Struggle for Life*. Darwin's theories met with skepticism from both scientists and theologians, but although specific questions about natural selection arose, the general concept of evolution became one of the foundations of modern biology.

Unlike early reactions to Darwinian evolution, the movement promoting creationism was not associated with an established church. By the mid-twentieth century, mainstream Christian theologians had accepted the idea of coexisting with Darwin. They considered other areas of science, such as genetic engineering, far more troubling than whether or not children should be taught evolutionary theory in science courses. When creationism appeared in the 1960's, it emerged among ordinary laypersons.

According to sociologist Dorothy Nelkin, the creationism movement began in California in 1963. Two events occurred, both in Orange County, a region of Southern California long known for ultraconservatism in both politics and religion. Ten men, all possessing graduate degrees in science, established the Creation Research Society (CRS). The goal of the CRS was to promote teaching creation science. Within ten years, the CRS claimed 450 regular members and 1,600 sustaining members.

At the same time, two Orange County women, Nell Segraves and Jean Sumrall, launched a campaign to require public-school textbooks to emphasize the theoretical nature of evolutionary ideas. With help from Walter Lammertz, a geneticist and founding CRS member, the women petitioned the state board of education and state attorney general. Segraves and Sumrall argued that just as it was forbidden to teach religion in schools, atheists should be prevented from promoting atheistic beliefs. Assistant Attorney General Norbert A. Schlei agreed it would be unconstitutional for a state to prescribe atheism, agnosticism, or irreligious teaching. Max Rafferty, then California superintendent of public instruction, promptly ruled that all California texts dealing with evolution must clearly show evolution as a theory.

In 1969, the State Curriculum Commission, a volunteer body, revised science text guidelines to include a formal recommendation that schools teach creation theory. This recommendation shocked the California State Advisory Committee on Science Education, but the issue did not erupt into full-blown controversy until November, 1972. At that time, hearings were held to solicit public opinion regarding creation science. Eventually, the California State Board of Education adopted a compromise solution: Potentially offensive statements would be edited to indicate their conditional nature.

As the creationist debate in California heated up, events elsewhere in the country seemed to indicate the evolution-versus-creation dialogue was winding down. A February, 1969, article in *Scientific American* reported upon the Tennessee legislature's repeal of that state's antievolution law and the Supreme Court's overturning of an Arkansas antievolution statute. The latter, the Rotenberry Act, had been passed in 1927 and was, in 1969, the only antievolution law to have been contested at the level of the U.S. Supreme Court.

An advocate of creationism talks to reporters after a 1986 court ruling requiring removal of textbooks from Tennessee schools for violating Christian beliefs. (AP/Wide World Photos)

The Rotenberry Act had been passed as part of a fundamentalist drive led by a former presidential candidate, William Jennings Bryan. When, in 1925, the AMERICAN CIVIL LIBERTIES UNION (ACLU) persuaded a Tennessee high-school teacher, John Scopes, to challenge recent legislation passed in that state banning the teaching of evolution, Bryan served as prosecutor.

Popular accounts of the trial give the impression that the ACLU won, but in fact the presiding judge refused to allow arguments concerning the scientific validity of evolutionary theory. Instead, he ruled only on whether or not Scopes had violated Tennessee law, which Scopes admittedly had, and Scopes was fined $100. Because the conviction later was overturned on a technicality, the opportunity to contest the act's constitutionality was lost.

Renewed Interest. After the SCOPES TRIAL, interest in both evolution and creationism waned until the 1960's. Following the California textbook controversy, however, antievolutionists gained strength nationwide. For the first time in fifty years, state legislators considered statutes that were either explicitly opposed to evolutionism or in favor of creationism. For example, legislation introduced in Arkansas mandated equal treatment for evolutionary theory and creation science. Governor Frank White signed the act into law on March 19, 1981, but less than a year later, on January 25, 1982, U.S. District Court Judge William R. Overton found the act unconstitutional as it served to advance religion. Despite this ruling, the 1980's saw increasing numbers of antievolution bills introduced and passed, primarily in the Southern United States. These were, however, voided almost as quickly as they became law.

The creationists of the 1980's were quite different from the antievolutionists of the 1920's and employed different tactics. Where fundamentalist views on evolution in the 1920's had been promoted by ministers and politicians, the 1980's creation-science advocates were purportedly men of science themselves. Henry Morris, one of the best-known spokespersons for the Institute for Creation Research, was the former head of the Department of Civil Engineering at Virginia Polytechnic Institute.

When engineers spoke out against evolution and presented what appeared to be compelling scientific arguments, they had more credibility than a minister arguing for biblical inerrancy. Engineers and other college-educated creationists marshaled an impressive array of what appeared to the nonscientist to be solid scientific reasons to support creationism and disprove evolution. These included both biological examples and references to the Second Law of Thermodynamics. Creationists issued challenges to evolutionists, offering a cash reward if the evolutionists could prove evolution did not violate the Second Law. After the challenge was issued in 1976, numerous proofs were submitted, but the creationists refused to accept any as valid.

Criticisms. Established science responded to the creationist threat in several ways. Critics held creationism up for ridicule as a pseudoscience because it failed to meet any of the standard criteria for judging scientific theories. In addition to noting the lack of empirical evidence to support creationism, critics argued that creation science was, in fact, indistinguishable from religious faith because it relied on a supernatural element, a divinity. Mainstream scientific journals refused to publish articles supporting creation science. In response, creation scientists published their own journals and condemned the prejudices of the establishment. The only place where creation science and evolutionary theory appeared within the pages of the same journal was a publication produced by the American Humanist Association, *Creation/Evolution*.

Moreover, the new generation of creationists learned from their mistakes. In an effort to get creation science into public schools, they downplayed religious aspects of creationism in courtrooms, claiming that it was a nondenominational concept. They also took advantage of U.S. attitudes regarding fair play and equal time. Creationists argued they did not want evolutionary theory out of schools but simply wanted to provide students with all available hypotheses. They argued that they were not against evolution but rather in support of creation. Nevertheless, creation science lost much of its momentum when television evangelism was rocked by scandals. The major wave of antievolutionist agitation peaked in the mid-1980's. Controversies surrounding television ministries may have caused people to examine fundamentalist movements more critically—just as in the 1920's, when similar scandals occurred. Court rulings against the promulgation of creation science seem to have further disheartened all but the most dedicated proponents of creationism. In any event, despite occasional local outbreaks of creationist fervor, by the 1990's, the controversy over creation science had receded from the public eye.

—*Nancy Farm Mannikko*

Credit card debt

SUGGESTED READINGS: Dorothy Nelkin's *Science Textbook Controversies and the Politics of Equal Time* (Cambridge, Mass.: MIT Press, 1977) gives an engrossing account of the origins of the modern creationism movement. Douglas J. Futuyma's *Science on Trial: The Case for Evolution* (New York: Pantheon Books, 1983) provides an interesting history of evolutionary theory and its critics. The anthology *God and Nature* (Berkeley: University of California Press, 1986), edited by David C. Lindberg and Ronald L. Numbers, contains fascinating studies describing interactions between science and religion throughout history.

Credit card debt: Credit card debt is the constantly fluctuating amount of money owed by individuals who use credit cards to purchase goods and services. As of 1987, such consumer credit indebtedness totaled approximately $150 billion among Americans, almost double the level of 1980, and the level of indebtedness expanded rapidly during the next several years. Some of this debt was incurred to purchase durable goods such as automobiles, home appliances, and consumer goods such as clothing; much of it was applied to nondurables, such as entertainment and food. The amount of debt during the 1990's, as a comparison, was about 15 percent of the gross national product of the United States, which measures the value of all goods and services produced in a year.

Almost 80 percent of families in the United States had at least one credit card by the early 1990's. Credit cards of various types were available to most working adults and even to many college students and teenagers. Credit cards (some of them technically called charge cards) are issued by different entities for different purposes. Bank cards are issued by banks and other lending institutions for consumers to use to purchase goods and services. The two most common types are VISA and MasterCard. Stores also issue cards, good only for purchases at those stores. Banks commonly charge retailers 2 to 3 percent of the value of a credit transaction to handle it for them through a bank card. Store cards are used only in the issuing stores, and those businesses operate their own billing and collection departments. A third type of card is the gasoline card, which operates like a store card.

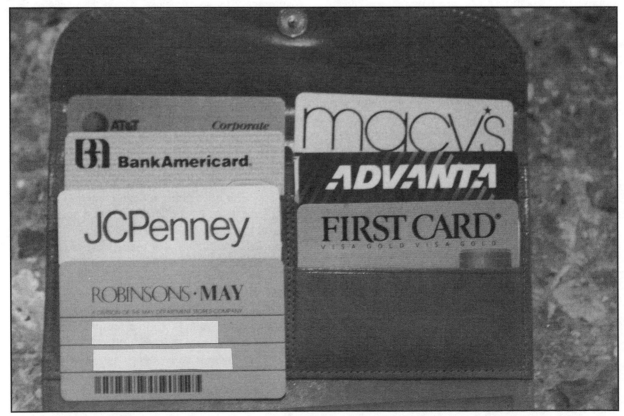

Credit cards can lead unwary consumers into substantial debt. (Yasmine Cordoba)

These three types of cards all charge interest to the consumer on outstanding balances. Many do not charge interest if the purchases are paid for in full at the end of a billing cycle. Some have annual fees associated with them, and consumers must weigh higher fees against the benefits of lower interest rates or lack of interest on payments made in full.

A fourth major type of card is the travel/leisure card, which was the first type of credit card to be used in the United States. Diner's Club is one of the most famous of these and was the first to be issued, in the 1950's; American Express is another well-known issuer. These true credit cards differ from charge cards in that they do not charge interest and require full payment at the end of a billing cycle, which typically is thirty days. They usually have higher annual membership fees and often charge a higher fee to retailers.

The economy benefits from the increased spending promoted by credit cards; however, such spending comes at a price. Consumers unwilling or unable to budget can get heavily into debt with credit cards. The large balances allowed and low monthly payments may appear to offer a good deal, but the interest rates charged on consumer debt typically are several percentage points higher than those charged on other types of debt. Some cards charge interest in the range of 20 percent annually.

Many households owe large amounts on credit cards, imperiling their financial status. Consumers become caught in a cycle of making minimum payments, which barely cover interest, and accumulating even more debt because credit card payments consume such a large part of their budget. Failing to pay credit card debt properly can ruin a person's credit, making important purchases, such as that of a home, more difficult. In addition, landlords often refer to a person's credit record to decide whether to rent to that person.

Economists worried during the 1990's, as the level of credit card debt skyrocketed, that an economic downturn might make many people unable to make their minimum payments. Credit card issuers might be faced with the choices of offering more generous terms, forgiving loans, or forcing BANKRUPTCY on cardholders. The issuance of credit implies a large amount of trust in borrowers; if large numbers of borrowers suddenly became unable to repay loans, as could happen if the unemployment rate rose significantly and many people lost their jobs, lenders could be put in danger of going bankrupt themselves.

Judicious use of credit cards can be an important tool in budgeting. It allows consumers to delay payment for some goods, which may make sense in the case of durables. For example, a family might choose to buy a new appliance, such as a washing machine, on credit rather than waiting to save the funds needed for the purchase. The appliance will be in use for many years, and the family can apply what they would have saved toward credit card payments. In this example, the purchase also might save money in the budget: Ownership of a washing machine might mean that the family does not have to pay to use machines at a laundromat.

Some credit cards also offer benefits such as extended warranty periods. Responsible use of a credit card also establishes a positive credit record that later can pave the way for bigger loans such as automobile and home mortgage loans. Moreover, credit cards can be used in emergencies to provide for essentials and can alleviate the difficulties and danger of carrying large amounts of cash.

Crime: One of the foremost social concerns of the American public. Fear of crime has prompted significant increases in police personnel and prison building and has caused responses to crime to be placed at the heart of many government services.

Crime Trends. Contrary to popular opinion, crime did not rise exponentially during the early and mid-1990's. Many crimes reported in the Department of Justice's Uniform Crime Reports (UCR) remained relatively stable during this time. Furthermore, although the murder rate in the United States rose sharply in the 1990's (from a low of less than five murders per 100,000 population per year, a level attained in the 1950's and early 1960's), it merely again reached levels observed the 1930's (of between nine and ten murders per 100,000 population annually).

The rise in crime over the levels experienced in the 1960's and 1970's, especially the increase in violent crime, produced an outcry from the American public. Three specific sources of crime, mostly interrelated, were at the center of the public reaction to crime: gang crime, crime in the inner cities, and crimes committed by teenagers and other young people.

GANGS have been a part of American cities for many years; the earliest studies of gangs date back to the 1920's. Gangs in Chicago, New York City, and Milwaukee proliferated during this time and continued to grow into the 1970's, when Los Angeles gangs began

A gang-related shooting in Chicago, 1929. (Archive Photos/American Stock)

to draw national attention away from gangs in Eastern cities. The difference between modern gangs and gangs of the past, however, lay in the level of violence they employed and in who the gang members considered to be acceptable targets of violence. Fueled by gang involvement in drug sales, the 1980's and 1990's showed a significant increase in the use of guns by gang members. In fact, a 1993 publication by Carolyn R. Block and Richard Block, "Street Gangs in Chicago," reported that a gun was the weapon used in almost all gang-related homicides in Chicago from 1987 to 1993. In the 1980's and 1990's, a new term was added to the English language as a result of gang activities: "DRIVE-BY SHOOTING." This crime typically involves gang members who drive past people or their residences and shoot at them from a moving vehicle. Inherent inaccuracies in shooting from a moving vehicle often cause bystanders to be shot rather than the intended targets.

Although crime figures for the mid-1990's showed a decrease in overall crime in the twenty-five largest U.S. cities, with 1994 showing the largest drop in more than a decade, crime in inner cities became a focus of many political and popular groups. Increasing violence, especially violence committed by gangs and younger teenagers, brought attention to the conditions of inner cities. This concern was enhanced by images of Los Angeles and Chicago "war zones" of drugs and gang violence and by the realization that smaller cities such as Little Rock, Arkansas, with a population of less than 200,000, were experiencing dramatic increases in violent crime and were developing serious gang problems.

Crimes perpetrated by those eighteen and under rose significantly during the 1980's and 1990's. From 1988 to 1992, the Uniform Crime Reports' "index crimes" (murder, rape, robbery, aggravated assault, burglary, theft, motor-vehicle theft, and arson) rose 5.4 percent for persons eighteen and older. During this same period, however, index crimes committed by persons younger than eighteen rose 12.3 percent. Even greater was the difference between the ages for violent crimes (murder, rape, robbery, and aggravated assault): Here the increase in crime commission for those eighteen and older was 18.8 percent, while the change for persons younger than eighteen was 47.4 percent. Although the number of crimes committed by those over eighteen years of age is still greater than those committed by younger persons by a factor of four to one, the dramatic increase in the number of violent crimes committed by juveniles indicated a level of acceptance of violence by the younger generation that seriously worried the American public.

Much of the blame for changes in American criminal activity during the 1990's was placed on crack, a potent form of COCAINE that is smoked rather than

PUBLIC OPINION, 1994: WHAT IS THE MOST IMPORTANT PROBLEM FACING THE UNITED STATES?

Crime; violence	49%
Health care	31
Economy in general	17
Unemployment	17
Poverty and homelessness	9
Drugs and drug abuse	8
Federal budget deficit	8
Education	6
Welfare	6
Ethics and moral decline	5
Dissatisfaction with government	3
Guns and gun control	3
International situation	3
Environment	2
Taxes	2
Trade relations; trade deficit	2
AIDS	1
Foreign aid; too much focus overseas	1
High cost of living	1
Immigration; illegal aliens	1
Medicare; Social Security	1
Racism; race relations	1
Recession	Less than 1%
Other	12%

Source: George Gallup, Jr., ed., *The Gallup Poll: Public Opinion, 1994* (Wilmington, Del.: Scholarly Resources, 1995).

Note: Total exceeds 100 percent because of multiple replies by some respondents.

U.S. CRIME INDEX OFFENSES, 1993

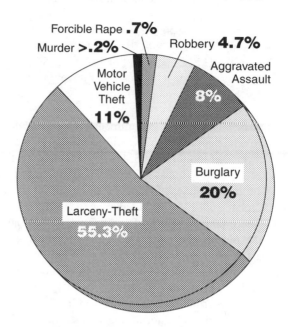

The annual Crime Index lists selected serious offenses used to gauge fluctuations in the overall crime rate.

Source: U.S. Department of Justice, Federal Bureau of Investigation, *Crime in the United States* (Uniform Crime Reports). Washington, D.C.: U.S. Government Printing Office, 1994.

sniffed. Processing cocaine into crack allowed it to be sold in much smaller quantities and for a lower price. The availability of crack for a few dollars per dose, compared with a hundred dollars or more for a dose of powder cocaine, changed the nature of crime surrounding drug sales. Prior to the development of crack, many persons committing crimes related to drug use were burglars. Robbery, which unlike burglary involves confrontation of the victim, often with a weapon, was inefficient for supplying a habit, because robberies typically net only a few dollars. The price of crack made robbery more attractive; small monetary gains were sufficient to support a habit, and direct collection of money negated the problem of fencing stolen property. The rise in robbery, however, brought with it a rise in crack-related violence and HOMICIDE that had not existed with burglary.

Cost of Crime. Direct costs of crime may be broken down into two categories: cost of government responses and cost to victims. There are other costs, such as higher prices of goods caused by shoplifting and the cost of private security, which are related to crime but are more indirect and difficult to link with the criminal event itself.

Cost of crime responses are mostly government costs in support of the CRIMINAL JUSTICE SYSTEM. According to the U.S. Department of Justice, $75 billion was spent by federal, state, and local governments in 1990 for law enforcement, criminal prosecution, and corrections.

The largest portion of governmental resources allocated to crime control is in law enforcement. The more than seventeen thousand U.S. law-enforcement agencies accounted for almost $32 billion in cost to taxpayers. The largest share of this cost was born by local governments, which contributed more than $23 billion to law-enforcement efforts. The fifty states added another $5 billion; the federal government contributed the least amount, at slightly more than $4 billion.

A total of $16.5 billion was devoted to processing suspected criminals through the U.S. court system. Although the contributions of the different levels of government were more balanced, local governments still contributed the greatest amount ($8 billion), while state governments added another $5 billion and the federal government contributed $3.5 billion.

Finally, cost of incarceration and other correctional programs added more than $26 billion to government expenditures on crime. State governments contributed the largest share to the correctional resources, $17 billion. Local governments contributed almost half of that, at more than $8 billion. The federal government once again contributed the least, at slightly more than $1 billion.

Information on costs to victims of crime is more difficult to obtain. As a result, much of the data on victim-related costs is based on estimates. The most reliable information on costs to victims concerns direct costs, which can be broken down into three categories: direct loss, loss of wages, and medical expenses. The largest portion of direct costs to victims is the direct economic loss as a result of the crime. Most of this cost (about $139 billion annually) is from property crimes (such as burglary, theft, and auto theft) resulting in lost money or goods. The one violent-crime exception

The scene of a 1992 homicide in New York City. (AP/Wide World Photos)

is robbery, which involves the taking of money or possessions from a victim. Both property-crime and violent-crime victims experience lost wages as a result of criminal behavior. Victims may have to take time off from work to file police reports, view suspects, or attend court. Additionally, violent-crime victims may

ARRESTS IN THE UNITED STATES, 1993 (ESTIMATED)

Total	**14,036,300**

Arrests for FBI "Index Crimes"

Aggravated assault	518,670
Arson	19,400
Burglary	402,700
Forcible rape	38,420
Larceny-theft	1,476,300
Motor vehicle theft	195,900
Murder and nonnegligent manslaughter	23,400
Robbery	173,620

Arrests for Other Crimes

All other offenses	3,518,700
Curfew and loitering law violations	100,200
Disorderly conduct	727,000
Driving under the influence	1,524,800
Drug abuse violations	1,126,300
Drunkenness	726,600
Embezzlement	12,900
Forgery and counterfeiting	106,900
Fraud	410,700
Gambling	17,300
Liquor laws	518,500
Offenses against family and children	109,100
Other assaults	1,144,900
Prostitution and commercialized vice	97,800
Runaways	180,500
Sex offenses (except forcible rape and prostitution)	104,100
Stolen property; buying, receiving, possessing	158,100
Suspicion (not included in totals)	14,100
Vagrancy	28,200
Vandalism	313,000
Weapons; carrying, possessing, etc.	262,300

Source: U.S. Department of Justice, Federal Bureau of Investigation, *Crime in the United States* (Uniform Crime Reports). Washington, D.C.: U.S. Government Printing Office, 1994.

Note: Arrest totals are based on data from all agencies reporting to the Uniform Crime Reporting Program and estimates for unreported areas. Because of rounding, figures may not add to total.

have to spend time at home or in hospitals recovering from injuries. Loss of wages adds another $3 billion to the cost of crime to victims. Finally, there are medical expenses that are incurred as a result of personal injury from crime. Medical expenses add another $6 billion to the cost of crime. Such estimates thus place the total cost of crime to victims at about $148 billion annually.

Causation. The cause of criminal behavior is the most elusive element of the study of crime. Since the earliest research on crime in the 1700's, people from many different fields have sought the source of criminal behavior. Possible causes range from inherited biological abnormalities, mental disorders, the environment in which a person lives, influences of peers or society, and even the system of democracy and justice itself. None of these, however, has proven strong enough to explain a significant portion of the differences between criminals and noncriminals.

The earliest exploration into criminal behavior took a biological approach. Publication of *The Criminal Man* by Caesar Lombroso in 1876 is considered the first attempt to study criminal behavior scientifically. Biological explanations of crime continued as the dominant paradigm through the early twentieth century. These criminologists expanded Lombroso's works to include inherited biological defects, feeblemindedness, and criminal body-typing. Although biological explanations continue to the present, other explanations now override biological ones in popularity.

Closely related to biological theories, psychological explanations look to the human brain for the causes of criminal behavior. Based in the works of Sigmund Freud and the early works on feeblemindedness, this perspective places the cause of crime in the brain functioning and thought processes of individuals. Although some biological links still remain in this perspective, most modern psychological theories focus on how individuals learn and how peers influence their behavior. This line of study is known as learning theory. Learning theories differ from other psychological theories in the proposition that criminal behavior is learned, like any other behavior, and that it is not the result of a physical or mental abnormality. The essence of learning theory is that criminality is the result of interaction with or reinforcement from individuals, factors that shape all behavior, including criminal behavior. Contributors to criminal behavior, therefore, are a person's peers and environment.

The majority of criminological explanations since the 1950's have focused on sociological influences.

REPORTED U.S. CRIMES CLEARED BY ARREST, 1993

Crimes of Violence

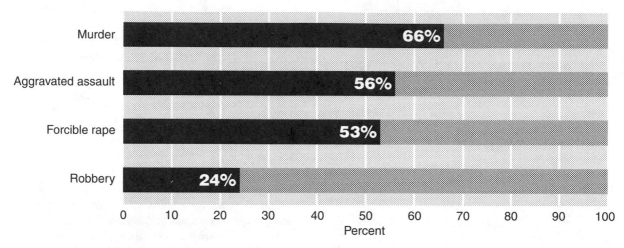

Crimes Against Property

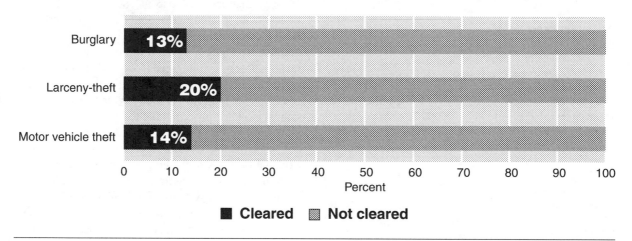

■ **Cleared** ▒ **Not cleared**

Source: U.S. Department of Justice, Federal Bureau of Investigation, *Crime in the United States* (Uniform Crime Reports). Washington, D.C.: U.S. Government Printing Office, 1994.

This is also the most diverse body of explanations. Attempts to explain criminal behavior focus on such factors as the environment in which people live, the strain placed on individuals between what society sets out as economic goals (clothes, houses, etc.) and the differential ability to obtain these goals, the development of a subculture of society conducive to crime, conflicts between different cultures within society, and the lack of internal and external controls on behavior that allow individuals to commit deviant acts.

The final source of criminological explanation comes from those who are critical of the government and criminal justice system and who place the cause of criminality upon the actions of the political and financial elite. This category of criminological explanation (known as radical criminology) is a strategy for analyzing crime and justice that attempts to explore connections between social phenomena and economic reality. Behavior that is examined as criminal under this set of theories includes: whether certain people (such as minorities, the poor, and drug abusers) and their behaviors are targeted by the government for law en-

Capital punishment is one of the most controversial topics in American criminology. (UPI/ Corbis-Bettmann)

forcement, while others (such as stockbrokers engaged in fraud, or corporations that violate safety or environmental laws) are not; whether the government commits criminal behavior on its own (such as police brutality or illegal acts in foreign countries); and whether the system of justice is fair.

At issue with all of these theories is that they cannot, by themselves, answer the question of what causes all crime. A single explanation is not sufficient to explain such a complex behavior, and no one has found an acceptable mix of the different theories that can explain a level of criminality sufficient for effective preventive measures.

Prevention. The idea of CRIME PREVENTION begs the question of what society is preventing if it does not know the cause of criminality. Nevertheless, myriad programs have been developed that purport in some way to prevent criminal behavior. Most of these programs are designed to "control" criminal behavior after a person has been brought to the attention of the criminal justice system, rather than to "prevent" criminal behavior before the fact. As such, the discussion here will first look at programs that can truly be classified as prevention and then turn to a discussion of programs more appropriately classified as "correction" or "rehabilitation."

Prevention has its roots in the control of juvenile behavior. Based on the notion that juveniles should be treated differently from adults, the first juvenile court statute was developed in 1899 in Illinois, with the mandate to control juvenile behavior after it had been brought to the attention of the criminal justice system; the statute was intended to prevent status offenders or those committing minor crimes from reaching the point of criminal acts. This philosophy still exists today; most prevention efforts are still aimed at juvenile delinquents.

True prevention programs must, by definition, attempt to influence people prior to the commission of delinquent acts. These people are typically referred to as "at-risk" juveniles because their personal characteristics, environment, or behavior are identified as predictive of delinquent behavior. They may also be predelinquent juveniles who have committed status offenses or other behavior indicative of the onset of delinquent behavior. Programs at this stage attempt to modify individual behavior or change to the environment so that such factors obstruct rather than promote delinquency. Identification of youth at risk can occur at the individual level or at the environmental level.

Typical preventive programs at the individual level target youths who are status offenders, who have exhibited problem behavior in school, or who are identified as people in need of supervision (or services). The most widespread and effective programs at this level fall into what is referred to as alternative schools. Youths who exhibit problem behavior at school are placed in special classes or are moved to other locations, where they receive greater supervision and where traditional school activities are augmented with special programs. These programs attempt to change problem behavior before the juvenile adopts delinquent attitudes and behavior.

Prevention programs at the community level cast a broader net in the juveniles they attempt to attract. Programs such as midnight basketball leagues attempt to provide alternatives to involvement in gangs or delinquent activities and provide juveniles with role models and supervision that they might not otherwise receive. Also effective at this level are Drug Abuse Resistance Education (DARE) and Gang Resistance Education and Training (GREAT) programs, which work with school-age children to prevent the acceptance of drug abuse and gang attitudes and to prevent juveniles from beginning these behaviors.

Corrective programs have the goal of making delinquent youths nondelinquent. These programs are exemplary of the rehabilitative model for shaping behavior. Corrective programs target juveniles who have been diverted from prosecution by the police or by the courts, or they may work with youths who have been found delinquent.

Corrective programs accept that the juvenile has adopted criminal attitudes and characteristics; such programs attempt to downplay or eliminate such attitudes or characteristics. For example, substance abuse programs attempt to reduce drug and alcohol addictions in juveniles, while training and education programs attempt to provide avenues for productive employment so that juveniles have the opportunity to leave their criminal tendencies and environment. Corrective programs may also incorporate activities of prevention, such as the handling of aggression in personal relationships.

By 1990, a new method of correction had become popular: the "boot camp." Based on the notion that initial military training had changed many people from "rowdy teenagers" to "productive citizens," states began to pattern programs after the models of Georgia and Oklahoma, which first began boot-camp programs

President Bill Clinton signs the 1994 Violent Crime Control and Law Enforcement Act. (Reuters/Corbis-Bettmann)

in the 1980's. In such programs, juvenile delinquents were placed in correctional facilities in which for three to six months they were taught respect and discipline through military marching and behavior, education, and work. By the time the 1994 Crime Bill offered funding for boot camps, almost all states had some kind of boot-camp program.

Politics and Crime. Public concern over crime in the early and mid-1990's brought a corresponding concern from political figures. In political campaigns throughout the country, crime became a pivotal issue for both sides. Building on the 1988 presidential race between George BUSH and Michael Dukakis, which featured a battle over prison furloughs for people convicted of murder, the 1992 presidential race between George Bush and Bill CLINTON put crime at the base of both parties' platforms.

In 1994, the U.S. Congress passed the most comprehensive crime-control bill in U.S. history. The VIOLENT CRIME CONTROL AND LAW ENFORCEMENT ACT (the Crime Bill), the result of six years of work within Congress, was designed to pour more than $30 billion into the justice system over a six-year period. This was to include more than $11 billion for additional police officers and law-enforcement programs, $10 billion for prisons and other correctional alternatives, and more than $6 billion in crime-prevention efforts and social programs designed to ease crime problems.

Soon after the Crime Bill was signed by the president, however, the nature of Congress changed. The 1994 congressional elections elevated Republicans from the minority to the majority party in Congress and ushered in the Republican "CONTRACT WITH AMERICA." Under Republican leadership, Congress vowed to rewrite the Crime Bill, removing many of the social programs and crime-prevention efforts and putting more force behind correctional systems and stern laws.

Crime-control efforts did not stop at criminal justice efforts of the federal government, however. Crime also became a true concern of leaders at all levels of government. Many states passed tax increases to support the expansion of police personnel or prison beds, and local governments began placing emphasis on reducing crime in high-crime neighborhoods at all costs.

Answers. The world continues to look for answers to the problems of crime, which plagues inner cities and shocks rural areas where the population thinks that crime will not reach.

Researchers and scholars faithfully look for the answers to these questions, and the criminal justice system continues to work on effective ways to deal with people who violate criminal laws. No acceptable answers have been found to questions about what causes crime, and such answers may never be found. Unless they are, people will continue to commit crimes, and they will continue to be processed through a less-than-perfect criminal justice system.   —*Jeffrey T. Walker*

SUGGESTED READINGS: The primary source of annual U.S. crime data comes from the *Uniform Crime Reports: Crime in the United States* (Washington, D.C.: Department of Justice). An alternative source of crime information is *Criminal Victimization in the United States* (Washington, D.C.: Department of Justice), also published annually. For a prophetic commentary on the current criminal justice system, proposed by a eighteenth century philosopher, read *On Crimes and Punishments* by Cesare Beccaria (Indianapolis, Ind.: Bobbs-Merrill, 1963). A good understanding of crime in America can be obtained by reading *Thinking About Crime*, 2d ed., by James Q. Wilson (New York: Basic Books, 1983). A philosophical and practical understanding of the police can be found in *Policing a Free Society* by Herman Goldstein (Cambridge, Mass.: Ballinger, 1977). *The Contours of Justice: Communities and Their Courts*, by James Eisenstein, Roy B. Flemming, and Peter F. Nardulli (Boston: Little, Brown, 1988), offers a fairly complete look at the American court system.

The process and philosophy of sentencing is documented in Robert Martinson's "What Works?—Questions and Answers About Prison Reform," *Public Interest* (Spring, 1974), and *Doing Justice: The Choice of Punishments*, by Andrew von Hirsch (New York: Hill & Wang, 1976). A thorough examination of prison, life in prison, and prison administration can be found in John J. DiIulio, Jr.'s *Governing Prisons: A Comparative Study of Correctional Management* (New York: Free Press, 1987). A look into the future of crime (some of which has already arrived) can be found in Georgette Bennett's *Crimewarps: The Future of Crime in America* (Garden City, N.Y.: Anchor Books, 1987).

Crime prevention: Efforts to reduce or eliminate criminal activity. Crime-prevention debates center on arguments over whether the application of punishment or the removal of motive and opportunity is the most effective method of combating criminal behavior.

Many crime-prevention programs aim to keep at-risk youth out of gangs and away from criminal influences. (UPI/ Corbis-Bettmann)

Deterrence. The deterrence model assumes that the pain (which in this case would be swift and certain punishment by the courts) outweighs any pleasure or gain the criminal might derive from illegal behaviors. Individual deterrence refers to the fact that punishment keeps offenders from committing the same crime again because the criminal is either in prison or—in the case of CAPITAL PUNISHMENT—dead. General deterrence involves setting an example that will keep others from engaging in criminal activity: If people observe that punishment is swift and certain, they will be hesitant to attempt the same behaviors.

Scholars are involved in an ongoing debate about whether punishment actually is a deterrent and, if it is, how much punishment is necessary to deter a person from crime. In a study of inmates in three states, 50 percent of California inmates, 34 percent of Michigan inmates, and 23 percent of Texas inmates stated that they believed they could commit the same crime again without getting caught. Imprisonment for this group may not seem to be an effective deterrent. Nevertheless, the United States has a higher proportion of its

population in prison than any other developed nation. During the year ending June 28, 1991, there were more than 20 million jail (operated by local governments) admissions and releases, with a midyear population of 426,479 inmates, representing one out of every 430 U.S. residents. During 1992, state and federal prison populations reached a new high of 883,593 inmates.

Research suggests that sanctions such as fines or imprisonment are not particularly effective in preventing street crimes, although they do appear to have a high probability of success in reducing corporate or WHITE-COLLAR CRIME. If it is true that people change their behaviors based on feelings of guilt, fear of getting caught, or desire to maintain reputations, then high-profile individuals would have the most to lose from the traditional penalties imposed on criminals. Such people may also be subjected to societal and peer shame as well as the prescribed prison term or fines.

It has been proposed that societies that rely on public shame followed by reintegration into society might have the lowest rate of crime. For example, compared to the United States, Japan appears to fit the model of

The Guardian Angels and other community groups represent a popular approach to crime prevention. (AP/Wide World Photos)

society that relies upon shame and reintegration to keep its crime rate low.

Street crimes such as auto theft, robbery, and vandalism, which require minimal resources for commission, and violent crimes such as assault, murder, and rape, are known as index crimes. In the United States, index crimes do not seem to be responsive to traditional measures of punishment or to the Japanese style of reintegrative shaming. This may be because of the fact that the individuals most likely to commit index crimes—males aged fifteen to twenty-five years old,

unmarried, unemployed, and with low educational and occupational aspirations or advantages—have the least to lose with regard to societal shame and to the likelihood of punishment.

Routine Activity Approach. With the goal of crime prevention in mind, some criminologists no longer focus on what motivates an offender but instead concentrate on how to minimize the opportunity for crime to occur. This approach assumes that the incidence of crime can be explained by three elements: the existence of likely offenders, the existence of suitable targets, and the absence of capable guardians. If suitable targets and the absence of guardians occur at the same time, and if there are likely offenders, there will most likely be an increase in crime.

People may unknowingly invite or tempt criminals by providing both target and opportunity. For example, self-service stores often place expensive, popular consumer items within easy reach and easy exit. This temptation helps to promote criminal acts that may not have occurred if the conditions to commit a crime had not been so tempting. This type of behavior extends to individuals who flash large amounts of money, leave their valuables in sight and unattended, or leave their keys in their car. Crime prevention from this perspective focuses on the structure of both temptation and control.

The concept of a guardian, someone who is nearby and in sight to discourage criminal activity, does not necessarily mean professional law-enforcement personnel. A guardian can be an ordinary citizen, a stranger, a friend, or anyone whose mere presence is enough to discourage criminal activity. The existence of localized community projects that encourage neighbors to be aware of one another's schedules, visitors, or unusual activities, such as NEIGHBORHOOD WATCH PROGRAMS, are a reflection of this type of crime prevention.

For much of American history, most neighborhoods were small and stable enough so that strangers were instantly identified and observed, keeping community property crime rates low. In the latter half of the twentieth century, however, neighborhood characteristics have changed. Working mothers leave many residential areas unattended during daytime hours, while a more mobile population means that strangers in an area are the norm, not the exception. In response, community action programs such as "Take Back the Night" have been promoted to construct a sense of community involvement in protection.

Neighborhood Watch programs may involve residential block meetings, election of officers, and the posting of signs warning anyone entering the neighborhood that the community members are on guard, protecting one another and notifying the police if they observe criminal activity. Community residents as well as community businesses may be encouraged to rearrange their schedules, rearrange their merchandise, and plan ways to discourage crime.

Natural Crime Prevention. "Natural" crime prevention involves informal crime prevention, which includes designing settings and environments that re-

duce crime unobtrusively and nonviolently. One example of this is the chain of 7-Eleven stores, which in the 1970's had a high rate of robberies. The chain's proprietors redesigned the floor plans of stores to reduce the chance of violent crime and petty theft. Cash registers were moved to the fronts of stores and put on raised platforms, with cash drawers out of the line of vision. The front doors became the only exits or entrances, making all entrances and exits visible. In addition, all merchandise, displays, and signs were removed from front windows so that the insides of stores could be observed from the street. Taxi drivers were invited to use parking lots in the evenings, with free coffee and restroom privileges. Finally, clerks were trained to make eye contact with all customers. These innovations, while relatively subtle, drastically reduced the incidence of crime in these stores.

Another environment-based concept was invented by C. Ray Jeffery and published in his book *Crime Prevention Through Environmental Design* (1971). This approach involves urban planning and environmental design. Specialists known as environmental criminologists can plan locations of homes, schools, business, and recreation areas before a community is actually constructed, with the goal of minimizing criminal opportunities. Design possibilities include such changes as eliminating high concrete walls, which can provide places to hide, and replacing them with low hedges that provide visibility; avoiding creation of vast unassigned public space that is difficult to monitor; designing housing for the elderly, with glass-walled recreation rooms on the ground floors to allow residents to keep watch; keeping schools away from shopping malls to minimize youths' opportunities for theft, vandalism, or drug use; and planning the routes that teenagers walk from housing areas to school so that they do not cross parking lots, which might provide opportunities for vandalism or car theft.

In addition to proactively "designing out crime," the new and seemingly more successful approaches to crime prevention are those attempting to bring the community and police together. Local substations may act as a combination police station or social service center. In some areas, civilians are being recruited as volunteer, unarmed, mobile patrol officers attached to the police department.   —*Sandra Harte Bunce*

SUGGESTED READINGS: Marcus Felson shows how simple changes in environment and activity patterns can reduce crime in *Crime and Everyday Life* (Thousand Oaks, Calif.: Pine Forge Press, 1994). For a history of American prisons, see Adam J. Hirsch's *The Rise of the Penitentiary: Prisons and Punishment in Early America* (New Haven, Conn.: Yale University Press, 1992). Martin Sanchez Jankowski provides a look at how gangs and communities relate to each other in *Islands in the Street* (Berkeley: University of California Press, 1991). Barry Poyner offers specific designs to prevent crime in *Design Against Crime: Beyond Defensible Space* (London: Butterworth, 1983).

Criminal justice system, Canadian: Canada differs from the United States in having a national criminal justice system. In the United States, the power to enact criminal law falls primarily to individual states, the federal government plays a limited role. In Canada, the criminal justice system is a matter of shared responsibility. The federal Parliament enacts all criminal law and sets the procedures to be followed in criminal matters, leaving to the ten individual provinces responsibility for administering justice and prosecuting offenders within their own borders. The federal attorney-general conducts criminal prosecutions in the Yukon and the Northwest Territories.

History. Before Canada became independent in 1867, British influence dominated all aspects of colonial life. Indeed, from the beginning of English settlement in British North America, it was accepted that the new colonies would adopt Britain's criminal legal system. British criminal law was also accepted in French-speaking Lower Canada—as Québec was then known—although the territory used the Napoleonic Code, while the British territories followed English COMMON LAW.

Passage of the British North America Act of 1867 made Canada an independent confederation. Section 91 (27) of this act conferred upon the new federal government legislative authority over "the criminal law . . . including the procedures in criminal matters." This was not an exclusive jurisdiction, however, as other sections of the same act gave the provinces exclusive jurisdiction over the administration of justice inside their territories, including the composition and maintenance of provincial courts and the right to make laws for imposing penalties in order to enforce local provincial laws.

At the time the act was passed, there was no controversy over whether primary legislative control over criminal law should be vested in the federal government. Framers of the act deliberately avoided the model of the U.S. CONSTITUTION, which vested all criminal-law power in the hands of individual states. The experience of the U.S. Civil War—which ended two years before the British North America Act was passed—may well have inspired the act's framers to give all criminal law-making authority to Canada's central government so that it would symbolize unified nationhood. One framer of the confederation stated that having a uniform system of law "would weld us into a nation."

One of independent Canada's first tasks was to mold the mass of preconfederation criminal laws into a single legal system. In 1892, the federal government enacted a national criminal code, which—after substantial revision in 1955—has remained the primary source of Canadian criminal law. The criminal code is not, however, the only source of Canadian criminal law. Other federal statutes have created under such criminal laws as the Food and Drugs Act, the Narcotics Control Act, the Young Offenders Act (which provided a legislative framework for the administration of youth justice), the Competition Act, the Income Tax Act, and the Corrections and Conditional Release Act.

Although criminal lawmaking is under exclusive federal jurisdiction, the provinces enact quasi-criminal laws relating to matters falling only within their territorial jurisdictions, delegating authority for their implementation to the municipalities. These provincial laws relate to health care, highways, education, and alcoholic beverage control.

Enactment of the Canadian CHARTER OF RIGHTS AND FREEDOMS in 1982 has had a profound impact on the tenets and philosophy of Canadian criminal law. Similar to the U.S. Bill of Rights—though arguably broader in scope—the Charter has an overarching effect on all Canadian laws, including criminal laws. Indeed, the Charter boldly proclaims itself the supreme law of the land, asserting that any laws inconsistent with its provisions are null and void (section 52). In some measure, the Charter has usurped the traditional Canadian notion of parliamentary supremacy. After the Charter's passage, judicial activism and intervention became hallmarks of the Canadian justice system. At every court level, the judiciary has asked whether government is properly exercising its criminal-law powers or if government intrudes upon the rights and freedoms of individuals.

Seeing itself as the guardian of Canadian constitutional values, the judiciary analyzes criminal laws to measure their intent against principles enunciated in the Charter. This should come as no surprise, as the

Charter itself guarantees such basic civil liberties as the presumption of innocence. Other specific guarantees include protection against arbitrary detention and unreasonable search or seizure, the right to be informed of reasons for arrest, the right to retain legal counsel and have a speedy trial, protection against self incrimination, the right not to be compelled to be a witness, and the right not to suffer cruel or unusual punishment.

Of particular importance is the Charter's section 7, which guarantees everyone "the right to life, liberty and security of the person and the right not to be deprived thereof except in accordance with the principles of fundamental justice." Canadian courts interpret the latter phrase as encompassing not only the procedural rights enumerated above, but also the power of the courts to review the "substance" of legislation. The principle contrasts sharply with the situation in the United States. Because criminal lawmaking power primarily rests with individual American states, the U.S. SUPREME COURT has been reluctant to make similarly far-reaching decisions in substantial criminal-law matters.

Practice and Principles. A "crime" may be defined as any act against society for which the accused is found both to have a guilty mind and to have performed a guilty act—as determined by the state. In other words, criminal offenses are set down in legislation, and the state itself—which represents society as a whole—is the victim, not the private individual. It is therefore the state that takes the initiative to see that justice is done. In practice, it is usually the police who lay charges and the Crown attorney who prosecutes the case on behalf of the state, leaving the individual victim of a criminal act merely one of many players in the system. To fulfill its role, the state spends vast resources to establish various institutions and staff them with persons dedicated to uphold the peace and promote lawfulness. The key personnel are the police, prison guards, parole officers, Crown attorneys, and the judiciary. The main institutions are the courts and prisons systems. In contrast with the United States, all Canadian criminal justice personnel, such as the Crown counsel and Crown attorney and all members of the judiciary, are appointed. U.S. county sheriffs, county prosecutors, and district and state judges are elected.

To balance the huge resources of the state, several fundamental justice principles protect the accused. The first is that the accused are presumed innocent until proven guilty. Further, the burden of proving guilt always rests with the Crown, which must prove all ele-

ments of a crime beyond a reasonable doubt. Finally, proof of guilt must be made at fair and public hearings. Distinctions between legal and evidentiary burdens must be made, as it is true that the evidentiary burden alternates between the prosecution and defense. After the Crown presents its evidence, the defense faces the evidentiary burden to raise a reasonable doubt; however, the legal burden never shifts from the Crown.

In some instances of sexual-assault crimes and crimes involving young persons, Canadian criminal law makes exceptions to full public hearings. Even in such cases, however, the hearings usually take place in open court.

Categories of Crimes. Canadian law recognizes three types of criminal offenses: summary conviction, indictable, and hybrid. Summary conviction offenses are relatively minor crimes that carry maximum penalties of $2,000 or six months imprisonment. Penalties for indictable offenses range up to life imprisonment and millions of dollars in fines. Hybrid offenses are those that the Crown attorney can choose to prosecute as either summary or indictable offenses.

Trials for summary conviction offenses must take place in provincial courts; they are presided over by provincial court judges or justices of the peace. Trial procedures depend on the seriousness of the individual offenses; in most cases, the accused can choose. However, trials for the most serious offenses, such as murder and treason, must be conducted by superior court judges, together with juries—unless both the Crown attorney and defence agree to nonjury trials. Other offenses may be heard by provincial court judges without juries, and the rest of indictable offenses are tried in manners chosen by the accused. Offenders convicted and sentenced to two or more years in prison are held in federally operated penitentiaries; those sentenced to shorter terms go to provincial prisons. Conditional release programs permit eligible offenders to be released after completing part of their sentence.

Reform. Criminal-law reform in Canada is an ongoing process. Government and committed nongovernmental bodies, academics, victims' groups, prisoners' rights groups and defence attorneys all share a desire to improve the criminal justice system. Like all large industrial nations, Canada faces problems in the administration of its criminal justice system. Trials are often delayed as backlogs build up in the courts. There are valid concerns over disparities in sentencing practices, gender bias, and over-representation of minorities and Native Americans within the prison population. Many Canadians believe that the system fails to deal effectively with crime because of its seeming overconcern for the rights of the accused, at the expense of the rights of victims. There is also concern that costs of the system are rising faster than its effectiveness in solving crime problems. —*Mark L. Berlin*

SUGGESTED READINGS: *Understanding the Canadian Criminal Justice System: Process Chart and Handbook* (Ottawa: Statistics Canada, 1995) and *Canada's System of Justice* (Ottawa: Department of Justice, 1993) are good reference sources. Basic introductory texts include Curt Griffiths and Simon Verdun-Jones' *Canadian Criminal Justice* (Toronto: Harcourt Brace, 1994) and Don Stuart's *Canadian Criminal Law: A Treatise* (Toronto: Carswell, 1995). Joel Pink and David Perrier's *From Crime to Punishment* (Toronto: Carswell, 1992) is an anthology of articles on various aspects of the criminal justice system.

Criminal justice system, U.S.: The United States criminal justice system enforces, interprets, and administers criminal laws through three primary agencies of social control: police, courts, and corrections.

Police. Law-enforcement officers are generally perceived by the public as encompassing one of two roles: "crime fighters" or "order maintainers." Police contribute to social control through enforcement of laws and maintenance of public order; their dual—and sometimes conflicting—role in the U.S. system is to safeguard legislated social norms and to deter future crime by arresting individuals who violate criminal laws.

The ambiguous nature of the role of the police is compounded by the amount of discretion allocated to officers. Discretion, which provides officers the freedom to use judgment in the performance of their roles, is a necessary authority given to law-enforcement officers. If officers were not allowed to use discretion, communities would likely become estranged from officers who stringently enforced all laws. Courts, jails, and prisons would become inundated and would be unable to function efficiently. Factors that often affect an officer's decision to employ discretion include the attributes of a crime, the policies of a specific department, and the relationship between an alleged perpetrator and a victim.

New programs are continually instituted by law-enforcement agencies to address the changing nature of crime. Community policing is a much-touted attempt on the part of law-enforcement agencies to involve community members as participants in addressing the specific crime problems in their neighborhoods.

The recruitment of officers from minority groups may increase community acceptance of police officers in minority neighborhoods. Diversifying the composition of police departments often results in improved policy effectiveness and community relationships. Another recent concept in law enforcement is "problem-solving" policing, an ideology that emphasizes that crimes may be caused by underlying social problems; the goal of this approach is to address such problems rather than to focus on individuals and specific criminal acts.

Police deviance, specifically POLICE BRUTALITY, became a national issue following the beating of Rodney King by Los Angeles police officers in March, 1991. Other types of police deviance include drug abuse and drug trafficking, abuse of authority, opportunistic theft, protections of illegal activities, and acceptance of money to influence the outcome of criminal cases.

Courts. The United States has a dual court system in which there is one federal court system and a separate court system within each of the fifty states. Unified throughout the nation, the federal court system is a four-tier structure consisting of magistrate courts, district courts, courts of appeal, and a supreme court.

The U.S. SUPREME COURT is the highest court in the nation and is the only court specifically mandated by the Constitution. The Court is composed of nine justices who are nominated by the president and confirmed by the Senate. Supreme Court justices are appointed for life, a policy designed to shield them from political influence.

In contrast to the federal judiciary, state court systems have diverse names and jurisdictions. Each state enacts its own criminal laws and designs its own methods of administering those laws. Generally, each state system has a lower, a trial, an appellate, and a supreme court. Most state court judges are elected by popular vote. The selection of state judges may thus be influenced by political popularity, often at the expense of judicial qualifications.

Reform of the organization and administration of the state courts has been advocated. In an effort to make the courts more effective in the distribution of justice, some reformists have focused on consolidating and simplifying court structures. Others have advocated a shift toward a unified court system.

The judge, the prosecutor, and the defense attorney are the major officials within the criminal court system.

Inmates at a shock incarceration "boot camp" in New York State. (Impact Visuals, Andrew Lichtenstein)

The prosecutor, who serves as the government's lawyer, is given broad discretion in filing criminal charges. In a criminal proceeding, the prosecutor presents the government's evidence and must prove the defendant's guilt beyond a REASONABLE DOUBT. The defense attorney, who serves as an advocate for the accused, presents evidence and makes arguments on behalf of the defendant. The defendant, however, has no obligation to present evidence and is presumed innocent.

An individual accused of a criminal charge may enter a plea of guilty or not guilty. The superabundance of cases in the criminal courts has prompted the widespread use of negotiated pleas of guilty, a process known as "PLEA BARGAINING." A plea bargain is an agreement between a prosecutor and a defense attorney that the defendant will receive a specific charge or sentence in exchange for a plea of guilty. The practice of plea bargaining has been criticized, both for permitting the guilty to receive more lenient sentences and for encouraging individuals who are not guilty to enter guilty pleas because of assured leniency. Defenders of the practice argue that it is a necessary evil in a time of overcrowded courts.

The defendant has a constitutional right to a trial before a judge or jury. The trial is an adversarial proceeding that is governed by legal procedures designed to ensure that the accused will receive a fair trial. These procedures, fashioned to safeguard rights of the defendant, have contributed substantially to the complexities of and delays within the court system.

Upon a finding of guilt, the judge has the duty to impose a criminal sanction, or sentence. Disparities in sentencing are among the most controversial issues in the criminal justice system. Critics have argued that a defendant's social class, race, and gender often unduly influence sentences, causing great variations in sentences handed out for similar offenses. Mandatory sentences have been implemented by the federal and some state courts to limit judicial subjectivity. This philosophy imposes a sentencing guideline that ensures that defendants with similar criminal histories who commit similar offenses will receive corresponding sanctions.

Corrections. Following a determination of guilt, individuals convicted of criminal offenses may be placed in a community-based correctional program or sent to prison. Among the most urgent problems facing

Chain gangs are still employed in some U.S. jurisdictions, as this 1995 photo of prisoners in Alabama shows. (Impact Visuals, Donna Binder)

the corrections system are the overcrowding of prisons and the concern that imprisonment often intensifies criminal dispositions. Therefore, alternatives to confinement have been vigorously sought.

Community-based correction programs are of a nonpunitive, rehabilitative nature. These programs allow communities to assume responsibility for dealing with offenders, reduce problems with reintegration of convicted offenders into the community, and provide offenders with only the amount of supervision they require.

Probation, the conditional release of an offender into the community under supervision, is the most commonly used alternative to confinement. After being granted probation, an individual agrees to abide by a variety of regulations and conditions of probation. Violations of any of the conditions may result in revocation of probation and subsequent commitment to a correctional institution.

According to Bureau of Justice statistics, the total number of convicted criminals incarcerated in federal and state prisons exceeds one million. The problem of overcrowded prisons has been approached by diverting convicted defendants from prison via intermediate sanctions, shortening the time served by individuals who go to prison, and increasing prison space through the construction of more prisons.

Intermediate sanctions include fines, restitution, community service, intensive supervision, house arrest, electronic monitoring, boot camps, and split sentences. The latter sanction entails "shock" incarceration; the offender serves a short sentence in prison, then serves the remainder of the sentence on probation. These sanctions can be used alone or in differing combinations. Several sanctions, such as house arrest and electronic monitoring, can be utilized with offenders who have been paroled from correctional facilities.

"Parole" refers to the release of an inmate from incarceration before the full sentence has been served. Parole is the most common manner for a prisoner to be released early from prison. One of the major concerns of parole authorities is to select those prisoners who will most likely succeed on parole. Risk-versus-need assessments have been adopted by some parole authorities to predict RECIDIVISM and to reduce the subjectivity involved in the parole process.

Overcrowded prison conditions are also the emphasis of ongoing litigation. Citing the Eighth Amendment's prohibition against CRUEL AND UNUSUAL PUNISHMENT, courts have addressed this concern by ordering prisons to reduce overcrowded conditions. Limited resources and escalating costs of prison construction have led some state governments to utilize private vendors to construct and manage prisons.

Private organizations can often build prisons faster and operate them more efficiently than the government can. Opponents of privatization, however, argue that inmates can suffer decreases in security and quality of services because of the emphasis that private vendors place on profit.

New prison construction may alleviate the affects of overcrowded conditions; however, it does not address

DISPOSITION OF MAJOR U.S. CRIMINAL CASES

Drug offenses

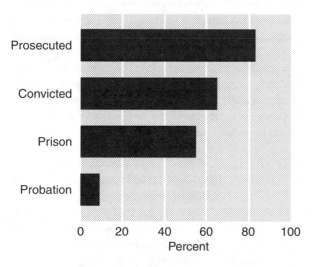

Violent offenses

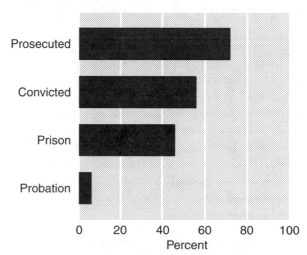

Property offenses — fraudulent

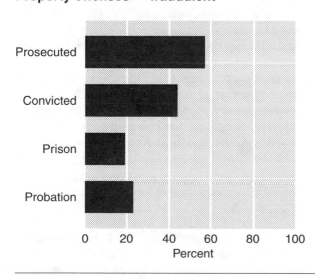

Other property offenses

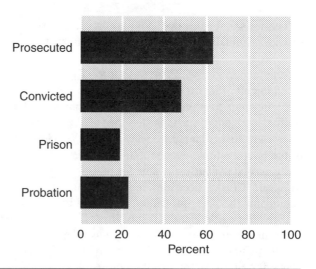

Source: U.S. Department of Justice, Bureau of Justice Statistics

the social impact of long-term incarceration. Prisons have been described as "total institutions," in which every aspect of an inmate's life is monitored and controlled. The process by which inmates learn how to live in a total institution is referred to as "prisonization." Through this process of inmate socialization, prisoners adapt to an inmate subculture and learn the attitudes, behaviors, and skills necessary to cope with imprisonment. The internalization of such behaviors and attitudes often impedes a prisoner's rehabilitation. While such attributes may be endorsed in the prison environment, they are often incompatible with reintegration into society. —*Kimberly Raines Greer*
Linda D. Ferrell

SUGGESTED READINGS: An overview of issues related to law enforcement can be found in John S. Dempsey's *Policing: An Introduction to Law Enforcement* (St. Paul, Minn.: West Publishing, 1994). Norval Morris and Michael Tonry address possible implementations of intermediate sanctions in *Between Prison and Probation: Intermediate Punishments in a Rational Sentencing System* (New York: Oxford University Press, 1990). In *Community-Based Corrections*, 2d ed. (Pacific Grove, Ca.: Brooks/Cole, 1991), Belinda R. McCarthy and Bernard J. McCarthy provide a discussion of agencies concerned with community-based programming.

Criminal procedure: Laws and rules regarding the apprehension, prosecution, and punishment of criminal suspects.

The laws and rules that apply to the various stages of U.S. criminal procedure are derived primarily from the Fourth, Fifth, Sixth, Eighth, and Fourteenth Amendments to the CONSTITUTION. The first ten amendments, the BILL OF RIGHTS, were adopted in 1791 in order to protect citizens from oppression by the federal government. Still, some of these protections were being denied in many states. The adoption of the Fourteenth Amendment in 1868, particularly its "DUE PROCESS" clause, became the basis for a series of SUPREME COURT decisions requiring states to grant defendants the basic protections provided by the federal government under the Bill of Rights.

Criminal procedure typically begins when the police focus upon a suspect. Their efforts to gather evidence for an arrest and eventual prosecution are governed by the law of SEARCH AND SEIZURE of the Fourth Amendment. Accordingly, all searches must be rea-

sonable and, in some cases, must also be accompanied by a search warrant issued by a magistrate. Over the years, the Court has noted several exceptions to the requirement of a search warrant, so that most legal searches are in fact not based on a warrant.

Once arrested, a suspect is taken into custody. At this stage, the suspect comes primarily under the protection of the Fifth Amendment's privilege against self-incrimination. This privilege—that the state cannot force an accused person to admit wrongdoing—was underscored by the Supreme Court's decision in the landmark case *MIRANDA V. ARIZONA* (1966), which required police to warn suspects of their right to remain silent before custodial interrogation begins. The so-called Miranda warnings also stipulate the suspect's right to have a lawyer (retained or appointed) present during questioning to further protect the privilege against self-incrimination. The right to a lawyer at this early stage is rooted in the Sixth Amendment right to counsel and the Fourteenth Amendment guarantee of due process; it extends far beyond custodial interrogation to include some post-conviction proceedings.

It is with the trial stage that the Sixth Amendment right to counsel is most often identified. Beginning with *GIDEON V. WAINWRIGHT* (1963), the Supreme Court has advanced rights of impoverished defendants to have counsel for any criminal trial that may result in imprisonment. Other important Sixth Amendment guarantees that apply to the states include the right to a JURY TRIAL and the right to a speedy trial.

The laws and rules concerning the punishment of convicted criminals fall under the Eighth Amendment's ban against CRUEL AND UNUSUAL PUNISHMENT and the Fourteenth Amendment's due-process guarantee. Thus, states have had to rewrite their death-penalty laws because the Court found them to be discriminatory, in violation of these amendments. Likewise, the improvement of certain prison conditions and disciplinary procedures have been ordered by the Court to avoid Eighth and Fourteenth Amendment violations.
—*Henry W. Mannle*

Crips: African American street gang that originated in South Central Los Angeles following the 1965 Watts riots. According to gang researcher Lewis Yablonsky, the origin of the name stems from a "crippled" member who had a cast on his leg. The Crips have spread to most major U.S. cities and have become notorious for engaging in acts of violence, robbery, drug dealing,

Los Angeles Crips members display their gang hand signals. (AP/Wide World Photos)

and other street crimes. The gang's bitter rivalry with the BLOODS, another powerful Los Angeles gang, has led to dozens of deaths.

Cruel and unusual punishment: Prohibition against particularly cruel or torturous punishment, established in the U.S. CONSTITUTION by the Eighth Amendment. In medieval and Renaissance Europe, convicted criminals were often tortured and put to death using exceedingly cruel methods. Criminals were burned to death, crushed to death, "drawn and quartered" (a practice whereby the criminal was pulled apart by horses) and punished in numerous other ways that modern society would judge to be inhumane. To prevent such brutal punishments, the Eighth Amendment guarantee

against both excessive bails and cruel and unusual punishment was included in the BILL OF RIGHTS.

Over the years, the interpretation of what constitutes "cruel and unusual punishment" has been addressed by the courts, and controversy remains. Using a standard of reasonableness, the judiciary seeks to interpret the prohibition against cruel and unusual punishment in light of what is acceptable in a civilized society, while maintaining an objective of justice for victims.

The U.S. SUPREME COURT has repeatedly cited the Eighth Amendment prohibition against cruel and unusual punishment in its decisions regarding the conditions and practices that are permitted and prohibited in dealing with inmates; numerous prison reforms have come about because inmates have raised the issue of cruel and unusual punishment to challenge conditions

Cryonics

and practices in prisons. In *Rhodes v. Chapman* (1981), for example, the Supreme Court stated that the punishment must not involve the "wanton and unnecessary infliction of pain" or be "grossly disproportionate to the severity of the crime warranting imprisonment." Such standards continue to evolve, but the Court has prohibited physical abuse (even where there is no significant harm) in disciplining inmates; the Court does, however, allow solitary confinement of prisoners.

In addition, the Supreme Court has examined the impact of the Eighth Amendment on several issues surrounding the death penalty. For example, although the death penalty *per se* has not been judged unconstitutional, it has been declared unconstitutional when it is imposed for the rape of an adult. The issue of cruel and unusual punishment has been raised in numerous death-penalty cases. For a short time (1972-1976), the death penalty was held to violate the Eighth Amendment ban against cruel and unusual punishment. In deciding FURMAN V. GEORGIA (1972), the Court ruled that capital punishment is a violation of the Eighth Amendment if it is imposed arbitrarily and unfairly. Consequently, states that imposed the death penalty reconstructed their death-penalty statutes to establish specific criteria governing its use. In GREGG V. GEORGIA (1976), the Court ruled that so long as states apply uniform standards that are legislatively determined the death penalty is legal. In the 1980's, courts were asked to consider whether a lengthy delay between the time the penalty is declared and the time it is carried out constitutes cruel and unusual punishment, as intervals of years or even decades between the sentencing and execution of condemned prisoners were not uncommon. In general, such delays have not been found to be unconstitutional.

In the 1980's, courts also examined some mandatory-sentencing laws, specifically habitual-offender statutes, as they relate to the issue of cruel and unusual punishment. In *Solem v. Helm* (1983), for example, the Supreme Court found that the imposition of a life sentence without the possibility of parole upon a nonviolent habitual offender was significantly disproportionate to the offender's crimes and thus violated the Eighth Amendment.

—*Mary Ann Eastep*

Cryonics: Process of freezing the body or the head of a person who has been declared legally dead. Based on cryobiology, the study of life at low temperatures, the hope is that both a cure for the terminal illness and technology for re-animation will be developed so that the deceased may be brought back to life and ultimately recover from whatever initially caused death. The cryonics movement was inspired by Robert C. Ettinger, a physics teacher from Michigan, who published *Prospect of Immortality* in 1964.

The cryonics process begins as soon as possible after a person (or animal, in some cases) is officially pronounced dead. The body is brought to a cryonics laboratory, where the aim is to maintain the supply of oxygen and nutrients to the brain for a short time after death in the hope that part of it survives, and then to preserve it by freezing. The process begins by cooling the body using an ice bath and heat exchangers, while a heart-lung machine keeps the blood circulating and administers oxygen. Finally, to maintain oxygen supply to the brain, the blood, which becomes viscous on cooling, is drained and replaced with glycerol, a blood substitute used in organ transplants. The body is then cooled to a temperature of two or three degrees Celsius. Over a two-day period, the body is cooled to the temperature of liquid nitrogen, minus 79 degrees Celsius, and cryoprotectant drugs are pumped into it. The body is then placed in a Dacron-wool sleeping bag, which remains soft and pliable at minus 196 degrees Celsius, and placed in a capsule containing liquid nitrogen. At minus 196 degrees Celsius, the boiling point of nitrogen, biological processes have stopped, and all that remains to do is to maintain the level of liquid nitrogen.

Cryobiologists assert that these procedures will not preserve the cells of a body, although it is possible to freeze some tissues successfully. For long periods, freezing can preserve egg cells, single-cell suspensions such as semen and white blood cells, and simple tissues such as skin, cornea, and pancreatic islets.

Cryonicists and biologists agree that it is the brain that contains essential information for personal identity. Yet, according to these researchers, cloning deoxyribonucleic acid (DNA) from body cells would not be sufficient to reproduce a human being, since the new person would be a "twin" and not the original. Moreover, biologists know that the brain contains about 10 billion neurons. If the oxygen supply to any of these neurons ceases, they die. Thus it is not clear how, even theoretically, preserving some of these neurons would preserve a person's brain function.

Most biologists do not believe that a person frozen by current methods could be restored to life—ever, by any technology—and thus cannot justify the cost of

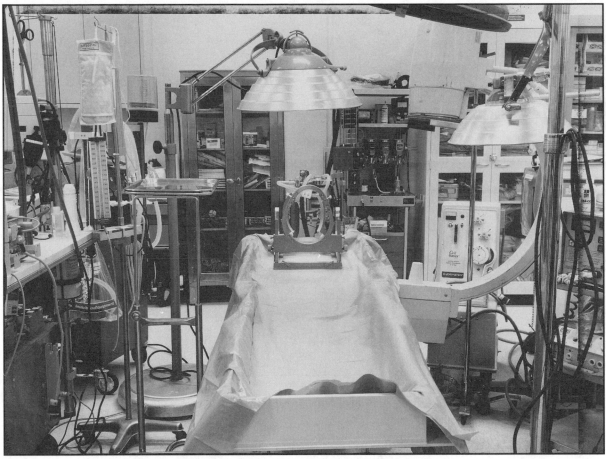

A cryonics laboratory. (Impact Visuals, Slobodan Dimitrov)

related research and experimentation. One major laboratory charges a hundred dollars to enroll in the program and $288 a year (until death); a neuro suspension (in which just the brain is preserved) costs an additional $41,000, while a whole-body suspension costs $121,000.

In 1967, Dr. James Bedford was the first person to be frozen. As of 1992, there were nineteen people in cryonic suspension in the United States. Aside from the cost and technical difficulties involved, some argue that cryonics symbolizes the ultimate denial of death in the twentieth century.

Cuba and the United States: Although the end of the COLD WAR greatly reduced tensions between the United States and most of the former Communist bloc, relations between Cuba and the United States have remained tense and, at times, intractable. The United States has continued to insist that Cuba adopt a plural-

istic political system and other reforms; without such changes, the United States has refused to lift the economic embargo that it imposed on the island nation after the 1959 revolution. In the 1990's, Cuba opened the island to foreign investment, but it has refused to accede to U.S. demands about how it should govern itself. Although diplomatic relations have been severed since 1961, the Cuban government has continued to negotiate with the United States over a host of thorny issues such as the status of refugees and immigration policy.

Early History. From the Spanish-American War in 1898 to Fidel CASTRO's successful insurrection against the dictator Fulgencio Batista in 1959, Cuban and U.S. fortunes were intimately tied. Cuba was the quintessential example of a client state, dependent on its more powerful neighbor ninety miles away. In a sense, the island benefited from its position within the U.S. sphere of influence in the Caribbean, but in other ways it did not. Cuba's chief task was to supply the North

Cuba and the United States

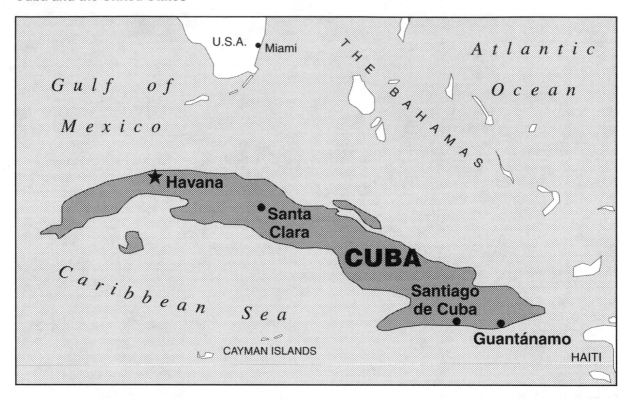

American market with sugar. U.S. companies invested heavily in this industry and other agricultural pursuits, and for those Cubans connected to the export sector, prerevolutionary Cuba was a profitable place. U.S. influence on Cuban political affairs ensured that politicians remained friendly to business interests.

After the 1930's, Washington preferred to work with Cuban military leader Batista to ensure political stability on the island. The island's status as a client state rankled many Cubans, who claimed that Cuba was little more than a U.S. colony and that Batista's corrupt and increasingly brutal rule had to be eliminated before meaningful change could come about.

A Revolution Meets with Hostility. Fidel Castro led a successful fight to overthrow Batista, and on January 1, 1959, Castro assumed power. The years immediately following the revolution were stormy ones for Cuba-U.S. relations. Cuba wished to assert its sovereignty—one of the main themes of the revolution was "Cuba for Cubans"—and any assertion of independence during the Cold War worried the Dwight D. Eisenhower Administration. As Castro consolidated his hold over Cuban society, he implemented a number of sweeping social, cultural, and economic reforms. His expropriation of large properties drew the wrath of both the Cuban middle classes and Washington. The United States

responded by cutting the island's sugar quota and eventually imposing a trade embargo. The embargo created havoc in Cuba, since the United States had been the island's chief trading partner, and virtually all of the island's industries were dependent on supplies and parts suddenly denied to Cuba. In response, Castro moved quickly to establish ties with the Soviet Union. Under Castro's authoritarian leadership, the nationalistic revolution turned progressively leftist, and on October 1, 1961, Castro declared himself a Marxist-Leninist. In January, 1961, Cuba and the United States severed diplomatic relations. Soon thereafter, Cuban exiles—with U.S. assistance—launched an unsuccessful invasion of the island at the Bay of Pigs; the invasion quickly became a fiasco, as Cuban troops routed the would-be liberators.

After the Bay of Pigs invasion, Castro was convinced that the United States was intent on destroying the revolution and that a much larger invasion, led by U.S. troops, was a foregone conclusion. He asked for and received nuclear missiles from the Soviet Union. When Washington learned of the missiles, President John F. KENNEDY ordered a naval quarantine of the island in October, 1962, and did not lift the blockade until he had been given assurance by Soviet premier Nikita Khrushchev that the missiles would be removed. In return, the United States agreed not to invade the island.

Antagonism Breeds Intrasigence. In a general sense, Cuba-U.S. relations have remained frozen, as the adversarial relationship established during the revolution's early years would fester over ensuing decades. Cuba, seeking to assert itself as a leader of national liberation movements, sought to spread the "idea" of socialist revolution to its neighbors throughout Latin America (and later to Africa). Castro thus provided assistance to revolutionary movements throughout the hemisphere. Conversely, the United States defended its economic and strategic interests and gave assistance to anticommunist regimes throughout the region. The United States did not give up entirely on the idea of overthrowing Castro; throughout the 1960's, Washington sanctioned a number of plots to assassinate Castro and other top leaders, and the CENTRAL INTELLIGENCE AGENCY (CIA) conducted punitive economic

sabotage operations against Cuba in the hope of spurring popular dissatisfaction with the revolution.

Thaws in bilateral relations, however, did occasionally occur. In 1973, for example, Washington and Havana penned an antihijacking agreement, and over the next few years, high-level talks took place to negotiate terms for normalization of relations. Those talks were terminated after the United States protested the Cuban decision to send troops to Angola in 1975. Diplomatic relations improved again during the Jimmy CARTER Administration, as a fishing agreement was signed and talks were resumed to explore the possibility of improving relations. These efforts, however, also failed, ostensibly over Cuba's involvement in Ethiopia.

Another stumbling block to improved relations was the unwavering position taken by many Cuban émigrés who objected to a change in policy toward the Castro regime. The Cuban American community, which resides predominantly in southern Florida, has been out-

Cuban president Fidel Castro waves to the crowd at a 1993 meeting of the Iberia-America Summit in Brazil. (Reuters/Corbis-Bettmann)

437

spoken about the general thrust of U.S. policy toward Cuba and about such vexing issues as immigration.

Cuban emigration to the United States has surged and ebbed over the years, reflecting internal and external factors that have at times made it possible for large numbers to leave the island and at other times have reduced the flow of refugees to a trickle. The early waves of émigrés in the 1960's were political exiles and members of the middle class; most of these people were opposed to the revolution's leftist drift. They were largely white, educated, and in possession of professional expertise, entrepreneurial skills, and capital. They became an increasingly potent force in U.S. domestic politics; any step taken by politicians to change the adversarial line initially adopted by the Eisenhower and Kennedy Administrations was successfully countered by intense lobbying efforts by Cuban American groups such as the Cuban American National Foundation. During the 1970's and 1980's, however, Cuban immigrants to the United States reflected a

Cuban refugees cross the Florida Straits in 1994. (Reuters/Bettmann)

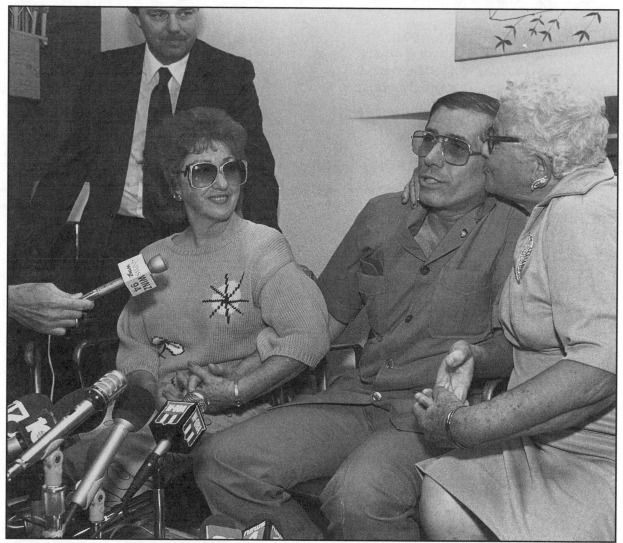

Ramon Conte Hernandez, the last prisoner to be held from the 1962 Bay of Pigs invasion, is welcomed by his family after his 1986 release. (UPI/Corbis-Bettmann)

more representative sample of Cuban society; the later immigrants tended to have more limited occupational skills, were more racially diverse, and possessed less education than their predecessors. In 1980, 125,000 Cubans emigrated during the Mariel boatlift alone.

The Ronald REAGAN Administration adopted a hard line against Cuba. No efforts were made to renew diplomatic overtures; Havana was once again charged with exporting revolution; its human rights record was roundly criticized; and travel restrictions were placed on U.S. citizens to deter tourism and deprive the island of foreign exchange. Despite the Reagan Administration's apparent hard line on bilateral relations, in 1987 Havana and Washington hammered out an immigra-

tion agreement whereby the United States agreed to accept up to twenty thousand Cubans annually. In return, Cuba agreed to repatriate twenty-five hundred refugees of the Mariel boatlift who had been deemed "excludable aliens" by the U.S. IMMIGRATION AND NATURALIZATION SERVICE (INS) because of their criminal records or mental illness.

History Repeats Itself. Cuba became increasingly isolated after the collapse of the SOVIET UNION and other socialist states in Eastern Europe after 1989. The drying up of Soviet aid proved to be an economic disaster, yet the George BUSH and Bill CLINTON Administrations refused to diminish economic pressure and maintained the embargo in place. The passage of the

PUBLIC OPINION, 1994: SHOULD THE U.S. CONTINUE ITS EMBARGO AGAINST CUBA WHILE FIDEL CASTRO RETAINS POWER?

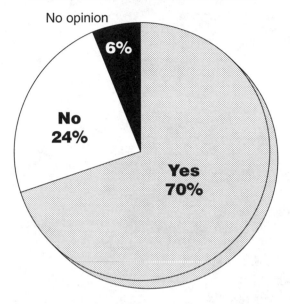

Source: George Gallup, Jr., ed., *The Gallup Poll: Public Opinion, 1994* (Wilmington, Del.: Scholarly Resources, 1995).

Cuban Democracy Act by Congress in November, 1992, tightened one of the loopholes of the embargo, giving U.S. presidents the power to ban all U.S. subsidiaries based in Third World countries from trading with Cuba.

Throughout 1994 and 1995, Cuba and the United States continued to wrangle over immigration policy, refugees, and human rights. Castro opened the floodgates of immigration again in the summer and fall of 1994, and thousands fled the island on homemade rafts. The Clinton Administration responded by picking up the rafters at sea and herding them into refugee camps at Guantanamo Naval Base and in Panama. To discourage refugees from leaving the island, Washington announced that the refugees would not be accepted in the United States, and it negotiated with Cuba to regularize the flow of refugees. In April, 1995, the Clinton Administration changed its policy when it proclaimed that refugees in camps in Guantanamo would be permitted to come to the United States. While this pleased many Cuban American groups who felt that an indefinite stay in the camps was inhumane, Clinton

also infuriated émigrés when he announced that future refugees fleeing the island the island would be returned.

Through the mid-1990's, Cuba-U.S. relations remained intractable, with little change forseeable. Although Cuba wished to end the embargo, it refused to negotiate the political direction of its revolution. For its part, the United States appeared willing to maintain its policy toward Cuba until either the revolution was overthrown by domestic opposition or until Fidel Castro's death—neither of which seemed imminent.

—Allen Wells

SUGGESTED READINGS: A thoughtful historical overview of U.S.-Cuba relations is Louis A. Pérez's *Cuba and the United States: Ties of Singular Intimacy* (Athens: University of Georgia Press, 1990). Jules R. Benjamin has written an authoritative history of the U.S. role in Cuba prior to 1959 in *The United States and the Origins of the Cuban Revolution: An Empire of Liberty in an Age of National Liberation* (Princeton, N.J.: Princeton University Press, 1990). A useful overview of diplomatic relations since the revolution is found in Philip Brenner's *From Confrontation to Negotiation: U.S. Relations with Cuba* (Boulder, Colo.: Westview Press, 1988). A compelling eyewitness account is provided by Wayne S. Smith in *The Closest of Enemies: A Personal and Diplomatic History of U.S.-Cuban Relations Since 1957* (New York: W. W. Norton, 1987).

Cuban-American Legal Defense and Education Fund: (CALDEF): Community organization. CALDEF was founded in the early 1980's to promote the legal rights and educational opportunities of Cuban Americans. Supporting issues of equal access to education, employment, housing, and justice, and addressing other social issues, CALDEF supports several social and political movements designed to enhance the quality of life for Cuban Americans. Primarily using the court system to fight its battles, CALDEF has been successful in winning many high-profile suits that involve mistreatment of both Cuban Americans and Cuban refugees living in the United States. CALDEF, headquartered in Fort Wayne, Indiana, also publishes newsletters and other informational materials.

Cults: Originally defined as any small religious group under strong leadership, the term has acquired a derogatory connotation since the 1950's and is aimed primarily at religious groups that do not belong to the main Western traditions. "Sects," a related term, is commonly used when categorizing such churches as Pentecostal and Quakers, which are offshoots of the Western religions of Catholicism, Protestantism, and Judaism. In contrast, many cults, such as the Hare Krishna movement, derive inspiration directly from Eastern religions such as Hinduism and Buddhism; others, such as Scientology, though of Western origin, have little in common with mainstream Western spiritual practices.

Much of the controversy surrounding cults has stemmed from the refusal of some young members to communicate with their families and the subsequent accusations by parents that cults are brainwashing their children. In the 1970's, many court cases against cults resulted from this claim. Many fundamentalist Protestants have also separately condemned cults, accusing them of perverting Christian values and promoting violence. This public association of cults and violence has been reinforced by several tragic events, notably the Charles Manson-inspired murders in the 1960's, the Jonestown suicides in the 1970's, and the Waco, Texas, killings in the 1990's.

Broad Trends in Membership. The 1950's and 1970's witnessed an upsurge both in the number of cults and their membership. Much of the recruiting took place on college campuses and continued through to the 1990's. The majority of new members are single adults aged between eighteen and twenty-five, mostly white, and are educationally and financially in the top half of the population. Jews are disproportionately represented.

Anticultists have exaggerated the numbers of cults and their membership. By the 1990's, approximately six hundred cults existed in North America, with a membership of between 150,000 and 200,000. About one hundred of these groups are purely ethnic in origin and make no attempt to convert outsiders. Though often overstated, the number of cults and their membership is steadily increasing. Neither fundamentalist rhetoric nor court cases have halted this upward trend.

The Appeal to Individuals. The psychologist Marc Galanter identified forces that most cults have in common and that probably have a strong influence in attracting new members and binding them into cohesive units.

First, a shared belief system provides the theory that satisfies an individual's need to explain life. Second, group cohesiveness gives individuals a sense of belonging and commitment. Third, codes of behavior are typi-cally very definite and strongly enforced in cults, which may provide security in a world of ambiguity and cynicism. Fourth, many cults have a charismatic leader who seems to show the way to some "promised land" and to whom mystical, often healing, powers are attributed.

Galanter also pointed to another force that can be strong at the time of an individual's first encounter with a cult, namely an altered consciousness: thinking and feeling differently because one is in an unusual environment. This altered consciousness can lead to an increased susceptibility to new explanations of old questions and to new lifestyles.

Reasons for Cults' Growth. The forces mentioned in the previous section can explain the appeal of cults to an individual, but they do not fully define why the number of cults and their membership has increased steadily since World War II. Sociologists, fundamentalists, and commentators have suggested many reasons for this growth. Many point to the social upheavals in the 1960's as a huge impetus for cult movements. While this is undoubtedly true, it was the 1950's, an extremely conservative decade, that saw a bigger rise. Brainwashing has been cited as a factor in attracting new followers, but this has been largely discredited in academic circles.

Other reasons can also be cited for the interest in cult membership. The West has a long-term interest in religions and spiritual ideologies from the East that dates back more than a hundred and fifty years. In 1965, a repeal of some immigration laws relating to people from Asian countries led to an influx of gurus and masters and a resultant increase in cults.

Certain fields of interest that grew following World War II led many people to experiment with cults. One is parapsychology, the study of hidden capabilities of the human mind. Another is the discovery of psychedelic drugs, most notable LSD, through which many people reported having mystical experiences, which in turn led them to a more rigorous investigation of spirituality through cults. During the 1950's and 1960's, alternative branches of psychology also came to the fore, including the humanistic, transpersonal, and Jungian schools. These emphasized the individual's self-growth and the holistic nature of personality and society and found many parallels with the Eastern religious traditions. Finally, the NEW AGE MOVEMENT borrows heavily from the East, especially in its metaphysical content, and both feeds off cults and stimulates new varieties and membership in cults.

Cults

The Prominent Cults. A defining line leads from cults to sects to religions. Which term is used will often depend on one's point of view. Cult members usually define their organization as a religion or spiritual practice; more traditional churches do not see them that way.

Over time, cults can gain acceptance and rise to the status of religion. Examples of this include Christian Science, Mormonism, and Jehovah's Witnesses. All three organizations began in the nineteenth century as offshoots of Christianity. All were derided and attacked, sometimes violently, from their inception. With time and increased membership, however, came some accommodation with and recognition from mainstream society.

Since the 1970's, three cults have stood out in the media as the embodiment of strangeness and have often been portrayed with sinister overtones: the UNIFICATION CHURCH, or "Moonies," the Hare Krishna movement, and the Church of Scientology.

The Moonies became famous for marriages arranged and presided over by their leader, the Reverend Sun Myung Moon; thousands were wed at the same ceremony. Anticult movements claimed a victory in the early 1980's when Moon went to prison on tax-evasion charges. Paradoxically, however, the sentence gained public sympathy for the leader, who many believed had been victimized by federal authorities. Furthermore, the prison sentence did not hurt the movement, which included five thousand members in the United States and many more in Korea and Japan by the 1980's.

Perhaps the most visible of the new cults during the 1970's and 1980's were the Hare Krishnas, whose male

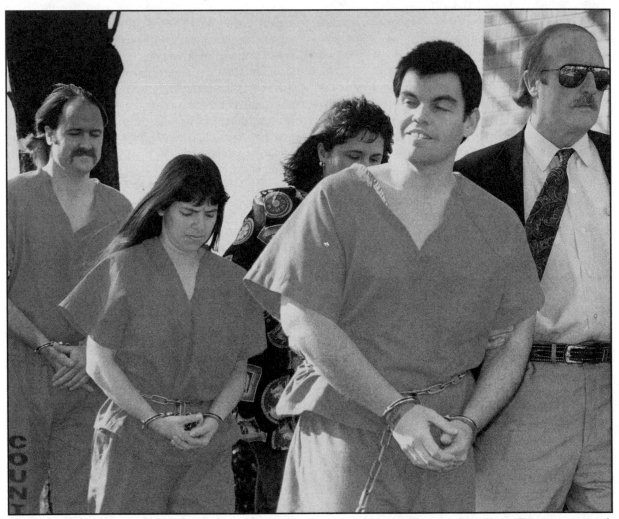

Members of the Branch Davidian cult are arrested following the 1993 destruction of their Waco, Texas, compound. (AP/Wide World Photos)

initiates shaved their heads, wore saffron robes, and walked the streets chanting praise to Krishna. By 1990, membership stood at three thousand initiates, with hundreds of thousands attending temples.

The Church of Scientology, founded by a science-fiction writer, L. Ron Hubbard, has a controversial history, but after numerous court cases, many including federal agencies, it has remained strong into the 1990's. Scientology's self-development courses are its structural foundation. Among its members are many celebrities who publicly praise Scientology's teachings.

Violence and Cults. There is an ongoing association of cults with violence, although public perceptions of the connection are exaggerated. Many religious organizations are labeled as cults after some act of violence, such as the 1979 JONESTOWN mass suicide of almost a thousand members of the Peoples' Temple, led by Jim Jones; in reality, however, this group was a part of mainline Christianity, being affiliated with the NATIONAL COUNCIL OF CHURCHES OF CHRIST IN THE U.S.A.

Another famous case involved David KORESH's Branch Davidians, who forced a standoff with federal agents in Waco, Texas, in 1993, that resulted in seventy deaths. While the cult was certainly guilty of stockpiling weapons and inflammatory prophecies, the federal authorities also were blamed for escalation of the conflict.

Though many cults undoubtedly produce megalomaniac leaders and strange beliefs and lifestyles, many others have mature and ethical leadership. By the mid-1990's, many of the knee-jerk reactions to cults had abated, and many people saw them as a visible face of pluralism in American culture. —*Philip Magnier*

SUGGESTED READINGS: J. Gordon Melton's *Encyclopedic Handbook of Cults in America* (New York: Garland, 1992) is a fair and accessible work on cults. Mark Galanter provides an analysis of both the individual and social psychology involved in *Cults: Faith, Healing, and Coercion* (New York: Oxford University Press, 1989). *Life 102: What to Do When Your Guru Sues You* (Los Angeles: Prelude, 1994), by Peter McWilliams, is a firsthand account of weird happenings in a cult. *The Joys of Sects* (New York: Doubleday, 1994), by Peter Occhiogrosso, gives a comprehensive overview of cults deriving from the world's major religions.

Culture of narcissism: Phrase first used by Christopher Lasch in his book of the same name published

in 1978. Lasch deployed the modern psychological diagnostic description of the narcissistic personality and applied it to contemporary American society, which he saw as increasingly preoccupied with the self. Often used by neoconservative or right-wing political thinkers, the term suggests a permissive society that absolves individuals of moral responsibility. According to this view, therapeutic ideologies, the cult of consumption, and changes in family life and in patterns of socialization are seen as creating a nation of disconnected individuals whose only ethic is that of immediate gratification. —*Margaret Boe Birns*

Culture-of-poverty thesis: Concept coined by anthropologist Oscar Lewis in 1961 to describe a self-perpetuating and self-defeating view of life. Lewis argued that this viewpoint, held by many poor people, ensures that they and their descendants will remain destitute.

While researching the life of poor families in Mexico, Lewis discovered that certain traits that were passed on from parents to children strongly contributed to the latter's being indigent as adults. In *Children of Sanchez* (1961), Lewis argued that most children in poor families were socialized to accept a set of VALUES and attitudes that made it difficult for them to escape POVERTY. Taking on their parents' worldview, they adopted a fatalistic approach to life and had trouble planning for the future, controlling their impulses, postponing gratification, developing self-discipline, or acquiring and saving money. This present-time orientation led many poor children to have low motivation in school and inadequate preparation for employment. Many members of this subculture felt helpless, dependent, and inferior. Moreover, since these poor families were often headed by a single female, they tended to provide little protection, privacy, or affection for children.

Lewis and other proponents of this explanation of poverty contended that the new norms, values, and aspirations that emerged among those experiencing extended periods of economic deprivation eventually became independent of the situations producing them, so that this self-sustaining system of values and behaviors passed from one generation to the next. These characteristics helped the poor cope with the stress of their situation, but they also kept them from escaping it. Lewis argued in several books that this culture of poverty existed throughout the world and was evidenced

The culture-of-poverty thesis asserts that the children of poor families are socialized to accept their circumstances.
(Impact Visuals/Thor Swift)

in the remarkable similarities in family structures, interpersonal relations, attitudes toward time, value systems, and spending behaviors of poor people in varied nations. The culture-of-poverty perspective was adopted by many of those involved in President Lyndon B. Johnson's War on Poverty, waged in the mid-1960's, as they confronted a cycle of dependency in which families receiving welfare benefits seemed to pass this practice on from one generation to the next.

Other scholars have challenged the culture-of-poverty theory. Some have argued that the poor do not have attitudes and values different from those of the nonpoor. They insisted that many people remained below the poverty line only temporarily and that most children of poor parents are able to break the cycle of poverty. Some critics have denounced the culture-of-poverty explanation for blaming the victim and for failing to consider the political, economic, and social conditions that cause and perpetuate poverty. Still other scholars have contended that it was welfare, rather than poverty itself, that produced this orienta-

tion toward life. By providing the poor with a minimal income, welfare encouraged its recipients not to seek employment, acquire skills, save money, or live responsibly. Finally, some investigators have argued that a culture of poverty persists among the poor not because particular traits are transmitted from parents to children but because the characteristics and attitudes of the poor are realistic and predictable responses to their circumstances.

Culture wars: Public arguments between antagonists whose worldviews differ as to how society should be ordered. Culture wars, a relatively recent phenomenon in American society, differ from cultural conflicts in which political and social hostility are rooted in different systems of moral understanding. In cultural conflicts, such as the common disputes between Protestants and Catholics, disagreements are based on a doctrine, ritual observance, or commitment to an organization. The term "culture wars" typically is applied to differences such as those between political liberals and conservatives, in which divisions are based on worldview and cut through organizational and doctrinal allegiances.

Currency exchange rates: Ratio expressing the number of units of one country's currency, or money, equal in value to one unit of another country's currency. An example is the number of Japanese yen that exchange for one dollar, alternatively expressed as the number of dollars that exchange for one yen. Currency exchange rates can be "fixed" or "floating." Under a system of fixed rates, all legal exchanges of currency must take place at a stated rate. Floating exchange rates, which were far more common by the end of the twentieth century, allow exchange rates to be set by the operation of a freely operating financial market.

Countries will sometimes alter their exchange rates, either through changing fixed rates or through buying or selling currency in international financial markets. In the process of devaluation, for example, a country makes its currency worth less in relation to other currencies, with the goal of making its products cheaper to foreign buyers, thus raising the level of exports.

Cyberspace: All areas of ON-LINE computer activity, including the INTERNET, E-MAIL, bulletin board services, and other network-accessible sources for computer data. The spatially oriented label illustrates the popular tendency for users to believe in the space that is projected by the network. The term was adopted from William Gibson's novel *Neuromancer* (1984); in the novel, cyberspace is a computer-generated land-

scape that users perceive of as occupying real space. People worldwide are able to communicate with one another through cyberspace; some see this phenomenon as a new frontier for mass communication, whereas others worry that it will have negative psychological and sociological effects.

A virtual reality aficionado enters the world of cyberspace. (Reuters/Bettmann)

D

Daigle v. Tremblay (1989): SUPREME COURT OF CANADA decision. Jean-Guy Tremblay was the father of Chantal Daigle's unborn child. The Québec couple had ended their relationship, and Daigle, then eighteen weeks pregnant, decided to seek an ABORTION. Tremblay obtained an injunction preventing the abortion on the basis that the fetus had a right to life that Tremblay was entitled to protect. The Supreme Court set aside the injunction, stating that Québec law neither recognized a father's interest in a fetus nor permitted a father to overrule a woman's decision to seek an abortion.

Date rape: Sexual assault that takes place within the private context of a social or romantic relationship. Only recently has date rape been identified and publicized as a crime punishable by law.

RAPE is identified as sexual intercourse against a person's will, either by force or the threat of force or when the victim is physically or mentally unable to give consent. If the offender and the victim are known to each other, the episode falls under the definition of "acquaintance rape." This association may be casual—such as persons who meet in class, at work, or in the course of normal business—or it may be more familiar, such as steady dates or former sexual partners. Date rape is thus a variety of acquaintance rape.

All crimes of rape are underreported in national crime statistics; estimates are that three to ten rapes occur for every one rape reported. Of the incidents that are reported to the police, the vast majority involve strangers. A number of major studies conclude that approximately nine out of ten occurrences of rape between acquaintances are never brought to the attention of law-enforcement agencies. Much of the information about the frequency of acquaintance rape comes from a 1988 study of more than three thousand female college students published as *I Never Called It Rape*. That investigation revealed that 15 percent of the college women surveyed had been raped and that another 11 percent were victims of attempted rape. Subsequent studies revealed similar responses, leading to the frequently cited statistic that one in four college women experiences acquaintance rape.

Colleges are prime locations for acquaintance rape, partly because of the large concentrations of young people, many of whom are looking for an active social life and many of whom accept gender stereotypes that prescribe an aggressive role for males and a passive role for females. According to the U.S. Bureau of Justice Statistics, the risk of rape is highest for women aged sixteen to twenty-four. Approximately half of the men arrested for rape are twenty-nine years old or younger. Social values that degrade women, such as the cultures of some FRATERNITIES and athletic teams, also contribute to the environment that encourages acquaintance rape.

Prosecution and conviction in cases of acquaintance rape have provided some complex issues for the CRIMINAL JUSTICE SYSTEM. Police and prosecutors are often reluctant to press charges when a case does not fit the common definition of rape—an act committed by an armed stranger, preferably against a woman of irreproachable behavior. Juries are often unwilling to convict in situations in which the defendant looks to be clean-cut or when the evidence appears to support a simple case of two differing interpretations of the same sexual encounter. Defendants often argue that a woman "implied" consent by her willingness to engage in some lesser sexual activities, by her dress, or by her visit to the defendant's apartment. Supporters of educating young people to the "no means no" standard of sexual conduct argue that such a rule would hold an accused rapist responsible, in that a reasonable person would not interpret "no" as consent.

Most colleges and universities have adopted education programs to provide their students with information about acquaintance and date rape and with strategies to minimize miscommunication about sexual expectations.

SUGGESTED READINGS: *I Never Called It Rape*, by Robin Warshaw (New York: Harper & Row, 1988), is the definitive study of date rape, based on a national survey funded by *Ms.* magazine. *Straight Talk About Date Rape*, by Susan Mufson and Rachel Kranz (New York: Facts on File, 1993), is a clear and informative source for teenage readers.

Socializing and heavy drinking by young adults still unsure of the limits of acceptable behavior can lead to date rape. (Impact Visuals, Brian Palmer)

Daughters of Bilitis (DOB): Lesbian group founded in 1955. The first homophile organization for women in the United States, the DOB was founded by Del Martin and Phyllis Lyon as a semisecret social club. The goal of the organization was to educate lesbians so that they could make "adjustment to society"; later, it was hoped, members could educate the general public toward the "breakdown of taboos and prejudices." In the repressive 1950's, these goals were radical. The creation of an organization to bring lesbians together was pathbreaking, even though the group did not engage in activism on behalf of lesbian rights. The DOB paved the way for later lesbian activism.

Davis, Angela (b. January 26, 1944, Birmingham, Ala.): Political activist. A 1965 graduate of Brandeis University who subsequently studied in Europe, Davis in the 1960's joined the Student Non-Violent Coordinating Committee (SNCC), the BLACK PANTHER PARTY, and the Communist Party. In 1969, her controversial politics led to her dismissal by California governor Ronald REAGAN from a teaching position at the University of California at Los Angeles, an action later overturned by California courts. Davis became a national celebrity in connection with the 1970 seizure of hostages at a California courthouse, a crime for which she had allegedly supplied weapons. She became a

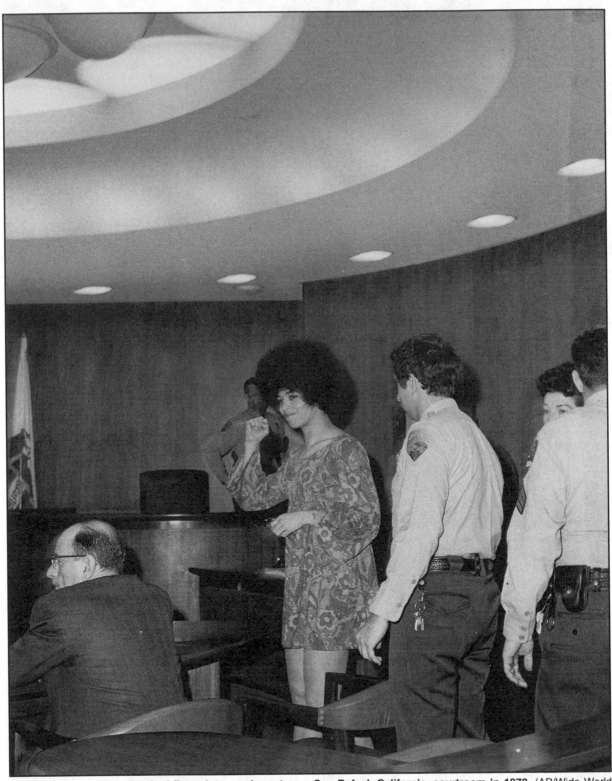

Angela Davis gives a clenched-fist salute as she enters a San Rafael, California, courtroom in 1970. (AP/Wide World Photos)

fugitive to avoid trial on charges of kidnapping, murder, and conspiracy; she was captured within two months but was acquitted of all charges in 1972. She subsequently founded the National Alliance Against Racist and Political Repression and remained active in political and feminist causes. Her major books include *Angela Davis: An Autobiography* (1974), *Women, Race and Class* (1981), and *Women, Culture, and Politics* (1989).

DDT (dichloro-diphenyl-trichloroethane): Insecticide created during World War II and banned by the U.S. Environmental Protection Agency in 1972. After the war, DDT's low cost, high toxicity, and suitability for aerial spraying encouraged its widespread use in agriculture and forestry to control pests and in residential areas and around bodies of water to control mosquitoes. By the late 1950's, many scientists had associated wildlife deaths with the spraying of DDT. Biologist Rachel Carson popularized the notion of harmful PESTICIDES, including DDT, in her controversial 1962 bestseller *Silent Spring*. The ban on DDT's use followed a decade of public protest and lawsuits.

Death, causes and rates of: Death will visit everyone; only the mode differs. In the past, communicable diseases and accidents were the main causes of death. In the late twentieth century, chronic diseases, cancer, and accidents rank as the leading causes.

Trends. In recent decades, the cause of death has changed. The number of deaths caused by diseases of the heart has increased to the point where cardiovascular disease has become the leading cause of death in industrial countries. At the turn of the century, pneumonia and influenza were the leading causes of death, followed by TUBERCULOSIS and diarrhea; diseases of the heart were only the fourth-leading cause. One hundred years prior to that, diseases of the heart were quite rare. The reasons for the ascendancy of HEART DISEASE are varied. Transportation and industrialization are primary reasons. Two hundred years ago, people walked and performed most work by hand; less than 3 percent of power was supplied by machines. One hundred years ago, the automobile was emerging, replacing the horse and augmenting the railroad. Long-distance travel was mechanized, but local movement was still mostly on foot. Industrialization was pervasive; more than two-thirds of all power was supplied by machinery. In contemporary society, in contrast, virtually all work is done by machines, and people travel extensively by automobile. The fact that walking has recently become a form of recreational activity attests the near-total reliance upon machinery and lack of exercise among most populations of industrialized societies. One result of this inactivity has been an increase in the rate of heart disease.

Pneumonia and influenza have been reduced to sixth place as causes of death. There are several reasons for this. One major factor is the development of drugs to treat pneumonia; over the past half-century, potent antibiotics have been found. These drugs, however, proved so successful that they have been taken for granted and abused. As a result, drug-resistant strains of bacteria have emerged that may well increase the death rate attributable to pneumonia in the future. A second factor has been the elimination of much industrial AIR POLLUTION throughout North America. One result of this clean-up has been a general decrease in the severity of cases of influenza and pneumonia. A third factor has been the development of vaccines for some types of lung diseases. Influenza mutates, meaning that new vaccines must be created annually.

The history of tuberculosis is similar. One hundred years ago, the disease was the second-leading cause of death in North America. During the intervening period, potent drugs were developed to treat the disease. Reliable screening methods were developed to enable medical professionals to diagnose and treat tuberculosis at an earlier stage, which led to a higher cure rate and reduced mortality. The incidence of tuberculosis declined to the point where it was thought to be completely controllable. In the 1980's and 1990's, however, tuberculosis re-emerged as a potent and deadly disease. Among some population groups—the homeless, individuals with AIDS, the malnourished, and intravenous drug users—it has become a leading cause of death.

Diphtheria, another communicable disease, ranked as the tenth-leading cause of death in 1900. As a result of the development of an effective vaccine and the diligence of pediatricians and public-health professionals, it has since become rare.

CANCER accounted for slightly more than 3 percent of deaths in 1900. In the intervening century, its incidence has increased sevenfold; by the late twentieth century, it accounted for almost one-quarter of all deaths and ranked as the second-leading cause of death in industrialized societies. The reasons for this are complex but revolve mainly around the spectacular development of new chemicals and their emission into the environment. SMOKING causes almost all new cases of lung cancer, the leading cause of death in both men and women. Dietary changes—increased use of refined carbohydrates and decreased amounts of fiber and vegetables in the diet—account for the development of cancer of the colon and rectum, the third-leading cause of death from cancer among both men and women. Among men, the second-leading site for fatal cancer is the prostate; among women, the second-leading site for fatal cancer is the cervix. A portion of the increased number of cancer deaths is attributable to identifying and then diagnosing neoplasms, new tissue growths, using improved and more sensitive methods of technology than were available in the past. The number of deaths has thus been attenuated somewhat by improvements in screening, early detection, and treatment; however, many forms of cancer are almost completely preventable by modifications in lifestyle.

Lifestyle also is a factor for three other leading causes of death: atherosclerosis, chronic liver disease, and suicide. Atherosclerosis, or hardening of blood vessels, is related to large dietary intakes of cholesterol, which is found principally in red meat, butter, and dairy products. Until the 1980's, Americans had increased their intake of these products. Recently, people have become conscious of the hazards of these substances and have begun to reduce their dietary intake. Chronic liver disease is primarily an outcome of years of excessive alcohol intake. When the liver is unable to keep up with the demands placed on it, the organ begins to fail. Like atherosclerosis, chronic liver disease can be avoided by judicious and early lifestyle modifications and changes in dietary habits.

SUICIDE is often considered to be a side effect of contemporary living. Pressures and stress often overwhelm people who opt to end their lives. There are clear cultural effects associated with suicide. Roman Catholics and Hispanics, who are primarily Catholic, have very low suicide rates because of religious teach-

More Americans have died in motor-vehicle accidents than in all the country's wars combined. (UPI/Corbis-Bettmann)

ings prohibiting the act. Whites have higher suicide rates than other racial populations. Suicide is a leading cause of death among teens; observers argue that this phenomenon is a harbinger of more serious problems in society related to the structure of the FAMILY.

Accident and Disease Statistics. Accidents are the fourth-leading cause of death in contemporary society; among children between the ages of one and ten, they are the leading cause. Most accidents occur at home; many of those involving children could be prevented by improved parental supervision and by the repair of unsafe conditions in and around the home.

Motor-vehicle accidents are another leading cause of death. In the United States alone, more than 3 million people have died in motor-vehicle accidents since the invention of the automobile; more people have died in motor-vehicle accidents than have died in all the wars in which the United States has been involved. Drivers between fifteen and twenty-one years of age and drivers above sixty-five years of age are more prone to motor-vehicle accidents than are middle-aged drivers. Young drivers have less experience and are more likely to make poor decisions when operating an automobile; older drivers frequently have impaired vision and hearing and tend to drive excessively cautiously, factors that often contribute to accidents.

Deaths also occur on the job, with accidents the number-one cause of occupational deaths. Unguarded machinery, poor maintenance, and carelessness are key contributing factors. Additionally, the use of alcohol and illegal drugs on the job impairs judgment and leads to many deaths. Exposure to chemicals and dusts indirectly contributes to deaths by initiating cancers or pulmonary diseases; for example, asbestos, formaldehyde, and polychlorinated biphenyls (PCBs) can cause cancer in the lungs and liver. Exposure to coal dust leads to anthracosis, and inhalation of silica dust causes silicosis; both are diseases of the lungs that are eventually fatal.

Social Patterns. Several studies have shown that married individuals live longer than single, separated, widowed, or divorced people, although the reasons for this are unknown. Men generally die sooner than women, with male life expectancy approximately seven years less than that of women. Different authorities have generally attributed the difference between men and women to innate biological factors or to environmental "wear-and-tear" factors such as job STRESS. Yet the life expectancy difference between men and women is beginning to shrink as women achieve greater equality in the job market; the "wear-and-tear" hypothesis is thus being accepted more widely by health professionals.

One of the most persistent patterns observed is that people in the lowest socioeconomic groups have the highest rates of mortality and morbidity. These higher morbidity rates are true for almost all diseases as well as for MENTAL ILLNESS and conditions such as DEPRESSION, schizophrenia, anxiety, worry, hopelessness, and unhappiness.   —*L. Fleming Fallon, Jr.*

SUGGESTED READINGS: *Pathways to Health: The Role of Social Factors* (Palo Alto, Calif.: H. J. Kaiser Family Foundation, 1989), edited by J. P. Bunker et al., studies the effects of societal conditions on public health and morbidity. J. M. Last and R. B. Wallace's *Public Health and Preventive Medicine* (Norwalk, Conn.: Appleton & Lange, 1992) looks at the effects of preventive approaches on mortality rates. M. E. P. Seligman's *Helplessness: On Depression, Development, and Death* (San Francisco: Freeman, 1975) examines the connection between mental health and death rates. D. L. Wingard's "The Sex Differential in Morbidity, Mortality, and Life Style" (*Annual Review of Public Health* no. 5, 1984) analyzes gender differences in life expectancy.

Death and dying: From the mid-twentieth century onward, death has no longer been viewed as a single event occurring at a specific moment in time. Rather, it has been revealed to be a process, a series of stages on a continuum. With the advances made in medical technology, it has become possible to sustain the bodily functions of a human being almost indefinitely. American society has thus become preoccupied—some even say obsessed—with the idea of forestalling death as long as possible. This preoccupation has led to debates. How far will society go to prolong human life? And at what cost—literally and metaphorically?

Defining Death. While each successive generation has had to face the enormous challenge of attempting to define death, the challenge increased exponentially with the development of sophisticated medical equipment aimed at prolonging life. Beginning with the heart-lung machines of the 1950's, rapid advances in medical technology have led to questions about the criteria used to determine death. Although new and improved treatments have prolonged the lives of many who would have died in the past, issues surrounding the quality of life have been a topic of increasingly

A cemetery in Syracuse, New York. (Diane C. Lyell)

heated debate. In the mid-twentieth century, death was no longer viewed as progressing neatly from CLINICAL DEATH, to BRAIN DEATH, to biological death, to cellular death. Clinical death occurs when spontaneous respiration and heartbeat cease irreversibly and leads to brain death, since the brain, at normal body temperature, cannot survive without oxygen for more than a few minutes. When the brain, which dies in stages, is completely dead, it is known as biological death. Cellular death is the last to set in, with different cells of the body dying at different times because of their varying makeup. For example, hair and nails may continue to grow after biological death has occurred. With mechanical support, brain death may occur while heartbeat and respiration continue.

While some researchers assert that death is not an event but a continuous process, others maintain that there is a point at which the human being must be considered dead. A question, though, remains: What is that point?

Even in the past, defining death was not a simple matter. In 1740, an article entitled "The Uncertainty of the Signs of Death and the Danger of Precipitate Interments and Dissections" set off a debate on the criteria of death. Putrefaction was considered the only sure sign of death, but even this criterion was attacked because putrefaction was also found in cases of gangrene. The fear of premature burial and premature cessation of medical care motivated the development of safeguards, which took such forms as the creation of mortuaries and legislation delaying burial for at least one day. These developments enabled people to observe the dead to make sure they actually were dead. As the medical profession advanced in terms of developing more thorough scientific standards, a consensus developed that medical knowledge could lead to the best protection against premature burial. In 1875, an article appeared in the *Dictionnaire Dechambre*, an encyclopedia of medicine, that discussed twenty-seven major signs of death. Agreement was slowly reached among physicians that the major signs of death were the irrevocable cessation of heartbeat, respiration, and consciousness.

In the late 1950's and early 1960's, there was an impetus to redefine death in terms of the brain rather than using the heart-lung definition. The explicit idea of brain death developed from the work of two French neurologists. In 1959, P. Mollaret and M. Goulon presented an article concerning grades of coma, the deepest coma being a state without movement, spontaneous breathing, reflex activity, or temperature regulation. Their assertion was that this was a state approaching conventional death except for the presence of a beating heart kept alive by artificially controlled lungs.

During the 1950's, organ transplant operations were also being conducted. In December of 1954, Joseph Murray and his colleagues performed the first successful kidney transplant operation. In December of 1967, Christiaan Barnard performed the first heart transplant. By the early 1980's, almost twenty-five different organs had been transplanted with varying degrees of success. Organs then needed to be available for transplantation. If a heart is to be used for transplantation, the donor must be maintained on a heart-lung machine. Other organs would also be of better quality if they were being supplied with oxygen until removal from the donor. The question arose of whether a patient could be defined as dead if the heart were beating, even if it were beating artificially.

Under these circumstances, it became imperative to define death in such a way as to protect the "dying patient" and to protect the surgeon from violating the law; and so as not to preclude a potentially life-saving operation for the patient who needed a new organ.

In 1968, the Ad Hoc Committee of the Harvard University Medical School to Examine the Definition of Brain Death presented a report in which they proposed criteria for determining brain death. The four conditions were: unreceptivity and unresponsivity; no movements or breathing; no reflexes; and a flat electroencephalogram. Evidence for the validity of the Harvard criteria came from a study of 2,500 comatose patients with flat electroencephalograms over a twenty-four-hour period. None of the patients not excluded by the Harvard criteria recovered. Furthermore, 128 autopsies on people who met the Harvard criteria showed that their brains had been destroyed. While the Harvard criteria became the standard reference point for the definition of death in the United States, the criteria have been constantly reexamined and reevaluated since their inception.

In Europe, instead of waiting twenty-four hours, if an individual fulfills the Harvard criteria, including a flat electroencephalogram at one point in time, an arteriograph is given that tests brain circulation, which should be nonexistent in brain death. (Blood flow is cut off because of the swelling of the brain cells.) The advantage to this procedure is that it takes only thirty minutes. It is a cumbersome procedure, however, and some American physicians feel the test may harm a brain that is not yet totally dead.

There have also been discussions of viewing brain death solely in terms of the neocortex (that portion of the cerebral hemisphere comprising most of the convoluted cortex and its associated white fibers), which would base the definition of death solely on a flat electroencephalogram. Since the brain stem is still alive, the person would have spontaneous respiration and certain brain-stem reflexes. To support their views, researchers have presented cases in which patients survived for months after neocortical death.

Many researchers have proposed frameworks that would enable the analysis of the various definitions of death. They discuss the concept of death and ask such essential questions as: Is life found in the flow of vital fluids? In the soul? In the capacity for bodily integration? In the capacity for social interaction? Once death has been defined, however, the locus of death must be determined. If one's concept of death concerns the loss of vital fluids, then one must look at the heart and lungs; if one is concerned with bodily integration, then one focuses on the total brain; if the concept is based on social interaction, then death would probably be found in the neocortex. For the soul, one might look for the pineal body (a gland-like structure in the brain that appears to be the major site of meatonin biosynthesis in most mammals and humans), as suggested by French philosopher and mathematician René Descartes. Next, the criteria of death must be decided: What specific tests—for example, the electroencephalogram—must be applied at the locus of death to see whether death has occurred?

The point in distinguishing the levels of death is that the criteria used in measuring death result from society's concept of death, rather than from society's needs for organs for transplantations or from economic considerations. However, most pieces of legislation concerning the definition of death are linked to the demand for organs.

In 1970, Kansas became the first state to legislate a definition of death; however, the statute was strongly

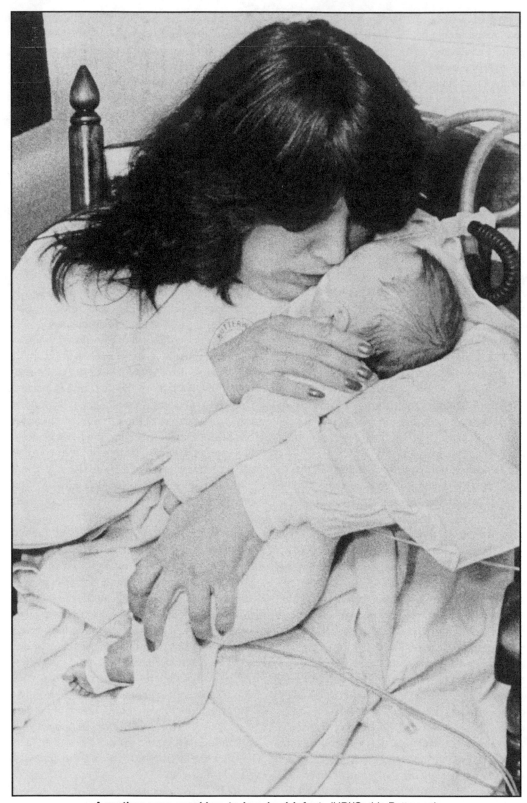

A mother says good-bye to her dead infant. (UPI/Corbis-Bettmann)

criticized on several grounds. Since the Kansas statute, more than seventeen other states have enacted definition-of-death laws, many of which have taken into consideration the criticisms of the Kansas statute. A model statute, it has been said, would clearly define death and would protect the rights of the dying.

Changing Attitudes Toward Death and Dying. Edwin Schneidman, a renowned thanatologist (one who studies death and dying) and the author of many works on the subject of SUICIDE, has dubbed the twentieth century "the age of death." He maintains that the Western world is perhaps more death-oriented in the twentieth century than it has been since the days of the Black Plague in the fourteenth century. Books and college courses in the field of thanatology have appeared all across the nation, and reports have indicated that lectures on death have begun to outdraw those on sex or politics on the national lecture circuit.

Some of the most popular items in the publishing world have become books professing to have found at least the first signs of scientific "proof" of life after death. Funeral homes have become big business. People are sometimes made to feel guilty if they do not make elaborate and often costly funeral arrangements; the funeral is viewed as one last statement to society about the quality of the deceased person's life and about the esteem the survivors felt for the person.

CRYONICS is the practice of freezing a dead person in the hope of bringing the person back to life at some point in the future. Soon after death, the body, or just the brain, is drained of blood, injected with preservatives, and put in a capsule of liquid nitrogen at very low temperatures, in a condition of "suspended animation," from which future scientists will "reanimate" the individual. The advent of cryonics in the 1960's reflected society's inability to accept death: Its attempted postponement at all costs became a logical extension of high technology's search for physical immortality.

Since the days of Charles Darwin, a change has clearly occurred in the relationship between man and God in the minds of some. Darwin's theory of evolution put in doubt the existence of a God-creator, and the Industrial Revolution made humankind less dependent on a scientific explanation for various diseases. By the beginning of the twentieth century, most infectious diseases were under control. New faith in progress, science, and technology became stronger with every invention and discovery. The relationship between man and nature had changed; humans were no longer part of nature but had the illusion that they could control it.

As the twentieth century progressed and the world became more industrialized, specialized, and impersonal, most people died in NURSING HOMES or hospitals instead of at home. Many lived out their final moments in a dehumanized state of loneliness and isolation and despair. The HOSPICE MOVEMENT (which maintains that dying patients are better cared for in their own homes rather than in hospitals or nursing homes), has emphasized quality of care rather than quantity, individual care instead of depersonalized efficiency, recognition of the person as a social being, of the person as a whole, mind and body, intellect and emotions, and by implication, recognition of death as part of life. This movement has been growing slowly and steadily since the 1960's and has been a welcomed alternative to the predominantly bureaucratic American way of dying.

With the advent of such forms of treatment as "bereavement counseling" and "grief therapy," and their increasing availability on the job as well as in the community, Americans learned that grieving—as well as dying—did not have to be faced in isolation. Society also learned that BEREAVEMENT was a process that deserved exploration and study. Researchers found that sometimes the bereaved individual does not reach a level of recovery from the loss. In some cases, grief reactions could be pathological; for example, grief reactions might be delayed, inhibited, or chronic. These patterns exaggerate the normal aspects of grief, which appear to be a working out of conflicting impulses. The DEPRESSION, panic, GUILT, and ill health that are felt in these distorted forms of grief do not differ in kind, but rather in duration and intensity, from normal grief reactions. Researchers discovered that there are stages of dying (and by extension, grieving) that most individuals experience. These are, according to a pioneer in the field of death and dying, Elisabeth Kübler-Ross: denial, isolation, anger, bargaining, depression, and acceptance. The stages are merely descriptive and are not meant to be normative. Nor do these feelings necessarily follow one another, but may exist contemporaneously.

In the twentieth century, though there are many levels and facets to this revolutionary shift in death-consciousness, some maintain that the overall meaning is probably one of gain and health and not of decadence and morbidity. Only in a mature culture, they say, can death come of age and be received and accepted as a natural companion of life. The death preoccupation in American society is viewed, then, as an

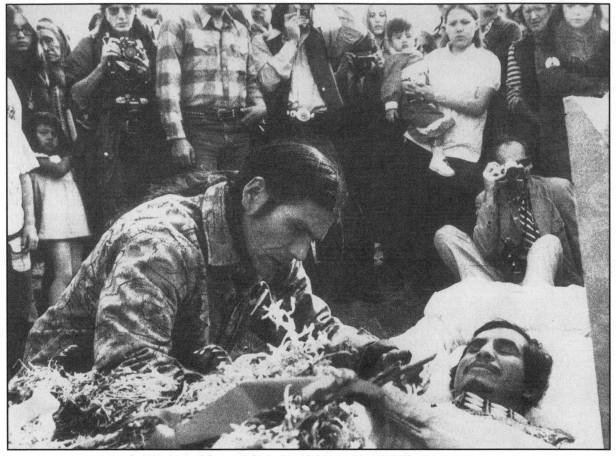

A 1971 funeral for a slain Indian rights activist. (UPI/Corbis-Bettmann)

awkward but significant rite of passage that affects and may well have epochal meaning for Western culture. Western civilization is impatient with limits; its paramount priorities are on action and power. Thus, it is not surprising that it has been slow to come to terms with death. To many, death appears as the very ultimate in passivity, impotence, and limit.

Death and Advanced Medical Technology. Before the twentieth century, little was written about the care of the dying. The absence of antibiotics, chemotherapeutic agents, and sophisticated medical procedures made illness more likely to be deadly and death more swift. Yet in just a few decades, technological advances in medicine dramatically transformed this situation. Infectious diseases, once life-threatening, became reversible, while degenerative and chronic diseases became the predominant causes of death.

By the mid-twentieth century, technological advances had come to the forefront with astounding results. In the decade of the 1950's, for example, besides the heart-lung machine (an artificial breathing technique developed for polio victims), the cardiopulmonary bypass machine and coronary angiography were invented. The 1960's saw even greater medical progress: Renal dialysis, ORGAN TRANSPLANTATION, cardiac-valve prostheses, external cardiac massage, coronary-care units, and nonsurgical life supports were all in use. Computerized axial tomography (CAT) scanners were developed in the 1970's.

A decade later, CAT's successor, the Nuclear Magnetic Resonance Imager (MRI), and the artificial heart made their way into medical use. Such developments influenced the care of the sick and dying and saved many lives. In cases in which they have not been able to prevent death, they have changed the manner in which it occurred.

Some argue that technology created some problems, particularly for the terminally ill patient, especially if the technological imperative was allowed to take precedence over the individual's values. By the 1950's, those techniques that had been developed to serve human interests, and which often did so brilliantly, began, in a moral sense, to override and even displace human priorities. Since then, while some therapies have eased pain and suffering, in other instances they have been used inappropriately and overzealously.

Critics also argue that enhancing the biological quality of life has often led to overutilization of intensive-care units. Initially, these units were designed to treat trauma and some postoperative cases, not the extremely ill. Yet intensive-care units began to fill with elderly patients, whose with underlying untreatable diseases (such as CANCER), and patients with loss of cerebral function. Such people, it is argued, would not benefit from the high concentration of medical techniques available in these units, nor would many of them approve of the procedures—ones that limit their freedom and dignity—if they were capable of choosing.

In their zeal to create new and better technologies, many doctors have promoted measures that have unintended consequences. These efforts have provoked a certain backlash of disapproval, such as growing resistance to cardiopulmonary resuscitation (CPR), a technique that has greatly increased survival from cardiac arrest, but has not yet found a way to deal with the brain damage resulting from diminished oxygen supply during the arrest.

The media has heightened society's awareness of and fascination with medical technology. Technology has proven itself to be extremely beneficial, yet there are many who maintain that its applications need to be controlled. They believe that technology is often used because it is available, not because its use is justified by patient need. Once this technology is applied without consideration of the ethics of the treatment, it is argued that the danger is that it may be used excessively or inappropriately. Such overuse is often prompted by physicians' training—which places great value on saving life at any cost—as well as by fears of MALPRACTICE suits and other factors.

Consumer demands have also promoted the use of medical technology. Technology offers the possibility of cure to patient and family, promising eternal hope. The desire for highly specialized techniques and procedures, however, sometimes generates expectations that are then translated into demands. In turn, hospitals often bend to such pressures and acquire technology to satisfy consumer demand. It follows that once the technology has been secured, it must be utilized to meet the costs of use and maintenance.

Another argument against high medical technology is that while many life-support systems and techniques are beneficial, too often they reinforce the notion that death can be avoided indefinitely. Often, skilled techniques and sophisticated therapies postpone important decision-making on the part of the physician and the patient's family.

While the dying still cling to life, the question of the point at which the terminal patient may refuse further treatment is one that has been hotly debated for decades. Pope Pius XII's statement in 1957 differentiating "ordinary" from "extraordinary" means has been used as a benchmark by many in deciding what is appropriate treatment. Catholic thinkers have struggled to define these terms more explicitly, however, since ordinary and extraordinary treatment are relative measures, and their definitions are open to a great deal of interpretation. What is ordinary treatment for one patient may be extraordinary for someone else. What a patient might see as extraordinary would not necessarily seem so to a physician. Thus the complexities of new and innovative techniques demonstrate how technology has confounded the issue of which treatments are suitable for which patients, especially for those who are dying. There are no fixed guidelines to decide what is suitable. If technology is a mixed blessing, it is because it has been developed and incorporated into hospital and medical practices at such a rapid rate that decisions on how to use it appropriately have lagged behind.

—Genevieve Slomski

SUGGESTED READINGS: Both *Death and Dying* by Barbara A. Backer et al. (New York: John Wiley & Sons, 1982), and *On Dying and Denying*, by A. D. Weisman (New York: Behavioral Publications, 1972), discuss the United States as a death-denying society. In *Death and Dying: Challenge and Change* (Reading, Mass.: Addison-Wesley, 1978), edited by Robert Fulton et al., historical perspectives on death and dying are discussed. What the dying have to teach health professionals, clergy, and their own families is examined in Elisabeth Kübler-Ross's pivotal works, *On Death and Dying* (New York: Macmillan, 1969) and *Questions and Answers on Death and Dying* (New York: Macmillan, 1974). Life after death is explored in Raymond A. Moody's groundbreaking work *Life After Life* (St. Simons Island, Ga.: Mockingbird Books, 1975) and Betty J. Eadie's *Embraced by the Light* (Placerville, Calif.: Gold Leaf Press, 1992). In *How We Die* (New York: Alfred A. Knopf, 1994), the physician Sherwin B. Nuland reflects on the dying process.

Death of God

Robert Jay Lifton's *The Broken Connection* (New York: Simon & Schuster, 1979) analyzes death from a philosophical perspective.

Death of God: Cultural phenomenon describing the collapse of VALUES once centered upon a divine being or source. The most famous expression of the death of God comes from the nineteenth century German philosopher Friedrich Nietzsche, who described how a society no longer committed to belief in God must be characterized by directionlessness, by the inability to know what is absolutely right or wrong, what is beautiful or ugly, what is ultimately true and what is not. Those who live in the wake of the death of God find themselves without a moral or spiritual compass.

To a considerable degree, modern and postmodern culture reflects this sensibility. The fact that so many people have adopted the view that knowledge and belief are relative to a person's interests and backgrounds, and that the values people hold dear are principally a reflection of time-specific preferences, would seem to indicate that Nietzsche's diagnosis of the contemporary scene is largely accurate. Value judgments are made without reference to or guidance from God. In many cases, people are unwilling to suggest that their views are absolute or universally binding. Instead, these views are seen as a reflection of the person holding them—they do not bear a direct relation to how the world "really" is or how the world ought to be.

In essence, when people refer to the "death" of God, they are referring to the fact that many traditional assumptions about the existence of God no longer hold. God, it is argued, is no longer an active presence in the affairs of this world. Once one grants the presupposition that God does not exist—or, at least, that God has no bearing on how one understands oneself and the world—then a number of other beliefs also begin to crumble. This is because the idea of God has been so closely linked to the way Western culture has understood itself and its practices. For example, for those who believe in God, morality is to be explained in terms of how God has made the world and the commands God has given with respect to how the world ought to function. If God is absent, however, then this basis or foundation for morality disappears as well. The world is stripped of ultimate purpose, and it also becomes difficult to argue that the world must function one way and not another. The way we live thus does not require any external or divine legitimation, be-cause we decide for ourselves what we shall do and become.

The death of God, therefore, is not simply about whether or not one will believe in a religious system. It also has to do with a reevaluation of the way Western society understands itself. In other words, the death of God entails a critical reexamination of the absolutes that have guided Western society in RELIGION, ethics, politics, and ART.

Declaration of the Rights of the Child (1959): Code adopted by the General Assembly of the UNITED NATIONS. The declaration sets forth ten principles supporting the rights of children in all nations, emphasizing the need to protect children from neglect, exploitation, and cruelty and the need to give children opportunities for development. According to the declaration, children are entitled to a name, a nationality, an education, and social benefits. The 1990 World Summit for Children addressed a number of issues relevant to the survival and welfare of children worldwide.

Declaration on the Rights of Disabled Persons (1975): U.N. document. Disabilities of one form or another affect more than 50 million people in North America, roughly 17 percent of the population. Three-fourths of these disabilities are the result of injury, disease, and war, while one-fourth result from congenital causes. Formerly known as the "handicapped," disabled persons have long been discriminated against in numerous ways. The inability to find adequate housing, jobs, and health care has plagued the lives of many of these persons. As the awareness about the plight of the disabled has grown, slow improvements in their situation have occurred. The UNITED NATIONS has made several declarations to provide leadership to urge member nations to adopt policies that provide protection for the disabled.

In the 1950's, the United Nations began to concern itself with the treatment of the disabled. Concerned with human rights in general, the organization saw the need to pass the Social Rehabilitation of the Physically Handicapped resolution in 1950 and augmented this with a further resolution on the rehabilitation of the disabled in 1965. As more attention was paid to the rights of the disabled, the United Nations then recognized the need for another resolution in 1971, the Declaration on the Rights of Mentally Retarded Persons,

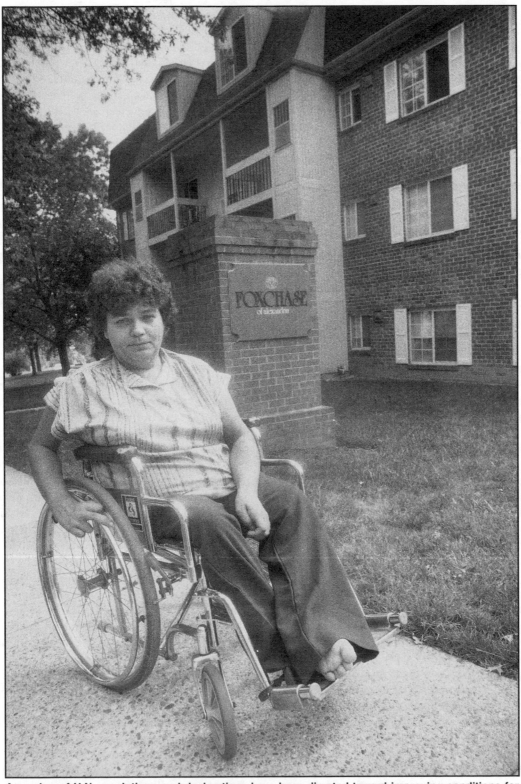

A number of U.N. resolutions and declarations have been directed toward improving conditions for people with mental or physical disabilities. (UPI/Corbis-Bettmann)

as a continuation of its efforts to ensure full human rights for all people. This foundational declaration laid out the essentials of human rights for all persons, especially the disabled, who were among the most likely to face discrimination.

The 1971 declaration lists proper medical care, physical therapy, education, training, rehabilitation, guidance, economic security, and a decent standard of living as essentials. The declaration also urged protections for the disabled in the form of laws prohibiting the exploitation, abuse, and degradation of the disabled. Further, the 1971 declaration urged protection under DUE PROCESS of law and required that diminished capacity be recognized as a disability in cases of law.

Directed at government policymakers, the Declaration on the Rights of Disabled Persons further refined the tenets set forth in the 1971 resolution. Acknowledging the technical challenges such mandates would have, the 1975 resolution calls for both national and international cooperation in establishing a standard by which the disabled are identified and protected. The declaration defines as disabled "any person unable to ensure by himself or herself, wholly or partly, the necessities of a normal individual and/or social life, as a result of a deficiency, either congenital or not, in his or her physical or mental capabilities." These individuals are to enjoy all human rights accorded to all citizens without distinction based on race, color, sex, language, religion, political or other opinion, national or social origin, economic status, or any other situation applicable to the disabled person and to his or her family. The declaration seeks to protect the dignity and respectability of the disabled and urges that all agencies involved seek to enable those suffering disabilities to live as normal a life as possible.

Defamation: Any form of public ridicule of an individual or group by another. Defamation can be "actionable," or an issue for a lawsuit, when the alleged ridicule can be proved to have been intentional or false and to have resulted in a direct loss of public favor, respectability, or opportunity of association with others. As in cases involving defamation's extensions, LIBEL and SLANDER, a plaintiff must prove both intent and damages for such an action to be successful.

Defense spending: The efforts to defend the interests of the United States in the world have been divi-

sive through the nation's history. After World War II, the United States threw off its isolationist past and developed a massive MILITARY apparatus to counter the Soviet Union. In the post-Cold War era, the United States has struggled to define how it will change this structure to adapt to changing realities.

The Defense Establishment. After the end of World War II, the wartime alliance between the Soviet Union and the United States began to crumble. The "COLD WAR" that emerged produced a concerted effort by the United States to contain the expansion of communism around the world. The centerpieces of this policy were efforts to provide economic aid to American allies and to establish a powerful peacetime American military presence around the world. President Harry S Truman, at one time content to trim the military, dispatched U.S. forces to defend South Korea against an invasion from North Korea in 1950. Threats to American allies in Europe and other parts of the world from Soviet expansionism created an atmosphere of continuing crisis between the two emerging superpowers. As one historian has observed, the result of the fear and suspicion between the Soviet Union and the United States was "a drastic militarization of the Cold War in the form of a conventional and nuclear armaments race, the frantic search for military alliances and the establishment of military bases." In the period from 1950 to 1954, the percentage of the United States gross national product (GNP) devoted to the production of defense-related items grew from 5.2 to 13.5 percent.

President Dwight D. Eisenhower, the hero of the allied defeat of Nazi Germany, moved the American military toward a more modern and mobile army. Faced with a series of crises with the Soviet Union, Eisenhower established a military policy based on American technological superiority and "massive retaliation" with NUCLEAR WEAPONS in response to communist expansion. As he left office in 1960, a somber Eisenhower warned Americans about the threat of a growing "military-industrial complex" that had developed in response to the efforts to contain the communist threat. This alliance of military officials, politicians, and defense-industry executives was seen by Eisenhower as a self-perpetuating "defense establishment" that could expand defense at the cost of other programs even in the absence of credible threats to NATIONAL SECURITY.

The 1960's were marked by the continuing expansion of Soviet military power and the quagmire in Vietnam. By 1968, American defense expenditures reached

A Michigan plant producing U.S. Army M-1 tanks. (Jim West)

$78 billion. In the 1970's, both Republican and Democratic administrations moved to upgrade conventional forces and modernize the American nuclear arsenal. The 1979 Soviet invasion of Afghanistan and the 1980 election of Ronald REAGAN brought about a new emphasis on defense spending and military preparedness. Reagan's top priority was to provide the American military with whatever resources were needed to counter perceived Soviet expansionism, and the increase in defense spending during the Reagan Administration was dramatic. Defense spending had grown in real terms by an average of approximately 2 percent from 1976 to 1980; from 1981 to 1985, the growth rate reached 8 percent. A large share of these increases was devoted to the expansion of research and development and further modernization of conventional and nuclear forces. By 1985, the fiscal restraints of the Gramm-Rudman deficit-reduction act and opposition from congres-

sional Democrats forced the Department of Defense to reevaluate its priorities.

Defense Politics. Debates about the proper amount of defense spending have influenced every presidential contest since the end of World War II. President John F. KENNEDY castigated the Eisenhower Administration for allowing the Soviet Union to surpass American superiority in nuclear weapons. The charge, later found to be false, illustrates how politicians have used defense policy for political ends. What makes defense spending so divisive in American politics are the so-called opportunity costs it imposes on society. A dollar devoted to military objectives is a dollar that cannot be devoted to social programs deemed important by voters. Attempting to balance the international threats and domestic realities is an age-old dilemma. Eisenhower's warning of the existence of a military-industrial complex illustrates how leaders have struggled with balancing military security with economic realities. Eisenhower realized that a robust defense should not be allowed to grow into a fiscal power that weakens the very national security interests it was designed to protect.

By the middle of the 1980's, many Americans began to call for reductions in military spending. Press accounts of thousand-dollar coffee makers, three-hundred-dollar toilet seats, and corrupt military contractors forced Washington to announce a new campaign to rein in procurement abuses. In 1986, polling indicated that almost 80 percent of the public believed that the PENTAGON had seriously mismanaged a budget that totaled approximately $300 billion. Forced to deal with the Reagan-era deficits, President George Bush moved with caution in the area of defense. Even with the collapse of the Soviet Union and the reemergence of long-standing nationalist conflicts around the world, public opinion still supported cuts in defense spending to deal with the growing budget deficit. The 1990 budget reversed ten years of growth by specifically targeting defense. Even the U.S. participation in the GULF WAR against Iraq was constrained by budget priorities. While constructing the multinational military coalition in response to Iraq's invasion of Kuwait, American officials were also forced to request financial contributions to support U.S. participation.

With the end of superpower conflict with the Soviet Union, many Americans felt that a "peace dividend" resulting from major reductions in military spending would help reduce the national debt and bolster domestic social programs. In fact, one of the biggest opponents of cuts in defense spending in this period was not the Pentagon but Congress. Attempts to close military bases deemed nonessential by the Pentagon were opposed by congressmen and congresswomen who feared the electoral wrath of constituents left jobless by the economic effects of the MILITARY BASE CLOSURES. In 1990, for example, Democratic Representative Patricia Schroeder of Colorado, a leading critic of Reagan-era defense-spending increases, praised plans to close bases to reduce the military budget. Her views changed a year later, when the independent base-closure commission targeted Colorado's Lowry Air Force Base near Denver. In an attempt to save the base, Schroeder issued a statement vowing to defeat the entire base-closing process by finding "anything wrong or questionable" in the Pentagon's base-closure plans.

The Bill CLINTON Administration also backed away from campaign promises to reduce defense spending.

Upon taking office in 1993, Clinton called for a "bottom-up review" of American defenses and capabilities. Clinton, though, made the decision to keep intact Pentagon plans to develop forces capable of fighting two regional conflicts at the same time. Despite the president's pledges to cut major programs, the early Clinton budgets did not result in deep defense cuts. Clinton refrained from openly confronting the military in his first years of office and, after the Democratic loss of the House of Representatives and the Senate in 1994 elections, he responded by adding $25 billion to his proposed defense budget. By the mid-1990's, many members of Congress began to call for increased defense expenditures. These proponents cited the ten-year reductions in the defense budget, the smallest active fighting force since before the Korean War, and the seventy-year-low share (about 4 percent) of GROSS DOMESTIC PRODUCT (GDP) devoted to defense.

Fearing the wrath of voters, both the Clinton Administration and the Republican-led Congress opposed efforts to halt production on a number of weapons systems that had been designed to counter Soviet threats. One such program, the Seawolf nuclear attack submarine, was designed to hunt and destroy a new generation of Soviet nuclear submarines. The new generation was never built, and the old Soviet fleet was consigned to port as a result of a lack of spare parts. Even the Defense Department's own review concluded that there was no need to continue the production of the Seawolf. Yet despite the project's apparent pointlessness, Defense Secretary William Perry in October, 1995, lobbied the Senate to save the program from elimination proposed by the House of Representatives. Such manueverings have led many observers to point to the maintenance of defense-related jobs around the country as the true reason for the existence of many large defense-related programs. —*Lawrence I. Clark*

SUGGESTED READINGS: An examination of the influence of defense spending on the post-World War II economy can be found in Ann Markusen, Scott Campbell, Peter Hall, and Sabina Dietrick's *The Rise of the Gunbelt: The Military Remapping of Industrial America* (New York: Oxford University Press, 1991). The integration of defense industries into the civilian economy is the topic of Jacques S. Gansler's *Defense Conversion* (Cambridge, Mass.: MIT Press, 1995). The impact of domestic politics on defense spending is outlined in Lawrence J. Korb's "Our Overstuffed Armed Forces" (*Foreign Affairs*, November-December, 1995). A critical examination of Pentagon funding can

A demonstrator calls for cuts in U.S. defense spending at a 1995 protest. (Jim West)

be found in Tim Weiner's *Blank Check: The Pentagon's Black Budget* (New York: Warner Books, 1990). For an extensive analysis of the "bottom-up review" of the Pentagon, see Michael O'Hanlon's *Defense Planning for the Late 1990s: Beyond the Desert Storm Framework* (Washington, D.C.: Brookings Institution, 1995).

Deficits. *See* Budget deficits

Deforestation: Depletion of the world's forests and woodlands as a result of cutting, burning, disease, flooding, erosion, or pollution. Considered by many scientists, environmentalists, and policymakers to be one of the most critical social and ecological problems facing the planet, global deforestation serves as a vivid illustration of the ways in which rapid population growth, poverty, increasing urbanization and industrialization, unsustainable agricultural practices, and the overconsumption of scarce natural resources can result in wide-scale environmental degradation.

Trends. Prior to the dawn of agriculture, the earth had a rich mantle of forest and open woodland covering; almost half of the area of the United States, three-fourths of Canada, almost all of Europe, and major portions of the rest of the world were originally forested. Since that time, the earth's forests have been reduced to a fraction of the area that existed in preagricultural times, constituting about 28 percent of the planet's total land surface as of 1992.

The deforestation of the earth's tropical forests has been particularly alarming. As of 1990, the Food and Agricultural Organization of the United Nations estimated that tropical forests covered about 7 percent of the earth's surface, with 52 percent of such forests located in South America and the Caribbean, 30 percent

A native uses a chainsaw to cut down a tree in the Brazilian rain forest. (UPI/Bettmann)

in Africa, and 18 percent in the Asia/Pacific region. Half of all tropical forests were located in four countries: Brazil, Zaire, Indonesia, and Peru.

Between 1980 and 1990, tropical deforestation averaged 15.4 million hectares per year, with South America and the Caribbean experiencing the most destruction (7.4 million hectares annually), followed by Africa (4.1 million hectares), and the Asia/Pacific region (3.9 million hectares). Brazil, for example, had by far both the largest total area of RAIN FOREST and the highest rate of deforestation, and subregions such as Southeast Asia, Mexico, and Central America had deforestation rates that were twice the average for the tropics. In total, more than 154 million hectares of tropical forests—almost three times the land area of France—were lost in the 1980's, at a rate of more than a hundred acres per minute.

Temperate forests (which experience moderate amounts of rainfall, seasonal winter temperatures, and the loss of their leaves) showed a small net increase in forested areas over the past decade as a result of reforestation efforts and decreased tree harvests. This improved picture, however, does not take into account the significant degradation and fragmentation of many of these areas, especially the disappearance of ancient OLD-GROWTH FORESTS (those that have a natural diversity of trees more than two hundred years old). Of the more than twelve million hectares of virgin temperate forest that originally occupied the Pacific Northwest, for example, less than 10 percent in the United States and less than 40 percent in British Columbia still remain.

Because British Columbia is logging the largest and most productive forest in North America at a rate of half a million acres yearly, some observers have characterized the Canadian province as "the Brazil of the North." With government and industry plans to log much of the remaining ancient woodlands underway, fierce political debates have raged in the Northwest among loggers, environmentalists, timber companies, and other constituencies concerned with jobs, forest harvests, ENDANGERED SPECIES, and environmental preservation. On the whole, few of the old-growth forests in temperate regions around the world are fully protected, even though the majority lie in industrialized countries such as Russia, Canada, and the United States.

Causes. In tropical areas, the conversion of forest to cropland for agriculture is by far the leading direct cause of deforestation. Population pressures, inequita-

ble land distribution, and the expansion of profitable export crops such as rubber, coffee, bananas, soybeans, pineapples, and palms have greatly reduced the lands traditionally available for subsistence farming, forcing many peasant farmers to clear virgin forest to grow food. In arid areas in Africa and Asia, high population density and low vegetation rates have also resulted in woodlands being cut down for fuel. More than two-thirds of the people in the developing world rely on wood for their immediate cooking and heating needs. During the 1980's, the forest cover around India's major cities dropped by at least 15 percent, and Delhi lost almost 60 percent of its surrounding trees.

In Latin America, another cause of deforestation has been the conversion of forests to pastureland for cattle ranching. In the 1960's and 1970's, pastureland in Central America increased by more than 50 percent, while woodlands declined by 39 percent. While beef imports to the developed world have since declined, much of this forest conversion was originally stimulated by U.S. and European demands for cheap beef, especially for the fast-food industry. Other causes of global deforestation include AIR POLLUTION, mining, fossil-fuel exploration, urban development, consumer demands for exotic tropical hardwoods and various paper products, dam construction, pesticides, and tree blights.

Consequences. Perhaps the most pressing environmental effect of tropical deforestation is its contribution to species extinction and declining BIODIVERSITY. Tropical forests contain at least one-half of the world's plants and animals, and the destruction of forest habitat results in loss of an estimated seventeen thousand species a year, many of which exist nowhere else. These forests hold much of the genetic material that underlies the evolution of biological life; they are also the principal source of thousands of oils, resins, gums, rubber latexes, nuts, fruits, vegetables, and medicinal plants on which humans depend. It is estimated that rain forests, which are appropriately described as "nature's medicine cabinet," contain some three thousand plants with cancer-fighting properties, as well as plants yet to be discovered that could provide the pharmacological ingredients for drugs necessary to treat many human diseases.

The other major environmental consequences of deforestation are its effects on the earth's climatic systems and its air, soil, and water quality. All forests, especially tropical forests, play crucial roles in the hydrological cycles regulating rainfall patterns, wind cir-

Logging has drastically reduced the size of forested areas in North America. (Ben Klaffke)

culation, and sunlight absorption, as well as the global cycling of carbon dioxide from the air for photosynthesis. When trees are burned or cut, they stop filtering carbon dioxide from the atmosphere and release their stored carbon back into the environment, thereby contributing to the carbon dioxide emissions that increase GLOBAL WARMING and air pollution. In addition, deforestation causes severe soil erosion and WATER POLLUTION, as both the soil and stored rainwater previously held by the tree roots wash away into rivers, lakes, and oceans, killing fish and plants, damaging coral reefs, aggravating droughts and floods, and reducing land productivity. Thus, in their ability to anchor many natural systems on which life depends, global forests literally form the roots and lungs of the earth.

Deforestation also has negative social impacts for the estimated 140 million people and one thousand indigenous tribal groups who live within the world's tropical forest zones. As forests are destroyed by outside forces, these peoples are often compelled to flee their homelands as refugees. Many die from exposure to infectious diseases to which they have no resistance, while others lose forever the knowledge of rain-forest management practices on which their local ecology and culture have traditionally rested.

Prevention Efforts. International efforts to protect endangered forests have increased significantly since 1980. Some preservationist groups have called for an immediate ban on the harvesting and sale of rain forest or old-growth timber, while others favor more moderate approaches using economic incentives and public relations to pressure countries into creating more forest reserves, reforestation projects, and "sustainable forestry" programs. The intent is to adopt ways to harvest forests profitably without clearing them for timber or farming, damaging the ecological functions they perform, or denying food, fiber, and income to those who must subsist from the forests' bounty. Efforts to finance such initiatives have come from international conservation banks and from debt-for-nature swaps via which environmental organizations agree to forgive a portion of a developing nation's outstanding foreign debt in return for promises to set aside forest areas as reserves. Nevertheless, activists say reducing beef and paper consumption, reforming existing forest management and agricultural practices, stopping the clear-cutting of old-growth timber, reducing global population growth and socioeconomic inequalities, protecting indigenous peoples and sustainable forest products, and replanting at least 100 million hectares

of trees worldwide are just some of the many efforts that must take place if the planet's remaining tropical and temperate forests are to survive destruction by the mid-twenty-first century.   —*Anthony E. Ladd*

SUGGESTED READINGS: A thorough overview of forests worldwide and sustainable resource use is provided in Alexander S. Mather's *Global Forest Resources* (Portland, Ore.: Timber Press, 1990). For an easy-to-read book on saving old-growth forests, see Seth Zuckerman's *Saving Our Ancient Forests* (Washington, D.C.: Living Planet Press, 1991). For a moving story of a Brazilian activist's struggle to save the rain forest, see Andrew Revkin's *The Burning Season: The Murder of Chico Mendez and the Fight for the Amazon Rainforest* (Boston: Houghton Mifflin, 1990).

Deism: Religious belief in which God is viewed as creator but is thought to be removed from, and uninvolved with, the universe. The term is derived from the Latin word *deus*, or "God." According to deist belief, nature contains all that one needs to know about God, and everything is governed by a divinely established "natural law" with which God never interferes. No provision is made for the miraculous. Deism flourished in England in the sixteenth and seventeenth centuries and from there came to America. Such prominent Americans as Thomas Jefferson and Benjamin Franklin were essentially deists.

Delano grape strike (Sept. 8, 1965-July 29, 1970): Labor conflict. This strike for better wages and working conditions against Coachella Valley grape growers was led by César CHÁVEZ's UNITED FARM WORKERS (UFW). The union maintained a nonviolent stance but was met with much resistance and some retaliatory violence from growers and from the Teamsters' union, which competed for the same workers. The UFW organized a 250-mile march from its base in Delano, California, to Sacramento in 1966; in 1968, the union called for a nationwide boycott of grapes. The pressure and the bad publicity engendered by the union's tactics brought the growers to sign a contract with the UFW in July of 1970.

Democracy: Derived from the Greek words *demos* (people) and *kratia* (from *kratos*, power); the literal translation is "rule of the people." In its commonly

Democracy

Democracy requires citizen participation. (James L. Shaffer)

accepted sense, however, "democracy" means not just any regime calling itself democratic; otherwise, the "people's democracies" of the Soviet era would qualify as democracies. A critical understanding of democracy takes the ideas and ideals of modern Western democracies as models. This conception can be best understood as liberal democracy, or, more precisely, constitutional liberal democracy. Each part of this term has a meaning essential to the whole.

The first element, "constitutional" government, means limited government—government restrained in practice by law and by written or, infrequently, unwritten constitutions. The rule of law is at the heart (but is not the whole) of the principle of limited or constitutional government. It means that all members of society are equally subject to the same law, and that governments must conform to preestablished, properly constituted law and cannot act through arbitrary orders and decrees.

Some form of separation of governmental powers is indispensable as a means of restraining government. Most essential is an independent judiciary, since an autocratic government might otherwise manipulate

law to illegitimate ends, undermining the rule of law. Under some political systems, called shared powers or presidential systems, a further SEPARATION OF POWER is established between the executive and legislative branches. In the American model, a system of CHECKS AND BALANCES restrains each branch of government. In parliamentary systems, legislative and executive powers are not as sharply separated as in shared powers systems, but there is a degree of separation. Executives are restrained by the possibility of their governments' collapse if they lose the confidence of parliamentary majorities.

The second element, "liberal," refers to the guarantee of certain individual rights, as opposed to group rights that characterized premodern societies or certain aspects of some otherwise liberal societies today. To the extent that group rights are substituted for individual rights, the "liberal" element of liberal democracy has been abandoned. This occurs when individuals are not treated according their abilities and behavior as particular individuals but rather as members of ascriptive groups—groups into which people are born and cannot leave, such as caste, sex, race, or ethnicity. Liberal societies maintain significant legal recognition of individual rights.

These individual rights are those that guarantee personal and political freedom, such as freedoms of religion, association, and expression. Liberal societies recognize a private realm into which the state may not intrude. The protection of liberal rights yields the open society, within which ideas and individuals move freely, citizens travel abroad and return unimpeded, and excessive restrictions do not bar foreigners from visiting.

An essential characteristic of liberal democracy is an autonomous civil society, a portion of society independent of the state. "Civil society" refers to self-organized, voluntary social activity, a vital force in the maintenance of limited government, since it forms centers of organizational, intellectual, and economic power independent of the state, capable of opposing government policy and influencing political change.

The third element, "democracy," refers to the right of all citizens to participate in the governance of the polity, including voting and holding office. Democracy is based on full, equal citizenship and equality before the law. Essential to democracy are free and regular elections with widespread participation by the electorate. Most institutions of modern democracies comprise representative government, not direct democracy, as practiced in ancient Greece.

Other Forms of Government. Liberal democracy can be best understood when contrasted with other forms of government in matters such as the relationship between governors and governed. Under authoritarian and totalitarian governments, governors dominate the governed, who have no recourse against state power and are accorded only those rights the state finds convenient. Under these governments, power flows from the top down. The governed are treated only as subjects—those subject to state authority—and are conceived of as passive receivers, not initiators, of government action.

Under liberal democracy, by contrast, the state is understood as the creature of the governed. Citizens

Voting in democracies is one reflection of the necessary mobilization of public opinion. (Jim West)

erect the state to serve their needs and can change it at will. The doctrine of popular sovereignty sees citizens as ultimate masters of their governors. Power flows upward from the governed to governors, for citizens must consent for authority to be legitimate. The sole purposes of government are protection of citizens' fundamental rights and promotion of the common good.

Problems of Democratic Rule. When Winston S. Churchill called democracy "the worst form of government, except for all the others," he was referring to the difficulties inevitably encountered by democracy. Principal among them is the need to reach agreement on public policy. While authoritarian governments have the advantage of depending upon few decision-makers whose decisions are final, democracies must aggregate the opinions of millions of citizens. This task is carried out through political parties and their leaders, linking the individual and interested groups to the public agenda.

Political parties, however, generally reflect social fissures, manifested as factions within a larger party, as small parties, or as interest groups and splinter parties. Somehow, these centers of opinion must reach decisions on legislation and executive action. While complete consensus is seldom necessary, democracy must restrain opposition within certain bounds if politics is not to be replaced by violence.

Difficulties associated with aggregating opinion are magnified in parliamentary regimes, in which legislative majorities supporting the government are required. Once parliament's support is withdrawn in such a regime, the government falls and another must be established—often with a new general election. If a parliament is composed of a number of parties refusing to cooperate, political instability results.

Such problems cannot occur in democracies built on the American model, since the executive has a fixed term of office. However, the American system has problems of its own. For example, complaints are often heard about "gridlock," the chronic inability of CONGRESS and the executive branch to agree on legislation. Critics argue, however, that the U.S. Constitution's framers intended that there be friction among the branches of government; the division of power ensures that vast power cannot easily be abused.

These problems are summed up in the description of democracy as "messy." Quality of debate may be low; decisions may be made slowly and reversed or amended; second-rate individuals may hold office; and cumbersome procedures may result in inefficiencies.

But most such problems must be accounted necessary evils. If vast numbers are to have a say in electing those wielding power and making public policy, smooth and neat processes cannot be expected. Churchill's backhanded defense of democracy retains its force; the alternatives are far less attractive. Experience suggests that if rulers are not surrounded by restraints, they will abuse their power.

Moreover, recent history reveals liberal democracy to be effective. In modern developed societies, there can be no legitimate government without recourse to democratic ideas and institutions. The stability of Western nations is among liberal democracy's major achievements; their prosperity is based upon this stability. The efficiency and effectiveness of authoritarianism is more apparent than real. One example is the environmental legacy of the Soviet era. Its governments could make decisions unhindered by "inefficient" democratic procedures; the result was environmental catastrophe on a vast scale.

Moral Dimensions. Liberal democracy is founded upon the idea that the primary purpose of government is the protection of citizens' fundamental personal and political rights. Regimes established upon this conception of justice, insofar as they are successful, must be accounted among the highest of humanity's moral achievements.

Democracy's moral dimension also regards the role of citizens. Alone among forms of political rule, democracy treats citizens as adults. Other forms of government are to some degree paternalistic, since they keep the portion of society excluded from self-rule in a state of political childhood.

In treating people as adults, democratic self-government constitutes the wholesale abandonment of political paternalism and marks the final step in political maturity. Actually or potentially, democracy elevates its citizens morally by calling upon them to think, judge, and act as rational adults, balancing personal interest with public good. As a form of government and a way of life, liberal democracy represents the political fulfillment of human aspirations to personal dignity. In promoting the public use of reason by its members, liberal democracy morally transcends regimes whose subjects are obliged merely to obey and be silent. When government demands obedience without informed consent, the human estate is degraded.

—*Charles F. Bahmueller*

SUGGESTED READINGS: No student of democracy can ignore Alexis de Tocqueville's classic *Democracy in America* (New York: Vintage, 1990). Robert A. Dahl's *Democracy and Its Critics* (New Haven, Conn.: Yale University Press, 1989) is a highly regarded contemporary statement of democratic theory; James David Barber in his *The Book of Democracy* (Englewood Cliffs, N.J.: Prentice-Hall, Inc., 1995) examines the development of democracy in a number of countries; Seymour Martin Lipset, ed., *The Encyclopedia of Democracy* (Washington, D.C.: Congressional Quarterly, 1995) is a remarkable compendium of scholarship on democracy.

Democratic Party: One of the two principal partisan organizations in U.S. politics. The Democratic Party has long based its popularity on appeal to the "common people," but its leaders coped with depression and war during the twentieth century by increasing the power of the federal government, the size of the federal bureaucracy, and the national debt.

Origins. Although both major parties of the twentieth century claimed a direct lineage to Thomas Jefferson's Democratic-Republicans of the 1790's, most political historians have concluded that the Democrats exhibited stronger roots to the supporters of Secretary of State Jefferson, who jousted with Secretary of the Treasury Alexander Hamilton for influence over President George Washington and the American people.

Jefferson's Democratic-Republican Party, which existed from 1789 to 1825, favored rule by informed white males, free speech and press, and no national debt. They preferred the French over the British, opposed tariffs that protected factories, advocated a narrow interpretation of the Constitution insuring states' rights, and composed a rural party that focused on agrarian rights.

Democratic presidential hopefuls at a 1988 forum. (AP/Wide World Photos)

Democratic Party

Early Successes. By 1820, practically every major politician belonged to Jefferson's party. The Jeffersonians, however, split into two groups during the early 1820's: National Republicans and Democratic Republicans. The latter became Jacksonian Democrats following Andrew Jackson's failed 1824 presidential campaign. Jackson, who received the highest total of popular and electoral votes, saw his victory disappear when the Speaker of the House of Representatives, Henry Clay, arranged a "corrupt bargain" with Secretary of State John Quincy Adams that made Adams president. An angry Jackson vowed revenge and coalesced regional factions led by Martin Van Buren of New York and John C. Calhoun of South Carolina into the modern Democratic Party.

The Jacksonians, like the Jeffersonians, were mainly farmers and frontiersmen, but the group also included urban immigrants and small businessmen. Jackson revolutionized the presidency by incorporating political advisers into the first White House staff, or "kitchen cabinet." He also introduced patronage into the federal government by replacing government workers with deserving Democrats. This "spoils system" was so effective that the party controlled the presidency, the Congress, and many state legislatures until the outbreak of the Civil War.

The Great Crisis. The first conflict occurred during the 1850's, when northern Democrats began joining the Know-Nothing Party who objected that Jackson's appeal to the common people had attracted millions of German and Irish immigrants. A more important division emerged over the issue of slavery and the influence of Southerners, whom Democratic abolitionists increasingly resented. As party unity declined, a new group called the Republicans filled the gap, electing Abraham Lincoln in 1860 and controlling the federal government for the next fifty years.

The Civil War nearly destroyed the Democratic Party, reducing its membership to northern "copperheads," who criticized Lincoln during the fighting, Southerners who supported the Confederacy, and immigrants. Able to elect only one president, Grover Cleveland, between 1856 and 1912, the Democrats resigned themselves to influencing Congress, which effectively controlled the federal government after the war. Critics stereotyped the Democrats as the party of "rum, Romanism and rebellion"—a thinly veiled reference to their opposition to prohibition and their unusual combination of Catholics and Southern Protestants.

National Democratic leaders seemed unsuited to the conservative, *laissez-faire* economics of Social Darwinism sweeping the country during the period, while Republicans developed governmental policies favorable to the rise of an industrialized and urbanized United States. The one Democrat conservative enough to win a presidential election, Grover Cleveland, experienced only moderate success mimicking Republican economic policy. Conversely, populists such as William Jennings Bryan, the Democratic presidential nominee in 1896, 1900, and 1908, seemed too radical for most voters.

The Democrats continued their minority status during the first third of the twentieth century. The split between Theodore Roosevelt and William Howard Taft in 1912 allowed Woodrow Wilson to become the second Democrat to capture the presidency since the Civil War. Wilson's election also produced the Democratic Sixty-Third Congress, which created some of the most significant legislation of the twentieth century. In 1913, Congress passed the Federal Reserve Act, providing a more elastic monetary supply, the Underwood Tariff, the first downward foreign tax revision since the Civil War, and the Norris Amendment, a predecessor to the income tax.

Wilson's zealous pursuit of U.S. participation in the League of Nations after World War I repelled many Americans. Voters identified his party with the failure to democratize Europe after the fighting stopped. Businessmen particularly criticized Wilson's domestic wartime socialism. Eventually, the electoral mood of the public again turned conservative. Too much Democratic progressivism and internationalism produced a backlash that returned the country to isolation and the Republican politics of business from 1918 to 1930.

With the Republicans firmly in control of both houses of Congress during the 1920's, the Democrats divided along urban and rural lines on the crucial issues of the day: the KU KLUX KLAN, IMMIGRATION, and PROHIBITION. These controversial issues tore at the fabric of the party for more than a decade. Three Democratic presidential nominees in a row lost to the Republicans; then came the Depression.

The GREAT DEPRESSION became as much of a realigning event for the Democrats as the Civil War had been for the Republicans. Beginning with Franklin D. Roosevelt's landslide victory over Herbert Hoover in 1932, the Democrats won seven of the next nine presidential contests. The party of Roosevelt also controlled at least one house of Congress in all but two elections between 1930 and 1994.

Bill Clinton's 1992 victory made him the first Democrat to capture the presidency since 1976. (Reuters/Bettmann)

The 1992 Democratic National Convention in New York City. (AP/Wide World Photos)

Roosevelt created both the modern presidency and the powerful federal government that dominated the country for the remainder of the twentieth century. He wielded executive orders with impunity and exhibited great political expertise in pushing the first key pieces of "NEW DEAL" legislation through Congress.

The New Deal produced many changes from the Republicans' *laissez-faire*, free-enterprise approach to American life. The NATIONAL LABOR RELATIONS ACT (1935) protected labor's right to organize. The SOCIAL SECURITY ACT (1935) offered senior citizens and unemployed persons financial support. The Home Owners Loan Corporation (1933) kept people off the streets and in their houses. The Works Progress Administration (WPA) established the principle that the federal government constituted the employer of final resort.

Most Americans now identified the Democratic Party with the programs that saved America from the ravages of the Depression. Republicans who fought the New Deal frequently lost their seats in Congress. Leading the country through World War II, Roosevelt became the only president to win more than two elections, winning in 1932, 1936, 1940, and 1944. When he died on April 12, 1945, he bequeathed the institutions that revolutionized America.

The presidents who followed Roosevelt in the twentieth century did not attempt to revoke legacies of the New Deal. Republicans Dwight D. Eisenhower, Richard M. NIXON, Gerald Ford, Ronald REAGAN, and George BUSH considered Social Security untouchable. Conversely, Democrats such as Harry S Truman, John F. KENNEDY, Lyndon B. Johnson, Jimmy CARTER, and Bill CLINTON tried to expand the federal government's role through national health-care programs, AFFIRMATIVE ACTION, Medicare, Medicaid, and such programs as the PEACE CORPS and the JOB CORPS. Liberal Democrats thus perpetuated the approach to government established by Roosevelt in the half-century that followed World War II.

Not everyone agreed with the philosophy that government could solve most or all problems through the "tax-and-spend" philosophy pursued by the Roosevelt Democrats. Congressional conservatives questioned the cost-effectiveness of the liberal agenda. The agencies Roosevelt and his successors created, they argued, were both unfair and expensive. Beginning in the late 1930's, these minorities began voting together as a conservative coalition, although liberals and moderates usually outvoted them. Throughout the 1950's and 1960's, these "right wingers" sometimes blocked liberal legislation and slowly gained influence and prestige. Setbacks caused by Republican scandals involving President Richard M. Nixon and Vice President Spiro T. Agnew in the 1970's did not deter them, although the Democrats continued to win solid majorities in Congress.

During the 1980's, however, Ronald Reagan led a conservative "revolution" that began shifting the balance of power away from Democratic liberals in Congress and the White House. With the national debt increasing to nearly $3 trillion, conservative Democrats again joined their Republican colleagues in calling for a balanced budget and an end to the welfare programs initiated by Roosevelt and continued by every president and Congress since the 1930's. Reagan Republicans such as Newt GINGRICH and Richard Armey continued to push the New Right's agenda before the voters.

The 1990's, like the 1850's, found the Democratic Party deeply divided, as liberals such as Massachusetts senator Ted KENNEDY attempted to stem the party's turn to the right. The 1992 presidential election provided a case in point, as Arkansas governor Bill Clinton captured the White House as a moderate while his party expanded its control over both houses of Congress. When the Democrats failed in 1994 to solve crucial problems such as health care and the national debt, however, they lost both of their congressional majorities to the Republicans for the first time in forty years. Unable to define itself clearly with one voice and failing to cope with the newly emerging political realities of the late twentieth century, the Democratic Party in the 1990's faced an uncertain future.

—J. Christopher Schnell

SUGGESTED READINGS: The most comprehensive study of the Democratic Party is Robert Rutland's *The Democrats: From Jefferson to Carter* (Baton Rouge: Louisiana State University Press, 1979). Wilfred E. Binkley offers an older but highly readable account in *American Political Parties* (New York: Alfred A. Knopf, 1958). Also see Kevin Phillips' *Boiling Point: Democrats, Republicans, and the Decline of Middle-Class Prosperity* (New York: Random House, 1993).

Demographics, Canadian: Demographics (or demography) is that branch of sociology that studies the quantitative aspects of human populations. Demographers use birth and death rates and other statistics to characterize a population. Statistics Canada is the fact-

Some 5 million Canadians of French descent live in Québec province; here, residents of Québec vote in 1995 on the issue of whether Québec should separate from Canada. (Archive Photos/Reuters/Mike Blake)

gathering agency of the Canadian government. The census has been conducted once every ten years since 1851, when the population was 2,440,000.

Canada is the second-largest nation in the world (after Russia) in terms of area. It is the thirty-fifth largest in population, with a 1991 population of 28,114,000, 51 percent of which is female and 49 percent of which is male.

Vital Statistics. The birth rate in Canada is 14.48 births per 1,000 population per year; this figure is higher than that for the United States. The death rate is 7.35 deaths per 1,000 population per year, lower than in most other industrialized nations. These factors combine with the net immigration rate (5.68 immigrants per 1,000 population per year) to produce a population growth rate of 1.28 percent per year. At the time of marriage, the average female is twenty-four, and the average male is twenty-seven.

The average Canadian resident can expect to live to the age of seventy-eight. The life expectancy for males is seventy-six, for females, eighty-two. The average age of all Canadians is 31.6 years. About 21 percent are under the age of fifteen, and 12 percent are sixty-five or over.

The Canadian infant mortality rate is 7.0 infant deaths per 1,000 live births per year. This figure is among the lowest in the world, even when compared with the infant mortality rates of other industrialized nations.

Native Canadians. The Canadian population is composed of many racial and ethnic groups. Native Canadians make up 1.5 percent of the population of the Dominion of Canada. They include indigenous Indians and Inuit (sometimes referred to as "Eskimos") who had lived in the area for thousands of years before Europeans arrived. These groups represent a small minority of the Canadian population as a whole, but they are a major element in the northern regions. They make up the majority of residents in the Northwest Territories and are a significant proportion of the population of the Yukon.

There are ten major tribes, or "nations," to which most of Canada's Indians belong: the Algonquin, the Athapaskan, the Haida, the Iroquois, the Salishan, the Sioux, the Tlingit, the Kootenayan, the Tsimshian, and the Wakashan. The majority of Indians in Canada live within reservations called "reserves"; there are 2,250 reserves throughout the nation. The average standard of living of Canada's Indians is substantially lower than that of the non-Indian population.

European Canadians. Approximately 40 percent of Canada's population have British, Scotch, or Irish ancestry. About 26 percent have descended from French colonists, and another 25 percent immigrated from other nations in Europe. Québec is the only province not populated by predominantly British, Scotch, or Irish persons. About 5 million of the 6.5 million Canadians of French ancestry live in Québec. Repeated attempts have been made by French-speaking groups to establish Québec as a separate, independent nation.

Each of such referendums has failed, the latest in 1995.

Large numbers of Europeans have been attracted to Canada by political and religious freedoms as well as by the hope of economic opportunity. About 4 percent of Canadians are of German descent, 3 percent Italian, and 2 percent are Ukrainian in origin. In addition, there are sizable numbers of persons from The Netherlands, Hungary, Poland, Greece, Norway, Sweden, and Portugal.

Other Canadians. About 7 percent of the people of British Columbia are of Asian ancestry. Vancouver has in recent years accepted numbers of Chinese from Hong Kong, many of whom were prompted to emigrate by the scheduled reversion of Hong Kong to the control of the mainland Chinese government in 1997. Toronto has fairly large numbers of Asian Indians, Chinese, and West Indians. Blacks make up less than 1 percent of the Canadian population. The majority of these are West Indian, including Haitians.

Distribution. About 77 percent of Canadians live in metropolitan areas, 23 percent in rural areas. About 80 percent live within a hundred miles of the border with the United States. The most populous province is Ontario, with 36.9 percent of the Canadian population.

ETHNIC ORIGINS OF CANADIANS

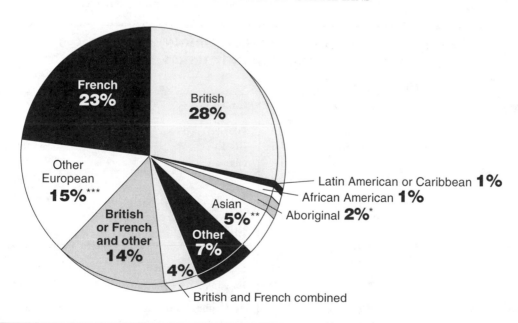

Source: Data are from "The Daily," Statistics Canada, February 23, 1993
*Includes American Indian, Inuit, and Métis   **Especially Chinese and Asian Indian   ***Especially German, Italian, and Ukrainian

Québec has 25.3 percent, followed by British Columbia with 12 percent. The smallest populations are in the Yukon Territory and the Northwest Territories, each with less than two-tenths of 1 percent of the Canadian population; Prince Edward Island has about six-tenths of 1 percent.

Ontario is the most urbanized province, with 80 percent of its population living in cities. The least urbanized province is Prince Edward Island, which is only 40 percent urban. The largest urban area is Toronto, Ontario, with a population of 3,893,046, followed by Montreal, Québec, with 3,127,242, and Vancouver, British Columbia, with 1,602,502. Other large Canadian cities include Ottawa-Hull, Ontario, with 920,000, Edmonton, Alberta, with 839,000, Calgary, Alberta, with 754,000, Winnipeg, Manitoba, with 652,000, and Québec, Québec, with a 1991 population of 645,000.

In terms of density, the most populated areas are Prince Edward Island, with 59 persons per square mile, Nova Scotia, with 34.4 persons per square mile, and New Brunswick, which has 21 persons per square mile. The least dense area is the Northwest Territories, with only 0.017 persons per square mile. The Yukon Territory has 0.07 persons per square mile, and Manitobe has 3.67 persons per square mile. Canada as a whole has a population density of only 7 persons per square mile, the lowest in the world.

Religion. There are numerous denominations, sects, and cults in Canada. National surveys indicate that 90 percent of the population identify themselves as Christians. More than 47 percent are Roman Catholic; 41.2 percent are Protestant (of these, 16 percent are in the United Church of Canada, and 10 percent are Anglican or Episcopalian; there are substantial numbers of Presbyterians, Lutherans, Baptists, Pentecostals, and Charismatics). About 1.5 percent are Orthodox, 1.2 percent Jewish, 0.4 percent Muslim, 0.3 percent Hindu, 0.3 percent Sikh, and 0.2 percent Buddhist. About 7.3 percent report having no religious identity whatsoever.

Education. Approximately 99 percent of Canadians age fifteen and above can read and write. Nearly 35 percent of Canadian females have at least a bachelor's degree from a college or university; more than 40 percent of Canadian males have completed four or more years of postsecondary education. Public schooling is available for the entire population. In some provinces, Catholic and Protestant schools are publicly funded. Canada has sixty-nine accredited colleges and universities, some of which teach entirely in the English language, some in French, and some of which are bilingual.

The Economy and Labor. About 66 percent of Canadian men and 56 percent of Canadian women are in the labor force. Fewer than 8 percent are unemployed. Ap-

CANADIAN POPULATION BY ETHNIC ORIGIN, 1986 AND 1991
TOP TEN SINGLE-ORIGIN ETHNIC GROUPS

1986 Group	Number	Percent	1991 Group	Number	Percent
British	6,332,725	25.3	French	6,146,605	22.8
French	6,093,160	24.4	British	5,611,050	20.8
German	896,720	3.6	German	911,560	3.4
Italian	709,590	2.8	Canadian	765,095	2.8
Ukrainian	420,210	1.7	Italian	750,055	2.8
Aboriginal	373,265	1.5	Chinese	586,645	2.2
Chinese	360,320	1.4	Aboriginal	470,615	1.7
Dutch (Netherlands)	351,765	1.4	Ukrainian	406,645	1.5
South Asian	266,800	1.1	Dutch (Netherlands)	358,185	1.3
Jewish	245,855	1.0	East Indian	324,840	1.2
Total population	**25,022,005**	**100.0**	**Total population**	**26,994,045**	**100.0**
Total single-origin population	**18,035,665**	**72.1**	**Total single-origin population**	**19,199,795**	**71.1**

Source: Susan B. Gall and Timothy L. Gall, eds., *Statistical Record of Asian Americans.* Detroit: Gale Research, 1993.

proximately 12.3 percent of Canadian families are below the poverty level. Statistics Canada considers a family as being in the low-income category if it must spend more than 58.8 percent of its annual income on the basic needs of food, clothing, and shelter. The poverty level for rural households is about 25 percent lower than for urban households. About 19 percent of poor families live in rural settings.

Projections. According to demographers, there will be more women than men in the labor force in Canada by the year 2020. Given current birth, death, and immigration rates, the Canadian population will continue to age far into the next century. Although such predictions could be modified by a host of factors, it seems certain that Canada will remain a world power with great natural resources and human potential.

—*Calvin Henry Easterling*

SUGGESTED READINGS: A solidly researched book that provides detailed statistics and facts about every province is *The Canadian Almanac and Directory* (Toronto: Canadian Almanac and Directory Publishing, 1996). For a fairly thorough but concise and easily readable background on Canada, see Desmond Morton's *A Short History of Canada* (Edmonton, Alberta: Hurtig Publishers, 1983). An interesting picture of the rich French influence on Canada can be found in Nancy Wartik's *French Canadians* (New York: Chelsea House, 1989). An illustrated and pungent explanation of the ongoing conflict between English-speaking and French-speaking Canadians in Québec is offered by Pierre Berton in *Canada Under Siege* (Willowdale, Ont.: McClelland and Stewart, 1992).

Demographics, U.S.: Quantitative aspects of the U.S. population. In the United States, the Bureau of the Census is the demographic fact-gathering agency of the government. The Census has been conducted once every ten years since 1790, when the population was 3,929,000.

Vital Statistics. The United States is the third most-populous nation in the world, with a 1990 population of 249,632,692, 51 percent of which is female and 49 percent of which is male. The U.S. birth rate is 15.48 births per 1,000 population per year; this figure is higher than in Western Europe and Canada. The death rate is 8.67 deaths per 1,000 population per year, about the same as in other industrialized nations. These factors combine with the net migration rate (3.41 immigrants per 1,000 population per year) to produce a

U.S. POPULATION BY RACE/ETHNICITY, 1990

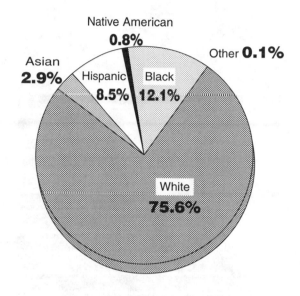

Source: Marlita A. Reddy, ed., *Statistical Record of Native North Americans.* Detroit: Gale Research, 1993.

population growth rate for the United States of 1.02 percent per year.

The average U.S. resident can expect to live to age seventy-six. The life expectancy for males is seventy-two; for females, seventy-nine. The average age of all Americans is thirty-four years. About 26 percent are under age eighteen, and 12.7 percent are age sixty-five or over.

The U.S. infant mortality rate is 8.36 infant deaths per 1,000 live births per year. This figure is favorable in comparison to Third World countries, but it is high in comparison with the infant mortality rates of other industrialized nations.

Native Americans. Native Americans make up 0.8 percent of the U.S. population. They include American Indians, Eskimos, and Aleuts. About half of the 2.2 million Native Americans live on or near reservations. There are three hundred such reservations, located primarily in South Dakota, New Mexico, Arizona, Utah, Washington, and Montana. Those who live outside the reservation sites reside primarily in urban areas of the western and central states. The largest concentration of Native Americans in an urban area is in Tulsa, Oklahoma.

AGE DISTRIBUTION OF THE U.S. POPULATION BY SEX, 1990

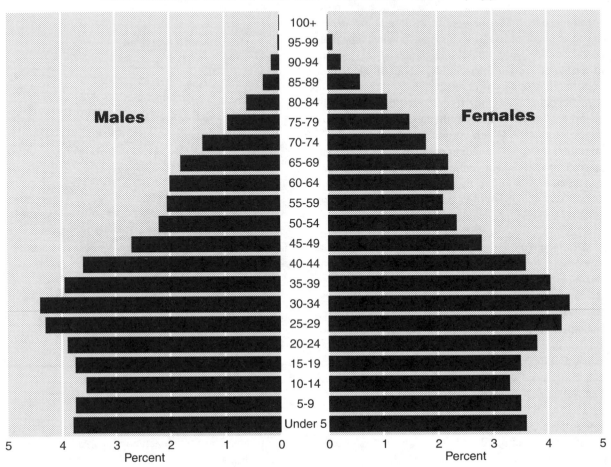

Source: U.S. Bureau of the Census.

African Americans. African Americans, most of whom are descendants of slaves, comprise 12.4 percent of the U.S. population, or 30,400,000. More than half live in the southern states; the others are concentrated in urban areas throughout the country. The most recent migration pattern for African Americans has been a movement away from northern industrial centers to the large cities of the South and West.

Hispanic Americans. Persons of Hispanic origin are those who classify themselves in one of the specific Hispanic categories listed on the census questionnaire. They may identify themselves as Mexican, Puerto Rican, Cuban, or "other." A person choosing the "other" category may self-identify with Central or South America or Spain. The Hispanic population was 22,354,000 in the 1990 Census, or 9.9 percent. The Hispanic population increased by more than 50 percent in the 1980's, largely as a result of both legal and illegal immigration. Mexican Americans make up 62 percent of the U.S. Hispanic population. They live primarily in Texas, New Mexico, Arizona, and Southern California. New York City and Miami have large concentrations of Puerto Ricans and Cubans.

Asian Americans. The 1990 Asian American population was 7,273,662, or 2.9 percent of the U.S. population. Asian Americans are the fastest-growing minority, having increased by more than 107 percent between 1980 and 1990. The "Asian American" label covers more than a dozen ethnic groups with diverse national origins, histories, religions, languages, and customs. The largest group is Chinese Americans, followed closely by Filipino Americans and roughly equal populations of Korean Americans, Japanese Americans, and Asian Indians.

European Americans. The vast majority of people in the United States are descended from Europeans. Large numbers were attracted to the country by political and religious freedoms as well as by the hope of economic opportunity. Before 1860, most immigrants were from England, Ireland, and Germany. Between 1860 and 1920, the majority of immigrants came from Russia, Poland, the Balkans, and Italy. In order, 13.1 percent of all immigrants to the United States have come from Germany, 9.9 percent from Italy, 9.5 percent from Great Britain, 8.8 percent from Ireland, and 6.4 percent from Russia.

Distribution. More than 79 percent of U.S. citizens live in metropolitan areas; more than 53 percent live in one of the forty-one metropolitan areas with popula-

tions of one million or more. The most populous states, in descending order are California, Texas, New York, Florida, Pennsylvania, and Illinois. The states with the smallest populations are Wyoming, Alaska, Vermont, Delaware, and North Dakota. More than 56 percent of the U.S. population lives in the southern and western sections of the country.

In terms of density, the most populated areas are the District of Columbia, with 9,883 persons per square mile, New Jersey, with 1,042 persons per square mile, and Rhode Island, with 960 persons per square mile. The least dense state is Alaska, with only one person per square mile. Wyoming has 4.7 and Montana 5.5 persons per square mile. The population center of the United States is approximately 9.7 miles northwest of Steelville, Missouri.

Religion. There are more than a thousand denominations, sects, and cults in the United States. National surveys indicate that 94 percent of the population ex-

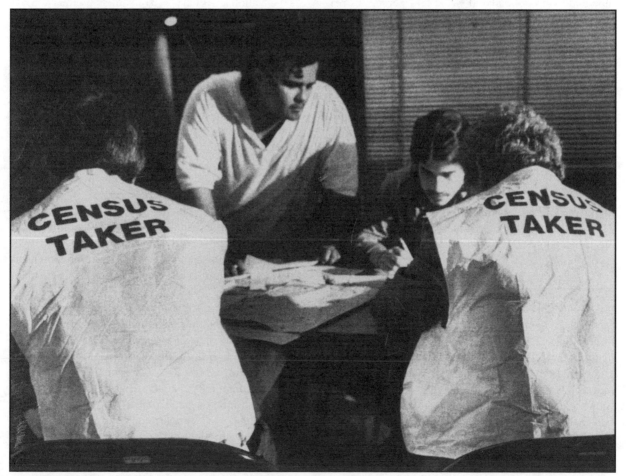

Officials gather information on U.S. demographics as part of the 1990 Census. (UPI/Bettmann Newsphotos)

press a belief in God and about 57 percent report that they either are members of a church or synagogue or have attended church within the last six months. Of these, 36 percent are Roman Catholic, 60 percent are Protestant, 6 million are Jewish, 2.6 million are Muslims, and 100,000 are Buddhists.

Approximately 87 percent of U.S. citizens identify themselves as Christian. The largest Christian organization is the Roman Catholic church, with about 57 million members in the United States. The largest Protestant denomination is the Southern Baptist Convention, which has 15 million members, followed by the United Methodist Church, with a membership of 9 million. Since the 1960's, there has been a shift in membership away from mainstream denominations toward evangelical and charismatic churches, whose members are "born again" and tend to be highly committed to their faith.

Education. Nearly 98 percent of Americans age fifteen and over can read and write; 80.2 percent of persons age twenty-five or over are high-school graduates; and 20.9 percent have at least a bachelor's degree from a college or university. Approximately 60 percent of all college students in the United States are female. An average of $4,700 is spend annually per pupil for public elementary and secondary schooling.

The Economy and Labor. About 76 percent of men and 60 percent of women are in the labor force. Approximately 6.7 percent are unemployed, and 14.5 percent are below the poverty level, which in 1992 was $14,335 of income per year for a family of four. More than 33 percent of all African Americans live below the poverty level, as do 29.3 percent of Hispanics and 11.6 percent of whites. Numerically, however, there are more poor whites than poor people of any other race.

Projections. There will be more women than men in the U.S. labor force by the year 2020. By the middle of the twenty-first century, non-Hispanic whites will no longer be in the numerical majority of the U.S. population, which will reach half a billion by the end of the next century. These predictions and many others are being made by social demographers who project current trends into the future. The actual direction of the future depends, of course, upon many factors. One certain fact, however, is that the United States will continue to be a nation of great diversity.

—*Calvin Henry Easterling*

SUGGESTED READINGS: A solidly researched book that provides detailed statistics and facts about every state and a multitude of comparisons of the states is *The World Almanac of the U.S.A.* by Allen Carpenter and Carl Provorse (Mahwah, N.J.: Funk and Wagnalls, 1993). An interesting warning about the dangers of overpopulation is sounded in Paul R. Ehrlich and Anne H. Ehrlich's *The Population Explosion* (New York: Simon & Schuster, 1990). Predictions and projections for the future may be found in *Toward the Twenty-first Century: A Special Report by the Population Institute to the 101st Congress* (Washington, D.C.: Population Institute, 1988). A classic and witty examination of the phenomenon of city dwelling is Herbert Gans's *The Urban Villagers* (New York: The Free Press, 1962).

Department of Defense, U.S.: Headquartered at the PENTAGON in Arlington, Virginia, the Department of Defense was created by the National Security Act Amendment of 1949. The basic structure was created as the National Military Establishment by the National Security Act of 1947. The new structure replaced the cabinet-level positions of secretary of war and secretary of the navy with a single secretary of defense. Responsible for the defense of the nation, the department consists of the Army, Navy, and Air Force. The Navy has responsibility for the Marine Corps and, during wartime, the Coast Guard. The Office of the Secretary of Defense and the Joint Chiefs of Staff assist and advise the secretary of defense and the president.

Department of Education, U.S.: Cabinet-level department that establishes federal education policy. The U.S. Department of Education was established with the passage of the Department of Education Organization Act. The first secretary of education was sworn in on December 6, 1979.

The department's mission is to ensure access to education and to promote educational excellence. The secretary of education is responsible for advising the president on education plans, policies, and programs of the federal government. The secretary's duties also include promoting the general public's understanding of the department's goals, objectives, and various programs; directing the department staff in the execution of various activities and programs; and performing specific duties involving the American Printing House for the Blind, Howard University, Gallaudet University, and the National Technical Institute for the Deaf, all of which are federally aided corporations.

The secretary of education is nominated by the president and must be approved by the Senate prior to taking office. The deputy secretary and undersecretary positions do not require Senate approval, but appointments are generally made as a result of collaboration between the secretary and presidential advisers. While upper-level positions are vulnerable to political currents and generally undergo total or near-total change with each incoming presidential administration, lower-level department positions are more stable. Regional offices of the department are located in ten cities: Atlanta, Boston, Chicago, Dallas, Denver, Kansas City, New York City, Philadelphia, San Francisco, and Seattle. These offices provide technical support to state and local educational agencies and serve as centers for the dissemination of information for institutions, agencies, and individuals.

Department of Health and Human Services, U.S.

(DHHS): Cabinet-level department of the executive branch of the federal government. The DHHS consists of five divisions: the Social Security Administration, the Health Care Financing Administration, the Office of Human Development Services, the Family Support Administration, and the Public Health Service. The DHHS is the main source of regulations affecting health care, and its secretary is the main adviser to the president on health and welfare issues. Branches of the DHHS are responsible for programs such as Social Security, Medicare, and Medicaid. The FOOD AND DRUG ADMINISTRATION (FDA), CENTERS FOR DISEASE CONTROL AND PREVENTION (CDC), and NATIONAL INSTITUTES OF HEALTH (NIH) are all under the direction of the DHHS.

Department of Justice, U.S.:

Agency of the executive branch of the U.S. federal government that represents the government's legal interests. The organization was created and placed under the authority of the attorney general, the federal government's chief legal officer, in 1870.

The Department of Justice investigates and enforces federal laws, supervises the federal prison system, pro-

The Department of Justice building in Washington, D.C. (McCrea Adams)

vides legal counsel in cases involving the federal government, interprets laws related to the activities of other federal departments, conducts all suits that are brought to the U.S. Supreme Court in which the federal government is concerned, and provides legal advice to the president and cabinet members.

The attorney general, with assistance from the deputy attorney general, the associate attorney general, and the solicitor general, oversees a department of over fifty-four thousand employees, including more than forty-two hundred lawyers. With the exception of the FEDERAL BUREAU OF INVESTIGATION (FBI), each division of the department is headed by an assistant attorney general. The department's field activities are carried out by U.S. attorneys and U.S. marshals. The attorney general, the solicitor general, the director of the FBI, and the district U.S. attorneys and marshals are all appointed by the president, with approval by the Senate.

The attorney general supervises and directs the Department of Justice, providing organization and direction to each of the various divisions and organizations that make up the department. Reporting directly to the attorney general are the FBI, the federal government's primary law-enforcement organization, the Office of Legal Policy, the Office of Legal Counsel, the Office of Professional Responsibility, and the Office of Intelligence Policy and Review. The solicitor general, the associate attorney general, and the deputy attorney general also report directly to the attorney general.

The solicitor general oversees all U.S. Supreme Court litigation that concerns the federal government. The associate attorney general is responsible for the Criminal Division, the IMMIGRATION AND NATURALIZATION SERVICE (INS), the Bureau of Prisons, the U.S. Parole Commission, the Pardon Attorney, the U.S. Marshal's Service, and the Board of Immigration and Appeal. The deputy attorney general is responsible for the Antitrust Division, the Civil Division, the Civil Rights Division, the Land and Natural Resources Division, the Tax Division, the Office of Justice Assistance, the Research and Statistics Office, the Community Relations Service, the U.S. Trustees, and the Foreign Claims Settlement Commission.

The Department of Justice represents the U.S. people through its detection and prevention of crime, regulation of aliens and immigrants, prohibition of the abuse or illegal use of controlled substances, enforcement of the civil and criminal laws enacted by Congress, assistance of communities experiencing racial tensions, protection of the economy from unfair business practices, application of the internal revenue laws to ensure that taxes are paid properly, and protection of civil rights. Further, its capacity as an adviser to the federal judiciary significantly influences U.S. constitutional government.

Department of National Defence, Canadian (DND): Canadian government agency responsible for protecting Canada's national sovereignty. The DND's headquarters are located in Ottawa, the national capital. The department is staffed by both military and civilian personnel. The minister of national defense, a civilian nominated by the prime minister, administers the department. The chief of the general staff, a senior military officer, advises the prime minister. The Canadian parliament annually debates the merits of providing funds to implement DND policies and activities, including Canada's participation in the NORTH ATLANTIC TREATY ORGANIZATION (NATO).

Depo-Provera: Injected contraceptive. Depo-Provera inhibits the secretion of gonadotropins, suppressing ovulation; the effectiveness of the drug depends on regular reinjections. Once Depo-Provera use is discontinued, the average woman requires about ten months to conceive. Women who use Depo-Provera have an increased risk of developing bleeding irregularities and osteoporosis. The product is convenient and well suited for individuals who have difficulty remembering to take oral contraceptives daily or for those who find the use of condoms or other barrier methods of contraception objectionable. While Depo-Provera prevents pregnancy, it does not protect against AIDS and other SEXUALLY TRANSMITTED DISEASES.

Deportation: Expulsion of aliens who are considered threats to public welfare or who are in the country illegally, usually to their native countries or the country from which they came. Immigration laws provide for the deportation of legally admitted aliens who are convicted of crimes against persons or property, who violate narcotics laws, or who engage in subversive activities. Naturalized citizens who lied in their applications for admission to the United States may also be expelled from the country. The IMMIGRATION AND NATURALIZATION SERVICE (INS) has primary responsibility for administering deportation procedures, with appeals possible to the federal courts.

Depression, economic: Situation in which national output declines substantially, with a consequent decrease in business activity, income, and prices and a significant increase in UNEMPLOYMENT. The most severe depression in U.S. history occurred in the decade following 1929. Since then, there have been several RECESSIONS (a milder economic malaise in which output declines perhaps 2 or 3 percent and unemployment rises to as high as 10 percent) but no real depression. Social problems arise from the unemployment, bankruptcies, debt foreclosures, and defaults that accompany depressions and recessions. Historically, the chief cause of economic depression has been decline in total spending for goods and services; however, depressions can also result from wars, revolutions, and other social upheavals.

Depression, psychological: One of the most common mental health problems. In the United States, the most medically recognizable form, major depression, affects between 10 percent and 25 percent of women and between 5 percent and 15 percent of men. Of these individuals, nearly 15 percent die by suicide.

In contrast to sadness, major depression is best characterized by a greater intensity and longer duration of intense feelings. Specific symptoms include a loss of interest or pleasure in activities normally enjoyed, change in weight or appetite, sleep disturbance, and fatigue. Feelings of guilt or worthlessness, ideas of suicide, agitation or, alternatively, slowed reactions, and difficulty concentrating are also common signs of major depression.

Depression has biological, behavioral, and environmental causes. It is associated with many kinds of causes and, therefore, it requires skilled diagnosis. Acute and chronic physical illnesses, stress, seasonal changes in light, sudden losses, and developmental life changes all can result in psychological depression. It appears to be more common for women than men; there is debate, however, as to whether lower diagnosis rates are truly the result of men experiencing less depression. Instead, it may be that men simply express depression differently than women—for example, as anger or through alcohol abuse. It should be noted, however, that for men, psychological depression can be quite devastating; men who attempt suicide succeed more often than women.

The treatment of depression can be ordinary or controversial, depending on the type of person being treated. With average adults, there is not much controversy. Normal treatment usually involves ruling out physical causes, such as major physical illnesses. Following that, psychiatric medication and therapy are typical courses of treatment. With children and the elderly, however, treatment is somewhat different.

Children are not identical to adults; thus, symptoms may be expressed differently. In addition to the symptoms mentioned, children may display psychotic features, aggression, accident proneness, or variable alterations in mood. Treatment is also different for children. It often involves family members' participation in psychotherapy, as well as the use of psychiatric medications for the child. Because of potential for the medications to affect development in children, the use of medication is somewhat controversial. Some argue that medications should be used just as aggressively as with adults; others suggest that medication should be a last course of action.

With elders, similar problems arise with treatment. Depressed elders are at a higher risk for suicide than younger people and so the delivery of rapid and effective treatment becomes even more critical. Medications and psychotherapy are helpful, however, they take time to have an effect. Additionally, physical health problems and the aging process change the way drugs are metabolized in the body and sometimes make antidepressants inappropriate. As such, physicians sometimes use shock treatment, more formally known as electroconvulsive therapy (ECT) to treat depression. ECT remains controversial because it has serious side effects such as memory loss, and its mechanisms for alleviating depression are not well understood. In the case of treating depression in those who cannot use or are not responding to other treatments, however, it presents a humane alternative to leaving a patient severely depressed and at risk for suicide.

Deregulation: Removal of governmental controls over private business practices and transactions. Deregulation typically occurs in response to a government's taking undue control of an industry; often, an industry's poor performance as the result of regulatory restrictions motivates such action.

The 1980's saw an increase in deregulatory actions

that affected a broad range of industries. Control of economic, organizational, and developmental matters was returned to the various industries including air transportation, shipping, and telecommunications. This move was a fundamental part of President Ronald REAGAN's "Reagan Revolution." Supporters see deregulation as returning rights that should belong to the private sector; critics counter that the government has a right to dictate business practices and that its proper role is to mitigate the actions of business, to the supposed advantage of consumers.

The U.S. government takes an active role in directing various industries. This control ranges from dictating what companies can charge their clients to demanding various testing and safety protocols. Deregulation allows companies to assume that control. For example, Congress created the federal Civil Aeronautics Board (CAB) and granted it sole power over the financial management of the air transportation industry. Its powers included the authority to aid and promote air travel in small communities, to give licenses to airlines, to accept or reject rate and fare proposals, and to approve or reject proposed mergers and consolidations of companies. Legislation in the late 1970's provided for the deregulation of the industry, and later legislation called for elimination of the CAB. While the air-transportation industry underwent such deregulation in the 1970's and 1980's, the federal government maintained a certain level of control. The FEDERAL AVIATION ADMINISTRATION (FAA) holds power to govern all commerce associated with air transportation, monitor air-traffic control, initiate work and testing that will bring about the production of advanced aircraft, and administer sanctions if regulations are not approved. The government has assumed this role to provide for the growth and safety of air travel.

Controversy concerning regulation ultimately concerns two opposing views of private industry—the view that private property is wholly owned by its owner, who enjoys the right to do with that property as he or she wishes, provided that it does not infringe on the rights of others, and the view that it is the government's right to control private property and to guarantee that the interests of the nation's citizenry are met by use of that property.

SUGGESTED READINGS: Robert Novak's *The Reagan Revolution* (New York: Dutton, 1981) offers insight into the conservative movement to deregulate industry and the ideology of the Reagan Revolution phenomenon. *Contrived Competition: Regulation and*

Deregulation in America by Richard Vietor (Cambridge, Mass.: Belknap Press of Harvard University Press, 1994) explores the relationship between the government and private industry, considering the effectiveness of regulatory actions. Gary Mucciaroni's *Reversals of Fortune: Public Policy and Private Interests* (Washington, D.C.: Brookings Institution, 1995) presents an examination of regulatory acts and the marketplace.

Desegregation: Efforts to end SEGREGATION of the races. In the aftermath of the Civil War and the ending of slavery in 1865, segregation between blacks and whites, especially in the South, became the norm in the United States. Although segregation was not usually mandated by law, few schools or other public facilities were integrated anywhere in the country. In 1896, the Supreme Court in PLESSY V. FERGUSON ruled that a Louisiana law permitting the provision of "separate but equal" public facilities for the races did not violate the Constitution. After the decision, Southern states enacted a wide range of JIM CROW LAWS mandating segregation in most walks of public life. Outside the South, few such laws existed, but social practice maintained fairly rigid segregation in the absence of law.

In the early twentieth century, civil rights advocates such as W. E. B. DU BOIS and other founders of the NATIONAL ASSOCIATION FOR THE ADVANCEMENT OF COLORED PEOPLE (NAACP) began a long political and legal battle to have legally mandated segregation declared a violation of the Fourteenth Amendment. In the 1940's and 1950's, Thurgood MARSHALL of the NAACP's Legal Defense Fund led a concerted legal battle against segregation in public schools; in 1954, the Supreme Court agreed with Marshall's arguments in the case BROWN V. BOARD OF EDUCATION OF TOPEKA, KANSAS. The Court's decision requiring desegregation in public schooling was met with widespread resistance in the South; when the ruling's provisions were interpreted to outlaw many aspects of de facto desegregation, many whites around the country also expressed hostility to the prospect of INTEGRATION. Nevertheless, backed by the power of law, desegregation forces made steady progress.

The courts eventually extended the logic of the *Brown* decision to ban virtually all legally mandated forms of segregation. During the 1960's, moreover, the federal government moved to outlaw segregation practices by private individuals and firms. These actions

A black girl and a white girl in a Virginia classroom examine each other on the first day of legally mandated school desegregation in 1954. (UPI/Corbis-Bettmann)

culminated in the passage of the CIVIL RIGHTS ACT OF 1964, which banned segregation and other forms of discrimination on a broad scale.

Spurred by the Civil Rights movement and other social-justice movements of the 1960's and 1970's, legislatures and courts acted to oppose segregation in virtually all walks of life. Most such efforts met with broad public approval, typically generating opposition only from avowed racists or from interest groups that perceived integration as a threat. However, some such governmentally mandated actions, notably efforts to integrate public schools by BUSING students to distant facilities and attempts to integrate workplaces and schools via AFFIRMATIVE ACTION programs, have gen-

erated heated controversies and have led to charges of rights abuses and "REVERSE DISCRIMINATION."

Developing nations: Term applied generally to the less economically advanced nations of Asia, Africa, and Latin America. Since World War II, these nations have tried to make the transition from economies producing raw materials for export to balanced economies that include modern industrial sectors.

Some developing nations, such as South Korea, Taiwan, and some Latin America nations, have made large strides toward the creation of developed economies. Yet despite aid programs by industrial nations, organizations such as the INTERNATIONAL MONETARY FUND (IMF) and the WORLD BANK, and the United Nations, many developing nations have seen their economies stagnate. Some observers argue that only a massive transfer of technology and investment from industrialized nations to developing nations can end the growing inequality between developing and developed nations.

Dieting: Deliberate efforts at weight loss. Billions of dollars are spent each year on weight-loss products and services; however, only about 5 percent of those people who lose weight maintain that weight loss. As a consequence of the widespread desire for thinness, quick weight-loss systems, which are often detrimental to one's health, have thrived. The most effective method of dieting involves lifestyle changes that include exercise, a balanced diet, and behavior modification.

The social standard of beauty has changed throughout history. In the 1900's, to be thin was considered unsightly and connoted a person at risk of disease. In the 1960's, the model Twiggy, who was naturally thin, became the epitome of beauty. Thus, the trend to reshape the body through dieting became popular and was fueled by the growing diet industry.

Common characteristics of fad diets are that they promote quick weight loss, focus on a limited food selection, highlight testimonials from famous people, require expensive supplements, and suggest that the diet is a cure-all. Fad diets generally fail because they are often nutritionally inadequate, lack a scientific basis, and do not address the basic lifestyle changes necessary to maintain a healthy weight for an individual.

Chronic dieting not only can have negative physical and psychological consequences but can also cause future weight loss to be even more difficult. Weight cycling, or the "yo-yo syndrome," can increase the risks of body-fat deposition and heart disease. Lean muscle mass is the primary metabolizing tissue in the body; the greater the ratio of an individual's lean muscle mass to fat tissue, the better. In a study on weight-fluctuating mice, it was demonstrated that each time the mice gained weight back, there was a greater percentage of fat tissue gained, and a lesser percentage of lean tissue, making future weight loss more difficult. Humans respond similarly.

An effective weight-loss program should include slow, steady weight loss, which means weight loss should be only one to two pounds per week. Regular physical activity is also important, because it not only uses up more energy but also provides the benefit of cardiovascular fitness. A variety of foods from the five food groups should be included on a daily basis in order to meet one's nutritional needs. Effective weight-loss maintenance should include physical activity, balanced diet, and permanent behavior changes.

Dillingham Report: Findings of the Immigration Commission of 1907 that concluded that unlimited IMMIGRATION created unmanageable social problems. The commission was created in response to the Immigration Restriction League, which wanted immigration restricted by requiring literacy tests for admission to the United States. The commission's exhaustive forty-two volume report examined the impact of immigration on American life; the findings revealed no evidence to correlate new immigration with feeble-mindedness, crime, epilepsy, or tuberculosis, but it nevertheless endorsed the use of literacy tests to stem immigration. The recommendation, implemented in the 1917 Immigration Act, is still a requirement for immigration to the United States.

Disability insurance: Economic benefit that provides income to a person unable to work as a result of an accident or illness. Payments continue as long as the disability lasts or for the maximum time period set by the applicable insurance policy. Disability insurance is usually purchased at work under a group plan, but it may be bought as an individual policy.

Disability rights: The struggle to obtain rights for the disabled revolves around basic issues regarding such revered American values as liberty and the pursuit of personal happiness. In fact, many of the "rights" sought by people with disabilities are simple aspects of life that are taken for granted by most able-bodied people.

History. During the mid-nineteenth century, special schools began to be established throughout the United States for deaf and blind people; the presidency of Abraham Lincoln was notable for the founding of a number of such schools. During the remainder of the century, more such schools were begun, primarily with assistance from philanthropists and often under the impetus of individuals with a personal association with these disabilities. For the most part, however, persons with disabilities were long merely tolerated and were kept out of sight.

Economic expansion, depression, and war dominated American social consciousness during the first half of the twentieth century. In the rebuilding that followed the conclusion of World War II, small groups of people began to meet and discuss issues related to disabilities. Parents of children with disabilities met to share experiences and provide support for one another. The notion of collective action began to permeate these meetings.

Advocacy groups began to form during this era. Many are still in existence, although many have changed their names. The Muscular Dystrophy Association of America, the United Cerebral Palsy Association, the National Federation of the Blind, and the National Association for Retarded Children all had their origins in the postwar era. Each had a different agenda and related to persons with different disabilities. Collectively, however, they began to raise a loud voice of protest about the manner in which disabled persons were treated. The groups raised money to support research concerning specific disabilities and provide recreational programs that were modified to make them accessible to disabled people.

The postwar era was also marked by technological innovations to help the disabled. Many everyday items and devices were modified to allow disabled people to utilize them. The control systems of automobiles were modified to allow those with handicaps to drive, giving many disabled persons additional mobility and, more important, freeing them from dependence on others. New applications were found for transistors, which were themselves fairly new in electronic markets. Disabled persons were given electronic assistance that allowed them to read, write, and—in some instances—talk. The development of such products and aids has been an important ongoing adjunct to the effort to improve the ability of the disabled to participate in society and to lead full, productive lives.

As late as the 1950's, there was widespread legal discrimination against disabled persons in the United States. Although the disabled were not denied the right to vote, seventeen states, for example, prohibited persons with epilepsy from marrying.

The collective attention of America became focused on CIVIL RIGHTS during the close of the 1950's and early 1960's, and the rights-centered activism that per-

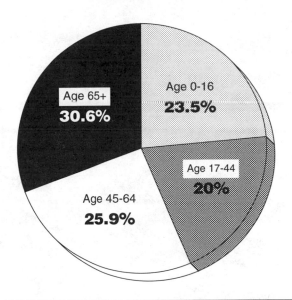

DISABLED U.S. CITIZENS BY AGE GROUP

Age 65+ **30.6%**

Age 0-16 **23.5%**

Age 17-44 **20%**

Age 45-64 **25.9%**

Source: From Gregory J. Walters, *Equal Access: Safeguarding Disability Rights.* Human Rights series, p. 3. Vero Beach, Fla.: Rourke Corp., 1992

Note: Total number of persons with disabilities in the United States: approximately 42.5 million

vaded many sectors of society soon spread to the disabled. Inspired by the example of the CIVIL RIGHTS MOVEMENT and related social justice campaigns, disabled Americans began to conduct letter-writing campaigns and to stage events such as "wheel-ins," public demonstrations in which people in wheelchairs blocked entrances to public buildings to draw attention to problems of access.

Many Americans became disabled in the 1960's and 1970's as a result of the VIETNAM WAR, and many disabled veterans became vocal activists upon their return, speaking out stridently against the social inequities visited upon the disabled. Members of such groups as the Disabled American Veterans and the Paralyzed Veterans of America drew substantial publicity to the plight of the disabled; because many members of these groups had acquired their handicaps in dramatic fashion while in the service of their country, they became the focus of much media attention.

The Americans with Disabilities Act. The AMERICANS WITH DISABILITIES ACT (ADA) was signed into law by President George BUSH on July 26, 1990, and

A computer controlled by acoustic signals developed for use by the disabled. (Reuters/Bettmann)

went into effect in January, 1992. Advocates hailed the legislation, which protects the civil rights of disabled persons, as the Emancipation Proclamation of the disabled.

The ADA defines a "disability" as a physical or mental impairment that substantially limits an individual's life activities. This definition includes people with impaired sight or hearing, muscular dystrophy or cerebral palsy, CANCER or epilepsy, emotional impairment or a low level of intelligence, or a cosmetic disfigurement. Individuals who have AIDS or who test positive for the HUMAN IMMUNODEFICIENCY VIRUS (which leads to AIDS) are included as being disabled. While this list

defines disabilities quite widely, it excludes drug users, compulsive gamblers, and individuals with sexual disorders. Under the ADA, being a member of a minority group is not synonymous with having a disability.

The ADA is intended to allow disabled persons to participate in all aspects of life to the greatest extent they can; according to its mandates, societal and physical barriers to such participation are to be removed on an accelerated basis. Employment opportunities, governmental services, public accommodations, transportation, education, and communication systems are to be made as accessible to the disabled as to those without disabilities.

Title III of the ADA requires that all public places make any necessary changes so that persons with disabilities can have equal access to facilities; denying such access is considered a form of discrimination. Places of public accommodation include sources of lodging such as motels, hotels, and inns; exceptions are made only for establishments with fewer than five rentable rooms in which the owner also resides. Places that offer entertainment or that serve meals or drinks are also covered. Auditoriums, convention centers, retail stores, service establishments, and professional offices must all be barrier-free. Transportation terminals, cultural facilities, schools, and social-service centers are also covered by the act. Indoor and outdoor recreational facilities, including camps, must have some barrier-free facilities to accommodate handicapped persons. Existing facilities can be renovated, but all new construction must be readily accessible to all. The only other exceptions to the ADA's requirements are made for buildings that have fewer than four stories or that are smaller than three thousand square feet in area.

There is some flexibility in how the act can be interpreted. "Reasonable" accommodation is just that: reasonable. For example, all of the trails and buildings of a summer camp need not be altered to provide access for wheelchair-bound persons; paving a portion of the trails and modifying some buildings to be barrier-free would be sufficient. Restaurants do not need to provide menus in Braille to accommodate blind customers; a server who can read the menu to sight-impaired customers is sufficient.

The ADA also makes it illegal to discriminate against disabled persons in terms of employment; however, the rule of reasonable accommodation also applies where the health or safety of others is potentially at risk. Thus, a blind person cannot serve as a rifle-range supervisor but may be fully qualified to teach basketry. A wheelchair-bound person would be inappropriate as a life guard but might be fully qualified as a computer-systems operator.

The ADA requires that public transportation be available to all persons. For those with a disability, this may mean special accommodations or vehicles. Municipalities are required to provide barrier-free transportation facilities. The ADA allows an exception where the financial burden to provide alternative services is excessive. This loophole has been exploited by some municipalities. All train and light rail (subway and trolley) stations must be accessible; there are no exceptions. Despite these seemingly stringent requirements, alternative transportation systems designed exclusively for persons with disabilities are seen as discriminatory by some critics.

Other Important Legislation. The needs of the disabled have been addressed from a variety of perspectives via numerous pieces of legislation. The following summary gives a sense of the time that has been required for disabled persons to achieve equal status; it also demonstrates the accelerating pace of relevant legislation that culminated in the 1990 passage of the ADA.

In the mid-1930's, the Crippled Children's Services were established by an executive order from President Franklin D. Roosevelt. The purpose of the program was to provide specialized medical care and rehabilitation for children with disabilities whose families were unable to pay for the services. These units still exist and continue to provide funding in every state.

An early attempt to address issues related to housing for disabled persons was the Housing Act of 1949. This act made persons with disabilities eligible to be included in housing projects funded with federal money. Eligibility for inclusion did not, however, guarantee access; up to 1964, virtually no housing units accessible to the disabled were built in the United States.

In 1956, the SOCIAL SECURITY ACT was amended to allow DISABILITY INSURANCE payments to persons aged fifty and above. Although this first step was initially hailed by advocates for the disabled, those under the age of fifty soon began to sound the battle cry of discrimination.

The Housing and Urban Development Act of 1965 included persons with disabilities by making them eligible for rent subsidies. This reprised a similar but unsuccessful attempt made in the Housing Act of 1949. One thousand housing units were constructed for the disabled between 1964 and 1975.

Title I of the ELEMENTARY AND SECONDARY EDUCATION ACT of 1965 pertained to handicapped children. The legislation attempted to ensure that children with LEARNING DISABILITIES or mental handicaps received equal access to all educational classes and facilities.

The ARCHITECTURAL BARRIERS ACT of 1968 required that any building that was constructed or leased using federal funds had to be accessible to the disabled. This act, however, was of limited value because it pertained only to public buildings. Further, military and private structures were not covered by the act, and enforcement of its provisions was lax.

Disability rights

The EDUCATION OF THE HANDICAPPED ACT of 1969 expanded the provisions of the Elementary and Secondary Education Act of 1965. This legislation mandated that public schools provide counseling services, extracurricular activities, physical-education classes, health services, and transportation for children with disabilities, in addition to providing them with basic educational instruction. The Federal Aid to Highways Act of 1973 required that all street or highway projects built with federal money allow complete access to all persons. The requirement for ramps on curbs at intersections was first promulgated by this act.

The outcry originally sounded after passage of the Social Security Act of 1956, which limited federal disability insurance payments to persons over the age of fifty, was addressed in 1973 with the passage of the REHABILITATION ACT. This legislation created and funded programs for persons with disabilities; it also contained an early outline of a civil rights platform for the disabled. Title V of the 1973 act states that no otherwise qualified handicapped individual can, on the basis of a disability, be "excluded from participation in, be denied benefits of, or be subjected to discrimination under any program or activity receiving federal

A 1972 rally at the Capitol by disability rights activists. (UPI/Bettmann)

financial assistance." The Rehabilitation Act also represented the first federal attempt to deny financial assistance to any school, hospital, housing project, or transportation or welfare program that did not make its facilities completely accessible to disabled persons. Like the 1968 Architectural Barriers Act, however, the Rehabilitation Act was loosely enforced. Enforcement failings contributed to the pressure that culminated in passage of the AMERICANS WITH DISABILITIES ACT in 1990.

Disabled persons became eligible for rent subsidies under the terms of the Housing and Community Development Act of 1974. For the first time, the federal government paid for alterative living arrangements that accommodated the needs of persons with disabilities. It also provided funds to modify existing housing units by removing barriers and constructing external means of access. This act has been termed the single most important piece of federal housing legislation for persons with disabilities.

The EDUCATION FOR ALL HANDICAPPED CHILDREN ACT was passed in 1975. The primary goal of the act was to provide complete access to education for every disabled person between the ages of three and twenty-one. The law contains specific requirements that school districts must meet as a condition of receiving or retaining funding.

The Developmental Disabilities, Rehabilitation, and Comprehensive Services Amendments of 1978 authorized vocational rehabilitation agencies for persons with disabilities. The amendments also established independent living programs for elderly persons who were blind and created advocacy programs for individuals with severe disabilities. The amendments also changed the definitions of developmental disabilities; more than two hundred different disabilities were specifically delineated in the legislation. Also in 1978, the Housing and Community Development Act sponsored eight demonstration projects that addressed the needs of disabled people by attempting to make them more independent.

In 1984, the VOTING ACCESSIBILITY FOR THE ELDERLY AND HANDICAPPED ACT was enacted. This legislation required that all polling places must be accessible to handicapped voters. It also required each state to have a reasonable number of polling places that are conveniently accessible to persons with disabilities. This act provided closure to 1974 class-action suits that first raised the issue of access to voting places.

Under the terms of the AIR CARRIERS ACCESS ACT of 1986, no air carrier may discriminate against any handicapped person. Compliance with this legislation has required the interiors of some aircraft to be redesigned to allow wheelchair access.

Notable Legal Cases. Many legal suits have considered the rights of the disabled and society's obligations to accommodate such rights. In 1971, for example, the Pennsylvania Association for Retarded Children filed and won a lawsuit against the Commonwealth of Pennsylvania (*PARC v. COMMONWEALTH OF PENNSYLVANIA*). The ruling became a landmark for its declaration that mentally retarded children were better served by placement in regular public-school classrooms than in special-education classes. For the first time, the courts had affirmed the right of mentally handicapped children to equal access to public education. Schools were prohibited from assigning children to special-education classes without first notifying parents; and parents were accorded the right to challenge such placement decisions. The concept of the "least restrictive environment" enunciated in the decision eventually evolved into the practice of "mainstreaming" children with disabilities.

The 1972 decision in *MILLS V. BOARD OF EDUCATION OF DISTRICT OF COLUMBIA* was a second important ruling. The court expanded the scope of previous rulings by extending the right of a public education to all individuals with disabilities. It also noted that a plea of "insufficient funds" on the part of school boards was not an acceptable excuse for denying disabled people equal access to education.

In 1972, a disabled attorney in Cleveland, Ohio, filed a class-action suit, *FRIEDMAN V. COUNTY OF CUYAHOGA*, arguing that a lack of access provisions for the disabled at the county courthouse abridged his First Amendment right to petition. He also argued that the barriers in the building violated his rights to equal protection, freedom of movement, and equal opportunity guaranteed by the Fourteenth Amendment. Cuyahoga County entered into a consent decree before a court verdict could be reached, promising to make all county-owned buildings accessible. Nevertheless, the case was widely quoted in subsequent legal briefs filed in support of access for disabled people.

In 1974, in another class-action suit, *Seph et al. v. Council of the City of Los Angeles et al.*, attorneys argued that because disabled voters could not enter polling places as a consequence of architectural barriers, their constitutional right to vote was violated. The presiding judge suggested that absentee ballots could be used to overcome the difficulty; the plaintiffs argued that forcing the disabled to use absentee ballots segregated them and discouraged them from voting. This issue was not completely resolved for another decade.

Ongoing Struggles. The term "handicapped" implies an impaired status or an incomplete person who is somehow second-class. The gradual replacement of the term "handicapped" with the more neutral "disabled"—a change reflected in the title of the ADA—has helped to remove some of the stigma associated with impairments. Moreover, much legislation and public consciousness-raising has helped to improve the position of the disabled in American society. Nevertheless, disabled persons face an ongoing, often uphill struggle in a world created largely by and for persons with few physical limitations.

—*L. Fleming Fallon, Jr.*

SUGGESTED READINGS: Edward Berkowitz's *Disabled Policy: America's Programs for the Handicapped* (Cambridge, England: Cambridge University Press, 1987) traces the political history of the disabilities movement; the writing is scholarly but accessible. Frank Bowe's *Handicapping America: Barriers to Disabled People* (New York: Harper & Row, 1978), though somewhat dated, is otherwise a classic on the issue of barriers faced by persons with disabilities. Charles Goldman's *Disability Rights Guide: Practical Solutions to Problems Affecting People with Disabilities* (Lincoln, Neb.: Media Publishing, 1991), written for students and professionals who interact with the disabled, is one of the best works on the topic.

Jean M. Knox's *Learning Disabilities* (New York: Chelsea House, 1989), with an introduction by former Surgeon General C. Everett Koop, discusses learning disabilities, their nature, possible causes, and potential treatments and is especially good for younger readers. The Resources for Rehabilitation's *Resources for People with Disabilities and Chronic Conditions* (Lexington, Mass.: Resources for Rehabilitation, 1991) is an excellent resource for both the disabled and students wanting to know more about disability issues.

Discrimination, racial: Unequal treatment of people based on their physical traits or cultural practices. Actions that deny members of a racial or ethnic group the opportunities that would be granted to similarly qualified members of another group constitute discrimination. The term "REVERSE DISCRIMINATION" is sometimes used to criticize programs designed to overcome the effects of past discrimination against racial and ethnic minorities.

Minorities. A racial or ethnic minority is a category of people whose physical appearance or cultural heritage is unlike those of the dominant group, making them targets for differential treatment. When individuals are denied jobs, choice of residential location, and access to higher education simply because of their membership in some racial or ethnic group, discrimination is at work. Chinese Americans, for instance, have distinctive physical traits and, for those who maintain a traditional way of life, cultural practices that can be used to distinguish them from other groups. Ethnic characteristics, however, should not be viewed as racial. For example, Jews are occasionally identified as a RACE although they are unique only in their religious beliefs and shared historical experiences.

A race is a category of people who share biologically inherited traits, such as skin color and facial features. Ethnicity, on the other hand, is shared culture, which includes language and religion. Race and ethnicity are not the same: one is biological, the other cultural. Discrimination can be based on either one or both. Therefore, the term racial discrimination can be applied to unequal treatment of people distinguished by physical traits or cultural practices.

Causes. A variety of perspectives have been used to explain discrimination. Psychological explanations of discrimination focus on the prejudiced person's personality. One prominent psychological explanation of prejudice and discrimination is the scapegoat theory, or the frustration-aggression explanation.

According to the scapegoat theory, discrimination occurs when people place the blame for their troubles on some relatively powerless group. Scapegoating typically occurs when an individual or group feels threatened but is unable to express aggression against the actual threat. A white supervisor earning low wages in a retail store, for instance, might understandably be frustrated with the situation. The individual, however, is more likely to direct anger at a subordinate minority coworker than at the powerful people who own the store. Discriminating against coworkers may not improve the individual's financial situation, but it will give a sense of superiority over someone else. Because they are often less powerful, racial and ethnic minorities are frequently used as scapegoats. The Jews of Nazi Germany were blamed for the country's economic troubles after World War I and became a socially acceptable target for persecution.

NOTICE

IT IS REQUIRED BY LAW, UNDER
PENALTY OF FINE OF $5.00 TO $25.00,
THAT WHITE AND NEGRO PASSENGERS MUST
OCCUPY THE RESPECTIVE SPACE OR SEATS
INDICATED BY SIGNS IN THIS VEHICLE.

TEXAS PENAL CODE; ARTICLE 1659, SEC.4
DALLAS CITY ORDINANCE; NO. 2904

A Dallas bus worker removes a sign requiring separate seating for whites and blacks following a 1956 Supreme Court ruling mandating desegregation. (UPI/Corbis-Bettmann)

A second approach traces the existence of discrimination to social conflict among various groups of people, rather than to personality needs. According to the conflict theory, a dominant group uses discrimination to suppress one or more subordinate minorities. The majority group may be motivated by a desire to increase control over valuable resources. To accomplish this end, the dominant group singles out a minority for discrimination in order to gain some material advantage. Discrimination against Asian Americans is exemplified by the Chinese Immigration Act of 1882, which was designed to exclude Chinese immigrants from competing with white Europeans. Eliminating or neutralizing a racial or ethnic competitor is especially effective when those with power are able to persuade the larger society that a certain minority should be subordinated.

A third approach suggests that discrimination, like other behaviors, is learned through socialization. While certain personalities may be prone to discriminate, a certain measure of discrimination is built into cultural values. According to the cultural theory, people learn to discriminate in much the same way that they learn the countless other aspects of their culture. Children learn from the social environment how to identify and behave toward specific minorities. When white children hear a parent object to Japanese Americans moving into the neighborhood, they are learning to dislike Asians. Even the use of language to categorize people as "white" and "nonwhite" creates the conditions for differential treatment. Learned as a part of everyday life, prejudice and discrimination are often simply a matter of conformity to social norms.

Social Costs. Discrimination has prevented people from gaining equal access to the resources necessary for entering mainstream life in the United States and Canada. For example, housing discrimination during the post-World War II era through governmental and private housing policies confined many African Americans to the deteriorating centers of large cities.

In this environment, many African Americans were unable to obtain the educational and employment skills necessary for them to take advantage of the opportunities that were unavailable to previous generations. As a result, they were—and, largely, still are—denied access to the jobs, schools, and services enjoyed by white Americans who moved to the suburbs.

The cumulative effects of discrimination can be so great that racial or ethnic minorities are denied access to many vital areas of life. Discrimination in employment is especially harmful because it denies people the money they could use to buy other valued resources, such as health care, housing, education, and political power. One indicator of the social costs of discrimination to African Americans is their rate of POVERTY. According to the U.S. Bureau of the Census in 1991, close to 31 percent of African Americans were living in poverty, compared to 10 percent of whites. Historically, Mexican Americans have been included in the farm-labor workforce and in other low-paying jobs in light industry, but they have been excluded from better-paying economic positions as well as from positions in the political and educational arenas.

Legal and Moral Issues. Racial discrimination can occur at two levels: legal discrimination and institutionalized discrimination. Legal discrimination involves unequal treatment of racial or ethnic minorities that is written into law. Through the first half of the twentieth century, legal discrimination was very common in the United States and Canada. For example, many state and local codes discriminated against African Americans in the areas of education, housing, jobs, and politics. In the U.S. in the 1950's and 1960's, many of these laws were repealed by the Supreme Court. For example, the 1954 decision in BROWN V. BOARD OF EDUCATION OF TOPEKA, KANSAS, declared segregated schooling discriminatory.

Institutionalized discrimination refers to unequal treatment of racial or ethnic minorities that is established in social traditions. Such traditions might include the school curriculum, testing procedures, and classroom activities that place some minority students at a disadvantage. The process of institutionalized discrimination can be subtle or unintentional. For example, union seniority systems that discriminate against promoting the most recently hired employees are common. Since many racial and ethnic minorities are new to jobs using seniority systems, their opportunities for promotion are limited even though race or ethnicity is not an explicit requirement for promotion.

On the surface, it might appear that the legal form of discrimination is the most problematic. Certainly, it has terrible consequences, but because legal discrimination is established by law, it can also be removed by law through the repeal of discriminatory legislation. Institutionalized discrimination, being more difficult to detect in practice, is very difficult to eliminate. Its elimination requires wide-ranging alterations in social traditions.

The removal of legal discrimination has not eradicated discriminatory practices that, over the generations, have become a routine feature of the social and economic lives of many racial and ethnic minorities. Therefore, the United States and Canadian governments developed other methods to compensate for the legacy of inequality. AFFIRMATIVE ACTION in the United States and employment equity programs in Canada are designed to ensure that minorities are not informally discriminated against in access to employment and educational opportunities. Affirmative action programs attempt to undo the impact of previous discrimination by establishing goals and timetables for including minorities in government agencies and other large organizations that receive federal funds.

Affirmative action programs have drawn criticism because what is considered "affirmative action" to one group is sometimes viewed as REVERSE DISCRIMINATION by another. The programs are controversial, in part, because those who believe they are being denied equal access to resources, for example, white males who must face new, government-mandated competition for jobs, are usually not the ones who engaged in past discrimination. The phrase "reverse discrimination" emphasizes the perceived loss of resources for those who may no longer discriminate but whose predecessors did. Therefore, they feel victimized and ask: Is affirmative action fair? Conversely, racial and ethnic minorities who suffer from the consequences of previous discrimination ask: How is the impact of past inequities to be diminished? There are no easy answers to these questions, but one thing is obvious: the definition of the word "discrimination" is likely to remain a controversial issue in the legal and social debate over race and ethnic relations. —*Michael Delucchi*

SUGGESTED READINGS: The dynamics and consequences of discrimination are examined in Adalberto Aquirre and Jonathan Turner's *American Ethnicity* (New York: McGraw-Hill, 1995). The various types of discrimination and prejudice in the United States are explored in Joe Feagin and Clairece Feagin's *Dis-*

crimination American Style: Institutional Racism and Sexism, 2d ed. (Florida: Krieger, 1986). The consequences of affirmative action with regard to race relations are described in Herman Belz's *Equality Transformed: A Quarter-Century of Affirmative Action* (New Brunswick, N.J.: Transaction Publishers, 1991). Sociologist William J. Wilson argues that differences in social class are becoming more important than differences in race to the status of African Americans in *The Declining Significance of Race: Blacks and Changing American Institutions*, 2d ed. (Chicago: University of Chicago Press, 1980).

Displaced Persons Act (1948): First refugee bill to pass the U.S. Congress after World War II. The act allowed 200,000 displaced persons to enter the United States provided they had security clearances showing that they were not communists. Refugees admitted under the act also had to assure immigration agents that they had jobs in the United States that would not displace American citizens. President Harry S Truman signed the bill, although he argued that it discriminated against Jews. The law provided that only refugees who had entered American-controlled areas in Europe before December 22, 1945, qualified for immigration; most displaced Jews did not flee Eastern Europe until 1946.

District attorney: Legal representative of the federal, state, or local government whose main task is to prosecute the accused in criminal courts and otherwise to represent the government. District attorneys work closely with police agencies in the process of investigation, indictment, and the trial of criminals. Such attorneys may also represent the federal, state, or local government in civil actions and other legal matters. District attorneys are usually full-time employees of the judicial districts that they represent and do not themselves take individual clients.

Divorce, marital: Legal termination of a MARRIAGE. Divorce is of concern for three primary reasons: the economic, social, and psychological effects of divorce on individuals and the implications these effects have for society; the financial and institutional burden on society's legal and human-service agencies; and the long-term consequences of divorce for society. Some

social scientists and political leaders are concerned that the social changes brought about by the high divorce rates of the last several decades have contributed to the decline of the American FAMILY.

Divorce Rates. The United States has one of the highest divorce rates in the world. The probability that a marriage will end in divorce in the United States is approximately one in two; in Europe, it is one in three to one in four. People are often surprised that the divorce rate is lower for first-time marrieds and higher for those who have been previously married and that those who cohabit prior to marriage tend to have higher divorce rates once they marry.

Divorce rates can be calculated in a variety of ways, but the two most reliable are the crude divorce rate and the refined divorce rate. The U.S. crude divorce rate in the early 1990's was 4.7 per one thousand persons per year, while the Canadian crude divorce rate was about half that of the U.S. rate. This means that for every one thousand U.S. citizens, 9.4 persons become divorced each year. The refined divorce rate is the number of

---

DIVORCE RATES OF SELECTED COUNTRIES

U.S. divorce rates are significantly higher than those of other developed nations.

	Divorces per 100 marriages
Austria	34
Belgium	31
Canada	38
Denmark	41
Finland	41
France	33
Germany	30
Great Britain	42
Hungary	28
Iceland	38
Netherlands	28
Norway	44
Russia	37
Sweden	48
Switzerland	36
United States	55 (1985 data)

Source: United Nations/*The Christian Science Monitor.* Based on 1990-1992 data except as noted.

divorces per one thousand married women above the age of fifteen; the refined divorce rate for 1991 in the United States was twenty-one.

Trends in Divorce. The U.S. Bureau of the Census and the National Center for Health Statistics are two reliable sources for information concerning the number of divorces. According to data available from these organizations and other sources, the U.S. divorce rate increased steadily before stabilizing in the early 1980's. In 1860, the first year records were kept, the annual divorce rate was one per one thousand marriages. Between the years 1920 and 1985, the divorce rate rose from eight to twenty-three per one thousand marriages. The divorce rate has been affected by social and economic conditions; for example, the rate tends to increase after wars. The divorce rate decreased during the Great Depression of the 1930's but increased greatly during the prosperous 1970's, peaking in 1981 with 1,213,000 divorces, or a refined divorce rate of 22.6. Since 1981, the divorce rate in the United States has been declining, but throughout the 1980's and early 1990's the rate varied little. During the 1970's

and through 1981, the divorce rate increased faster than both the total population and the married population. In the United States, the 1970's was truly the decade of divorce; the number of divorces skyrocketed from 708,000 in 1970 to 1,189,000 in 1980.

Determinants of Divorce. Some of the most significant variables affecting the probability of a couple's divorcing are the age at first marriage, race, frequency of church attendance, educational attainment, income, religion, and region of the country. Age at first marriage is the strongest predictor of divorce in the first five years of marriage. Those who are under the age of twenty when they marry are two to three times more likely to divorce than those who marry at the age of twenty or older. The divorce rate for blacks is twice as high as for whites and Hispanics. Those who attend church services two to three times a month are significantly less likely to divorce than those who never attend or who attend sporadically. The divorce rate is highest for women who have not graduated from high school. The higher one's income, the less likely one is to divorce. Protestants have a higher divorce rate than

Approximately half of all U.S. marriages end in divorce. (Michele L. McGrath)

MARRIAGE ANNULMENTS GRANTED TO U.S. CATHOLICS, 1970-1994

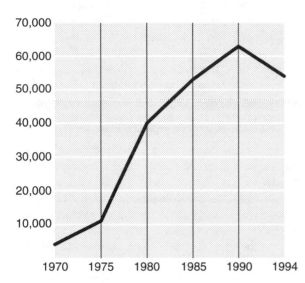

Annulment rates increased steadily in the 1970's and 1980's but declined in the early 1990's.

Source: Annual Catholic Almanac/*Newsweek.*

Catholics, while Catholics have a higher divorce rate than Jews. Those with no religious affiliation have the highest rates of divorce. The highest divorce rates in the United States are found in the West, followed by the South, Midwest, and Northeast.

Consequences of Divorce. Those who separate or divorce frequently experience guilt, loneliness, anger, remorse, and depression. Divorced individuals have higher annual death rates. Divorced men have a higher annual death rate than divorced women. Divorced women generally experience a decrease in their standard of living, while divorced men often experience an increase in their standard of living.

The consequences for children of divorced PARENTS vary depending primarily on the sex and age of the children. Younger children, especially those under the age of five, seem to have more negative short-term reactions to divorce. Teenagers also experience adjustment problems, but they are generally better equipped to express their anger, shame, and sadness to their parents. Boys tend to have more adjustment problems. Boys adjust better when in the custody of their fathers, while girls adjust better when in the custody of their

mothers. Researchers have found that the duration of post-divorce parental visits, rather than the frequency of such visits, is related to better father-child relationships.

No-Fault Divorce. Before 1969, U.S. divorces were granted under traditional fault-based law only if one of the spouses was found to be "at fault" (guilty of adultery, cruelty, desertion, neglect, or something of a similar nature) while the other spouse was found to be innocent. In 1969, California became the first state to enact a "no-fault" divorce law, which eliminated the need to prove fault and added "irreconcilable differences" as an acceptable reason for termination of a marriage.

All fifty states now have some type of no-fault divorce while also retaining some types of fault divorce. Lawmakers intended no-fault divorce to help reduce the conflict and hostility that normally surround the dissolution of a marriage. No-fault procedures have streamlined the dissolution process and reduced some of the bitterness that accompanies divorce, but no-fault has also had some unintended consequences: For example, no-fault laws are alleged to have contributed to declines in the economic position of women and children, thrusting many into poverty. Researchers have confirmed that the changes brought by no-fault procedures have contributed to the increased number of divorces seen in the United States beginning in the 1970's. —*William L. Smith*

SUGGESTED READINGS: Economic adjustment after divorce is the topic of Lenore Weitzman's *The Divorce Revolution: The Unexpected Social and Economic Consequences for Women and Children in America* (New York: The Free Press, 1985). How children are affected by divorce and advice on how parents and children can deal with divorce and remarriage are discussed in Frank F. Furstenberg and Andrew J. Cherlin's *Divided Families: What Happens to Children When Parents Part* (Cambridge, Mass.: Harvard University Press, 1991). The economic, political, social, and ideological factors that influenced the rise in divorce rates are examined in Cherlin's *Marriage, Divorce, Remarriage*, Rev. ed. (Cambridge, Mass.: Harvard University Press, 1992).

The lasting wounds of divorce and the long-term impact it has on children is the focus of a ten-year study conducted by Judith S. Wallerstein and Sandra Blakeslee presented in *Second Chances: Men, Women, and Children a Decade After Divorce* (New York: Ticknor and Fields, 1989). The economic consequences of no-fault divorce and the laws governing divorce are presented in Allen M. Parkman's *No-Fault Divorce: What Went Wrong?* (Boulder, Colo.: Westview Press, 1992). John Gottman constructs a theory of marital stability in *What Predicts Divorce?: The Relationship Between Marital Processes and Marital Outcomes* (Hillsdale, N.J.: Lawrence Erlbaum, 1994).

Divorce, parental: Legal efforts by minors to terminate their biological parents' custodial rights. Parental divorce entered the public consciousness in 1992 when Shawn Russ, a twelve-year-old Florida boy known in legal proceedings as "Gregory K.," won a court order removing him from his mother's home, where he had been routinely abused and neglected. Parental divorce proceedings differ from the more common removals of children from abusive or neglectful homes at the behest of social-service agencies in that the children themselves help to initiate the proceedings. The crucial issue in this regard is whether children are entitled to legal standing, or recognition as parties to, rather than mere subjects of, legal proceedings.

Opponents of the extension of standing to children argue that minors are too intellectually and emotionally immature to be trusted to exercise such legal power responsibly; such critics typically cite the possibility that children so empowered might initiate frivolous legal proceedings in an effort to frustrate the exercise of ordinary parental rights. Advocates of the extension of standing argue that such fears are groundless and that many children urgently need the recourse provided by legal standing to protect themselves from abusive parents. According to such advocates, many children are routinely ill-served by social-service policies that stress "family reunification," thus often returning abused children to the custody of their abusers; in such cases where child-welfare agencies do not act in a child's best interests, advocates say, children should have the legal right to protect themselves. The National Child Rights Alliance, an advocacy group founded in 1986 by adult survivors of parental abuse, provides legal assistance to children in parental divorce proceedings.

DNA testing: Method of forensic science. DNA (deoxyribonucleic acid) is an ideal compound with which to identify victims and suspects in criminal cases because it is unique to each person. When other evidence is absent, however, the reliability of DNA testing has been questioned.

Four kinds of building blocks, called nucleotides, make up the DNA that is present in each cell. The nucleotide sequence in DNA determines a person's genetic identity. Since everyone (with the exception of identical twins) has a unique DNA sequence, forensic scientists have begun using DNA testing to identify suspects and victims at crime scenes. If investigators collect enough DNA, they can use it to create a characteristic "profile" of the person from whom the DNA came. Fingerprints have long been regarded as virtually irrefutable proof in the identification of victims and suspects at crime scenes; DNA testing is being introduced into courtrooms as a similarly irrefutable form of biological identification in criminal cases.

Courts have used DNA testing as evidence since 1986. When DNA testing clearly excludes a suspect, the evidence has generally been accepted as conclusive. Because the technique is relatively new, however, defendants usually contest the reliability of DNA testing when a possible match occurs.

Three arguments have typically been raised to contest the use of DNA evidence as conclusive proof in criminal cases. First, DNA testing does not absolutely link suspects to a crime scene. The DNA profile created as court evidence is not an individual's actual DNA sequence. Since the DNA molecule is billions of nucleotides long, the actual sequence would be impractical to determine. Instead, the profile is made by cutting DNA samples into fragments. These fragments create a highly individualized profile when highlighted with the appropriate markers. The profile is so individualized that the likelihood of anyone having a similar pattern at the same crime scene is extremely remote.

A second reason DNA testing has been attacked in court is the potential for DNA to become contaminated before its analysis. The technique is sensitive to other sources of DNA. Such contamination can interfere with the interpretation of the subsequent profile and can increase the potential pool of suspects that might match the pattern that is developed.

A third argument used against DNA testing in the courtroom has been directed at the reliability and reproducibility of the testing itself. Standard procedures for processing DNA in criminal cases are lacking. This is a critical step, since the methods of handling and processing biological samples can influence the quality of DNA that is collected from them and, consequently, the appearance of the subsequent profile. In addition, the making of DNA profiles destroys the original DNA samples. This means that when small amounts of DNA are present, it is impossible to conduct independent DNA tests for comparison.

Ethical questions about the invasion of privacy and of civil liberty have been raised by the suggestion that law-enforcement officials create data banks of DNA patterns, much as they have created a nationwide data bank of fingerprint patterns. The resolution of both the technical and ethical questions surrounding DNA testing will likely be an ongoing process.

Doe v. Bolton (1973): U.S. Supreme Court case in which the Supreme Court declared unconstitutional a Georgia law limiting the conditions under which an abortion could be performed. Georgia law required a woman seeking an abortion to have residency in the state and required a physician's approval and the concurrence of a second doctor for an abortion to be legal; it also restricted abortions to certain hospitals. As in the better-known companion case ROE V. WADE, the Court in *Doe* by a vote of 7 to 2 found the law a violation of the Fourteenth Amendment's due-process guarantees. The majority opinion was based on the Court's finding of a right to privacy protected under the Fourteenth Amendment's provision that no citizen can be deprived of life, liberty, or property without DUE PROCESS of law.

Dole, Robert "Bob" (b. July 22, 1923, Russell, Kans.): U.S senator and presidential candidate. Dole was born in Russell, Kansas, where his father ran a small dairy business. A prominent local athlete in high school, he enlisted in the U.S. Army in World War II

Bob Dole celebrates his victory in the 1996 "Super Tuesday" Republican primary. (Archive Photos, Reuters, Luc Novovitch)

and fought on the Italian front in 1945. Shortly before the end of the war, he suffered serious wounds that almost killed him and left his right hand permanently disabled. His recuperation from his wounds consumed four years, and his life has never been free from physical pain since.

Dole entered Republican politics in Kansas in the 1950's and won a seat in the House of Representatives in 1960. He moved on to the Senate in 1968, quickly gaining a reputation as a hard-hitting Republican stalwart. Richard NIXON selected him to head the Republican National Committee in 1971, and Gerald Ford picked him as running mate in 1976. Although Ford and Dole were defeated, Dole's performance in a debate with Democratic vice presidential candidate Walter Mondale, in which Dole attacked the Democrats as the "party of war," intensified the sense that the senator fought hard in a partisan battle.

In 1984, Dole became the majority leader of the Senate, succeeding Harold Baker of Tennessee. When the Democrats regained control of the Senate in 1986, Dole retained his post as leader of the Republican minority. In 1988, Dole made a run for the Republican presidential nomination against George BUSH. After winning the Iowa caucuses, however, Dole lost bitterly in the New Hampshire primary in which he accused Bush of lying. Nevertheless, Dole subsequently provided the Bush Administration with strong support, and Dole's second wife, Elizabeth, served as secretary of labor in Bush's cabinet.

After the 1992 election of President Bill CLINTON, a Democrat, Dole organized Senate Republicans into an effective opposition force. He helped to defeat the ambitious health plan that the president and First Lady Hillary Rodham Clinton put forward in 1993, and he saw the Republicans regain control of the Senate and the House in the 1994 elections.

In 1995, Dole announced his candidacy for the 1996 Republican presidential nomination and quickly established himself as the front-runner. His assets include his strong roots in the REPUBLICAN PARTY, his success as the party's Senate leader, and his reputation as a master of Washington deal-making. Despite his abilities, both Republican and Democratic critics expressed doubts about Dole's advanced age, his capacity to rein in his quick and acerbic temper, and his devotion to conservative principles. To counteract the latter perception, Dole moved strongly to the right throughout 1995 in an effort to preempt challenges from Republican rivals. In the 1996 primaries, he fended off early challenges from Pat Buchanan, Steve Forbes, and Lamar Alexander to capture the 1996 Republican presidential nomination. In May, he resigned from the Senate to focus his energies on the presidential campaign.

Dolphin-free tuna: Tuna netted in the ocean by methods that do not cause the unintentional killing of dolphins. Traditionally, many commercial fishermen set their nets around pods of dolphins to catch yellowfin

Some makers of canned tuna promote their products as dolphin-free. (Yasmine Cordoba)

tuna swimming below the dolphins. As a consequence, many dolphins were killed in the fishery—an estimated 133,000 in 1986 alone. Environmentalists' protests included boycotts of canned tuna. The U.S. government responded by requiring fishermen, domestic and foreign, to follow practices that would release the dolphins while retaining most tuna. In 1991, an estimated 35,000 dolphins were killed. Reduced tuna catches, however, forced many U.S. fishermen out of the industry, leaving a void quickly filled by foreign fishermen.

Domestic violence: Physical, emotional, psychological, and sexual abuse occurring between domestic partners. Husband-to-wife abuse is reported much more frequently than the reverse. When a wife is violent toward her husband, it is most often thought to be in self-defense.

Causes. For centuries, women have occupied a lower social status than men. Biblical accounts and descriptions of women emphasize the appropriateness of blaming and punishing women for transgressions; Eve receives the primary blame for eating the forbidden fruit in the Garden of Eden. Women, like cattle, were long considered a man's possession, necessary principally for child-bearing. A Roman husband could legally kill his wife. Under English common law, a husband had the right to "physically chastise" a disobedient wife provided that the stick he used was no thicker than his thumb, a custom that allegedly gave rise to the phrase "rule of thumb." As recently as the 1970's, a Pennsylvania town ordinance prohibited a husband from beating his wife after 10:00 P.M. on Sundays, presumably implying that the practice was permissible at other times.

Many historians have argued that the reason men have maintained a dominant position is that economic and social circumstances operate both directly and indirectly to support a male-dominated social order and family structure. Historically, men have been responsible for earning and overseeing a family's finances. This, in turn, amounts to a degree of power and authority over the wife and children.

Aside from the economic advantage men usually have, the adult male is, on average, six inches taller and twenty-five pounds heavier than the adult female. In addition, the male's secondary sex characteristics give him a larger upper body and larger muscles in his arms and legs. Most men are also socialized to be aggressive and competitive. They are often given the message that

a "real man" will always be in control of a situation and will maintain power and control over those around him. Thus, abusive men have learned that when all other sources of masculine identity fail, they can always rely on being tough as a sign of manhood. Many such men see other people, including their wives, principally as objects to be exploited and manipulated.

Characteristics of Batterers. While there is no single pattern that characterizes all men who batter, several common characteristics have been identified. An abusive man is often a lonely individual with poor social skills. His wife is not only his best friend but also often his only friend. The abusive husband has few supportive relationships and has unrealistic expectations of his wife, who is expected to meet all of his needs. Abusive husbands tend to be jealous and insecure and to have problems with self-esteem. The abusive husband will attack his wife if he perceives that she is not providing for his immediate needs appropriately and acceptably, and he often views his wife's refusal to have intercourse as reason to beat and intimidate her. (In many states, a wife can now charge her husband with "marital rape.")

Most men who batter their wives were either abused as children or witnessed violence between their parents. Abusive husbands generally learn to be aggressive from violent role models; this factor is especially important in efforts to reduce domestic violence, because such violence is often the "family secret," something that goes on strictly behind closed doors and is rarely—if ever—talked about.

The majority of men who batter are not "in touch" with their feelings. Although men as a group tend to deny their feelings and try to appear rational and unemotional, men who batter are even more controlled; they thus often have trouble expressing what they are feeling. At the same time, they tend to be emotionally insulated from the feelings of their victims. They often blame their victims for their own aggressive behavior and show a lack of genuine remorse and guilt over what they have done. These men are often impulsive and have a low level of tolerance for frustration. They are unable to handle stress, tension, and anxiety and need immediate gratification. A trivial event can set them off, and there is frequently little connection between the trigger incident and their reaction.

Characteristics of Battered Women. Many women are brought up to be passive, accepting, and subservient to men. They are taught to be accommodating and frequently have difficulty with enforcing personal

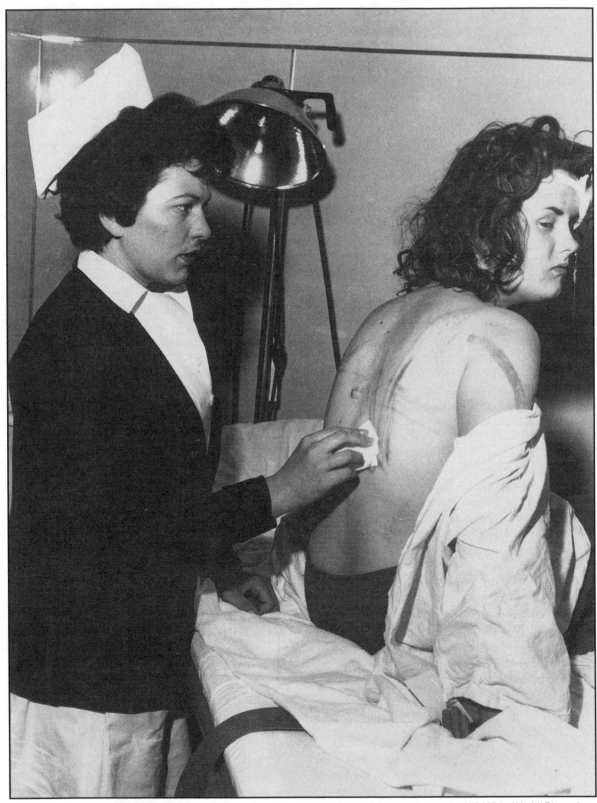

A nurse treats a domestic violence victim whose husband whipped her with a belt. (AP/Wide World Photos)

boundaries. Such women tend to perceive themselves as helpless, powerless, unworthy, and unimportant. Abused women thus often have poor self-images based on feelings of embarrassment, fear, guilt, humiliation, and intimidation. Their experience with violence and societal pressure to be submissive often make it difficult for them to think about leaving an abusive situation.

It is a myth that battered women enjoy being abused. Like battering men, abused women often have a family history of violence, intimidation, dependency, and isolation. Because of these experiences, battered women frequently have difficulty with self-assertion and have internalized feelings of helplessness. Many believe they deserve the abuse they receive. Moreover, many battered wives feel that they have few options. Many are said to develop learned helplessness; the psycho-emotional abuse they receive convinces them that they are incompetent and that they are unable to control what happens to them. They believe that they cannot protect themselves from further attacks, both physical and emotional, and are incapable of controlling the

events that may bring about more abuse.

Many abused women are not passive. They call the police, go to shelters, get court orders, and propose changes in the relationship. Yet they are frequently constrained from getting what they want by social, legal, and cultural forces. Many believe that their husbands will reform. Many avoid divorce because it would leave their children without a father or is against their religion. In addition, many abused wives fear for their lives if they ask for an end to the relationship.

Phases of the Violent Relationship. Abusive patterns tend to occur in three stages. The tension-building phase is a time of increasing tension between the couple. The husband intimidates his wife with verbal assaults and minor physically abusive acts; the wife tries to calm him down and reduce the stress. If she is unsuccessful, the acute battering phase begins, in which the batterer lashes out in blind rage, often causing serious injury to the victim, who is unable to control the situation. In the "honeymoon" phase, the abuser tries to make amends for his abusive behavior by pleading for forgiveness, offering gifts, and promising that it will never happen

A 1995 domestic-violence awareness rally held to protest the verdict in the O.J. Simpson trial. (Impact Visuals, Slobodan Dimitrov)

again. Because he is often convincing and she often believes that she can control such situations in the future, she stays, and the cycle begins again.

Treatment and Prevention. Three beliefs underlie prevention and treatment of domestic abuse. First, those seeking help are taught that spousal abuse is unacceptable. Second, abused wives are taught that they are not to blame for their victimization. The third tenet, taught chiefly to batterers themselves, is that the perpetrator must accept responsibility for his behavior and be willing to change. In order to accomplish these goals, a treatment program must include cognitive, behavioral, and affective components.   —*Sander M. Latts*

SUGGESTED READINGS: Lenore Walker's *The Battered Woman* (New York: Harper & Row, 1979) describes many aspects of domestic abuse. *Dating Violence: Young Women in Danger* (Seattle: Seal Press, 1991), edited by Barrie Levy, looks at abuse issues in dating. *Getting Free* (Seattle: Seal Press, 1986), by Ginny NiCarthy, covers such issues as getting help, whether to leave an abusive relationship, and how to protect children. Richard Gelles and Clair Cornell's *Intimate Violence in Families* 2d ed. (Newbury Park, Calif.: Sage, 1990) is an excellent reference that covers all aspects of family violence.

Domino and containment theories: Related concepts that largely shaped U.S. foreign policy during the Cold War era. Application of both theories involved U.S. military and economic aid to foreign governments in order to check communist expansion. The United States developed its foreign policy against what it saw as an aggressive post-World War II communist military threat posed by the Soviet Union, which emerged from World War II as a leading military power, and the People's Republic of China, which became a communist state in 1949.

In 1947, George F. Kennan, an influential diplomat and former ambassador to the Soviet Union, wrote an article entitled "The Sources of Soviet Conduct" for the journal *Foreign Affairs.* Keenan proclaimed that the Soviet system counted on external conflict for internal control of its people and commented that "any United States policy toward the Soviet Union must be that of a long-term, patient but firm and vigilant containment of Russian expansive tendencies." Kennan thus gave a name to postwar U.S. foreign policy.

In the late 1940's, the U.S.-sponsored MARSHALL PLAN, which involved economic aid and investment, and the NORTH ATLANTIC TREATY ORGANIZATION (NATO) became the cornerstones of containment in Western Europe and the Mediterranean. Critics have asserted that the Marshall Plan and NATO alienated the Soviet Union, making any sort of constructive engagement with the Soviets problematic. Defenders of the containment policy point to the relative peace and prosperity that prevailed in Western Europe during the postwar era.

In Asia, the United States twice went to war in the interest of containment. The Korean War in the early 1950's and the VIETNAM WAR in the 1960's and early 1970's were both fought to check communist expansion. The domino theory is most closely associated with the Vietnam conflict; it was often conjectured that if South Vietnam were to fall to communist North Vietnam, then the other states in Southeast Asia would topple like a line of dominoes. By this logic, the Harry Truman Administration had pledged aid to France in controlling Indochina in the late 1940's. In a 1961 visit to South Vietnam, Vice President Lyndon B. Johnson stated that the United States would have to win in Vietnam or fight "on the beaches of Waikiki." When Johnson became president, his devotion to the domino theory led to a fateful U.S. military escalation in South Vietnam. The domino fell on April 30, 1975; none followed.

In sum, the domino and containment theories were applied with some success in thwarting communist expansionism, especially in Europe. Such efforts, however, had little success in thwarting communist-inspired wars of national liberation, especially in Asia. In the long run, internal economic and political pressures, rather than external military pressure, restrained Soviet expansionism and brought the Soviet communist regime down.

SUGGESTED READINGS: Thomas G. Paterson's *Meeting the Communist Threat: Truman to Reagan* (New York: Oxford University Press, 1988) explains containment policies by presidential administration. Stanley Karnow's *Vietnam: A History* (New York: Viking Press, 1984) traces the Vietnam conflict from its colonial roots to its conclusion and discusses the domino theory.

Dothard v. Rawlinson (1977): U.S. SUPREME COURT case. In *Dothard*, the Court ruled that height and weight requirements for prison guards in Alabama discriminated against females and were therefore a violation of Title VII of the CIVIL RIGHTS ACT OF 1964. Diane Rawlinson had been rejected for failing to meet minimum height and weight requirements for a position as a correctional counselor; the Court found that the size

U.S. entry into the Vietnam War was endorsed by believers in the domino theory. (UPI/Corbis-Bettmann)

requirements had a disproportionate effect on women applicants. The court also ruled that Alabama's regulation prohibiting women from "contact positions" in male maximum security prisons was a reasonable security precaution and therefore constitutional.

Double jeopardy: Clause in the Fifth Amendment to the U.S. CONSTITUTION providing two important protections to accused persons. Under the double jeopardy clause's provisions, an individual may not be prosecuted for the same offense following an acquittal or conviction. In addition, the clause prohibits multiple punishments for the same offense.

The double jeopardy clause was adopted to protect citizens from repeated attempts by the federal government to convict or punish them for the same crime. Though some states provide protection against double jeopardy in their respective constitutions, others did not, since the states were not bound by any of the amendments to the U.S. Constitution at the time. The adoption of the Fourteenth Amendment in 1868, however, stipulated that no state could "deprive any person of life, liberty, or property, without DUE PROCESS of law; nor deny to any person within its jurisdiction the EQUAL PROTECTION of the laws." The "due process" and "equal protection" clauses of the Fourteenth Amendment became the judicial vehicle by which the prohibition of double jeopardy as well as other safeguards covered by the first eight amendments were eventually determined by the Supreme Court to be binding on all states.

Criminal proceedings against the accused begin with an arrest and continue through several stages, such as the preliminary hearing and grand jury. Since the prohibition against double jeopardy does not apply until the trial, a person may, for example, be reindicted for the same offense if a grand jury fails to indict the accused on the first attempt by the prosecutor. The prohibition against double jeopardy begins, or "attaches," when a jury is sworn or, in a bench (nonjury) trial, when the first witness is sworn to testify.

The meaning of "double jeopardy" goes beyond prosecution more than once for the same offense. Thus, a defendant who is convicted or acquitted of murder may not be retried for a lesser included offense arising out of the same act (for example, manslaughter). Nor may an individual convicted or acquitted of a lesser offense (for example, joyriding) be retried for a greater offense arising from the same set of facts (for example, grand auto theft). If the same act is a crime

under both state law and that of any political subdivision (city or county), the defendant may not be prosecuted in more than one jurisdiction.

There are, however, circumstances that constitute a waiver of double jeopardy protections. Whenever the court grants a defendant's motion for a mistrial (such as when a jury cannot reach a verdict or there is prosecutorial misconduct), the defendant may be retried again for the same offense. Similarly, if a defendant has been convicted and files a successful appeal, the defendant may be retried for the same offense. Finally, under the doctrine of dual sovereignty, a defendant may be prosecuted in both state and federal court, or by two states, for an offense arising from the same set of facts (such as interstate kidnapping).

Dow Jones Industrial Average (DJIA): Economic indicator. The DJIA is the most frequently cited indicator of the value of the STOCK MARKET. It is based on the stock prices of thirty large, well-established industrial corporations, representing about one-fifth of the market value of stocks sold on the New York Stock Exchange. Expressed in points rather than dollars, the DJIA is calculated by adding the prices of the thirty stocks and dividing by a number that is adjusted to account for splits, substitutions, and dividends. Dow, Jones & Company first published a stock average in 1884, but the current method for determining the DJIA was established in 1928. In 1995, the DJIA reached 5,000 for the first time, and a movement of one point was equal to about six cents in the price of an average stock.

Downsizing: Business practice. Downsizing, in usage that became common in the 1980's, refers to reducing the size of a business operation. It often implies a reduction in employment; in fact, downsizing came to be taken as a euphemism for a large-scale reduction in a workforce. Some companies use downsizing to reduce the ranks of middle management. Others use outsourcing as a means of downsizing, eliminating jobs at the production level by having some stages of manufacturing performed by outside contractors (often overseas) with lower costs.

Drafts and draft resistance: Conscription, or the forced induction into military service to fill manpower needs, has been used in the United States since 1862.

A Detroit protester expresses his feelings about a possible draft during a 1986 visit by President Ronald Reagan. (Jim West)

A draft resister burns his draft card at a 1970 antiwar protest in Dallas. (AP/Wide World Photos)

Its use has triggered resistance throughout American history, especially during major wars.

The Confederacy enacted the first American draft in 1862 during the Civil War. Loopholes existed allowing purchased exemptions, resulting in the popular phrase, "Rich man's war, poor man's fight." Resistance forced the elimination of many loopholes, but thousands continued to avoid military service. In some rural areas, conscription officers were harassed or killed.

The Union followed the Confederate lead, enacting the Conscription Act of 1863. As in the Confederacy, the draft was resisted; of the 776,000 men selected, 161,000 failed to report for service. The largest Civil War draft protest was a July, 1863, New York City riot that lasted four days and killed 105 people, the deadliest riot in American history.

The Conscription Act of 1917, enacted to supply soldiers for World War I, registered all males between the ages of twenty and thirty, later extended to include ages eighteen to forty-five. Of the twenty-four million men registered for the draft, almost five million actually served. Three million refused to register; some were arrested and some fled, but most went undetected. Another 338,000 men registered but failed to appear after their summons to serve; most were never caught.

The Selective Training and Service Act of 1940, the first American peacetime draft, was a response to the assumption that America would soon be involved in the war that had erupted in Europe in 1939. Because of the perception that World War II was a "just" war, resistance was not widespread. Many men, however, did take advantage of the loophole excluding married fathers from the draft, a fact evidenced by increased U.S. marriage and birth rates between 1940 and 1943.

In the Civil War, World War I, and World War II, conscription was a temporary answer to a crisis. Afterward, it was allowed to lapse. The first permanent U.S. peacetime draft was the Selective Service Act of 1948, which was enacted as a consequence of COLD WAR fears of war with the Soviet Union.

During the Korean War, the director of the draft observed that no one wanted to be in the military. When the government began to issue draft deferments for college students, millions enrolled—a pattern repeated during the VIETNAM WAR, which provided the best-remembered instances of U.S. draft resistance. By the end of 1972, about thirty thousand U.S. draft resistors were living in Canada. During the war, roughly half a million U.S. men committed draft violations; twenty-five thousand never registered, and thousands more burned their draft cards in protest.

The argument for conscription has always been the necessity of filling manpower needs during wartime. The government has often attempted to portray draft resistors as traitorous slackers who are nothing less than enemies of the state, which is fighting for survival. Arguments against the draft have included conscription's bias toward the economic elite and against minorities, youths, and males. Many draft protestors have also challenged the justness of certain U.S. wars, especially the Vietnam War, and have challenged the government's right to conscript during peacetime.

Dress codes in schools: Having almost disappeared in the antiestablishment 1960's, school dress codes reappeared in full force in the 1990's in response to parental concerns about DRUGS, CRIME, and GANGS on campus. Proponents cite safety concerns and economic and academic reasons as arguments in favor of such codes, while opponents claim that mandatory codes infringe upon students' rights.

For parents and school administrators, the most compelling argument concerns safety. Schools have adopted codes that range from banning certain items of clothing, to requiring students to wear identification tags, to mandating school uniforms. Uniforms make schools safer because anyone not wearing them can be spotted quickly, making it easy to find outsiders. Moreover, weapons are harder to conceal in uniforms, and students wearing uniforms are not robbed of expensive clothing and jewelry. The influence of gangs is decreased by uniforms, since gang members are no longer able to set themselves apart by their distinctive clothing or colors.

Dress codes also make financial sense to many parents. Uniforms are more economical to purchase than school clothes and save parents the daily hassle over what to wear. Designer labels and expensive status symbols are prohibited, thus eliminating PEER PRESSURE and competition over pricey apparel that many students cannot afford.

School officials tend to favor dress codes because they believe it enhances academic performance and discipline. Administrators believe clothing regulations decrease distractions, help students to concentrate on learning, and reduce group conflicts. Teachers often remark that students who are better dressed behave better, and administrators contend that distinctive school uniforms help to create a sense of community within a school.

A list of clothing banned by various school districts ranges from the ordinary to the exotic. Commonplace items include blue jeans and baseball caps. More up-scale entries include jewelry, gold chains, and designer sunglasses. Designated as gang-related garb are leather jackets, professional sports team jackets, bandannas, and earrings worn by men. Also prohibited are suggestive or revealing outfits. The most common sources of controversy, however, are shirts with messages emblazoned on them.

Shirts bearing messages fall under the category of communicative dress, that is, dress that communicates speech. The simple banning of messages that appear on students' shirts can thus infringe on students' First Amendment rights to free speech. It is on this point in particular that much opposition to school dress codes exists.

In TINKER V. DES MOINES INDEPENDENT SCHOOL DISTRICT (1969), the U.S. Supreme Court established the right of students to freedom of expression in schools unless the exercise of that right intruded on the rights of other students, the requirement of appropriate discipline, or the work of the school. School officials sometimes attempt to ban shirts with messages by arguing that the mode of communication interferes with the school's educational mission. Opponents of school dress codes argue that restricting students' choice of clothing inhibits their individuality and freedom of expression. Among the most vocal opponents is the AMERICAN CIVIL LIBERTIES UNION (ACLU), which decries the message that dress codes send: that in order for students to have safety, they must give up their rights.

Drive-by shootings: Criminal incidents involving the firing of a weapon from a moving vehicle. The practice is generally associated with gang-style shootings; instances have been recorded since motorized vehicles have been in common use. In its earlier and most common forms, drive-by shootings are intentional assaults and killings directed at specific individuals or targets. In recent decades, however, such shootings have occasionally been random in nature, having neither specific motives nor a specific target. Increasingly, innocent persons have been wounded or killed in such assaults; particularly in GANG-ridden inner-city neighborhoods, drive-by shootings are significant causes of public fear and property damage.

Dronenburg v. Zech (1984): U.S. District Court case. The case of James L. Dronenburg, who was discharged on April 21, 1981, lasted three years and resulted in a major articulation of U.S. court policy.

Dronenburg was an exemplary naval petty officer and Korean-language specialist at the Defense Language Institute in Monterey, California. During a purge of homosexuals at the Institute, he was discharged from the U.S. Navy after admitting to having had sexual relations on two occasions with another serviceman. Known homosexuals had long been banned from the U.S. armed services. Naval regulations stated, "Homosexuality is incompatible with naval service. The presence in the naval environment of persons who engage in homosexual conduct or who, by their statements, demonstrate a propensity to engage in homosexual conduct seriously impairs the accomplishment of the naval mission."

Dronenburg's appeal claimed that the discharge violated his constitutional rights to PRIVACY and EQUAL PROTECTION under the law. Hearing the case in the U.S. Court of Appeals for the District of Columbia were Robert Bork, who was later rejected by Congress for appointment to the Supreme Court, and Antonin SCALIA, who was successfully appointed to the Supreme Court by President Ronald REAGAN in 1986. The Court of Appeals decided against Dronenburg on August 17, 1984, and he was denied a rehearing that November. In the opinion, the court stated that the evolving right to privacy in American jurisprudence did not encompass HOMOSEXUALITY, that judicial restraint was necessary regarding possible reinterpretation of the Fifth Amendment's DUE PROCESS clause, and that democratic principles validate the majoritarian disapproval of homosexual behavior.

The Court of Appeals' affirmation in *Dronenburg v. Zech* was one of a series of decisions in which the military ban on homosexuality has been challenged in the courts. *Dronenburg v. Zech* was a setback for the GAY RIGHTS MOVEMENT, and it set the foundation for later affirmations of the ban. Subsequent cases have had varying outcomes, however, and though Dronenburg lost his appeal, the tendency in the courts has increasingly been to question the foundation and rationale of the military's policy. The issue of homosexuality in the military drew much attention during the

1992 presidential campaign and the opening years of the Bill CLINTON Administration, when pressure from the courts led to the adoption of the so-called "don't ask, don't tell" policy. Nevertheless, the revised standard still allowed for discharges on the basis of homosexual conduct or tendencies, and the issue was not put to rest.
—*Barry Mann*

SUGGESTED READINGS: Allan Berube offers a comprehensive history of military policy and procedure involving homosexuality in *Coming out Under Fire: The History of Gay Men and Women in World War Two* (New York: The Free Press, 1990). Mary Ann Humphrey's *My County, My Right to Serve: Experiences of Gay Men and Women in the Military, World War II to the Present* (New York: HarperCollins, 1990) is an anthology of first-person accounts about being gay in the military. *Conduct Unbecoming: Gays & Lesbians in the U.S. Military* (New York: St. Martin's Press, 1993) is Randy Shilts's exhaustive look at the issue, full of case histories.

Drug babies: Infants born to women who use legal and illegal DRUGS. Such children frequently have physical and mental impairments. A national debate over how to protect the unborn from drug exposure intensified in the 1990's, when a growing number of babies were born addicted to crack COCAINE.

Maternal cocaine abuse can result in the birth of babies with life-threatening cardiovascular and central nervous system complications, while babies born to alcoholic mothers often suffer from abnormalities resulting from fetal alcohol syndrome such as prenatal growth deficiencies and microcephaly. Women who smoke during pregnancy deliver infants with significantly lower birthweight than do nonsmoking women.

The combined costs for treating premature or critically ill drug-exposed newborns, for establishing effective treatment facilities for women in recovery, and for hearing cases in civil and criminal court were estimated to be in the billions. The influx of "cocaine babies" into public schools led to speculation about the negative long-term effects they would have on the schools and on society at large.

Debates over how to reduce the incidence of prenatal drug exposure focused on how health professionals and the civil and CRIMINAL JUSTICE SYSTEMS should respond to women who use drugs during their pregnancies. Proponents of the disease model of addiction argued that pregnant and postpartum drug-addicted women need treatment, parent training, and other sup-

port. Those who believed that such drug abuse is a form of fetal and CHILD ABUSE called for criminal charges and civil sanctions.

Fetal abuse, child endangerment, and feticide are some of the criminal charges that have been brought against drug-addicted pregnant women. One of the earliest cases, *Johnson v. State of Florida* (1989), involving a woman who used cocaine during her pregnancy, resulted in a conviction for delivery of a controlled substance to a minor. The conviction, however, was overturned in 1992 by the Florida Supreme Court, which held that "delivery," as used in the state statute, did not refer to substances received by a fetus from its mother through the umbilical cord.

Those who opposed the criminalization of perinatal drug abuse asked whether fetuses have rights, when such rights are acquired, and whether any such rights can ever supersede the rights of mothers. Ensuing arguments over these questions closely parallelled those related to the contentious debate over ABORTION, including whether there is a right to life and a right to be born healthy.

The most widely used civil penalty involves the loss of custody of drug-exposed newborns, with babies frequently taken into protective custody by social-service agencies immediately after birth. Some mothers never attempt to regain custody of their babies; those newborns, who are left behind in hospitals, known as "boarder babies," form an ongoing problem for overcrowded foster-care systems.

Key to the controversy over the most effective and societally acceptable response to pregnant and postpartum drug abusers is the juxtaposing of maternal and fetal rights, inevitably leading to litigation and legislation.

SUGGESTED READING: Sandra Anderson Garcia discusses perinatal drug abuse in "Maternal Drug Abuse: Laws and Ethics as Agents of Just Balances and Therapeutic Interventions" in *The International Journal of the Addictions* (1993).

Drug czar: Unofficial designation given the director of the U.S. Office of National Drug Control Policy, a cabinet-level organization established to coordinate "Federal, State, and local efforts to control illegal drug abuse and [devise] national strategies to effectively carry out antidrug activities." When Congress created the office by the Narcotics Leadership Act of 1988, it envisioned the drug czar (a presidential appointee

Drug Enforcement Administration

needing Senate confirmation) as an antidrug crusader who would rally the public behind the WAR ON DRUGS. From the outset, however, the czar's power and influence were more apparent than real. William J. Bennett, the first czar, came closest to achieving the intent of Congress, but he resigned in frustration. Another George BUSH appointee, former Florida governor Bob Martinez was rarely consulted during his tenure as drug czar; Lee Brown, Bill CLINTON's choice to head the office, had to preside in the wake of a staff cut that reduced his personnel from 112 to 25.

1968 to 1973 and then to the DEA, which was organized to coordinate national, state, local, and international antidrug efforts in the WAR ON DRUGS. The DEA's activities have expanded since its inception, a fact reflected in the agency's growth from nearly 1,500 officers in 1973 to more than 3,500 in 1992 and in the number of arrests, which increased from 7,500 to 25,000 during those same years. Critics have charged that the DEA spreads its efforts too thin by attacking all criminal drug activities instead of focusing on large trafficking organizations.

Drug Enforcement Administration (DEA): U.S. law-enforcement agency created July, 1973. The DEA is the principal federal agency charged with implementing "narcotics and controlled substances laws and regulations," a task managed by the Treasury Department's Federal Bureau of Narcotics from 1930 until 1968. Responsibility passed to the Department of Justice's Bureau of Narcotics and Dangerous Drugs from

Drug legalization: Controversy over the implications and consequences of legalizing various illegal DRUGS. Would legalization result in an increase in drug use? Would it reduce drug-related crime? Debate swirls around such questions. While most of the attention has focused on MARIJUANA, the legalization of other drugs, such as COCAINE, HEROIN, hallucinogens, and amphetamines, has also been debated.

COCAINE AND MARIJUANA CONFISCATED BY THE DEA, 1978-1990

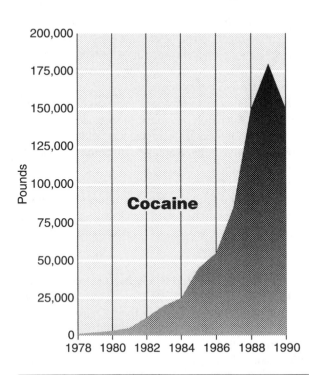

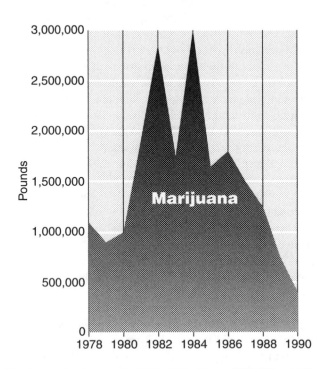

Source: U.S. Department of Justice, Bureau of Justice Statistics, *Drugs, Crime, and the Justice System.* Washington, D.C.: U.S. Government Printing Office, 1992.

PERCENTAGE OF NATIONAL OPINION RESEARCH CENTER RESPONDENTS WHO OPPOSE MARIJUANA LEGALIZATION

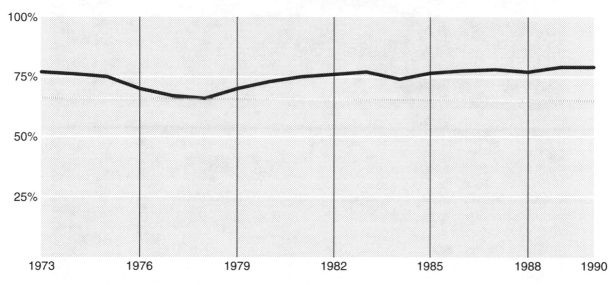

Source: U.S. Department of Justice, Bureau of Justice Statistics, *Drugs, Crime, and the Justice System.* Washington, D.C.: U.S. Government Printing Office, 1992.
Note: Based on interpolated NORC data from a number of sources.

History. During the 1800's in the United States, "medicinal" tonics and elixirs containing drugs such as morphine and cocaine were sold to the public by traveling salesmen in the patent medicine industry. With the passage of the Harrison Act in 1914, which restricted the importation and distribution of narcotics and cocaine, the United States entered into an ongoing era of efforts to control the importation, sale, and use of mood-altering drugs. The passage of the Marijuana Tax Act in 1937 placed controls on marijuana distribution. In the mid-1960's, the government identified and placed restrictions on a number of drugs, referred to thereafter as controlled substances. The Comprehensive Drug Abuse Prevention and Control Act of 1970 identified five schedules into which controlled substances were to be placed based upon their potential for abuse and medical utility. Drugs in Schedule I, considered to be the most dangerous and thus are the most tightly controlled, include heroin, LSD, and marijuana.

During the late 1960's and early 1970's, there was a move to decriminalize drug use. In fact, based in part on a report from the National Commission on Marijuana and Drug Abuse, the federal government in 1972 affirmed its support for the decriminalization of pos-

session of small amounts of marijuana. Beginning with Oregon in 1973, eleven states eventually downgraded the possession of small amounts of marijuana, typically from a misdemeanor to a violation.

By the end of the 1970's, this decriminalization "campaign" had lost some of its momentum. In the 1980's, the Republican administrations of Ronald REAGAN and George BUSH argued for increased criminalization, including heavier sanctions for drug distributors. In fact, federal antidrug legislation in 1988 provided for the death penalty for high-level drug traffickers.

The controversy over legalization, however, continued into the 1990's, with proponents arguing that it would ease the drug problem and opponents arguing that it would exacerbate it. Proponents suggested various policies, making distinctions between legalization and decriminalization (elimination versus reduction of the criminal status of a drug), as well as between selected or controlled legalization (elimination or reduction of the criminal status of particular drugs, with regulations, for example, taxing use or sale, or restricting use by age).

Arguments for Legalization. Advocates argue that the criminalization of drugs is undesirable and harm-

National Organization for the Reform of Marijuana Laws (NORML) executive director Gregory Porter, a leading advocate of drug legalization, at a 1992 rally. (AP/Wide World Photos)

ful. One set of arguments centers on "citizens' rights." Citizens, it is said, have the right to protection from state interference in behaviors or lifestyles that do not pose any serious societal harm. This view is typically set forth in regard to the legalization of marijuana, backed by studies indicating that the use of small amounts of marijuana is relatively safe healthwise, is not classically addictive, does not produce violent behavior, and, in fact, does have some medical utility, for example, the alleviation of nausea caused by chemotherapy for cancer patients and in the treatment of glaucoma. A related argument is that criminalization may violate the right to religious freedom. An example is the historical use of PEYOTE in the religious ceremonies of some Native American tribes, a practice that had been criminally sanctioned in many states. In 1994, however, President Bill CLINTON signed into law the RELIGIOUS FREEDOM RESTORATION ACT, exempting peyote from antidrug laws when it is used in Native American religious ceremonies.

Another "rights" argument is that because the prevailing view is that ADDICTION is a medical disease, criminalization of drug use runs afoul of the SUPREME COURT ruling in *Robinson v. California* (1962) that it is unconstitutional to criminalize a condition or status, such as addict or alcoholic. Rather, people with a disease, the argument continues, have a right to treatment.

More common among prolegalization social scientists are cost-benefit analyses. One line of reasoning is that criminalization has failed to stop drug sales or use. According to proponents, there is no evidence, for example, that rates of marijuana use are significantly affected by legislation that either increases or decreases penalties for such use. Relatedly, it is suggested that criminalization drains law enforcement resources, with little gain. For example, if personal use of marijuana is not particularly harmful, is it wise to use scarce dollars to enforce the law against marijuana use rather than against more harmful crimes?

Other prolegalization views focus on the extent to which criminalization causes other crimes. Studies show that heavy drug users engage in a large amount of CRIME. According to proponents, however, crime rates in the United States have historically been high, regardless of the level of drug use at a particular time. Advocates believe that legalization, along with treatment, would eliminate the need for addicts to live a criminal lifestyle, including buying and using illegal drugs and engaging in predatory crimes to pay for them. Legalization would also mean safer methods and conditions for taking drugs for those addicts unable to quit using. Additionally, with taxes or registration fees, legalization would actually increase government revenues. At the same time, legalization would take the huge profits out of the illegal drug industry, a criminal network that has expanded globally and is involved in a sizeable amount of crime and VIOLENCE.

Arguments Against Legalization. Opponents of drug legalization point to the many harms that illegal drugs bring to individuals, families, and society at large. Illegal drug use, it is argued, is responsible for illness, injury, and even the death of countless individuals, and has destroyed the motivation and chances for success of others. Children living with parents who are drug addicts, or who are born to women who took drugs during pregnancy, are harmed by others' drug use. Further, in this view, society is weakened to the extent to which its members are rendered less capable by the use of drugs.

Like proponents of legalization, opponents point to research showing an enormous amount of drug-related crime and violence. The opponents argue, however, that illegal drug activities cause other crime and that the arm of the law should be fully extended to control drug use and sale.

Another argument against legalization is that the addictive effects of most illegal drugs make them subject to compulsive or obsessive use. With legalization, such drugs would be more accessible, opponents argue, and use would increase. The proliferation of and problems associated with alcohol and tobacco, both legal and addictive drugs, serve as examples. It is also pointed out that during PROHIBITION (of alcohol), ushered in through the Eighteenth Amendment in 1920 and repealed in 1933, the rate of alcohol consumption actually declined.

Opponents of legalization may also view addiction as a disease requiring treatment, but see that as compatible with a law enforcement approach to illegal drug activities. As illustrated in diversion programs set up in some jurisdictions, the CRIMINAL JUSTICE SYSTEM and the treatment community have joined forces to allow some arrestees (for example, drivers under the influence of intoxicants) to avoid going to trial if they enter and complete a drug treatment program. Additionally, some offenders may be sentenced to a treatment program, or have such treatment be a condition of their probation or PAROLE.

It is also suggested that there is an important moral message in the criminalization of drugs. If a society believes that the recreational use of mood-altering, potentially addictive, drugs is harmful to current and future generations and to the social fabric as well, then it is society's duty to subject such behavior to formal as well as informal sanctions. To legalize drugs would be akin to encouraging and facilitating their use and would create a market that could only thrive through the continuance of demand for its product.

Ongoing Policy Shifts. By the beginning of the 1990's, the "War on Drugs" of the previous decade had waned. President Clinton streamlined the federal office in charge of drug policy, cutting back both its budget and staff. The president also announced a shift in antidrug resources, with more emphasis on prevention and treatment than in the preceding "law enforcement" years. Following a leveling off of drug use among U.S. youth throughout most of the 1980's (and actually a notable decline for marijuana use), there were again signs of an upswing in use in the early 1990's. The effects of the 1980's "war" were evident in U.S. federal prisons, where, in the late 1980's, more than one-third of the inmates were drug offenders. The conservative public mood in the early 1990's, backed by a sympathetic 1994 Republican Congress, was reflected in the relative silence of proponents of legalization. It was clear, however, that the war against drugs had not been won under traditional criminalization policies.   —*Kathryn Ann Farr*

SUGGESTED READINGS: Erich Goode discusses U.S. drug policies and several forms that decriminalization might take in *Drugs in American Society* (New York: Alfred A. Knopf, 1993). A review of arguments and evidence regarding efforts to control marijuana is offered in Mark Kleiman's *Marijuana: Costs of Abuse, Costs of Control* (New York: Greenwood Press, 1989). In his article "Drug Prohibition in the United States: Costs, Consequences, and Alternatives" in *Science* (no. 245, 1989), Ethan Nadelmann presents arguments in favor of drug legalization.

Drug testing: Employer-conducted testing for drug abuse. Issues of constitutional rights have been raised against the assertion that drug testing is necessary to protect the health and safety of the public.

Background. Despite efforts by the government and other societal institutions to reduce drug abuse in the United States, more than 11 million Americans reported the use of one or more illicit drugs in the 1992 National Household Survey on Drug Abuse. In that same year,

93 percent of companies with more than five thousand employees reported some type of drug-testing program. Drug testing is also performed on participants in most major athletic events, especially international contests such as the OLYMPIC GAMES. Such testing includes analysis for STEROIDS and other performance-enhancing substances as well as for the recreational DRUGS normally monitored in employee testing.

During the 1970's and 1980's, rapid automated screening methods for analyzing urine for the presence of drugs were developed based on a technique called enzyme immunoassay. Reports of widespread drug use by American troops in Vietnam and a widely publicized drug-related accident aboard an aircraft carrier in the early 1980's led to the institution of mass drug screening in the U.S. military. Media coverage of a series of civilian transportation disasters and the drug use of prominent sports figures inspired the Ronald REAGAN Administration to issue a 1986 Executive Order requiring federal employees in security-sensitive or public-protection jobs to be tested for drugs. The Omnibus Transportation Employee Testing Act of 1991 mandated drug and alcohol testing for all federal employees of the Department of Transportation (DOT); commercial interstate truck drivers and aviation, railroad, and mass-transit employees were all eventually included under the act's provisions.

Arguments Against. Opponents of mandatory drug-testing policies argue that employee drug use is a personal matter that is of concern to the employer only when job performance is seriously impaired. Violations of DUE PROCESS, PRIVACY, and EQUAL PROTECTION rights have been claimed, not only by labor unions and the AMERICAN CIVIL LIBERTIES UNION (ACLU) but also by individual employees.

The Fourth Amendment to the U.S. CONSTITUTION protects citizens from "unreasonable searches and seizures." Legally, a drug test is considered a search. Government workers are more clearly protected by this amendment than private employees are, but any unreasonable and arbitrary testing requirements could be grounds for contesting the results of a test in court. Courts have generally held that a "reasonable search" is one premised on a "reasonable suspicion" of an employee's drug use when such use creates a performance problem, safety hazard, or security risk.

Controversy has often arisen over the integrity of testing processes and the accuracy and use of results. Many drug-testing programs require witnessed specimen donation to insure against adulteration of the specimen by the donor. Most employees regard observation of the urine-collection process by a stranger as an invasion of privacy. Violations of privacy rights also involve the failure to maintain confidentiality of records and the unauthorized release of test results.

The Constitution requires the U.S. government to provide "due process of law" before depriving any individual of life, liberty, or property. This means, for example, that a fair decision-making process must be followed before the government takes any punitive measures that could result in wrongful discharge, intentional infliction of emotional distress, or DEFAMATION of character. Although constitutional protection applies mainly to governmental actions, courts have come to expect a similar fairness in employer-employee relations. Due process is also pertinent to debates over the accuracy of drug testing. Debates regarding accuracy involve not only such issues as whether a positive result is correct but also the use of such a result as concrete evidence that the person tested was under the influence of a prohibited drug. A positive urine drug test shows the presence of a substance at or above a certain threshold concentration, but such a result cannot be used to prove impairment, the dose taken, or the exact time the drug was consumed by the user.

Equal-protection rights are likely to be violated if an employer discriminates against a particular group or type of employee, particularly if discrimination has been based on gender, minority, or disabled status. Some employee drug-test results have been challenged because a positive sample would violate the Fifth Amendment right to avoid self-incriminating testimony. This challenge, however, has not met with success, since courts have consistently ruled that drug test results are not admissible as testimony.

Arguments for Drug Testing. Proponents of drug testing regard SUBSTANCE ABUSE by workers as a serious threat to the safety of their fellow employees and citizens. Employees with abuse problems increase a company's health and disability insurance costs and can be a threat to the security of sensitive government agencies and corporations. These arguments have proved most persuasive to both the courts and the public when applied to workers in health care, public transportation, law enforcement, or any occupation in which performance impairment could lead to a disaster. Drug testing in athletic events is based on universal rules of fair play and the desire that the contest be held on a "level playing field."

Proponents argue that drug-testing laboratories are highly accurate when testing is performed according to rigorous standards of quality. The most important of these are that the testing procedure provide for confirmatory testing of all positive screening results by an alternative method and that a chain of custody (documentation of who has transported and handled the specimen so that tampering or mislabeling of specimens can be checked) be maintained. According to proponents, any drug-testing program should also have an official written policy available to any employee or job applicant. This written policy should provide adequate notice of testing procedures and circumstances, list drugs to be monitored, and outline steps to be taken in the event of a positive result. This last requirement also should include an appeal process guaranteeing an employee's right to contest or explain results. If legitimate prescription drugs such as pain-relievers, tranquilizers, and sedatives are also monitored, a medical review officer should be designated to review positive results and determine if a legitimate

U.S. BUSINESSES WITH DRUG-TESTING PROGRAMS

Industry	Percentage of Businesses with Testing Programs	Total Number of Businesses in the Industry
Mining	21.6	31,600
Communications and public utilities	17.6	37,500
Transportation	14.9	153,500
Manufacturing:		
Durable goods	9.9	193,900
Nondurable goods	9.1	141,200
Wholesale trade	5.3	467,900
Finance, insurance, and real estate	3.2	403,900
Construction	2.3	458,100
Services	1.4	1,553,400
Retail trade	.7	1,101,800
All establishments	3.2	4,542,800

Source: U.S. Department of Justice, Bureau of Justice Statistics, *Drugs, Crime, and the Justice System.* Washington, D.C.: U.S. Government Printing Office, 1992. Primary source is Bureau of Labor Statistics, 1989.

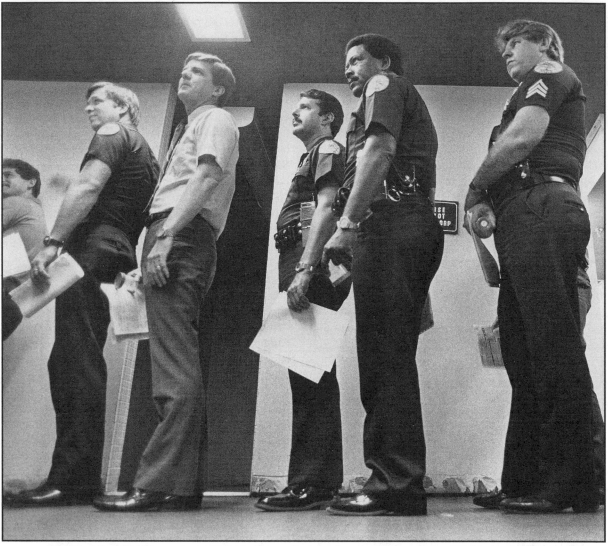

Miami policemen line up to participate in a voluntary drug-testing program. (UPI/Corbis-Bettmann)

medical use is warranted. Many workplace policies call for rehabilitation and treatment rather than outright dismissal when an employee tests positive for a prohibited drug.

In 1988, the federal DEPARTMENT OF HEALTH AND HUMAN SERVICES (DHHS) issued its Mandatory Guidelines for Federal Workplace Drug Testing Programs, which provided standards for all federally regulated drug testing. One year later, the DOT issued procedures for transportation workplace drug testing that mandated preemployment and random testing, testing during periodic physicals, and testing after accidents. The regulations include descriptions of laboratory testing procedures and guidelines for assurance of laboratory quality, use of testing controls, and reporting re-

sults. The DHHS regulations (known as "NIDA guidelines" because they originated with the NATIONAL INSTITUTE ON DRUG ABUSE) were mandated for laboratories wishing to do such testing. A system of inspections was set up to provide approval for laboratories doing federal drug testing. Once approved, laboratories are known as NIDA or SAMHSA (Substance Abuse and Mental Health Services Administration) laboratories. Although these rules are not mandated in the private workplace, they have been adopted by many laboratories that test both the public and private work forces.

Summary. The constitutional and human rights issues of mandatory drug testing have been reviewed in many court cases. The legal basis for such testing is secure when it is performed according to the rigorous rules established by NIDA guidelines and when an adequate policy to protect employee rights is in force. In the absence of a national testing policy applicable to both the public and private workplaces, however, controversy will likely continue to swirl around drug-testing policies and the rights of the persons being tested.

—*David J. Wells*

SUGGESTED READINGS: Issues of societal protection versus violation of individual rights by mandatory drug testing are discussed by Edward J. Imwinkelried in "False Positive" (*The Sciences*, September/October, 1987). Regulations for testing federal employees are given in "Mandatory Guidelines for Federal Workplace Testing Programs, *Federal Register*, vol. 53, 1988, and vol. 59, 1994. Two books by David G. Evans, an attorney who specializes in drug testing and drug-free workplace law, deal with the legal aspects of drug testing and how to set up such a program: *Drug Testing Law, Technology, and Practice* (1991) and *Designing an Effective Drug-Free Workplace Compliance Program* (1993) (both published by Clark Boardman Callaghan: Deerfield, Ill.). A discussion of preemployment drug testing, "Financial Viability of Screening for Drugs of Abuse," by Michael A. Peat, was published in *Clinical Chemistry*, vol. 41, no. 5 (1995).

Drug trade: Consumer-driven global industry with an annual revenue amounting to billions of dollars. The extensive use of DRUGS since the 1960's has provoked a debate over DRUG LEGALIZATION that involves political, economic, and moral issues and cuts across partisan and ideological lines.

Background. Until the twentieth century, Americans used drugs for medical and recreational purposes on a fairly wide scale. Doctors routinely prescribed opiates because they successfully relieved pain, treated gastrointestinal disorders, tranquilized anxieties, and calmed hyperactive children. The medical profession welcomed COCAINE as an effective prescription for hay fever, sinusitis, and as an energizing tonic. Both doctors and unlicensed healers and hucksters dispensed opiates, cocaine, and other powerful drugs. Coca Cola contained cocaine until 1903; it was also not uncommon to find cigarettes and cigars laced with the drug. Morphine was prescribed to cure opium addiction; HEROIN to prevent morphine addiction; and cocaine to remedy all of the other addictions. Although several states passed largely ineffective antinarcotic laws, no vigorous federal legislation controlling the production, distribution, or consumption of most drugs appeared until the Harrison Act of 1914. At that time, roughly a half-million addicts and millions of provisional users had nearly unlimited access to practically any drug.

Challenges to this casual approach to drugs began to appear in the late nineteenth century as temperance movements organized to rid the nation and the world of various evils, especially alcohol and narcotics. Greater awareness of the potency of drugs led physicians, pharmacists, manufacturers, and the federal government to begin regulating these products, the earliest example being the Pure Food and Drug Act of 1906. Thus began the first in a series of government actions designed to establish control over drug activities from raw material to consumption. Gradually, a Washington bureaucracy emerged to define what could be legitimately ingested, when they could be legally taken (for medically acceptable reasons only), and who could dispense these drugs and how. The Harrison Act went beyond the scientific rationale of the Pure Food and Drug Act, which was designed to protect society's physical well-being, to safeguard society's moral health as well. This soon became the prime objective of drug legislation as the national government sought to label addicts as people predisposed to crime and other aberrant acts. Enforced initially by the Treasury Department's Bureau of Internal Revenue, antidrug laws would be implemented by the newly created Bureau of Narcotics (now the Drug Enforcement Administration) after 1930. Headed by Harry J. Anslinger from its inception until 1962, the bureau aimed to root out all dangerous drugs by strict enforcement and through a public relations campaign to deny drug habitués any semblance of respectability.

Although many would challenge the narrowing range of permissible drug behavior, middle America generally endorsed—unlike with alcohol PROHIBITION— the government's definition of acceptable drug activities into the 1960's. The counter-cultural movement launched during that decade extolled the virtues of drugs and helped to spread usage into mainstream society. By the 1970's, growing antagonism to now-fashionable drug practices, especially among the young, resulted in a crusade known as the WAR ON DRUGS. Since then, the United States has been engaged in battles to persuade the American people that the war needs to be fought and can be won, if not unconditionally at least decisively; and to convince traffickers in illicit drugs that they cannot prevail. Victory in both battles presumes the cooperation of most

Americans, who will not only be called upon to refrain from personal drug usage but to disdain the drug indulgences of others.

Production and Distribution. The labeling of drugs is no small task given that both scientific and social definitions need to be considered. Drugs originate in fields and pharmaceutical laboratories. Some are natural, others synthetic; some are legal, others illicit. All are produced and marketed based on manufacturers' perceptions of consumer demand. Some drug entrepreneurs are legitimate, others criminal. The bulk of some drugs are domestically produced (for example, marijuana, PCP, and LSD), while the preponderance of others are of foreign origin (for example, opiates and cocaine). Some drugs designed for legitimate purposes (for example, amphetamines or "uppers," and depressants or "downers") end up in the illicit market. All illicit drugs get to the consumer via illegal networks, local GANGS, and individual distributors.

MARIJUANA is a major agricultural crop in the United States. Many farmers in the 1960's grew it to supplement income or to supply themselves and friends. By the late twentieth century, it had become one of the top three crops in California, where annual harvests reap more than $2 billion and the national income from it is estimated to be many times more. Thousands of marijuana "plantations" have been uncovered in the national forests, and many more remain hidden. As government crackdowns became more frequent, many growers turned to greenhouses and other covered facilities for increased security. In urban areas, and increasingly in rural locations too, drug laboratories in private homes and apartments sprouted up to produce METHAMPHETAMINES and other drugs. As with marijuana or other domestically produced illegal drugs, there is very little investment, substantial return, and limited risk. Many "designer drugs" are so new that they have not been designated illegal. What amounts to cottage industries often distribute what they produce and sometimes farm-out sales to bikers or inner-city gangs, but larger international organizations have also entered this lucrative market.

Opiates (opium, morphine, heroin) and cocaine are the principal commodities of international drug traffickers. More than 90 percent of the world's opium is produced in the Golden Triangle (Laos, Thailand, and Burma, now Myanmar) and the Golden Crescent (Iran, Afghanistan, and Pakistan). Until the 1980's, most opium leaving the Golden Triangle made its way to Bangkok or Hong Kong and thence to the West Coast of the United States or to Europe and finally to the American East Coast.

The MAFIA in Sicily and New York and the Corsican syndicate operating in Marseilles controlled the majority of the drugs entering the United States until the 1970's. Since then, organized crime in the former Soviet Union has taken over much of the Golden Crescent trade, and Nigerians have become leading middlemen in the opium trade between Asian producers and European and American consumers. International Chinese secret societies dominate distribution of opiates in the United States, with increasingly large amounts smuggled from Canada and Mexico. In Vancouver, Hong Kong-Chinese and Vietnamese-Chinese gangs compete to ship Golden Triangle drugs to American markets via desolate border regions in Idaho, Montana, and North Dakota. In Mexico, Asian drug lords utilize well-established local cocaine cartels to smuggle opiates north.

Most of the world's coca leaves are grown in Peru, Bolivia, Ecuador, Colombia, and Chile, where they are also refined into cocaine. Thereafter, Colombian cartels (mainly the Cali and Medellin) and Mexican cartels (chiefly in Tijuana, Sinaloa, Ciudad Juarez, and the Gulf cities) manage the marketing of the drug. The Mexican traffickers, who account for approximately three-fourths of all cocaine sold in the United States, became major actors in cocaine distribution when the American government began to close off the traditional cocaine points of entry in south Florida and the Caribbean in the late 1980's. Subsequently, Colombian cartels farmed out distribution to the Mexicans, who could move the drug up the "Pacific corridor."

Consumption and Prohibition. Given the illegal nature of the drug trade, the amount of drugs imported and consumed cannot be determined with precision. In the late 1980's, a Senate Task Force for a Drug-Free America estimated that 23 million Americans used drugs at least monthly, a number that corresponds with a 1995 assessment that roughly 10 percent of the American population has a regular appetite for illegal drugs. A heated debate has been unfolding since the 1970's between those who demand prohibition of all drugs deemed to be dangerous and those who claim that legalization of proscribed drugs will benefit society.

Prohibitionists argue that the War on Drugs must be fought to protect society from the health problems, accidents, loss of productivity, criminal activity, and suicides associated with drug use. Moral considerations were foremost in the mind of former Drug Czar Wil-

Policemen examine eight tons of confiscated hashish. (Reuters/Corbis-Bettmann)

New York City drug dealers pose for a photo in 1983. (UPI/Corbis-Bettman)

liam J. Bennett when he contended that "drug use—especially heavy drug use—destroys human character. It destroys dignity and autonomy, it burns away the sense of responsibility, it subverts productivity, it makes a mockery of virtue." Liberals commonly join with conservatives to stamp out drug use for other than acceptable medical purposes.

Legalizers stress the practical and civil-rights advantages of ending the War on Drugs. Conservatives William F. Buckley, Milton Friedman, and Paul Craig Roberts look at the war as unwinnable, costly, and socially damaging. Legalizing drugs would prevent the crime and gang activity associated with drugs, reduce the jail population, unburden the court system, allow the police to focus on serious crime, and save billions of dollars. The AMERICAN CIVIL LIBERTIES UNION (ACLU) and most civil libertarians maintain that DRUG TESTING, heavy-handed enforcement policies, and the denial of personal freedoms necessitate an end to the conflict. Moreover, legalization would not lead to greater drug use, any more than readily available tobacco and alcohol result in mass ADDICTION or inebriation. Columnist George Will has countered by stating that we can change our attitudes about drugs if politicians have the courage to guide the people out of the abyss. Why accept socially destructive behavior simply because it is difficult to harness? This is parried with, why attempt to control behavior that need not be ruinous? As with SLAVERY, ABORTION, and other core issues, drug use will continue to be hotly debated.

Canada. In many ways, Canadian thought about and handling of drugs have paralleled the U.S. positions.

Until the early twentieth century, Canada did not restrict drug use; however, reformers in Canada and other industrial nations eventually succeeded in forcing their governments to regulate drug trafficking and consumption. The 1908 Opium Act and subsequent antidrug statutes aimed to control drugs deemed to be dangerous. As in the United States, drug users were pictured as depraved junkies and were subjected to stiff jail sentences when convicted. Although the Narcotic Control Act of 1961 continued to specify harsh punishments for nearly all drug transgressions, it in fact only targeted major traffickers and allowed the CRIMINAL JUSTICE SYSTEM discretion in dealing with minor offenders. The Royal Canadian Mounted Police (RCMP), the agency that deals with drug enforcement in Canada, collaborates with the U.S. DRUG ENFORCEMENT ADMINISTRATION (DEA) in attempts to halt trafficking and consumption in both countries. The RCMP's thousand-person Drug Enforcement Directorate plays the central part in implementing Canada's National Drug Strategy, launched in 1987, which resembles the U.S. War on Drugs. Yet Canada's attempt to eradicate drugs has raised issues of costs, both economic and political. —*Thomas D. Reins*

SUGGESTED READINGS: The most thorough historical survey of the drug problem in the United States is physician David F. Musto's highly readable *The American Disease: Origins of Narcotic Control* (New York: Oxford University Press, 1987). Economists Daniel K. Benjamin and Roger LeRoy Miller argue that control over drug policies should be the responsibility not of the national government but of the states in *Undoing Drugs: Beyond Legalization* (New York: Basic Books, 1991). A detailed discussion of the chemical, psychological, and social consequences of the most frequently used legal and illegal drugs can be found in Richard G. Schlaadt and Peter T. Shannon's *Drugs* (Englewood Cliffs, N.J.: Prentice-Hall, 1990).

The classic commentary on drug users and their opponents is psychiatrist Thomas Szasz's *Ceremonial Chemistry: The Ritual Persecution of Drugs, Addicts, and Pushers* (Garden City, N.Y.: Anchor Press, 1974). William O. Walker chronicles historical and contemporary drug trafficking in the Western Hemisphere in *Drug Control in the Americas* (Albuquerque: University of New Mexico Press, 1989). Drug trafficking in Asia is diligently examined in Alfred W. McCoy's *The Politics of Heroin: CIA Complicity in the Global Drug Trade* (Brooklyn, N.Y.: Lawrence Hill Books, 1991). The best one-volume pro-and-con discussion of drugs is Neal Bernards' *War on Drugs: Opposing Viewpoints* (San Diego: Greenhaven Press, 1990). The entire Winter, 1991, issue of the *Journal of Drug Issues* provides Canadian perspectives on the drug quandary there.

Drugs, addictive: Substances that cause physical or psychological dependency. People can become addicted to a wide range of drugs, including barbiturates, opiates, and alcohol.

Introduction. Drug addiction is measured relative to a person's reaction to drug use. Such reactions include the body's need for increasing amounts of a drug (tolerance), the body's predictable response of discomfort whenever the drug is unavailable (withdrawal), and the user's psychological craving for the drug (habituation). Stimulants such as COCAINE, depressants such as HEROIN, and hallucinogenic drugs such as LSD can produce these reactions.

It is helpful to distinguish between drug use, drug abuse, and drug addiction; "drug use" is not synonymous with "drug abuse." Drug abuse can be defined only with reference to the culture and society in which the drug is taken. Drug abuse is using an illicit drug, such as cocaine in the United States, or using a substance the use of which is legal under medical supervision, such as barbiturates in the United States, without medical supervision. For example, the Peruvian Indians of the Andes Mountains ingest cocaine by chewing coca leaves, a process that helps them to adapt to life in the mountains. Scientists believe that the alkaloids in the coca leaves may aid respiration at higher elevations. The peasants have larger hearts and higher red-blood cell counts than nonmountainous people. These people, by definition, are not drug abusers, as they are not using either an illicit drug or a licit drug in an illegal manner. Certainly, they do not think of themselves as drug abusers. They are, however, addicted to cocaine.

Drug addiction involves some level of dependence on a drug, reflecting either the need or the compulsion to continue taking the drug, continually or periodically. The drug is typically taken either to maintain or to modify a particular mood or state of mind, and such use may be harmful to either the individual or society. "Drug abuse" is therefore also not synonymous with "drug addiction." Some, if not many, drug abusers stop taking drugs, on a permanent basis, often without treatment, before they experience any dependency; that is, before they are addicted.

A customs agent guards a seized shipment of heroin. (AP/Wide World Photos)

Drug Addiction: Crime or Disease? There is a long-standing and widespread debate about whether or not the "drug problem" is or ought to be considered a crime or a disease. Several legal distinctions have been made. Narcotics addiction has been classified as a disease by the U.S. Supreme Court (*Robinson v. California*, 1972), which ruled that punishment for this condition would be cruel and unusual as the addict cannot control his condition. The creation of the NATIONAL INSTITUTE ON DRUG ABUSE (NIDA) in 1973 represented the formal recognition by the federal government that drug abuse was a health problem. In contrast, the possession or sale of a wide range of specific substances is illegal and dealt with as a crime problem handled by the CRIMINAL JUSTICE SYSTEM.

The level of drug abuse and drug addiction is often related to the amount of crime in society. A greater proportion of criminals in recent decades are drug abusers, often dependent upon a variety of addictive drugs. To support their drug habits, drug abusers and addicts often engage in home burglaries, armed robberies, and other forms of theft, in addition to more directly drug-related activities such as dealing and possessing illicit drugs.

Opponents of the system contend that as long as drugs are criminalized, their possession and sale remain illegal, and law enforcement and the criminal justice system remain in the forefront of efforts to control illicit drugs, America will continue to have a widespread crime problem. These critics call for the legalization of illicit drugs as an effective way to fight crime. An alternative opinion is that the legalization of drugs may result in a decrease in crime but at the expense of a massive public health problem. For example, ACQUIRED IMMUNE DEFICIENCY SYNDROME (AIDS) is, in many cases, transmitted to other people through the reuse of contaminated needles used for intravenous injections of various drugs such as heroin. In some areas, one-half or more of AIDS cases result from use of contaminated needles, mostly by heterosexual users of illicit drugs. Although the level of drug abuse as well as drug addiction is apparently higher in the United States than in any other industrial society, the drug problem is not solely an American issue but is of concern globally.

History and Development. A historical account of the evolution of the U.S. response to drugs offers insight not only into past and present drug use, abuse, and addiction but also into the changing nature of American society itself.

Beer and wine, naturally fermented products of grain and grapes, date back to ancient times. Distilled alcohol, first widely available in the nineteenth century, was a result of certain technological developments; distilled spirits made people feel good and were initially thought to be beneficial. As the devastating effects of distilled gin and other distilled spirits became apparent, however, society slowly attempted to limit and even prohibit their use.

As beer and wine are naturally fermented products, so narcotics and stimulants are natural attributes of the poppy and coca plant. In the mid-nineteenth century, the development of organic chemistry led to the production of morphine from opium. In conjunction with the development of the hypodermic needle, morphine addiction became widespread. Next, heroin was developed from morphine; then cocaine, the active ingredient of the coca leaf, was isolated. Cocaine addiction spread, again in conjunction with the hypodermic needle. The evolution of addictive drugs—beer and wine to whiskey, opium to morphine to heroin, and coca to cocaine—was largely technologically driven. This ascent reached its most potent form in crack cocaine, a product of folk science, not organic chemistry.

Americans have been taking drugs to modify moods since before the Civil War. Until early in the twentieth century, opiates were a common ingredient in an array of patent medicines. Used by "respectable society," these substances were readily available to be purchased legally over the counter. As waves of immigrants poured into the United States, cities grew, and the country industrialized. Spurred on by journalists and moral reformers, Americans began to associate drug abuse and addiction with minorities and lower-class city dwellers. In the process of romanticizing the past, the tranquillity of rural, small-town life appeared in marked contrast to the poverty, crime, and unemployment—and drug abuse and addiction—seen as characteristic ills of urban living.

With the passage of the Harrison Act in 1914, the possession of narcotic drugs without a doctor's prescription became illegal. MARIJUANA was declared illegal in 1937. Following World War II, heroin use, especially among teenagers, rose in many large American cities. In the 1960's, many American soldiers were introduced to heroin, which was readily available in Vietnam. Cocaine has been in use in the United States since the 1950's, but its high price limited its use. By the mid-1980's, however, crack cocaine crystals, a relatively inexpensive drug, were being smoked in drug pipes in urban American cities, especially by younger users.

Recent drug policy reflects a combination soft-line and hard-line philosophy. For example, the Anti-Drug Abuse Act of 1988 provides for treatment on request to anyone desiring to overcome a drug problem. At the same time, vigorous and expanded law enforcement to interdict supplies and arrest dealers and users has been the primary goal of federal, state, and local governments. The mixture of policies is also seen in the fact that several states have decriminalized the possession of small amounts of marijuana for personal use, with no evidence that there has been any significant increase in the abuse or in addiction to other mood-altering drugs. Simultaneously, the federal government was steadfastly opposing all attempts to liberalize any laws against marijuana possession.   —*Charles E. Marske*

SUGGESTED READINGS: Norman Zinberg's *Drug, Set, and Setting* (New Haven, Conn.: Yale University Press, 1984) examines the reluctance of American physicians to engage in serious research on drugs. *Drug Trafficking* (San Diego: Greenhaven Press,

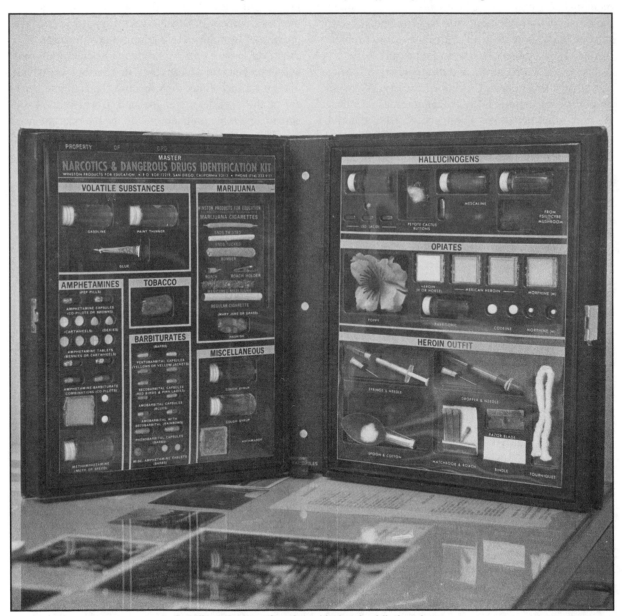

A police display of various kinds of addictive drugs.

A teacher lectures students on the dangers of addictive drugs. (James L. Shaffer)

1991), edited by Karin Swisher, discusses a number of current controversies surrounding drug use in America. Edited by Doris MacKenzie and Craig Uchida, *Drugs and Crime* (Thousand Oaks, Calif.: Sage, 1994) offers a useful analysis of the relationship between drugs and crime as well as a series of evaluative studies analyzing a number of policy initiatives.

Drugs, prescription: Controlled substances used legally for medicinal purposes. Access to prescription drugs is restricted to individuals with written authorization (a prescription) from a physician or dentist licensed to practice medicine or dentistry. They may be legally used only for specific situations (called indications). Prescription drugs are contrasted with over-the-counter drugs, the sales of which are not restricted.

Survey of Major Drugs. Prescription drugs can be categorized in several different ways: the site where the drug acts; the molecular structure of the drug; the type of problem or disease the drug addresses or is used to treat; the potential for addiction or abuse; the form in which the drug is provided; the annual sales of the drug; or the cost of the drug. Major drugs can be defined in terms of the volume prescribed or consumed, the dollar cost, or the importance in curing or addressing medical conditions.

The most frequently prescribed drugs in the United States vary from year to year. During the 1990's, there has been relative stability in the types of drugs prescribed: medications to control heart conditions, ulcer drugs, antibiotics, and antidepressants. Heart disease is the most frequent cause of death in the United States. It should not be surprising, therefore, that drugs to regulate heart activity, enhance the strength of heart-muscle contractions, improve the functioning of cardiac muscle on a molecular or tissue level, or simply to stimulate the heart as a whole account for a significant portion of prescribed drugs. Individuals of all ages are exposed to stressful situations that, in turn, can contribute to ulcer disease. The standard treatment usually includes drugs that reduce the production of acid by cells in the stomach. Two drugs of this variety can typically be found in the top ten most-prescribed list.

As a class, antibiotics are probably the most commonly prescribed drugs. There are, however, many different varieties of antibiotics, each useful for specific bacteria, diseases, or situations. Antidepressants are the other class of drugs commonly encountered in the most-prescribed list. There are usually two in the top ten. While the specific drug products have changed, this has been a constant finding since approximately 1970.

Measured in terms of dollar cost or revenue to pharmaceutical manufacturers, the major drugs parallel the classes already described. A drug's patent status, however, has a clear impact on cost. Pharmaceutical products can be protected by a patent, which lasts for seventeen years. During this time, manufacturers are afforded legal protection via the patent. Other companies can neither make nor sell the drug without permission from the patent holder. This creates a monopoly for the developing company. The theory behind patent protection is to allow companies to recover the often enormous costs (measured in billions of dollars) associated with developing, testing, and marketing a new drug. At any time, companies are free to set their own prices. When a patent expires, however, other companies are free to make and market previously protected drugs, referred to as generic drugs. Competition usually drives prices down. From the perspective of consumers, a major drug that loses patent protection will

usually remain a major drug as it continues to be widely used. From the perspective of specific manufacturers, a drug that loses patent protection typically does not contribute to corporate revenue at the same level as it did while being protected by a patent.

A drug's effectiveness in curing or addressing medical conditions is probably the most enduring measure of importance. As long as a drug continues to successfully address its indications, it will be used. Such use usually continues until a newer, more effective drug is developed; a cheaper but equally as effective drug is developed; an alternative mode of therapy is developed that renders the drug obsolete; or the bacteria against which the drug is effective become resistant, rendering the drug ineffective. The occurrence of one of these factors is usually behind the decline in usage of a drug.

Consumer Issues Regarding Efficacy. Efficacy is the maximum ability of a drug or treatment to produce a result, regardless of dosage. Different drugs may have the same efficacy but require different dosages of drug to attain the same effect. This rather technical issue has an impact upon consumers in terms of economics and choice.

Pharmaceutical manufacturers are in business to sell their products. To achieve their goal of sales, companies attempt to influence purchasers, hoping to persuade individuals to purchase their particular products. Magazines, television, and other media are used to deliver messages directly to consumers. This is relatively new; until the 1980's, such activity was not considered to be professional. Pharmaceutical manufacturers also try to influence the decisions of physicians in a number of subtle but completely legal ways. They provide information on drugs, free samples, support scientific meetings, and sponsor educational activities in hospitals. Individual physicians must assume the responsibility to come to their own conclusions about the activities of pharmaceutical manufacturers with which they come into contact. Consumers often enter the picture without knowledge of either pharmaceutical company activities or their physicians' reactions to them. Depending on the mind-set of the physician, an individual consumer may have limited choices for medications.

The other relevant aspect of efficacy involves economics. Different drugs may have nearly the same efficacies. Different drugs, however, may also have different costs. Left to their own choices, consumers may opt for the drug with the lowest price, but this may be a false economy. A fairer comparison would involve the total cost of achieving a given level or extent of efficacy rather than the cost per unit of medication.

Dangers Associated with Prescription Drugs. Prescription drugs are regulated in the United States and Canada, in part, to protect consumers. One hazard associated with many drugs is addiction. Addiction is defined as a physiological need to consume additional quantities of a substance because interrupting the supply of drug leads to physiological pain and discomfort. There is also usually a psychological component to addiction: Without the addictive substance, an individ-ual is not able to function normally. Many prescription drugs, such as analgesics, steroids, and antidepressants, have addictive potential.

Analgesic drugs relieve pain. In healthy people, some analgesics have the potential to induce a feeling of euphoria. In those suffering from pain, they have the ability to relieve the pain; if the dosage is incorrectly set at too high a level, these people may also experience euphoria. As patients recover from acutely painful conditions, the level of pain experienced decreases. Pain-relieving medications must be accordingly reduced. If

Alcohol and prescription drugs can be a dangerous mix. (James L. Shaffer)

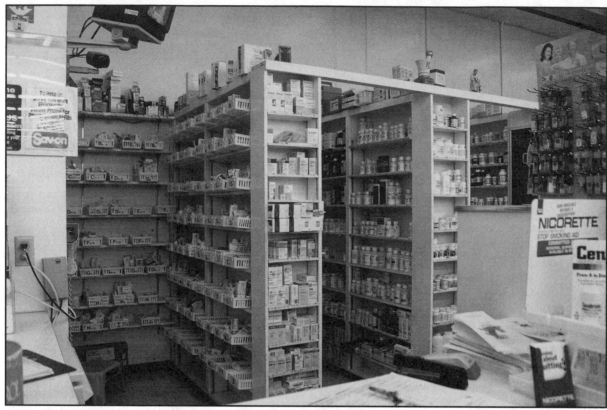

Prescription drugs are legally available only at pharmacies and other authorized dispensaries. (Yasmine Cordoba)

initial dosages are allowed to continue, the potential for addiction increases as actual pain decreases. Specific examples of analgesic medications that have addictive potential include narcotics (codeine and morphine) and synthetic opioids (meperidine).

STEROIDS comprise a potent class of molecules. Naturally occurring steroids are necessary for conception, embryonic maturation, and the development and maintenance of secondary sexual characteristics; most steroids are made by the adrenal glands. Therapeutically, they are used to reduce swelling in tissues, notably the brain and lungs. Physiologically, they have addictive potential without necessarily causing psychological dependence, although psychological dependence is fairly common. Addiction can be avoided by using the lowest possible dosage to achieve the desired therapeutic effect for the least amount of time and then tapering the dosage over a period of time rather than abruptly stopping administration. Some tissues in individuals who use steroids for long periods of time become physiologically dependent on the steroids. An example of this dependence is provided by an asthmatic who uses a steroid inhalant to open lung tis-

sues. After prolonged use, the adrenal gland is unable to respond to normal bodily demands for steroid production and a state of adrenal insufficiency can result. Psychological dependence can arise from the ability to breathe without obstruction. Rapid withdrawal can cause a rebound exacerbation of the disease that has the possibility of being fatal.

Antidepressants, by definition, create a feeling of well-being in most people and have been designed to elevate moods. This feeling of well-being has great potential for physiological and psychological addiction. Antidepressant drugs are usually prescribed for brief periods, typically not exceeding a few months.

Consuming two or more drugs simultaneously can lead to drug interactions and unwanted effects. Ingesting two or more drugs simultaneously is called polypharmacy. An example of drug interactions includes phenobarbital (a drug used to treat some types of epilepsy) interfering with the absorption of griseofulvin (used in the treatment of fungal infections). Cholestyramine is used to treat people with elevated levels of serum cholesterol, but it also interferes with the absorption of tetracycline (an antibiotic), digitoxin (used to strengthen weak heart muscles) and warfarin (used as an anticoagulant or "blood thinner"). Isoniazid, which is used to treat tuberculosis, inhibits the metabolism of phenytoin, a drug used to treat epilepsy.

One substance that interferes with many prescription drugs is alcohol. The effect may be unpleasant. Drinking alcohol while simultaneously taking the antibiotic cephamandole, the antibiotic moxalactam, or the amoebicide metronidazole will result in nausea, vomiting, and general discomfort. Mixing alcohol with barbiturates can lead to coma or death.

In theory, any drug can be tampered with or adulterated in its package. This is exceedingly rare with prescription drugs because of their restricted sales. Tampering is more common with over-the-counter, or nonprescription, drugs.

A final danger is allergy. Many people are sensitive to drugs. Drug reactions range from red, flushed skin to anaphylactic shock and death. Other adverse drug reactions include rash, heart irregularities, nausea, vomiting, high or low blood pressure, and headache. Individuals experiencing any unusual reaction to a drug should report them to a physician. It is also critical to share information concerning drug reactions with any hospital or doctor an individual encounters in the future. —*L. Fleming Fallon, Jr.*

SUGGESTED READINGS: *Lippincott's Illustrated Reviews: Pharmacology* (Philadelphia: J.B. Lippincott, 1992), edited by R. A. Harvey and P. C. Champe, is a technical text that can be easily understood by the general reader. *Physicians' Desk Reference*, fiftieth ed. (Montvale, N.J.: Medical Economics Company, 1996), updated annually, contains all the package inserts and other data about all prescription drugs available in the United States as provided by drug manufacturers.

Drunk driving: Operation of a motor vehicle while under the influence of alcohol. Alcohol and drug use contribute to more than half of all U.S. traffic fatalities each year. In the mid-1980's, for example, a person died every twenty-seven minutes in the United States as the result of an alcohol-related automobile accident. Extensive campaigns by anti-drunk-driving organizations such as MOTHERS AGAINST DRUNK DRIVING (MADD) and Students Against Drunk Driving (SADD), as well the passage of more stringent laws in some states, led to a reduction in the fatality rate in the 1990's. Nevertheless, thousands of drunk drivers remained on American roads.

Critics alleged that the persistence of drunk driving was largely the result of insufficient legal penalties. Although some states required incarceration of convicted drunk drivers for up to two months, several states did not mandate jail terms for drunk driving offenders. By 1990, twenty-nine states did have license-revocation laws giving police the right to seize the license of a driver who refused or failed a blood-alcohol test. Other widely utilized punishments include fines, community service, and license suspensions.

These traditional methods have not been especially effective in deterring drunk-driving offenders from repeating their crimes; repeat offenders are responsible for more accidents (and fatalities) than first-time offenders. One original and particularly effective prevention program was instituted in Orange County, California. First-time offenders between the ages of sixteen and twenty-one had to tour a local morgue, view a graphic slide show, and witness the autopsy of a person who had died a drug or alcohol-related death. Although approximately 30 percent of first-time offenders typically become repeat offenders, fewer than

U.S. DRUNK DRIVING ARRESTS, 1993

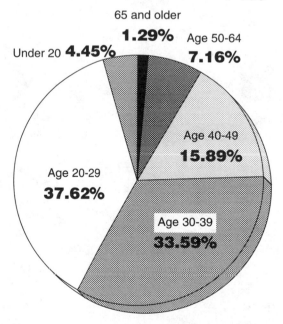

Source: U.S. Department of Justice, Federal Bureau of Investigation, *Crime in the United States* (Uniform Crime Reports). Washington, D.C.: U.S. Government Printing Office, 1994.
Note: Total 1993 arrests: 1,229,971.

Civil rights pioneer W. E. B. Du Bois in 1915. (UPI/Corbis-Bettmann)

2 percent of the Orange County youths were arrested for the offense a second time.

Other regions have far less impressive records. In Alabama, for example, one driver was found to have been convicted of drunk driving more than twenty-five times in a fifteen-year period, even though he had not held a valid state driver's license during that time. In Nassau and Suffolk counties of New York state, more than 6,800 warrants for drunk drivers were outstanding in the early 1990's; under lenient New York laws, however, these offenders were able to continue to drive legally.

Even when drunk drivers receive full sentences for their crimes, many are released early to relieve prison overcrowding and make room for "more dangerous" criminals. Because of the widespread popularity of social drinking, especially among young people, and the relatively light punishments and low rate of convictions, drunk driving has continued to be a serious social problem.

Du Bois, W. E. B. (William Edward Burghardt) (February 23, 1886, Great Barrington, Mass.— Aug. 27, 1963, Accra, Ghana): Scholar, social activist, and philanthropist. Du Bois is best known for his influential role as one of the founders of the NATIONAL ASSOCIATION FOR THE ADVANCEMENT OF COLORED PEOPLE (NAACP) and as editor of its publication *The Crisis*. He introduced the notion that black society should be led by a group of well-educated men, "the Talented Tenth." A prolific writer, Du Bois continues to influence individuals through his works, including *Black Reconstruction in America*, *The Souls of Black Folk*, and *The Philidalephia Negro*. His most notable achievements include earning a doctorate from Harvard University, helping to found the Niagara Movement, and being involved in virtually every major event leading to the modern CIVIL RIGHTS MOVEMENT.

Due process: Basic right guaranteed by the Fifth, Sixth, and Fourteenth Amendments of the U.S. CONSTITUTION. The Fifth Amendment provides that "no person shall . . . be deprived of life, liberty, or property, without due process of law."

Due process is understood to mean that legal proceedings should follow the rules and procedures ("the law of the land") established for protecting individual rights. Due process protections such as the right to a fair and speedy trial are among the most powerful restraints on government interference in the rights or property interests of citizens. A basic principle of democratic society is that of limited government. This means that individuals should basically be left alone unless the government can demonstrate legal cause that they should not be.

The importance of due process can be seen in the fact that it is a fundamental right protected by the BILL OF RIGHTS, the first ten amendments to the CONSTITUTION. The Bill of Rights establishes certain basic rights such as FREEDOM OF SPEECH, the right to assemble, the right to worship, and the right to due process. By guaranteeing individuals these and other basic liberties, the Bill of Rights is vital to the maintenance of a free and democratic society; its provisions include protections against arbitrary or unreasonable government intrusion in individuals' private lives.

The famous nineteenth century statesman and orator Daniel Webster defined due process as that "which hears before it condemns, which proceeds upon inquiry, and renders judgement only after trial." Although due process rights remain central to the functioning of America's legal system, the courts have not interpreted the protection of these rights to be absolute or unlimited. The question facing judges and administrators is this: What measures need to be taken to insure that the laws of the land are executed in a fair and equitable manner?

As questions of due process touch a wide range of legal issues, judges and administrators each day face difficult decisions concerning how to balance the rights and interests of society and those of the individual. The courts must simultaneously protect basic constitutional rights, including due process and other individual liberties, and the interests of society. Although individuals value their freedom and the protection of their rights, in some situations, individuals seem willing to surrender certain personal freedoms to governmental authority in exchange for peace and security. Many people, for example, willingly pass through metal detectors or submit to searches prior to boarding planes in the name of public safety.

Common sense would indicate that certain situations virtually require that individual rights be limited, especially when their exercise would threaten the rights and safety of others. Judge Oliver Wendell Holmes contended that the misuse of individual rights can in some situations create a "CLEAR AND PRESENT DANGER" for others. Regarding the limits of the right of free speech,

David Duke announces the 1980 founding of his National Association for the Advancement of White People. (UPI/ Corbis-Bettmann)

U.S. secretary of state John Foster Dulles explains plans for containing communist expansion in the Middle East. (UPI/Corbis-Bettmann)

in the landmark ruling *Schenck v. United States* (1919), Holmes noted that no one should have the right to shout "Fire!" in a crowded theater and then claim a constitutional right to do so as a defense for the act.

Duke, David (b. July 1, 1950, Tulsa, Okla.): Politician and white supremacist. A onetime official of the KU KLUX KLAN and the founder of the National Association for the Advancement of White People, Duke achieved national notoriety when he won election to the Louisiana state legislature, where he served from 1989 to 1992. Although he claimed to have moderated his views, his identification with racial extremists made him a lightning rod for protests by civil rights groups. In 1991, he was defeated in a campaign for Louisiana's governorship.

Dulles, John Foster (b. February 25, 1888, Washington, D.C.—d. May 24, 1959, Washington, D.C.): U.S. diplomat. Dulles, the son of a Presbyterian minister, is best known as Dwight D. Eisenhower's secretary of state (1953-1959) and as a symbol of the COLD WAR with the Soviet Union. He coined the term "brinkmanship" for risking conflict and the phrase "massive retaliation" for immediate nuclear response to aggression. His detractors viewed him as an inflexible anticommunist moralist. His defenders cited his closeness to Eisenhower and his sharp legal mind, which had a penchant for clear and simple expressions.

Dying. *See* **Death and dying**

E

E-mail: Electronic mail, messages sent and received by computers connected to a network. Before the advent of widespread computer networks, e-mail was restricted to computers with only local linkage. Global computer networks have since linked millions of computers. Among the problems created by global networks are the protection of confidential information and copyrighted works, the dissemination of COMPUTER VIRUSES, and the dissemination of pornography and other criminal activities. Legal problems associated with e-mail include the assignment of liability for legal violations and damages and decisions about where jurisdiction over a violation resides.

Earned Income Tax Credit: Financial benefit provided by the U.S. government to low-income wage earners. Unlike exemptions and deductions, which lower a person's taxable income, the credit is applied directly toward INCOME TAXES owed to the government. The Earned Income Tax Credit is intended to serve as an added incentive for people to work rather than to collect WELFARE benefits. As a general rule, only wage earners who are heads of households, that is, married or the parent of a dependent child, are eligible for the credit, but Congress has occasionally extended the eligibility to also include single, low-income workers.

Although widely acknowledged as one of the most successful and popular tax policies undertaken by the U.S. government, the Earned Income Tax Credit has not been without controversy. Its origins lie in the social programs of the late 1960's and early 1970's. Senator Patrick Moynihan and others proposed a Family Assistance Plan that would guarantee that each low-income family received a set amount of money annually. This program proved impossible to pass in Congress, but both Democrats and Republicans agreed on the Earned Income Tax Credit. Rather than being a handout, it would be a reward for working. Initially, many taxpayers overlooked the credit, but a vigorous publicity campaign by the INTERNAL REVENUE SERVICE (IRS) caused more claims to be filed.

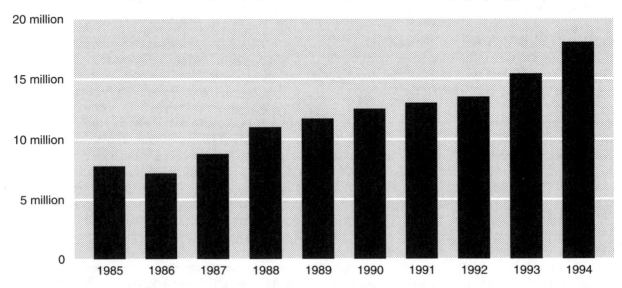

FAMILIES RECEIVING EARNED INCOME TAX CREDIT, 1985-1994

Source: Internal Revenue Service.

The IRS, in fact, pushed the program so strenuously that the promotion backfired. By the end of the 1994 tax year, reports of widespread fraud led to the IRS being forced to delay refunds that involved the Earned Income Tax Credit until Social Security numbers reported for dependents could be cross-checked with the Social Security Administration. Thousands of claims had been filed claiming nonexistent dependents. Honest taxpayers found themselves having to wait several months for refunds and, in some cases, having to provide additional documentation to prove their status as parents.

Requirements for the credit as well as the amounts provided have changed from year to year to keep pace with INFLATION. For the 1996 tax year, for example, for a person with two children and a taxable income between $8,600 and $11,300, the Earned Income Tax Credit would be $3,110. The credit for childless couples was considerably lower, with a maximum possible credit of $314. Using the example of the maximum possible credit for a family with children, according to the 1996 tax tables, a worker with two dependents would not incur any tax liability until income exceeded $13,250. In practical terms, this meant that any person eligible for the $3,110 credit would not only have any income tax withheld from paychecks returned but would also receive an additional $3,110 from the federal government. The credit thus provides a powerful financial incentive for a low-income person to keep working, even if the job pays only MINIMUM WAGE or provides less than full-time hours. Even critics of the Earned Income Tax Credit admit that it is a highly cost-effective method to help the poor.

Earth Day: Event designed to promote environmental awareness and CONSERVATION through educational activities and individual action. Earth Day was initially observed in the United States on March 21, 1970, and internationally on April 22, 1970. U.S. senator Gaylord Nelson is recognized as the founder of Earth Day, now observed annually on April 22 throughout the United States, Canada, and a growing number of other countries.

The event began as a grassroots movement on several American college campuses. It has grown to involve an army of volunteers, government agencies, civic groups, and social organizations, dedicated to protecting the earth by encouraging environmental responsibility and stewardship.

Earth Day observances are as varied as the communities and groups organizing them. They are as simple as a tree or garden planting or as organized as a roadside or waterway cleanup. They take the form of classroom projects, public proclamations, and eco-oriented contests. They also include events requiring year-round planning, complete with entertainment, hands-on demonstrations, and displays presented by environmentalists and businesses promoting environmentally friendly products.

The overall focus is on such issues as the prevention of WATER, soil, and AIR POLLUTION; habitat and wildlife preservation; and the protection of nonrenewable resources.

Participants are urged to seek and support environmental legislation. In the United States, the first Earth Day helped inspire the CLEAN AIR ACT, the CLEAN WATER ACT, and the establishment of the Environmental Protection Agency (EPA).

Earth Day activities faltered in the ensuing years. However, in 1991, a tax-exempt, not-for-profit corporation was developed as a national clearinghouse for Earth Day activities. Headquartered in Washington, D.C., Earth Day USA assists Earth Day organizers with the promotion and development of related events. It offers low-cost fact sheets, posters, and public service announcements, along with organizer's manuals. Earth Day USA also hosts conferences for organizers, and collects and disseminates Earth Day activity information in a national Earth Day calendar.

"More than just a day—a way of life!" is Earth Day USA's ongoing slogan, adopted to encourage organizations and individuals to integrate their concern for the environment into every daily decision. In 1995, to commemorate Earth Day's twenty-fifth anniversary, Earth Day USA adopted the slogan "The Time Has Come," along with the theme "Energy Efficiency." An "Earth Pledge" was also developed, and special projects were launched. A March for Parks was introduced as a fund-raising effort administered by the National Parks and Conservation Association. Project Earthlink, a massive public-education program on global change, was created and sponsored by thirteen federal agencies.

Other anniversary promotions have included Sun Day 1995, which was designed to focus attention on renewable energy and energy efficiency and to foster initiatives to promote sustainable energy policies; Ecothon, an education and fund-raising effort involving thousands of citizens, schoolchildren, and environ-

Children plant a tree in a Detroit park during the 1990 observance of Earth Day. (Jim West)

mental groups; Earth Day Energy 2000, a five-year program to assist communities in implementing energy efficiency projects; and Earth Day Energy Fast, a program for taking individual and collective action to reduce energy consumption.

Earth First!: Environmental group founded in 1980. More a network than a formal organization, Earth First! exemplifies "radical environmentalism," which rejects hierarchical structures and political compromise and embraces grassroots organizing, litigation, and CIVIL DISOBEDIENCE. The group earned notoriety for its advocacy of "monkey-wrenching," or sabotage employed for environmental ends. Earth First! members have been charged with erecting human and physical barricades, spiking trees, and damaging logging and earth-moving equipment. Often criticized, even by other environmental groups, Earth First! is

nevertheless credited with drawing press attention to particular issues, delaying or preventing acts of wilderness destruction, and having provided a radical context that often makes the policy proposals of mainstream environmental groups appear less extreme.

Earth Summit (1992): Worldwide conference held to discuss ENVIRONMENTAL ISSUES. Held in Rio de Janeiro from June 3 to June 14, 1992, the Earth Summit drew ten thousand delegates from 170 nations to discuss environmental topics of global concern. The central issue was how to promote sustainable development, progress and economic growth that does not cause irremediable environmental damage. The summit quickly polarized along economic and geographical lines, with the wealthy developed nations of the Northern Hemisphere generally calling for tighter restrictions on land use and industrial emissions, and the

Earth First! activists raise a banner at the Lincoln Memorial in 1987. (UPI/Corbis-Bettmann)

King Carl Gustaf of Sweden addresses delegates at the 1993 Earth Summit. (AP/Wide World Photos)

poorer nations of the Southern Hemisphere calling for foreign aid as the price of such regulation. The George BUSH Administration was broadly criticized both in the United States and abroad for its refusal to support many of the summit's proposals.

Eating disorders: Abnormal eating and DIETING habits that adversely affect an individual's health. The most common types are ANOREXIA NERVOSA, characterized by self-imposed starvation and severe weight loss, and bulimia, technically known as BULIMIA NERVOSA, characterized by rapid ingestion of large amounts of food (binge eating) followed by forced vomiting (purging), the use of laxatives or diuretics, and excessive exercise.

Characteristics of Eating Disorders. About one hundred years ago, anorexia nervosa was given its name by Sir William Gull, a British physician who first described the symptoms of this life-threatening disease. Anorexia means loss of appetite, but anorexics are often hungry; they deny their hunger and refuse to eat. Anorexia victims are extremely thin and have in-

tentionally achieved their physical condition by an abrupt and severe weight loss. They display a fear of gaining weight, even when they are emaciated. A disturbed body image, hyperactivity, fasting, vomiting, and compulsive and obsessive behaviors regarding food and eating are all characteristics of this disease. Female anorexics also cease menstruating. Anorexics are usually proud of the discipline and self-denial required for their rigid dieting.

Bulimia, from the Greek meaning "ox hunger," or insatiable appetite, is a related eating disorder. Unlike anorexics, bulimia patients may appear physically normal and be of average weight. Bulimics display recurrent episodes of binge eating and purging (usually in private), an obsession about their weight, and a feeling of lack of control about their binge eating. They often feel shame and embarrassment about their eating habits and may suffer from low SELF-ESTEEM.

Prevalence and Trends. The incidence of anorexia and bulimia has been increasing since the 1970's. Studies indicate that approximately eight million American teens and adults show some symptoms of eating disorders. Many high school and college students display disordered eating and dieting habits, such as extreme food restriction, binge eating, purging, and compulsive exercising. It is estimated that from 26 percent to 79 percent of college women practice binge eating. Although many individuals practice disordered eating, far fewer have actually been diagnosed and treated for an eating disorder. It can be difficult to accurately classify an eating-disordered patient since the major symptoms of these conditions may coexist or follow one another. For example, 47 percent of anorexics also have symptoms of bulimia, while from 30 percent to 80 percent of bulimic patients have a history of anorexia. Using stringent definitions of these conditions, from 1 percent to 3 percent of Americans are affected by eating disorders. Recent statistics suggest that from 3 percent to 5 percent of women between puberty and age thirty are bulimic and 1 percent are anorexic.

The spectrum of individuals who suffer from these disorders has expanded since the 1970's. Affluent, white, upper-middle-class female adolescents and young women are still the major victims, but these disorders now claim boys and men, people of color, older adults, and individuals across the socioeconomic spectrum. Approximately 5 percent to 10 percent of individuals with eating disorders are male. There have also been increases in the numbers of subclinical eating disordered or exercise-addicted men and women who lead apparently healthy and productive lives and who never seek treatment.

Causes of Eating Disorders. The causes of eating disorders are complex and not often easily identified. A combination of personal, psychological, physiological, and cultural factors contribute to the condition. It is ironic that eating disorders are most prevalent in societies in which food and food choices are abundant. However, the American culture, as well as that of other developed countries, puts great emphasis on thinness. Messages from the media, in regular programming as well as advertisements, highlight the cultural norm. Slim people are shown to be happy, successful, fit, and popular. This cultural preference is not in tune with reality. At the same time that thinness has become an ideal, Americans have gained more weight; 25 percent to 30 percent of adults are classified as overweight or obese. In various surveys, up to 80 percent of women are dissatisfied with their bodies and wish to lose weight. The ideal for men has also evolved into a thin, muscular body type, and men are increasingly feeling the pressures, long felt by women, to attain a body that

fits society's expectations. Overweight individuals are sometimes perceived as being incompetent, nonproductive, and lacking willpower. Social acceptability and economic security are perceived to hinge on one's appearance.

Because individuals, especially women, consider thinness to be an ideal, many people diet in order to control their weight and appearance. Many girls begin lifelong dieting practices when they reach puberty. Men begin dieting and often include rigorous exercise programs in an effort to become slim and fit. Some individuals begin to practice unhealthy methods of weight control, such as starvation, self-induced vomiting, and abuse of laxatives and diuretics, forerunners in the development of chronic eating disorders. Individuals at risk for developing eating disorders include those for whom body image or the need to maintain a certain weight becomes a critical factor in daily life. Eating disorders are frequently seen in wrestlers, ballet dancers, models, gymnasts, and long-distance runners.

While the underlying factors that lead to anorexia may not be known, anorexia is often precipitated by a specific event or circumstance. The stress of a new school or job, high expectations of achievement by family, physical changes associated with puberty, leaving home to attend boarding school, or even a chance remark about a person's weight or figure by a well-meaning relative or friend have each been identified as initiating factors. Adolescence is a particularly stressful time in which young people begin to notice that their lives and their bodies are rapidly changing. In an attempt to cope with STRESS and regain some control over their lives, young teens often begin harmful dieting practices. After the loss of a few pounds, the feelings of being special and gaining control may result in a relentless pursuit of additional weight loss.

Individuals who succumb to bulimia usually suffer from low SELF-ESTEEM. Like anorexics, they are predominantly female, but they tend to be young adults rather than teenagers. Instead of starving, bulimics turn toward food during stressful situations. They feel out of control during their eating binges. GUILT usually follows such binges, and bulimics try to rid themselves of the food and prevent weight gain by resorting to self-induced vomiting, laxatives, and strenuous exercise. Bulimics are not proud of their behaviors and often practice their binge eating and purging activities in isolation.

Treatment and Prognosis. About 40 percent of those diagnosed with anorexia recover after undergoing treat-

Overeating, along with various medical conditions, can cause obesity. (AP/Wide World Photos)

ment, 30 percent show improvement, and the remaining 30 percent never recover. About 9 percent of anorexics die from their condition. Treatment is multifaceted and long term, often taking two to three years, and sometimes longer. It is usually begun in an in-patient setting using a combined approach offering nutritional therapy to prevent starvation and psychological counseling to try to discover the underlying reasons for the disorder as well as to suggest coping mechanisms. FAMILY THERAPY is an important aspect of the treatment because family members may have inadvertently contributed to the condition and because family members may help the anorexic in the recovery process.

Although bulimia is not as life-threatening as anorexia, it is still a serious problem; continued bulimic practices can lead to health risks. Most of the health problems stem from the forced vomiting; these include demineralization and decay of teeth from exposure to acidic stomach contents, electrolyte imbalance, swelling of the salivary glands, and bleeding and tears of the esophagus. Treatment of bulimia proceeds on an outpatient basis and is geared toward fostering self-acceptance and establishing measures that will eliminate the binge-eating-and-purging cycle. Nutritional counseling and identification of alternate strategies for dealing with stress are important facets of the treatment. There is a range of estimates regarding the recovery of bulimics, depending on the treatment program and the length of the followup period. On the average, about 40 percent of bulimics recover, perhaps 40 percent improve significantly, as evidenced by a marked reduction in binge eating and purging, and the remaining patients show little sign of progress or substitute an exercise disorder for their eating disorder.

As long as society values thinness, Americans will continue to diet. Many will embark on destructive eating and DIETING habits that, in some cases, will give rise to chronic, disordered eating, which can be serious and life-threatening. Some experts have speculated that eating disorders will decline only when the attitude of Americans toward their bodies becomes more positive and realistic and when health, rather than thinness, becomes the ideal.   *—Barbara Brennessel*

SUGGESTED READINGS: Case histories that illuminate the complexities of eating disorders are featured in Suzann Abraham and Derek Llewellyn Jones's *Eating Disorders: The Facts* (New York: Oxford University Press, 1992). Raymond Lemberg has edited a collection of articles on eating disorders and has included a directory of treatment programs in *Controlling Eat-*

ing Disorders with Facts, Advice, and Resources (Phoenix, Ariz.: Oryx Press, 1992). A concise psychological and biological overview of anorexia is presented in R. L. Palmer's *Anorexia Nervosa: A Guide for Sufferers and Their Families* (New York: Penguin Books, 1988). The increasing problem of exercise disorders and their association with eating disorders is thoroughly analyzed in *Compulsive Exercise and the Eating Disorders: Toward an Integrated Theory of Activity* (New York: Brunner/Mazel, 1991), by Alayne Yates.

Economics: Economics studies the production and distribution of goods and services, primarily involving people buying and selling, borrowing and lending, and working and consuming. Social issues related to economics include POVERTY and inequality of incomes, INFLATION, depressions and UNEMPLOYMENT, resource depletion, environmental protection, and the proper role of government.

In the United States and Canada, production and distribution of goods and services are accomplished primarily through the activities of business firms. Firms employ workers, buy or lease capital goods such as machinery and buildings, and buy other inputs such as raw materials, fuel, electric power, and transportation. These expenditures are made in order to produce things that can be sold at a price sufficiently high to cover all the costs and yield a profit to the owners of the firm.

Firms must decide which products to produce, the quantities of each, and exactly which inputs to use. Products must meet the desires of buyers if they are to be sold at profitable prices. Firms must operate efficiently in order to keep costs lower than selling prices. They employ engineers to help achieve technological efficiency and personnel experts to help their human resources work efficiently. Economics assumes that these other helping disciplines do their jobs and looks at the results of profit-seeking behavior by firms.

Problems of Specialization. Modern industrial economies achieve efficiency through a high degree of specialization. Firms are specialized in what they produce. Workers become highly specialized in the activities they perform. Consider, for example, all the specialties among medical doctors. Specialized workers often use specialized equipment, as in an electricity generating plant or petroleum refinery. Such specialization increases efficiency and enables the economic system to

Consumer spending helps to drive the economy. (Yasmine Cordoba)

be highly productive, pay high wages, and permit most consumers to enjoy comforts, luxuries, and LEISURE TIME.

Specialization also raises two major problems. The first involves information. Firms need information about production processes and about the prospective demand for their products. Each worker must decide what specialized occupational activity to pursue, a decision that often entails undergoing lengthy and strenuous training and preparation. Making such choices can be stressful for young people passing through high school and college. No one knows with certainty which specialties will be in demand or how well suited he or she will be to a particular job. People have freedom to try different jobs, shifting from one to another, to find out what they are good at and like doing. Such exploration, however, is expensive in terms of both time and money when each new choice involves extensive retraining.

The second problem associated with specialization is motivation. Even if people know which jobs need to be filled and which products are in demand, they must have some incentive to enter these jobs and produce these products. The principal motivator is the opportunity to earn a high income. Firms that produce products that are strongly desired by consumers, using efficient methods, will earn profits. Competition among firms will prevent these profits from becoming unreasonably large. Workers who find jobs for which they are well suited and do these jobs well will receive high incomes. Conspicuously high labor incomes go to entertainers and athletes, corporate executives, and professionals such as doctors and lawyers. The prospect of earning a high income is an incentive for people to train themselves for success in these activities.

The Problem of Fairness. Human beings differ in intelligence, physical strength and dexterity, energy, and personality traits. These differences can be the basis for differences in earning power. Many people are either too young or too old to be capable of earning substantial incomes from selling their own services; their support must come from family members, from government transfer programs, or (for the elderly) from past savings. Some human differences are genetic, from body build to susceptibility to alcoholism. Other differences reflect the family environment in which a child is born and reared. High-income families, for example, are more likely to attend to their children's health and education. To overcome income inequalities from such sources, governments provide health and education services for young people.

The notion that some inequalities in income are unfair is reflected in "progressive" taxation, in which higher-income taxpayers pay higher percentages of their income as taxes. Carried very far, however, such taxes can damage people's incentives to work, save, and invest. The development of LABOR UNIONS also arose from beliefs that the labor market was unjust and income inequalities are in some sense unfair. Part of the motivation to join labor unions comes from the feeling that wage earners are treated unfairly in comparison with salaried executives and the owners of business.

Unfairness in income distribution may occur because of DISCRIMINATION. Women, ethnic and religious minorities, and handicapped persons in particular have been victimized by discrimination. Antidiscrimination programs such as AFFIRMATIVE ACTION attempt to curb such unfairness. Proving discrimination, however, can be difficult and costly. Some people believe that protection against discrimination is too broad. When the United States EQUAL EMPLOYMENT OPPORTUNITY COMMISSION classified alcohol and drug abuse as protected disabilities, many people objected, believing that persons with abuse problems should take personal responsibility for them.

Traditionally, issues of social justice were linked closely to ownership of property. Karl Marx, the principal intellectual source of COMMUNISM, argued that private ownership of the means of production (land and capital goods) was unjust. In Marx's view, capitalists (who owned the means of production) performed no useful service but received substantial benefits. In contrast, workers were exploited, receiving low pay

U.S. autoworkers protest job losses associated with competition from foreign automakers. (AP/Wide World Photos)

Stock markets are an efficient means of raising funds and establishing the value of businesses.
(AP/Wide World Photos)

for working long hours. Efforts to apply Marx's theories in the Soviet Union and China led to oppressive, totalitarian governments that, in most observers' opinions, failed to provide either prosperous economies or social justice. Most countries had abandoned communism by the early 1990's, with Cuba as a notable exception.

People may receive high incomes from ownership of property, but property ownership requires management. Investors or owners may be involved in the internal decision making of a firm. Their decisions affect the flow of capital, moving it into sectors of the economy where it contributes most to meeting consumer desires efficiently. In the United States, as of the early 1990's, more than three-fourths of income from private sources came from labor services. Property incomes were not a large proportion of the total.

Some people believe it unfair that persons born in a prosperous, developed economy will have lives that are far more comfortable than those of persons born in low-income environments such as rural China, Bangladesh, or Egypt. Many people from poor nations (particularly Mexico) try to emigrate to the United States. Those admitted legally usually improve their economic condition and give their children better opportunities. Large-scale IMMIGRATION, however, can create social problems. Many immigrants into the United States and Canada do not speak English and are not familiar with the laws and customs of their adopted countries. The period of adjustment can be lengthy, and during it, recent immigrants may suffer from social alienation.

Working-age immigrants expect to work, and most find jobs, often because they are willing to do things that established residents are unwilling to do. Agricultural labor is one important example. Competition from immigrants tends to keep wage levels down, so labor organizations have tried to restrict immigration. Both the United States and Canada restrict the number of immigrants and try to favor those who will be productive workers and those who already have family members in the country. Controversial policies were adopted in the 1990's to restrict government services for unauthorized immigrants and for legal aliens who did not become citizens.

Poverty. In many parts of the world, such as Asia, Latin America, Africa, and the Middle East, the majority of people live in POVERTY. Their homes are shacks or huts without gas, electricity, or indoor plumbing. Their food supply is barely adequate at best and may be insufficient to support life during times of famine.

INFANT MORTALITY rates are high, and ILLITERACY is widespread.

Two centuries ago, this was the condition of the average person in every part of the world. Incomes and living conditions in Europe and North America have improved enough that most people are far removed from such traditional poverty. The cure for mass poverty was economic growth.

Economic growth was aided by saving and by investment in capital goods. Another contributor was technological improvement, which brought new products and new methods of production. Dramatic recent examples include COMPUTERS, telecommunications, and medical science. A third source of growth was improvement in the quality of human resources, primarily through EDUCATION.

All these factors had to be brought together by effective forms of organization. Some countries experimented with socialist or communist forms of organization, in which many types of production were owned and managed by government. By the 1990's, however, such experiments were viewed widely as unsuccessful, a shift of opinion dramatized by the end of formal COMMUNISM in Eastern Europe and the former Soviet Union. A dilemma of economic growth is that saving must occur to stimulate investment in new technology or human resources, but until growth occurs, people are too poor to be able to save.

In the United States and Canada of the late twentieth century, few people experienced the kind of poverty characteristic of Bangladesh, Egypt, or Bolivia. More than 10 percent of the United States population, however, was classified in official statistics as living in poverty. Two broad categories of poor people can be identified. The first consists of persons who cannot engage in productive work, such as the very old, very young, sick, disabled, and handicapped. Since the 1930's, extensive programs of government transfer payments have been directed toward relieving their potential suffering.

The second category consists of persons who have made choices unfavorable to their earning potential. They may engage in CRIME and VIOLENCE, resulting in criminal records that limit employment opportunities. They may forgo education or refuse to exhibit honesty, punctuality, dependability, or courtesy, all of which are demanded in the workplace. A rising rate of childbirth among unmarried young women has led to poverty for many of the children and their young mothers, who may be unable to work because of child-care responsibilities or who may have left school. Some people are poor because drug or alcohol abuse has resulted in a poor employment record.

During the 1990's, both Canada and the United States experienced controversies over "WELFARE" and "ENTITLEMENTS" PROGRAMS. These programs provided either cash payments or subsidized services to low-income persons. Such programs were criticized as encouraging or rewarding choices that resulted in poverty along with providing aid to those who were in need through no fault of their own. Unfortunately, no one has figured out how to curtail assistance to adults deemed undeserving of aid without also harming their children. Efforts to deal with this problem included promotion of birth control (and in some cases abortion) and attempts to encourage marriage and develop parenting skills among young people.

Governments have tried to reduce poverty by promoting the formation of labor unions strong enough to negotiate wage increases and by enacting MINIMUM-WAGE legislation that forbids private employers from paying low wages. Both measures, however, tend to reduce job opportunities, particularly for workers with little skill or experience. A more promising approach is to provide education so that people will be qualified to hold better-paying jobs.

Business Cycles, Inflation, and Unemployment. Production and employment are relatively sensitive to variations in what economists call "aggregate demand"—spending for goods and services by households, businesses, government, and overseas buyers. A decrease in aggregate demand is likely to cause business firms to reduce production and lay off workers; as a consequence, UNEMPLOYMENT will rise.

The worst such experience occurred between 1929 and 1933, when U.S. aggregate demand fell by nearly half, and one-fourth of the labor force was unemployed. Similar conditions prevailed around the world.

If aggregate demand rises too rapidly, business firms will raise prices and the economy will experience inflation, as occurred during the 1970's and early 1980's. In between these extremes are economic conditions that, on the whole, policymakers consider to be acceptable. If aggregate demand, often measured by GROSS DOMESTIC PRODUCT (GDP) in current prices, rises between 4 percent and 8 percent per year, unemployment and INFLATION tend to stay at tolerable levels.

The harm that unemployment causes to the unemployed is easy to observe. U.S. workers (and those in many developed countries) who are laid off usually can collect unemployment compensation from the government. This form of temporary transfer payment may replace about half of lost income.

High levels of unemployment usually imply that the economy is producing less than it could. A zero rate of unemployment is infeasible because of the constant adjustments made by businesses and individuals. Inflation, at the modest levels usually experienced in the United States and Canada, does not usually reduce total output. As business firms increase prices, they also pay higher wages. The process is stressful for many people, however, because they cannot be sure that their incomes will keep up with price increases. Inflation, therefore, is perceived as a social harm.

Government efforts to keep aggregate demand in the acceptable range involve demand management policies. One type is fiscal policy. Government can attempt to stimulate aggregate demand either by spending more itself or by reducing tax rates, so that individuals and businesses have more to spend. Such actions are likely to be politically popular, although they tend to involve deficit spending and increasing the public debt. Government can restrain aggregate demand by spending less or increasing tax rates. Such measures are not politically popular. It is not surprising, therefore, that the United States government's budgeted expenditures exceeded its revenues every year after 1969. Efforts to balance the budget in the early 1990's were controversial.

The other type of demand management is monetary policy, which is administered by the FEDERAL RESERVE (often called the "Fed")—the central bank of the United States. The Fed can stimulate aggregate demand by increasing its loans to banks or its purchases of government securities from the public. The Fed can create new money through these actions, increasing the lending power of ordinary commercial banks and reducing INTEREST RATES.

Despite constant political controversy, demand management policies in the United States have been relatively successful. After World War II, economic recessions were infrequent and brief. Following the inflation of the 1970's and early 1980's, much of it attributable to excessive creation of money by the Fed, aggregate demand growth has been held within reasonable bounds. In the period from 1984 to 1993, unemployment averaged 6.5 percent of the labor force, and prices increased at a rate of 3.8 percent per year.

Overpopulation, Resource Depletion, and Pollution. In the eighteenth century, English clergyman-

Even in prosperous societies, some people are unable to find work. (Jim West)

Alan Greenspan took over as chairman of the Federal Reserve Board in 1987. (Reuters/Corbis-Bettmann)

economist Thomas Malthus warned that increases in economic productivity would tend to lower death rates and cause rapid population growth. With limited supplies of land and natural resources available, food production might not keep pace with the growing need. As Malthus warned, world population has grown rapidly, but technological advance has increased greatly the productivity of farmers. In the United States, farmers were only about 2 percent of the labor force in the late twentieth century, but they produced enough to feed the entire population and send substantial amounts to other countries. Improved processing methods have reduced the waste from spoilage, contamination, and pests.

The world petroleum crisis of the 1970's led many people to fear that nonrenewable resources were being depleted at an alarming rate and that supplies soon would run out. Free market forces, however, have many self-correcting tendencies. As resources are depleted, their prices tend to increase, encouraging buyers to find substitutes and encouraging producers to find more efficient ways of producing. The prospect of still higher prices in the future encourages private owners of resource-bearing lands to withhold some supplies for future availability. Some resources, however, are not suitable for private ownership. Ocean fisheries are a good example. Such resources present depletion problems calling for governmental action.

In Europe, the United States, Canada, Japan, and many other countries, economic prosperity has led to declining birth rates, slowing population growth and reducing the alarm. Forecasters for UNITED NATIONS agencies began to predict that world population might reach a stable level by the middle of the twenty-first century, but at a total of about ten billion, about twice the level of the 1990's.

Economic growth involves many production processes that pollute the environment. Increasing farm production involves use of chemical inputs such as fertilizers, insecticides, and herbicides that pollute streams and underground water. Burning fossil fuels (coal and petroleum) adds pollutants to the atmosphere.

The United States government established the Environmental Protection Agency (EPA) in 1970. Its operations have helped bring significant improvement to air and water standards. Critics charged that its programs and ENVIRONMENTAL LEGISLATION sometimes imposed costs larger than their benefits. The CLEAN AIR ACT of 1990, which led to widespread shutdowns of coal mines, was an example.

Medical Care. In Western countries, medical care traditionally has been provided in the free market in the same manner as other services. People went to the doctor or the hospital, were treated, and paid a bill for their care. In the United States in the 1940's, tax loopholes encouraged many employers to offer medical insurance as a fringe benefit. Many European countries (as well as Canada) adopted programs of socialized medicine, providing taxpayer-financed care for which the customers paid little or nothing in direct charges. In 1965, the U.S. government established two far-reaching medical programs, MEDICARE and Medicaid. Medicare, an adjunct to the SOCIAL SECURITY SYSTEM, provided large subsidies for the medical care of elderly persons. Medicaid subsidized medical expenses for low-income families. Medicare is paid for in part by Social Security taxes and fees imposed on beneficiaries, but its costs have far exceeded these revenues and have been borne by general revenues from taxpayers. Medicaid is financed entirely out of general tax revenues.

Such forms of subsidies for medical care increased demand for medical resources and drove medical costs up at a rapid rate. The heavy burdens on the government's budget were one motivation for U.S. president Bill CLINTON's 1994 proposals for increased government intervention in medical services. Economists noted that when consumers do not pay directly for services received, they have very little incentive to try to economize on those services. Experiments with group programs such as HEALTH MAINTENANCE ORGANIZATIONS (HMOs) were one method of trying to achieve better cost control.

Free Markets Versus Government Intervention. In 1776, Adam Smith published *The Wealth of Nations*, celebrating the values of free competitive markets. He saw the market as a social system in which people's desires for personal gain would encourage them to be productive and serve the needs of others. The free market system flourished in North America, aided by abundant land and natural resources, a firm British legal tradition stressing PROPERTY RIGHTS and individual liberty, and strong religious values and family ties. Critics have argued that free market institutions encourage greed and unscrupulous conduct. Workers will be exploited and abused, they predict, and consumers will be victimized by FRAUD and dishonesty.

Economists have compiled lists of "market failures" calling for government intervention. One of the most compelling is the need for "demand management" to avert DEPRESSIONS and INFLATION. Experience has shown, however, that people who work in government also are motivated by self-interest. Government programs are likely to be influenced by special INTEREST GROUPS (often well-organized producer groups) that can manipulate government policies to yield higher prices and incomes for themselves at the expense of the general consuming public. Moreover, governments may resort to coercion and force; in fact, systems of taxation rely largely on coercion.

By the 1990's, people in many parts of the world were expressing disillusionment with extended government economic activity. They recognized that competition helps to decentralize power. Competition among sellers protects consumers, particularly when sellers are seeking repeat business. Competition among employers protects workers, who can change jobs if they are discontented. Competition among lobbyists and political parties helps to keep the political process responsible to the citizens.

Modern economic life is stressful. Workplace stresses can be reduced by labor unions that introduce elements of DUE PROCESS into decisions about employment. The government's "safety net" of transfer payments to compensate for hardships associated with unemployment, old age, and general economic disaster helps many people recover from temporary distress. Neither business firms nor government programs, however, remove the importance of families, religious congregations, charities, philanthropic foundations, clubs and interest groups, fraternal and service clubs, and mutual support systems such as Alcoholics Anonymous.
—*Paul B. Trescott*

SUGGESTED READINGS: One of the best books for introducing the study of the problems enumerated here is Paul T. Heyne's *The Economic Way of Thinking*, 7th ed. (New York: Macmillan, 1994). Heyne uses almost no graphs and avoids economic jargon. Several books concentrate on current economic problems or controversies; one of the best is Ansel M. Sharp, Charles A. Register, and Richard H. Leftwich's *Economics of Social Issues*, 11th ed. (Burr Ridge, Ill.: Irwin, 1994), which includes substantial chapters on poverty and discrimination, education, crime, pollution, international trade policy, medical care, the role of government, and the national debt.

A shorter book with a similar approach is *The Economics of Public Issues*, by Roger LeRoy Miller, Daniel K. Benjamin, and Nobel Prize winner Douglass C. North (New York: HarperCollins, 1993). A vigorous liberal viewpoint is offered by Alan S. Blinder in *Hard Heads, Soft Hearts: Tough-Minded Economics for a Just Society* (Reading, Mass.: Addison-Wesley, 1987). A good counterweight, critical of most forms of governmental economic intervention, is *Free to Choose*, by Nobel Prize winner Milton Friedman and his wife Rose (New York: Harcourt Brace Jovanovich, 1980).

Living in the Environment, 8th ed., by G. Tyler Miller (Belmont, Calif.: Wads-worth, 1994) provides a wealth of information on population, resource depletion, and environmental problems. A controversial study critical of many programs aimed at poverty and discrimination is *Losing Ground: American Social Policy, 1950-1980* by Charles Murray (New York: Basic Books, 1984).

Ecosystems: Natural areas defined to include biotic (living) and abiotic (nonliving) components. The biotic component consists of all plants and animals of the area that interact to form the community; the abiotic component consists of the air, soil, rocks, and water that surround the community. The members of the community interact with their nonliving environment as well as with one another. Together, biotic and abiotic components function to form an ecosystem. Ecosystems include forests, streams, rivers, lakes, swamps, marshes, bays, beaches, coral reefs, and oceans. There is general agreement that human activities have altered many ecosystems.

Ecstasy: Illegal synthetic drug with stimulant and hallucinogenic effects, chemically related to amphetamines and mescaline. Because it alters ego states and lowers defenses, it was used experimentally in selected clinical settings until it was made illegal in 1985. Also known as "Adam" and the "love drug," Ecstasy is used in small doses at "raves" and other parties to induce feelings of euphoria, love for others, increased energy, loss of inhibition, and increased sexual desire. Side effects can include panic, muscle spasms, impotence, and hypertension.

Ecumenical movement: Movement among mainline Christian churches to create a unified state of all believers, whether Catholic or Protestant, with those involved desiring to rise above doctrinal differences and differences in practice and liturgy. The ecumenical movement (from a Greek word meaning "the whole

A police officer displays confiscated Ecstasy with an estimated value of $12 million. (Reuters/Corbis-Bettmann)

Edelman, Marian Wright

habitable earth") began with the missionary movement of the early twentieth century, which required cooperation among various denominations to achieve long-lasting results. The missionary movement remains an important part of modern Christianity. The World Council of Churches is an outgrowth of the ecumenical movement.

Edelman, Marian Wright (b. June 6, 1939, Bennettsville, S.C.): CHILDREN'S RIGHTS advocate. A Yale

University law-school graduate and the first African American woman admitted to the bar in Mississippi, Edelman first defended children in the HEAD START program in Jackson, Mississippi, for the NATIONAL ASSOCIATION FOR THE ADVANCEMENT OF COLORED PEOPLE (NAACP). From 1968 to 1973, Edelman was a partner in the Washington Research Project of Southern Center for Public Policy, which became the parent organization of the CHILDREN'S DEFENSE FUND, incorporated in 1973 with Edelman as president. Through the Children's Defense Fund, Edelman seeks

Children's Defense Fund founder Marian Wright Edelman. (UPI/Bettmann)

to make it "un-American" for any child to grow up poor, lacking adequate health care, food, shelter, child care, or education. Her major books include *Families in Peril: An Agenda for Social Change* (1987) and *The Measure of Our Success* (1992).

Education: Since the 1960's, education in the United States and Canada has undergone significant and often controversial changes. In both countries, schools have had to adjust to greater recognition of minority rights, increases in IMMIGRATION, and globalization of the economy.

Increased racial and ethnic diversity in Canadian and U.S. schools created the need to develop programs and curriculum changes that better met the needs of different racial and ethnic populations. In general, the intent of program and curriculum changes occurring in the last quarter of the twentieth century has been to promote educational and social equity between minorities and majority populations.

Reasons for Controversy. Proposed changes in education policies and curriculum often create community controversy. Historically, formal education has been accepted as a way for societies to pass on knowledge from generation to generation. Formal education is also expected to prepare youths for future jobs and their future roles as citizens. In both the United States and Canada, formal education is also expected to be a social leveler. This means that formal education is viewed as an avenue any individual can freely take to advance in social status. As a result of the high expectations Canadians and Americans have of formal education, there is often conflict between the more functional needs and goals of employers and the broader goals of creating social equality.

While it is generally accepted that families have the primary responsibility for teaching children VALUES

Public education has undergone many changes since this turn-of-the-century photograph was taken. (Corbis-Bettmann)

and social norms, formal education is expected to pass on broader cultural norms and expectations as well as the knowledge and expertise no one family can be expected to attain. In culturally diverse societies, proposed changes in education policies and curriculum create controversy because not everyone will agree with or support such changes. In democratic societies, such changes are often decided by a voting majority of citizens, so that education policies are often political in nature.

Neither the United States nor Canada has a federal system of education. In the United States, public education is the responsibility of the states, and school systems are governed by locally elected boards of education. Local control of school policy, spending, and curriculum has remained the backbone of U.S. education through the mid-1990's. Canadian education is also a local rather than federal matter, with governance of education resting with each province.

Formal education became even more critically important in the latter half of the twentieth century, as technological change and the globalization of the economy required that people acquire even more skills. Prior to the 1960's, many people could find family-supporting jobs without completing a secondary education; by the 1990's, post-secondary education had become a normal requirement for family-supporting jobs. In other words, the relationship between the amount and quality of formal education and the standard of living one could expect to attain became stronger.

When it is determined that educational policies and curriculum give unfair social or economic advantage to particular groups, or when it is determined that not enough graduates possess adequate skills to meet employer needs, such policies and curriculum come under serious attack. Remedies for unfair policies are debated and often modified before they are adopted. Those who oppose educational changes often want to maintain the status quo.

Integrated Education. Before the 1950's, African Americans in the South were generally not allowed to attend the same public schools as whites. Although northern public schools did not intentionally segregate by race, northern black children often attended mostly black schools because housing DISCRIMINATION often kept African Americans in separate neighborhoods. The landmark 1954 U.S. Supreme Court decision in *BROWN V. BOARD OF EDUCATION OF TOPEKA, KANSAS*, which ruled that "SEPARATE BUT EQUAL" education was un-

constitutional, required public schools to integrate. Supporters of integrated education believed that segregated black schools were inferior in educational quality to white schools. Moreover, supporters of integrated education claimed that the unequal quality of education that African Americans received kept them from competing for jobs and college entrance on an equal basis with whites.

Southern schools were nevertheless quicker to integrate than those in the North. Many northern school systems claimed that, because racial SEGREGATION was not the result of intentional school policies, they did not have to integrate; however, a 1973 Supreme Court ruling required northern U.S. public schools also to integrate as well. Forced INTEGRATION often resulted in racial confrontations in northern cities such as Boston when black children were bused into mainly white neighborhood schools. Controversy continued over forced integration into the last decade of the twentieth century. In addition, since many middle- and upper-income whites sent their children to private schools or moved to suburbs to escape increasing urban crime and forced BUSING, many black children ended up being effectually resegregated. As a consequence, in order to keep up with the intent of integrated education, black children were bused even farther from their homes. Beginning in the late 1970's, as a result of "WHITE FLIGHT" and increased immigration, the majority of children attending city schools became racial, ethnic, and non-English-speaking minorities. In addition to the issue of costs, many Americans also questioned whether integrated education really increased black student achievement. Many early studies of the effects of integration on minority academic achievement indicated little or no improvement had taken place. However, later studies indicated that longer-term improvement did occur.

After U.S. public schools began to integrate, some parents and educators claimed that minority children were less likely to do as well as whites because racial and ethnic discrimination had kept their families from achieving the same levels of social and economic status as white families. Education programs were thus developed to compensate for the social and economic disadvantages minority children often faced when they entered white schools.

The first direct federal legislative intervention in public education took place through the ELEMENTARY AND SECONDARY EDUCATION ACT (ESEA) of 1965. The ESEA made federal funds available for educa-

Opening day of the 1954-1955 school year in a Washington, D.C., school that had formerly been for whites only. (UPI/Corbis-Bettmann)

tional programs targeted at economically disadvantaged students, generally minority children. Three of the most prominent efforts evolving from ESEA were the BILINGUAL EDUCATION, Head Start, and Title I compensatory programs.

The purpose of U.S. bilingual education was to provide instruction to students in their native languages and in English. Bilingual education was controversial; many people believed that bilingual education's purpose was to teach non-English-speaking children enough English to be moved into classes with English-speaking students. Others, however, believed transitional bilingual education programs caused students to feel ashamed of their cultural identities. Those who opposed transitional bilingual education programs supported more comprehensive bilingual education programs that taught all courses in both languages to encourage biculturalism.

Head Start programs were created to provide a broad range of services aimed at disabled and low-income children before they entered primary schools. Head Start programs aim to improve the intellectual development, SELF-ESTEEM, and physical and mental health of such students in order to better prepare students from disadvantaged backgrounds. The controversy surrounding Head Start programs has focused on whether such programs made any real difference in the education of affected students. By the 1990's, studies showed, Head Start students did have higher academic achievement levels than children of similar backgrounds who did not attend Head Start programs.

Chapter I programs were remedial programs funded by the federal government and targeted to primary and secondary students from low-income families. Examples of Chapter I programs included reading, language, and math-tutoring programs. The underlying assumption of Chapter I programs was that students from economically disadvantaged families would not receive as much reinforcement of educational skill development as students from higher-income families.

Finances. The cost of providing primary and secondary schooling is a major source of controversy surrounding public education. U.S. public education is primarily funded by a combination of local property and state taxes. Several school spending issues are controversial. First, wealthier communities can choose to spend more on education than other communities. In 1993, for each of the 42.5 million children in U.S. public schools, an average of $5,598 was spent on education; however, the range of costs was from $3,419 in Utah to $10,062 in New Jersey. Moreover, there is further variance in spending between communities within states.

Variance in school spending is controversial because some people claim that wealthier communities can provide higher quality education through higher spending. Others, however, have claimed there is not a direct relationship between spending and student achievement. From the 1960's onward, lawsuits were filed against states seeking to equalize spending between districts. By 1989, eleven state school-finance systems were declared unconstitutional; others were

Average Salaries of U.S. Public School Teachers, 1969-1970 to 1991-1992 (in 1991-1992 Dollars)

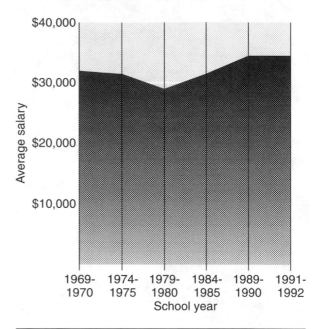

Source: National Center for Education Statistics, *Digest of Education Statistics, 1992.* Primary source: National Education Association.

U.S. Public School Expenditures, 1960-1991

In constant 1991 dollars

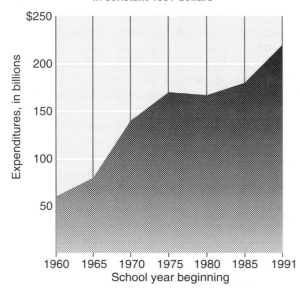

Source: National Center for Education Statistics, *Digest of Education Statistics, 1992.*

found to be legal. The differing results were based on each state's constitution. Generally, the determinant was whether or not the state guaranteed "equality" or "equity" of spending and how each term was defined relative to education. "Equality" was generally defined as connoting equality of opportunity, while "equity" was generally defined more specifically, in terms of dollars spent per pupil.

Second, many people who do not have children in schools believe that funding schools from property taxes places an unfair burden upon them. In the 1980's, an economic RECESSION initiated various plans to reduce property taxes by reducing or controlling educational spending. Some state legislatures put a limit on annual increases in educational spending, mandating that increases not exceed the INFLATION rate. In other states, more drastic action to eliminate property taxes as a source of school funding occurred.

Quality of Education Issues. In the 1980's, the U.S. system of public education came under severe criticism. In 1983, the DEPARTMENT OF EDUCATION published a study, *A Nation at Risk*, which claimed that U.S. students were falling behind those of other developed countries in academic achievement. The study also claimed that because the quality of education U.S. students received was lower than in previous years, U.S. employers would not be able to find enough qualified workers; because U.S. employers would not be able to hire workers with high enough skills, the study predicted, they would not be able to compete in the global economy.

The study touched off a great debate and triggered numerous other studies about how to fix U.S. primary and secondary public education. It was estimated that between 1983 and 1985, more than 350 studies of education issues were conducted. One response that received strong support from business leaders was to place more emphasis on the teaching of basic skills such as reading, writing, and math (this was popularly called the "back-to-basics" movement). As a result of business concern about the skill development of U.S. students, business and school partnerships increased dramatically in the late 1980's and 1990's. School and business partnerships were an effort of business leaders more directly to teach U.S. educators what their businesses would require from graduates.

Although many Americans supported improving educational programming and curriculum to help students to develop higher skill levels, controversy also arose over this issue. Those who raised questions about the need to focus on skill development expressed the opinion that too much emphasis on skill development might reduce emphasis on social development. As a result of the focus given to the need to increase skill development, a national program of education standards was initiated by the passage of the "Goals 2000" legislation in 1994. Goals 2000 established yearly goals for each state for standards of student achievement. Because Goals 2000 was the first attempt to establish national educational standards, its passage, while receiving bipartisan support at the federal level, was controversial; many feared the implementation of standards would lead to development of a national curriculum and increased federal control of education.

Private Schooling. Another response to the question of how to fix public education was to allow more children to attend private schools. Since U.S. public schools were funded from tax dollars and private schools were not, it was proposed that parents be allowed to choose to send their children to private schools and receive tax credits for doing so. Proponents of school choice argued that students who attended private schools did better on standardized academic tests and that allowing parents to choose between public and private schools would force public schools to compete for students with private schools. The school-choice argument based its claims on free-enterprise ideology, which asserts that competition increases quality.

Opponents of school choice argued that since many private schools were related to organized RELIGION, funding private schools from tax dollars was an unconstitutional violation of the doctrine of SEPARATION OF CHURCH AND STATE. Opponents of school choice also argued that even with tax credits, lower-income families would not be able to afford to send their children to private schools, meaning that wealthier families would benefit most from school-choice programs. Moreover, critics argued that the reason private-school students did better on academic tests than public-school students was because more upper- and middle-income students attended private schools. Finally, opponents of school choice argued that expanding school-choice options would allow more people to avoid racial and ethnic INTEGRATION.

The school-choice movement received substantial support from those who already sent their children to private schools and from parents who wanted to do so. By the mid-1990's, states such as Minnesota and Wisconsin passed laws allowing parents to receive tax credits for sending their children to nonreligious private schools.

School Prayer. As controversy continued over the quality of public education, other critics came to the fore claiming that students did not do well because they lacked moral and ethical instruction and discipline. Since separation of church and state was required in U.S. public schools, children were not allowed to recite prayers during the school day. Religious conservatives argued that prayer in public schools would reinforce the moral and ethical development of students. Opponents of SCHOOL PRAYER argued that the Constitution guaranteed the right to religious privacy, that families had the primary responsibility of religious teaching, and that school prayer would force children to recite prayers that might not agree with their personal beliefs. Even if children were allowed the choice of remaining silent during prayer recitals, critics argued, those children who did not want to participate in praying would feel compelled to do so in order to fit in with others.

Students at all grade levels are exposed to perspectives from a variety of cultures. (Don Franklin)

Multicultural Education. Before the 1980's, the majority of immigrants to the United States were Europeans. By the mid-1990's, however, the majority of U.S. immigrants were from Asian and Central American nations. The pace of immigration had more than doubled from the 1960's, and IMMIGRATION accounted for approximately a third of the annual increase in U.S. population. Between 1986 and 1991, therefore, while overall student enrollment in U.S. public schools increased by only 4 percent, the number of students with limited English skills rose by more than 50 percent. The changes in demographic makeup of U.S. immigrants, increases in minority birth rates, and decreases in birth rates among whites caused the Department of Education to predict that almost half of the nation's students would be minorities by the year 2020.

As more children from diverse racial and ethnic backgrounds entered U.S. schools, other critics began to question the accuracy of programs and curriculum they labeled "Eurocentric." Curriculum and programs called "Eurocentric" were those that focused mainly on European history and Western civilization and literature. Many people from more diverse racial and ethnic backgrounds claimed that traditional subjects as taught in U.S. schools did not give realistic, accurate, or appropriate recognition to the historic contributions of many races and cultures. Critics of the traditional curriculum also claimed that such curriculum had a white, middle-class bias. Further, critics argued that U.S. public schools were predominantly run by white educators who did not understand or respect the cultural differences among ethnic and racial minorities. By teaching such biased curriculum to students from different cultures, critics claimed, educators were sending the message to students that their own cultures were not only different but also inferior.

MULTICULTURAL EDUCATION curricula and programs were developed in response to such concerns. Multicultural education's primary purpose was to teach students about the language, culture, and customs of diverse groups. The underlying assumption of multicultural education was that the more students learned about people from different cultures, the more they would accept and respect different people.

Yet multicultural programs also created controversy. Those who opposed multicultural education typically claimed that the purpose of public education was to encourage children to form a common cultural identity and allegiance. Opponents of multicultural education claimed that such programs encouraged students to reject the idea of a common culture and encouraged the maintenance of separate ethnic communities. Further, maintenance of separate ethnic communities, opponents argued, went against the "MELTING POT" idea to which the United States had long aspired. Those who favored multicultural education claimed that the United States had always been a pluralistic society in which many ethnic groups came together but were not always allowed to "melt." Moreover, proponents of multicultural education claimed, such programs would help children understand that being culturally "different" was normal, both in the United States and in the rest of the world.

Canadian Education. While Canadian education was also subject to many of the same controversies as U.S. education, BILINGUAL EDUCATION became Canada's most controversial issue after the 1960's.

Whereas U.S. bilingual programs generally offered instruction in both the student's native language and English, Canadian bilingual programs generally offered a choice between French or English instruction. Although the majority of Canada's population spoke English, French speakers were the majority in the Québec province. Many of Québec's French-speaking business and political leaders believed that English and French bilingual education threatened the future of French-Canadian cultural identity. Because English was the language used in the Québec business community (even though the majority of the province's people were of French descent), more and more parents of French descent were choosing to send their children to English-speaking schools. As a result, the French separatist PARTI QUÉBÉCOIS government passed legislation in 1977 that required children of French origin and children of immigrants to attend elementary and secondary French-language schools. The 1977 legislation caused controversy throughout Canada's English-speaking regions, because the federal government guaranteed parents the right to choose between English or French instruction. By the 1990's, 80 percent

More than ten thousand students demonstrate in Montreal in 1968 to protest the Canadian government's policies on higher education. (UPI/Corbis-Bettmann)

of Québec's people were French-speaking. Increases in Canadian immigration and declining birth rates among French Canadians caused more language controversy in the 1990's, as new minority groups in Québec preferred to send their children to English-speaking schools. —*Sandra J. Callaghan*

SUGGESTED READINGS: A social history of U.S. education through the early 1970's is provided by David B. Tyack in *The One Best System* (Cambridge, Mass.: Harvard University Press, 1974). Ronald P. Formisano's *Boston Against Busing: Race, Class, and Ethnicity in the 1960's and 1970's* (Chapel Hill: University of North Carolina Press, 1991) portrays white resistance to forced busing. *The Great School Debate: Which Way for American Education?* (New York: Simon & Schuster, 1985), edited by Beatrice Gross and Ronald Gross, provides a forum in which leading educators and researchers debate the issues.

John E. Chubb and Terry M. Moe present the case for privatizing American public schools in *Politics, Markets, and America's Schools* (Washington, D.C.: The Brookings Institution, 1990). *Multiculturalism and Education: Diversity and Its Impact on Schools and Society* (New York: State University of New York Press, 1994) gives the arguments for and against multicultural education. Marc V. Levine thoroughly describes the history of the language controversy in Canada and its relationship to education in *The Reconquest of Montreal: Language Policy and Social Change in a Bilingual City* (Philadelphia: Temple University Press, 1990).

Education Amendments Act, Title IX (1972): U.S. federal legislation intended to guarantee equality between men and women in their access to sports and related programs. For many years, women and girls were broadly denied access to participation in many school-sponsored sports programs. Even when females were permitted to participate in a sport, they were often forced to practice and play under conditions far inferior to those given to males. For example, a boys' basketball team might practice and play in a school's main gymnasium, while the girls' basketball team might practice and play in a smaller, older facility. School districts would often spend hundreds of thousands of dollars on boys' sport programs and virtually nothing on girls' programs.

Title IX of the Education Amendments Act of 1972 changed the manner in which female athletes were treated in the schools and was directly responsible for the evolution of women's athletics. The section that dealt specifically with athletics stated that: "No person shall, on the basis of sex, be excluded from participation in, be denied the benefits of, be treated differently from another person or otherwise be discriminated against in any interscholastic, intercollegiate, club, or intramural program offered by a recipient (federally assisted educational programs)." All schools, with rare exceptions, are recipients of federal monies in some form, so the act applied to almost every U.S. school.

Passage of Title IX, however, did not necessarily guarantee compliance. Many schools chose to ignore the law and complied only when juries and courts ordered them to do so. Schools filed challenges to the law, and to the concept that girls and women have a right to compete, with the courts. The NATIONAL COLLEGIATE ATHLETIC ASSOCIATION (NCAA) spent hundreds of thousands of dollars to lobby members of congress against passage of the original legislation. When this strategy failed and Title IX was passed, the NCAA sued the Department of Health, Education, and Welfare in 1976 to try to stop the law's implementation.

Title IX appeared to be a threat because it meant that men would have to share the larger gymnasium, use the pool at inconvenient times, and share financial resources with women. This was probably the hardest pill to swallow for male-dominated athletic programs, as it was usually the male sports such as football and basketball that generated the income to support the less-popular male and female sports.

In spite of these hurdles, over the years Title IX has led to a significant increase in sport participation by women. In the 1990's, nearly 40 percent of all high-school athletes are women, and the number of women participating in intercollegiate athletics has increased more than threefold since the passage of Title IX. The law has not, however, completely leveled the playing field. Female coaches are still paid less than their male counterparts, and women receive a disproportionately small amount of money for their athletic budgets and scholarships. As the number of women participating in sport has increased, however, rates of compliance have also increased.

Education for All Handicapped Children Act (1975): Federal legislation enacted in 1975 that is commonly referred to as the "EHA." The EHA broadened the Education Amendments of 1974 to meet the needs of exceptional students. The major provisions of the law mandate that all students from ages three to twenty-one (even though most states offer services from birth) be educated in the least restrictive environment possible, require an individualized education plan or program to be developed for each exceptional student, and provide that funds be made available to state and local education agencies.

Education of the Handicapped Act (1969): U.S. federal legislation. The Education of the Handicapped Act expanded the provisions of the ELEMENTARY AND SECONDARY EDUCATION ACT of 1965; the 1969 act mandated that all public schools provide counseling, physical education, health, transportation, and other services to students regardless of disability status. The act was amended in 1975 and again in 1978 to cover more than two hundred types of disabilities.

Edward Books and Art v. the Queen (1986): SUPREME COURT OF CANADA case. The *Edward Books* decision upheld the legality of a provincial statute requiring the Sunday closing of retail establishments. The court ruled that the legislation, which had been criticized as a violation of the religious-freedom guarantees of the CHARTER OF RIGHTS AND FREEDOMS, was not an effort to promote religion but had been enacted for the secular purpose of providing uniform holidays for retail workers.

Egan and Nesbitt v. Canada (1995): SUPREME COURT OF CANADA decision in which the court upheld policies limiting spousal benefits to heterosexual couples. The court admitted that treating homosexuals differently might in some situations constitute discrimination violating the Canadian CHARTER OF RIGHTS AND FREEDOMS. In *Egan*, however, the court stated that discrimination occurs only when a person is treated differently because of an irrelevant personal characteristic; in these cases, the policies gave effect to the social objective of supporting heterosexual couples. This objective was accepted as a rational basis for differential treatment.

Ehrlich, Paul (b. May 29, 1932, Philadelphia, Pa.): Ecologist, educator, and writer. Ehrlich is the author of

Population-control pioneer Paul Ehrlich in 1970. (UPI/ Corbis-Bettmann)

numerous scientific papers and popular nonfiction works (many cowritten with wife Anne Ehrlich). A professor at Stanford University, he is probably most widely known for the 1968 book *The Population Bomb*. Ehrlich is a major proponent of the idea that humans have overpopulated the planet and are using the earth's resources at a rate faster than they can be replenished. He argues that humankind must control population growth to prevent large-scale famine and chaos. Ehrlich was a major force in the founding of the advocacy group ZERO POPULATION GROWTH.

Eisenstadt v. Baird (1972): U.S. SUPREME COURT case that allowed unmarried persons access to contraceptives on privacy grounds. The Court reasoned that the right to privacy means that individuals, married or single, have the right to be free from unwarranted governmental intrusion into matters affecting the decision to bear or beget a child. The decision effectively

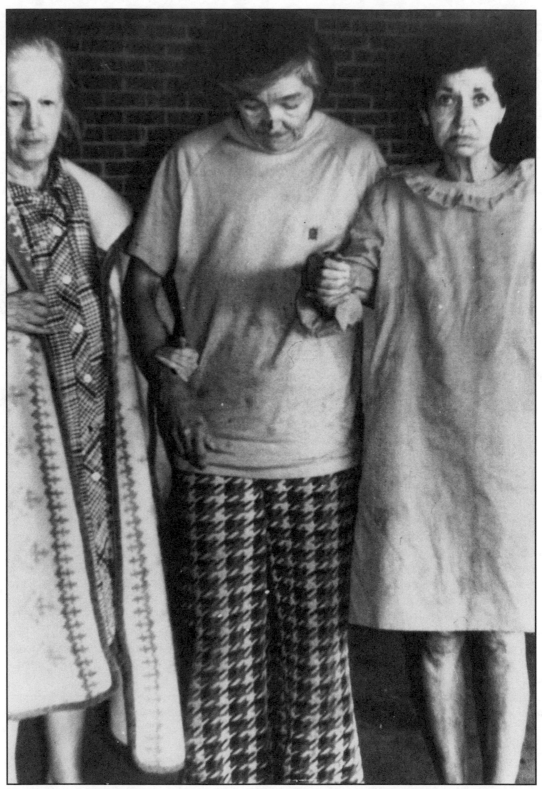

Three elderly women after their 1985 release from a New Jersey rooming house in which they were held captive and forced to sign over their Social Security checks. (UPI/Corbis-Bettmann)

barred a state from prohibiting access to contraceptives by adults.

Elderly abuse: Maltreatment of older people by their caregivers, typically spouses, children, relatives, or retirement-home employees. The abuse of the elderly may come in different forms and shapes. The most common forms of elderly abuse are physical and psychological abuse, financial or material abuse, and neglect. Physical and psychological abuses are deliberate harms inflicted upon the elderly by some family or other caregivers; such offenses sometimes include sexual victimization. Elderly people are also often financially exploited; they are common targets of confidence schemes, and their assets are often appropriated by unscrupulous insurance companies, real-estate agencies, retirement homes, relatives, and friends.

Elders, Joycelyn (b. August 13, 1933, Schaal, Ark.): Health educator and U.S. public official. In 1993, President Bill CLINTON appointed Elders sur-

geon general of the United States, making her the first African American and the second woman to hold that position. As surgeon general, she disseminated information about health problems, called for taxes on alcohol, studied the possible legalization of drugs, and worked to prevent teenage pregnancy. Her impolitic words about teaching children about masturbation led to her 1995 resignation and return to the University of Arkansas for Medical Sciences.

Electoral college: Body that elects the U.S. president and vice president every four years. The Founding Fathers incorporated the device into the Constitution to ensure that the nation's elite, rather than its common people, would choose its leaders. During every presidential election, voters in each state choose a number of members of the electoral college equal to the total number of that state's U.S. senators and representatives. These "electors" then cast votes for presidential and vice-presidential candidates. Electors usually vote to reflect the will of their state's citizens as expressed in the popular vote, but they are not required

Joycelyn Elders testifies at her 1993 Senate confirmation hearings. (Reuters/Corbis-Bettmann)

Acclaimed novelist Ralph Ellison. (UPI/Corbis-Bettmann)

to do so. Critics have called for the abolition of the electoral college, which they claim is a historical relic that has the potential to frustrate the will of the people.

Elementary and Secondary Education Act

(1965): Federal act that provided more than $1 billion to U.S. schools. Previous attempts to fund education had foundered on issues of local control and the provision of assistance to private schools, especially parochial schools. President Lyndon B. Johnson, a former schoolteacher, supported the legislation, which passed in 1965. The final bill appropriated funds based on the number of children from low-income families within a school district. Local officials retained the right to select textbooks and determine course content. While private schools could not receive direct funding, they did receive access to educational services such as media centers.

Ellis Island:

Twenty-seven-acre island in Upper New York Bay that served as the main IMMIGRATION center on the eastern coast of the United States from 1892 until 1943. From 1943 until 1954, it was used as an immigrant detention center and was then closed. Upon debarking on Ellis Island, immigrants were examined by medical personnel and immigration officials. Successful applicants entered the United States, whereas others were returned to their homelands. Approximately twenty million immigrants passed through Ellis Island. The Ellis Island Immigration Museum was opened to the public in 1990.

Ellison, Ralph

(March 1, 1914, Oklahoma City, Okla.—April 16, 1994, New York, N.Y.): Writer and teacher best known for his first and only novel, *Invisible Man* (1952). Combining modernist devices with a jazz-influenced prose style, the novel depicted the alienated condition of the young black man in American society. The novel, a landmark of American literature, established Ellison as a standard-bearer for the black intellectuals of his day. In 1953, Ellison became the first African American to win the prestigious National Book Award.

Employment benefits:

In addition to wages, employers often provide workers with a variety of fringe benefits. These benefits include optional items, such as production bonuses and health insurance, in addition to government-mandated programs, such as payment of unemployment and disability insurance premiums. Employee benefits constitute an additional expense to employers that can amount to as much as 40 percent above the actual hourly wages paid. This means, for example, that if an employee is paid ten dollars per hour in wages, providing various fringe benefits for that employee can result in the actual labor cost being fourteen dollars per hour. Industries that compete for highly skilled employees generally provide the most liberal benefits, while many low-wage industries provide few benefits beyond those required by law.

Background. For many years, the traditional employment benefits package consisted of employer-paid health and life insurance, a certain number of paid vacation and holiday days annually, a set number of paid sick days annually, and perhaps a pension plan. Typically, an employee would be granted forty hours of annual paid vacation time and forty hours of annual sick leave; the employee would be responsible for a portion of health- and life-insurance premiums. An employee would also be expected to pay a percentage of medical expenses.

Most employee benefits are voluntary rather than mandated by state or federal law. Employers are not required to provide paid vacations, holidays, sick leave, or health and life insurance that covers the employee away from the work site. The fact that many employers try to include benefits for their workers can be attributed in part to the force of custom in industrialized societies and in part to the competition for good workers within the labor market. Prospective employees often cite the availability of benefits, such as insurance, as a reason for picking one employer over another.

While it is true the most generous employee benefits are often provided by large corporations, it is possible to find a full range of benefits in almost any setting. Small businesses, particularly those employing professionals or workers in the skilled trades, may strive to provide an attractive employee-benefits package in hope of recruiting and retaining skilled personnel. Employment benefits can also vary widely within the same industry, even among employers of approximately the same size, depending on factors such as the local labor market. Production bonuses, for example, are found in many different settings. A production bonus is paid when the work performed exceeds certain minimum standards for either quantity or quality. A factory may pay employees a production bonus for assembling a large number of products, while a restaurant may reward waiters or waitresses who exceed sales goals.

Certain employment benefits, however, have come to be associated with specific settings. Colleges often provide tuition credits for support staff, while some retailers give employee discounts on merchandise. The food-service industry, which as a whole is notorious for providing few benefits, traditionally allows employees to eat meals for free or at reduced rates.

In addition to financial benefits, such as subsidized insurance or production bonuses, many companies provide other benefits intended to enhance employee morale or maintain employee health. Some businesses supply exercise equipment that allows employees to exercise on their lunch breaks or before or after work, while others arrange for discounted or free memberships at local health clubs and gyms. Quad/Graphics in Pewaukee, Wisconsin, is an example of a firm that goes further in rewarding healthy behavior; the company pays a two-hundred-dollar bonus to any employee who quits smoking and remains a nonsmoker for a year.

Legally Required Benefits. With a few exceptions, such as extremely small family-run businesses, all employers must participate in several government-mandated employee benefit programs. Almost all employers, for example, must pay federal SOCIAL SECURITY and MEDICARE taxes. Social Security provides benefits to employees when they reach retirement age or if they become disabled for a reason not related to their occupation. Social Security also pays benefits to a worker's children under the age of eighteen if the worker dies. Medicare provides health benefits for retirees. Employers must also participate in state-regulated unemployment and disability insurance plans. Unemployment insurance provides an income for workers if they lose their jobs through no fault of their own, such as through a reduction in the workforce or a company going out of business. Disability, or WORKERS' COMPENSATION, pays an income to workers if they become unable to work as a result of an injury or illness contracted on the job.

Areas of Conflict. Both voluntary and government-mandated employment benefit programs experienced rapid changes in the 1990's. As the business climate became increasingly competitive, many employers began to vary their benefit packages either in an attempt

to control costs or to provide wider choices for employees. Changes in the labor market, such as the entry of an increasing number of women, also contributed to changes in the types of employment benefits offered. By the mid-1990's, the range of employee benefits available to workers had, depending on the industry, both expanded and contracted.

Health-care benefits became a key issue for many employers and employees as health-care costs escalated. Many employers began trying to control costs by eliminating or reducing the health-care plans available to employees. Industries that had once been known for their generous benefits packages, such as automobile manufacturing, began curtailing employee benefits. Companies that had once allowed employees to accrue many weeks of accumulated sick leave and vacation days began to place caps on them. Employees have discovered that they can no longer count on being paid for unused vacation days when they terminate employment, nor can they save sick days to use as terminal leave prior to retirement. Many employers no longer carry unused sick leave or vacation over from one calendar year to the next; if an employee does not use it, it is lost.

At the same time, employee demand for new forms of benefits, such as on-site child-care facilities, led employers to develop benefits packages that permitted employees to select from a variety of options. These so-called cafeteria plans allowed the employees to decide for themselves which of a variety of health plans they prefer, whether or not to participate in retirement plans, and so on. Ironically, while benefits in employment in the traditional manufacturing sector of the economy were often being reduced, employers in other areas, such as fast food, began to discover that in order to keep as many employees as they needed to operate effectively, they had to increase the benefits they offered. Many fast-food franchisers now offer permanent employees benefit packages as attractive as those once offered by higher-status employers.

Concerns regarding the costs of employment benefits were not restricted to the private sector. In the 1990's, many states passed legislation that changed eligibility requirements and payment schedules for both unemployment insurance and disability compensation. States once known for their relatively liberal policies raised the number of weeks a person had to be employed to qualify for unemployment benefits or instituted measures to prevent seasonal workers from collecting such benefits. Legislators in Michigan, for

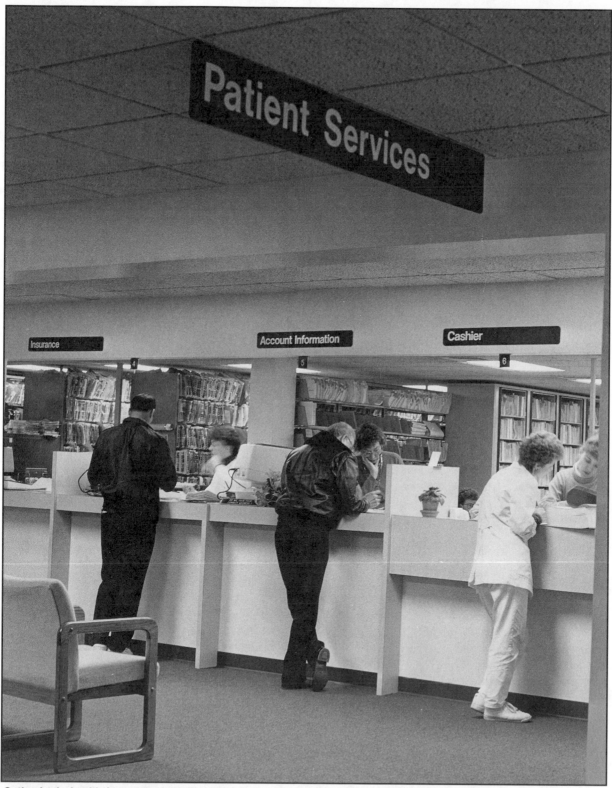

Cutbacks in health insurance benefits mean that more employees have to pay medical expenses out of their own funds. (James L. Shaffer)

example, made optional the payment of unemployment insurance premiums by employers in industries that operated seasonally, such as ski resorts. State legislators also debated altering the requirements for disability insurance to provide greater flexibility for employers. Critics of both of these trends, that is, the reduction of benefits and the loosening of state oversight, argue that such changes unfairly penalize the workers who can least afford to lose income. While some seasonal workers are employed in the skilled trades as construction workers, many others are in low-wage areas, such as farm labor or the tourist service industries. In addition, some analysts believe changes that eliminate unemployment compensation for seasonal workers will ultimately result in an adverse effect on these seasonal businesses. Unable to save enough to tide them over periods of unemployment, seasonal workers will seek year-round employment in other industries.

Long-term Outlook. As the United States and other industrialized nations move away from heavy manufacturing and toward service-based economies, changes in employment will be reflected by changes in employment benefits. The fear of many social scientists is that a loss of employer-provided benefits will be accompanied by a reduction in government-provided benefits, which could force many workers to accept lower standards of living and a reduced quality of life. When confronted with a competitive labor market, however, even industries long notorious for providing few benefits tend to change; this fact seems to indicate that such an overall reduction in employment benefits may be unlikely.   —*Nancy Farm Mannikko*

SUGGESTED READINGS: In *1001 Ways to Reward Employees* (New York: Workman Publishing, 1994) Bob Nelson provides creative examples of cost-effective employee benefits; Joseph D. Levesque's *The Human Resource Problem-Solver's Handbook* (New York: McGraw-Hill, 1992) reviews legal aspects of employee management and describes what benefits are legally required. In *Managing a Diverse Workforce: Regaining the Competitive Edge* (Lexington, Mass.: Lexington Books, 1991) John P. Fernandez discusses the impact of demographic changes in the workplace on issues such as benefits that attract and motivate employees.

Employment Division v. Smith (1990): U.S. Supreme Court decision that upheld Oregon's right to apply a state antidrug policy to state employees who, as members of the NATIVE AMERICAN CHURCH, were required to use peyote during religious rituals. Two state employees were fired when DRUG TESTING revealed that they had been using a controlled substance. The employees argued that they had used PEYOTE as part of a religious ritual and that the First Amendment protected their right to exercise their faith freely. The Court, however, ruled that the religious significance of peyote was irrelevant as long as the state law was not an attempt to regulate religious beliefs.

Employment Equity Act (1986): Canadian AFFIRMATIVE ACTION law designed to promote employment of specific groups of people judged to be disadvantaged. The act applies to banks, transportation companies, and other federally regulated companies with one hundred or more employees. The law requires such bodies to institute positive policies and practices to ensure that persons in designated groups achieve employment, promotion, and training proportionate to their representation in the workforce. The designated groups included women, aboriginal people, persons with disabilities, and other members of racial and ethnic minority populations. A 1990 study found that 365 employers and 635,000 jobs came under the act's authority.

Endangered species: Organisms that are at risk of extinction. In the United States, such animals are protected by the ENDANGERED SPECIES ACT, which regulates the taking of such species and forbids the destruction of their habitats. Initially expected to protect showy mammal and bird species, the act actually shelters a wide array of insects and plants, and the consequences of protecting habitats have been far more intrusive than initially envisioned.

Background. Before 1964, the federal government had historically provided little protection for wildlife aside from laws to prevent poaching on national park land. In that year, the Bureau of Sports, Fisheries, and Wildlife (now the U.S. Fish and Wildlife Service) listed sixty-three species as endangered in its "redbook." In 1966 and 1969, laws were passed allowing the Department of the Interior to protect species on the redbook list through acquisition of habitat; however, protection of endangered species did not extend to private lands until Congress passed the Endangered Spe-

Some species of tigers are among the world's most endangered animals. (Yasmine Cordoba)

cies Act in December, 1973. By this time, public awareness of the plight of the bald eagle, whales, whooping cranes, and some other large birds and mammals had grown; the issue was legitimate in the legislators' eyes, and the act passed by a large majority.

This act established the responsibilities of both the Fish and Wildlife Service (birds, terrestrial and freshwater species, the manatee, sea turtles on land, and sea otters) and the National Marine Fisheries Service (marine species except birds) to administer federal government efforts to conserve endangered species' habitats and regulate collection and CONSERVATION efforts. All federal agencies were directed to assist them in this effort. In 1988, amendments to the Endangered Species Act required the secretary of the interior to report every two years to the appropriate committees in both the Senate and the House of Representatives on the status of efforts to develop and implement recovery plans for all listed species.

Few citizens were aware of the Endangered Species Act before 1978. The Tennessee Valley Authority (TVA) had begun construction of the Tellico Dam project some years earlier, and a small fish, the snail

darter, was discovered at this very site just before the act became law. Opponents of the Tellico Dam requested that the Fish and Wildlife Service list this fish as endangered in 1975. At that time, the dam appeared to threaten the only known population of snail darters with extinction. A civil suit based on the Endangered Species Act was taken all the way to the Supreme Court, which ruled that it was the intent of Congress to prevent extinction regardless of the cost—more than $50 million had already been spent on the Tellico Dam. Tennessee senator Howard H. Baker, Jr., circumvented this by gaining legislation exempting the Tellico Dam from the ESA. More snail darter populations, however, were located in adjacent streams, and the fish was dropped to "threatened" status in 1984. This Supreme Court ruling of 1978, and a subsequent ruling in 1995 confirming the act's authority to regulate habitat on private property, confirmed the act's ability to insist that species be protected regardless of the cost.

Scientific Perspective. The Endangered Species Act attempts to conserve the ecosystems upon which endangered species and threatened species depend. Endangered species are listed because their populations

Several species of owls are listed as endangered. (AP/Wide World Photos)

are in imminent danger of going extinct; threatened species face less serious threats but could eventually become endangered. The regulatory agencies have criteria for listing, reclassifying, and delisting a species. Also, most state wildlife regulations recognize the federal endangered and threatened categories for species that fall within their state borders, as well as species in need of concern (SINC), although the latter category affords far less protection.

While extinction is a natural process, extensive expansion and development by humans has led to a higher rate of extinction within recorded history, nearly always through the destruction of habitat. Because most bird species are conspicuous and were de-

scribed at an early time, the extinction of the dodo bird from Indian Ocean islands and the passenger pigeon from North America were two examples of extinctions publicly recognized as having been caused by human activities and settlements. Many large mammals, including the wolf, bears, elk, and bison, had been extirpated from many states, surviving in small numbers in secluded reserves. The science community recognized, however, that most endangered species would be less glamorous invertebrates and plants, some of which would be lost before they were ever described or examined for properties useful to humans.

Because funds are limited, a recovery priority system was established in September, 1983, to rank endangered species. The scale first groups listed organisms into three clusters based on their immediate threat of extinction (high, medium, and low). Within each category, organisms are assessed for "recovery potential"—is there a reasonable chance to prevent extinction and perhaps achieve species recovery? Preference is given to saving organisms that represent the only surviving members of their genus. Second priority goes to saving a full species, and least priority is given to preserving subspecies. The priority recovery system results in eighteen levels. The black-footed ferret holds a high priority, while the Oregon silverspot butterfly has a lower recovery priority. Although the priority system helps direct attention to the most critical species, the costs of promoting recovery still vary widely with details of the species' situation.

Determining what constitutes a genuine full species or subspecies can be a difficult and controversial scientific issue. Although several millions of dollars were spent buying Florida land to save the dusky seaside sparrow, the population continued to dwindle until only one individual remained. Upon its death, university researchers examined its deoxyribonucleic acid (DNA) and declared it nearly identical to other common subspecies of seaside sparrow. The question of what constitutes a species or subspecies with a distinct evolutionary future is central to the problem of the PRESERVATION of endangered species.

Species status reports are compiled for listed species indicating whether the population is improving, stable, declining, unknown, or extinct. The difficulty of determining whether a species is extinct is shown in the case of the black-footed ferret. After researchers failed to livetrap or observe this prairie animal, it was presumed extinct until a farm dog carried in a specimen. Black-footed ferrets are now bred in captivity for reintroduction into the wild. Extensive research and survey work is required to assess correctly the changes in wild populations. The agencies admit that it is not reasonable to expect that all listed species will eventually be restored and dropped from the endangered or threatened list. In some cases, the critical habitat or resources are no longer available, and merely sustaining the rare population and preventing its extinction may be the best outcome that can be achieved.

Approved recovery plans are developed for the majority of species with highest priority. In 1990, when nearly six hundred species were listed, more than 350 had approved recovery plans. Nearly 60 percent of endangered species were animals, and about 40 percent of the animals were showier birds and mammals. More plants, however, have been on the endangered species list for three years or more.

Elimination of human activities cannot always save endangered species. The drastic reduction in American bison more than a century ago is most likely the ultimate reason for the decline in the American condor that apparently survived on bison carcasses. This giant bird now has little chance of surviving without constant human support. The Oregon silverspot butterfly survives in eight small populations, all dependent upon a violet species that survives only in open coastal grassland. Since the violet was dependent upon natural fires to prevent other plants from taking over—and since wildfires are now rare and rapidly stamped out—the threat to the butterfly is from natural succession. While the Endangered Species Act prevents landowners from destroying the environment, it cannot force owners to work against nature to preserve the successional stage that the butterfly needs.

Although species recovery takes a long time, and the expenditure of much money has not guaranteed recovery, several recovery successes received much publicity. Both the bald eagle and the peregrine falcon made a substantial comeback. The red wolf was successfully reintroduced into the Southeast, and the American alligator is no longer endangered. The Aleutian Canada goose population had dropped to nearly two hundred geese nesting on three islands when listed in 1967; after agencies acquired habitat, controlled predators, and reintroduced geese, the population returned to nearly six thousand nesting on eight islands, and the species was reclassified as threatened. Most biologists, however, are convinced that the rate of extinction of unknown and unlisted species far exceeds these successes.   —*John Richard Schrock*

SUGGESTED READINGS: *Endangered and Threatened Species Recovery Program*, prepared by the U.S. Fish and Wildlife Service (Washington, D.C.: Government Printing Office, 1990), is a report to Congress required by the Endangered Species Act; it describes briefly the recovery priority system and provides appendices of approved recovery plans, the status of their development, state-by-state listed species, and recovery status for listed species. Rocky Barker's *Saving All the Parts: Reconciling Economics and the Endangered Species Act* (Washington, D.C.: Island Press, 1993) is a fairly evenhanded account of the complex economic, social, and scientific issues involved in the day-to-day applications of the Endangered Species Act in the Northwest

Endangered Species Act

United States. "The Butterfly Problem," by Charles C. Mann and Mark L. Plummer (*Atlantic Monthly*, January, 1992), is a controversial article questioning whether we can afford to try to save every species.

Endangered Species Act (1973): U.S. law calling for the protection of species threatened with extinction. Early in the twentieth century, many people became concerned with the fate of other species in the face of human population growth, and various laws to conserve species were passed. The Pittman-Robertson Act (1937) attempted to ensure that game animals would be available to future hunters. The Endangered Species Preservation Act (1966) legislated land purchases for the PRESERVATION of any native species in danger of extinction, not merely game animals. The Endangered Species Conservation Act (1969) expanded the authority of the 1966 act.

The Endangered Species Act of 1973 was the culmination of earlier attempts. It established rules for protection of ENDANGERED SPECIES that remained in effect for more than two decades. The act gave the secretary of the interior ultimate responsibility for species conservation, but all federal agencies were charged with their protection. Federal activities could neither harm individual members of an endangered species nor damage their habitat.

The act established two categories of risk—"endangered," for species in imminent danger of extinction, and "threatened," for species in less immediate jeopardy. A 1978 amendment required that a recovery plan be developed for each endangered species and that the plan be followed until the species was judged to be out of danger. At that time, the species would be downgraded (from "endangered" to "threatened") or removed from the list ("delisted").

The Endangered Species Act has always been controversial. One extreme position contends that the act has not saved a single species. Another claims the act has been instrumental in saving numerous species ranging from whooping cranes to sea otters.

To political conservatives oriented toward economic growth, the act has stood in the way of progress. The delay in construction of the Tellico Dam to protect a tiny fish species (the snail darter) is often given as an example. Conservatives also often argue that the act is unfair to property owners, punishing them for noncompliance with endangered species regulations rather than compensating them for income lost in compliance.

Conservationists, on the other hand, argue that the act is neither efficient enough nor sufficiently strong to save species. The procedures for listing species are difficult and time-consuming, prompting critics to comment that a species could go extinct while waiting to be listed. In addition, the target populations in the recovery plans for some species were set lower than the actual population sizes at the time of listing. (The target population is the population level meant to ensure the species' survival; setting it below the size of the endangered population seems to some to be counterproductive.)

There have been signs of compromise between the two sides. For example, both have suggested that punishment for noncompliance should be replaced with tax breaks and other incentives to conserve species. Yet whatever its shortcomings, the Endangered Species Act has helped call attention to the plight of species in danger of being pushed off the earth by the growing human population.

SUGGESTED READING: The National Research Council's Committee on Scientific Issues in the Endangered Species Act, Board on Environmental Studies and Toxicology, Commission on Life Sciences, makes recommendations for renovation of the act in *Science and the Endangered Species Act* (Washington, D.C.: National Academy Press, 1995).

Engel v. Vitale (1962): U.S. SUPREME COURT case. One of a series of Supreme Court decisions dealing with church-state relations in the area of public education, the *Engel* case set new limits on government sponsorship of "voluntary" school prayer, thereby igniting an ongoing public debate.

The First Amendment to the U.S. Constitution contains two statements concerning the relationship between government regulation and private religious practice: the "establishment clause" prohibits government from sponsoring or favoring a particular religious organization or activity, while the "free-exercise clause" guarantees the right of private religious practice. The framers of the amendment assumed the two clauses to be complementary, in that restriction of government intrusion into religious matters was thought to be an important element in the protection of individual religious freedom. The *Engel* case, however, brought the two clauses into conflict by suggesting that the restriction of school-sponsored prayer was itself a violation of the right to religious free exercise.

The origins of the case lay in a decision made by a Long Island, New York, school board to adopt a twenty-two-word prayer recommended by the state board of regents. The prayer had been composed so as to be denominationally "neutral" and was not to be made a compulsory exercise: Any student not wishing to participate was free to refrain or even to leave the classroom. Opposition to the board's decision came in the form of a class-action suit organized by a group of parents, in concert with the AMERICAN CIVIL LIBERTIES UNION (ACLU), against the president of the school system. Lower state and federal courts had ruled in favor of the school board's policy, but the opponents continued to appeal the decision until 1962, when *Engel* was argued before the Supreme Court.

During oral arguments, attorneys for the school board asserted that a tradition existed from the time of the Founders that acknowledged the concept of a Supreme Being to be a necessary component of a democratic society. The board's attorneys thus suggested that the regents' prayer was nothing more than an exercise of public patriotism. They further argued that no individual rights were violated in the exercise of that observance, since the school board's policy did not compel participation, but that the majority's right to free exercise of religion was being hampered by a minority.

Opponents of the prayer charged that, by composing its own prayer, the state was establishing its own religion by "turning its schools into churches and its teachers into priests." Furthermore, the opponents drew on a remark made in a previous case by Justice Felix Frankfurter that "nonconformity is not an outstanding characteristic of little children"—thus, even though the prayer was officially voluntary, students would find it difficult to refrain from participating in a context where such a refusal might become a public spectacle. This, asserted the opponents, amounted to a compulsion of a different kind.

A majority of the court sided with the opponents. The opinion, authored by Justice Hugo Black, asserted that neither content nor circumstance were enough to free the activity from the Constitution's prohibition against establishment. "Government," he wrote, "should stay out of the business of writing or sanctioning official prayers and leave that purely religious function to the people themselves." Thus the Court chose to reaffirm the traditional relationship between the establishment and free-exercise clauses, in which governmental prerogatives are restricted so that individual rights might predominate.

The debate on school prayer did not end with the *Engel* case. Numerous attempts have been made to reintroduce school prayer through "moment of silence" laws and calls for a constitutional amendment; however, no successful attempt has been made to circumvent the standards set out in the *Engel* decision.

English as a Second Language (ESL): Term used to describe the teaching of English to people whose native language is not English. The United States and Canada, being immigrant nations, have long histories of ESL teaching, ESL theory, and ESL practice. The distinction is sometimes made between teaching English as a second language and teaching English as a foreign language (EFL). Many people live in English-speaking countries who speak little or no English; for such people, however, English is not a foreign language. They typically have a limited proficiency with English. Students with limited English proficiency are sometimes described as limited English proficients, or LEPs. One may also argue that English may not be a student's second language but rather a third, fourth, or so on, but the term "ESL" is what is most widely used.

English has become the most widely used international language of business, commerce, and science. ESL teaching, therefore, is practiced around the world as well as in countries where English is the native language and is taught to immigrants and language minorities.

That many people want or need to learn English is not in dispute; controversy has long existed, however, about how best to teach English to nonnative speakers and about the political aspects of language teaching. Teachers have often disputed the effectiveness of what may be called the grammar-based approach, which focuses on the rules of English, on systematic study, and on rote learning, versus what may be called the whole-language approach, which focuses on speaking, reading, and writing English in more natural contexts, without concentrating on grammar and usage. A considerable body of research exists on proper methods of teaching English or any other language as a foreign language. The research does not offer answers that firmly and generally settle the controversy, although it tends toward the whole-language approach, but the research does present a number of specific and practical methods for teaching. Many ESL teachers and researchers argue that dogmatism distorts the extremes of both the whole-language and the grammar-based methodologies.

ESL programs are offered in a variety of settings. (Dick Hemingway)

The political aspects of ESL teaching can be traced to issues of race, class, and culture. Those who are learning English often belong to what, in the English-speaking country, are cultural and racial minorities, and they are often poor. Some teachers and leaders in the field of ESL teaching have criticized ESL programs for instilling ideology as well as language; often this ideology is criticized as demeaning to the language learner. For example, in the United States, it was a common practice until the 1960's or even later to punish students who used a language other than English on school grounds.

English-only movement: Political effort initiated in the early 1980's to establish English as the official language of the United States. The English-only movement has roots in the anti-immigrant legislation of the early twentieth century, when immigrants from Southern and Eastern Europe potentially threatened the Anglo-Saxon culture and language heritage of the United States. Supporters of the English-only movement in the 1980's attempted to restrict bilingual and multicultural efforts among Latino populations of the United States.

In 1968, Congress passed the BILINGUAL EDUCATION ACT to increase the effectiveness of public school education among immigrant Hispanic groups. The Supreme Court further bolstered the Bilingual Education Act in *LAU v. NICHOLS* (1974) when it required schools to offer special assistance to students with limited English skills. Congress clarified the intent of the Bilingual Education Act in 1978 when it passed amendments emphasizing that the objective of the law was to provide students with the opportunity to achieve competence in the English language and, subsequently, a better occupational position in the American economy.

In spite of the fact that Congress suggested that bilingual programs were intended as transitional measures to aid immigrants in their efforts to accommodate to the American culture, proponents of the English-only movement viewed such programs as attempts to erode the Western heritage of the United States and replace it with a new multilingual and multicultural heritage. Prior to 1980, most efforts to restrict the use of languages other than English had been isolated and occurred at the state level. In the 1980's, the English-only movement shifted to the national level. Senator S. I. Hayakawa, a California Republican, introduced a proposed amendment to the U.S. CONSTITUTION that would have declared English the official language. Attacking what he referred to as "ethnic chauvinism," Hayakawa argued that it was language that made an American society out of a hodgepodge of various races and nationalities. Hayakawa further emphasized that if America were to continue to be the world's "melting pot," English had to be maintained as the official language. The bill died without further action, but it began a decade of national debate over the status of the English language in the United States.

In 1983, John Tanton of Michigan furthered the discussion when he formed an organization, U.S. English, to promote legislation declaring English the official language of the U.S. and an end to government policies that required printing documents in many languages. Although the movement has been unable to pass an amendment to the U.S. Constitution, it has had greater success at getting states to consider their arguments. Opponents argued that the debate had little to do with the maintenance of an American language but with the desire to exclude Hispanic populations from the political and economic structure of the United States. The debate continued into the 1990's and was symbolized by California's passage of PROPOSITION 187, which denied government benefits to illegal immigrants.

Enola Gay exhibit controversy (1994-1995): Turmoil surrounding the display of the airplane used to drop the first ATOMIC BOMB used in war. Objections by veterans groups and members of Congress forced the Smithsonian Institution to redesign a proposed exhibit that would have considered the controversial question: "Was the atomic bombing of Japan necessary to end World War II?"

On August 6, 1945, the *Enola Gay*, a U.S. Army Air Force B-29 bomber, dropped an atomic bomb on the city of Hiroshima, Japan. After the atomic bombing of Nagasaki, Japan, less than a week later, the Japanese surrendered, ending the war. To mark the fiftieth anniversary of the occasion, the Smithsonian Institution's National Air and Space Museum in Washington, D.C., planned an exhibit focusing on the delivery of the bomb, the destruction experienced at Hiroshima, and the decision to employ the atomic bomb against Japan.

The museum planned to display the forward fuselage of the *Enola Gay* and artifacts of the destruction borrowed from a Hiroshima museum, including the steps of a stone building that had been permanently imprinted with the shadow of a person sitting there as the intense heat of the bomb's explosion reached the site.

The most controversial aspect of the exhibit was the discussion of an Allied invasion of Japan as an alternative way to bring about an end to World War II. Initially, the script for the exhibit suggested there would have been about 31,000 casualties in the invasion, and contrasted this with the estimated 200,000 people who were killed, injured, or missing after the explosion of the bomb.

During the summer of 1994, veterans organizations charged that the exhibit, as proposed, portrayed Japan as the victim of a nuclear attack rather than as an aggressor in the war. In addition, they challenged the accuracy of the casualty estimates, suggesting many more American soldiers would have died in an invasion of Japan. One Smithsonian official summed up the situation by saying, "The veterans want the exhibit to stop when the doors to the bomb bay opened. And that's where the Japanese want it to begin."

In September, 1994, Smithsonian officials released a revised script for the exhibit, increasing the casualty estimate to 268,000 for the first phase of the invasion and up to one million if a second phase was required. This flexibility with the numbers strengthened the charge that the exhibit was historically inaccurate, and the criticism continued. Several members of Congress expressed public outrage, suggesting that the exhibit was still too sympathetic to the Japanese who were killed in the bombing and failed to describe either the atrocities committed by the Japanese during the war or the surprise attack on Pearl Harbor that had provoked U.S. involvement.

By the fall, Smithsonian officials had announced the deletion of all the controversial material from the exhibit. On November 17, 1994, a group of fifty historians released a letter criticizing the Smithsonian for yielding to pressure from the veterans groups. After five revisions of the script and the resignation of the National Air and Space Museum's director, Martin Harwit, the exhibit opened in June, 1995. The forward fuselage of the *Enola Gay* was the centerpiece of the exhibit, which also included a fifteen-minute video presentation featuring the remembrances of the flight crew. The revised exhibit, however, avoided discussion of alternatives to the bombing.

Entitlement programs: Benefits an individual can claim by virtue of personal identity or actions. The evolution of entitlement in Western industrialized nations parallels the notion of citizenship, which has been expanded since the eighteenth century to include civil, political, and social rights. Today, some argue, the rights of citizenship have taken on greater value and meaning than property rights and hereditary status.

History. The twentieth century has been marked in Western countries by expansion of social rights, or entitlements. In the United States, this process surged forward in response to the GREAT DEPRESSION. The SOCIAL SECURITY ACT of 1935 authorized establishment of America's largest entitlement program: Old Age, Survivors, and Disability Insurance (OASDI), commonly known as SOCIAL SECURITY. In 1965, the act was amended to include the next largest entitlements, Medicare (health insurance for the elderly) and Medicaid (health insurance for the poor). Unemployment compensation, another social insurance program, is also authorized under the act.

"Social insurance" entitlement programs are distinguished from "public assistance" or welfare programs in that eligibility for benefits is based not on income or assets but on prior contributions. In addition to contributions, beneficiaries must demonstrate that they have met the program's categorical requirements. In order to receive retirement benefits, a Social Security participant must both demonstrate retirement status (that he or she is not working) and meet age criteria (currently sixty-five years for full benefits).

The Social Security Act authorizes two public assistance programs, AID TO FAMILIES WITH DEPENDENT CHILDREN (AFDC) and Supplemental Security Income (SSI). Beneficiaries of these programs must meet both categorical and resource requirements for eligibility. AFDC is provided to low-income parents of dependent children. Those eligible for SSI are aged, blind, or disabled. In addition to these categorical requirements, both programs require incomes well below the federal poverty threshold and minimal assets. Although the federal contribution in these programs is constant, states vary in the levels of funding they assign. For example, SSI recipients in Alaska and California receive more than recipients in other states.

Programs authorized by the Social Security Act are the largest and most visible entitlements in the United States. They are not, however, the only means by which the government transfers funds to individuals. The federal retirement program is the nation's fourth largest entitlement. In addition, farm price supports, FOOD STAMPS, veterans benefits, and student loans rep-

Entitlement programs such as Aid to Families with Dependent Children are often controversial. (Jim West)

The 1935 Social Security Act established the largest U.S. entitlement program. (UPI/Corbis-Bettmann)

resent significant entitlements. More than half of the households in the U.S. benefit from some form of government transfer, often through reduced taxation of their income.

The nation's tax code also establishes entitlements, although most of these are less visible and controversial than spending programs. The tax code provides income support to homeowners through the mortgage interest deductions, to future retirees through special treatment of private pensions, to low-income workers through the EARNED INCOME TAX CREDIT, to parents through dependent care deductions, and to businesses through an elaborate system of tax abatements. In 1995, special tax treatment of private pensions was the nation's largest tax expenditure ($104.5 billion) followed by the mortgage interest deduction ($53.5 billion). Government revenue lost through tax expenditures is summarized annually in a report by the House Committee on Ways and Means known as "the green book."

Canadian experience with entitlements parallels that of other Western industrialized nations. Unlike in the United States, where entitlements were dramatically expanded by a single piece of legislation, social rights in Canada grew incrementally following World War II. The resulting system of income maintenance consists of "demogrants," social insurance, social assistance, and income supplementation. Demogrants provide universal, flat-rate payments. The largest are Old Age Security, paid to Canadians aged sixty-five and older, and Family Allowances, paid to all families with children under the age of eighteen. Demogrants are subject to the progressive income tax. Canada offers three programs of social insurance: Unemployment Insurance, the Canada Pension Plan, and Worker's Compensation. Where retirement coverage was a central aspect of the U.S. Social Security system, the Canada Pension Plan was not adopted until 1965. Social Assistance programs in Canada offer means-tested support to the needy and are administered at the provincial level. Canada also offers Income Supplementation to the elderly through a guaranteed income supplement and to low-income families with children through a tax credit.

Entitlement programs establish a legal right to goods or services provided by the government. From a budgetary perspective, they constitute "mandatory spending." The proportion of the U.S. budget devoted to these mandatory items has increased dramatically, from 29.6 percent in 1963, to 61.4 percent in 1993. Both entitlements and interest on the national debt doubled as proportions of the federal budget during this period. In 1992, President Bill CLINTON appointed a Bipartisan Commission on Entitlement and Tax Reform. With thirty-two members of Congress and distinguished private citizens the commission carefully examined the status of entitlements in the U.S. budget and concluded that "the Nation cannot continue to allow entitlements to consume a rapidly increasing share of the Federal budget." Another call of alarm was issued in 1995 by the Medicare Board of Trustees, which projected bankruptcy for that program by the year 2002.

Arguments Against Entitlements. The criticism of entitlement that marked the 1990's is attributed by some to renewed faith in capitalism in the wake of the Soviet Union's dissolution. In this context, the psychological argument against entitlements often carries great weight. Proponents of this view argue that entitlement programs create a "psychology of entitlement," undermining citizens' motivation to work. Entitlement programs are seen as contributing to the decline of the United States as a major world economic power by reducing the productivity of its workers. Under this view, the nation expanded its entitlement during an era of unprecedented prosperity. Wealth permitted Americans to be generous, but in today's fiscal environment such generosity has become prohibitively expensive. This argument is often used in support of "WORKFARE" proposals to add job or community service requirements to welfare.

A second argument against entitlement programs stems from observations about their dramatic growth. Since the 1940's, the U.S. has seen what many describe as an "explosion in entitlement spending." This unparalleled growth is not surprising, since OASDI paid few benefits prior to 1940, and Medicare and Medicaid were established in 1965. Demographic trends, such as the aging of the U.S. population, economic trends, such as the dramatic increase in the cost of health care, and social trends, such as decreased tolerance and concern for disenfranchised populations, have combined to lead the nation's politicians to consensus on the need to control or reduce entitlement spending.

Focusing on Social Security, other critics of entitlement argue that the program takes from low- and middle- income workers to finance the retirement of affluent elders. Arguing that Social Security should be means-tested, proponents note the regressive nature of the payroll tax and the special tax treatment of benefits. Social Security benefits are financed through a payroll tax, known as the Federal Insurance Contribution Act (FICA). It is regressive in that its burden falls heaviest on low-income workers. FICA tax is a flat percent (15 percent in 1995) of gross salary up to an income cap. The result is that low-income workers pay taxes on total income, while highly paid workers enjoy tax-free income for the amount above the cap. Prior to 1984, Social Security benefits were not subject to income tax. In 1983, the Social Security Act was amended to permit taxation of 50 percent of benefits. Under the Clinton Administration, that proportion was increased to a maximum of 85 percent for upper-income beneficiaries.

Arguments in Favor of Entitlements. Richard Titmuss articulated a philosophical defense of entitlement of his 1970 book *The Gift Relationship: From Human Blood to Social Policy.* Titmuss argued that in industrial societies, entitlements serve an integrative function, establishing a moral community in which assistance from strangers replaces the one-on-one assistance characteristic of earlier times. Thus the welfare state offers the support and concern needy people once derived from long-standing family and friendship ties. Without it, the capitalist system would run unchecked, leaving a trail of broken, battered, and abused humans in its wake.

In additional political arguments, proponents of specific entitlement programs emphasize the vulnerability of those served. Supporters of Social Security entitlement note the tremendous variation among America's elderly. A few may be affluent, but more are poor or economically vulnerable. Social Security benefits are computed using a progressive scale, so low-income workers receive proportionately more than upper-income workers. The elderly as a group are not more affluent than other adults. In 1994, the median income for households headed by the elderly ($17,160) was 56 percent of the median for all U.S. households. Further, deep pockets of POVERTY persist among the elderly, with the very old, single women, and ethnic minorities especially vulnerable. Rather than means testing Social Security, proponents of this view would favor eliminating the program's regressive features by reducing the cap on the FICA wage base or subjecting all benefits to income tax.

Other advocates of entitlement programs argue that the controversy surrounding their future represents an insidious form of class warfare. In support, proponents of this view note that the combined tax expenditures for private pensions and home-mortgage interest deductions roughly equal the amount spent on all means-tested entitlements. While means-tested programs such as AFDC and SSI are harshly criticized, tax expenditures that transfer income to the middle and upper classes are seldom subjected to debate.

—*Amanda Smith Barusch*

SUGGESTED READINGS: For a detailed theoretical critique of the U.S. system of entitlements, see Neil Gilbert's *Welfare Justice: Restoring Social Equity* (New Haven, Conn.: Yale University Press, 1995). Wallace C. Peterson's *Transfer Spending, Taxes, and the American Welfare State* (Boston: Kluwer Academic Publishers, 1991) also offers a thoughtful critique. More broad theoretical material can be found in both John Rawls's classic *A Theory of Justice* (Cambridge, Mass.: Belknap Press of Harvard University Press, 1971) and Richard Titmuss' *The Gift Relationship: From Human Blood to Social Policy* (London: Allen & Unwin, 1970). For details on entitlement spending and tax expenditures, see the House of Representatives Committee on Ways and Means's *Where Your Money Goes: The 1994-95 Green Book* (Washington, D.C.: Brassey's, 1994). This report is issued annually.

Entrapment: Luring of a person into the commission of a crime in order to prosecute the person for it. Claims of entrapment are often used as a legal defense by defendants who argue that police have gone beyond the scope of creating an opportunity to commit a crime and have actually encouraged criminal activity. The validity of the entrapment defense has been upheld by court decisions. Although the concept of entrapment is not specifically set forth in the U.S. CONSTITUTION, there are some constitutional underpinnings to the defense. According to the Constitution, police must act within the principles of "DUE PROCESS" when enforcing the law. In essence, the due process requirement means that there must be a fundamental fairness (which is sometimes difficult to define, and often difficult to apply to the enforcement of laws) in police proceedings. This is especially true of crimes in which the primary victim is the offender. In order to ensure that the government does not abuse its power to arrest and charge citizens with crimes, the state is forbidden from implanting or manufacturing crime in innocent minds. For example, if police do not have evidence of illegal activity, they may not get it by creating an outrageous set of circumstances that would encourage law-abiding citizens to break the law.

An example of successful use of the entrapment defense can be found in the SUPREME COURT case *Sherman v. United States* (1958). The defendant was suspected of dealing heroin, but the police had no evidence to support their suspicions. In order to obtain the evidence to make an arrest, an informant who had met Sherman in a doctor's office, where both were being treated for drug addictions, asked Sherman to help him find some narcotics. After trying to avoid the issue on several occasions, Sherman was finally convinced by the informant to obtain narcotics, and Sherman was arrested. The Supreme Court found that the police had gone too far in their efforts to enforce the law. In its decision, the Court stated that "the function of law enforcement is the prevention of crime and apprehension of criminals. Manifestly, that function does not include the manufacturing of crime."

Another notable case, *Jacobson v. United States* (1992), dealt with the purchasing of child PORNOGRAPHY through the mail, a federal offense. After the defendant had ordered magazines showing nude teenage boys, the law with respect to child pornography changed, and it became illegal to receive such materials. Jacobson's name was found on a mailing list, and law-enforcement agents encouraged Jacobson to purchase child pornography by repeatedly sending advertisements and solicitations to him. After more than two years of refusing the offers, he finally agreed to order a magazine and was arrested. In this case, the Court found the defendant was not predisposed to committing the crime but had been lured by agents of the government to do something he would not ordinarily have done.

Victims of sting operations, including government officials who believe that they have been "set up" by police, often raise the defense of entrapment. The difference between creating an opportunity for a crime to be committed—an accepted part of police "sting" operations—and actually inducing an innocent party to commit a crime is often subject to interpretation. The use of videotape in such cases has been effective in shifting the interpretation of such issues to the courts.

Environmental illnesses: Diseases, illnesses, or physical conditions that are directly or indirectly linked to environmental degradation. Environmental illnesses usually represent themselves in floral and

faunal populations as the direct result of the effects of natural and synthetic pollutants on the environment. Natural pollutants include pathogenic bacteria and protozoa, volcanic ash, and forest fires; synthetic pollutants are human-generated organic and inorganic materials released into the environment. The severity and extent of pollutant-related illness is dependent on the amount of contaminant released, the extent of exposure, the pollutant's chemical and physical properties, and the susceptibility of the exposed biota.

Environmental issues: Topics pertaining to the quality and quantity of aspects of the physical environment in which people live. Since the early 1960's, concern has risen that the activity of an increasingly industrialized society has harmed numerous aspects of the environment, often adversely affecting human health as well. Major issues include ozone depletion, GLOBAL WARMING, AIR and WATER POLLUTION, toxic chemicals, the depletion of forests, fresh water, and other resources, the loss or endangerment of many species of life forms and of biological communities, and population growth.

Humans have altered the world since the beginning of their existence, but it was only in the 1960's that large numbers of people across North America became concerned about the cumulative impact of their activities. Rachel Carson is widely credited with beginning this movement with her 1962 book *Silent Spring*, which pointed to the harm pesticides had inflicted on bird populations.

In the years following the publication of Carson's book, many Americans became concerned about other aspects of the environment as well. New environmental organizations were formed, existing ones grew, and numerous pieces of important legislation were passed.

Global Problems Affecting the Western Hemisphere. The hole in the ozone layer was first hypothesized in 1973, when a researcher discovered that the CHLOROFLUOROCARBONS (CFCs), propellants used in aerosol cans, were lingering in the earth's upper atmosphere. There, they destroy the layer of ozone that lies eight to thirty miles above the earth's surface and that shields it from the sun's deadly ultraviolet light. In 1984, a team of British scientists discovered a temporary 40 percent loss of ozone—the first proof of the theory, which was subsequently confirmed by other scientists many times over. The best-understood effect

Environmental activists celebrate Earth Day at a 1990 rally in Washington, D.C. (UPI/Corbis-Bettmann)

of this loss of ozone has been an increase in skin CANCER: 800,000 new cases diagnosed per year by 1991, and an estimated 2,100 percent increase in deaths, at a rate of 10,000 per year.

By 1978, the United States banned CFCs in aerosols. Further action was stalled by Ronald REAGAN's presidency until 1985, when, as a result of a lawsuit by the National Resources Defense Council (NRDC) and other pressures, the Environmental Protection Agency (EPA) was forced to take up the development of CFC regulations again as part of amendments to the CLEAN AIR ACT.

In 1985, a hole was discovered in the ozone shield over Antarctica; by 1991, scientists discovered that the entire shield was vanishing twice as fast overall as had been anticipated. U.S. industry stopped CFC production in 1988. International efforts to reduce CFCs gave birth to the MONTREAL PROTOCOL in 1990, which called for a global ban on CFCs and other similar compounds.

In 1979, a U.S. Department of Energy (DOE) report declared global warming the most important environmental issue. Global warming occurs because human activity, particularly since the Industrial Revolution, has added gases to the earth's atmosphere, the environmental layer that allows sunlight to pass through it to warm the earth. Organic carbon released from the burning of coal, oil, and natural gas has been the chief culprit, but other compounds, including CFCs, contribute. With their addition, the sun's warmth is increasingly trapped in the atmosphere. Temperatures globally have risen, but fluctuations occur from year to year, and some scientists, particularly those associated with related industries, contend that warming has yet to prove a long-term trend. Others say the risks are so serious that even if doubt remains, countries should work to reverse it.

The consequences of global warming could be grave. If the world's climate warms by even a few degrees, polar ice caps will partially melt, causing sea level to rise. Coastal areas would flood and agriculture would be required to relocate, both causing large-scale disruption of settlement patterns. The world's fish stocks could be drastically affected, and a number of species would be lost as well.

The solution to this issue is not simple. Transportation, industry, and heating in Western society have been built on these forms of energy. Partial attempts at curbing emissions have been contested by those industries most affected. Even if industrialized nations could

change their habits, many THIRD WORLD NATIONS in the process of development are unlikely to do so. Nor is energy the only issue. The loss of forests worldwide impedes the absorption of atmospheric gases and increases world temperatures, and few governments—including the United States and Canadian—have the desire or power to stop global DEFORESTATION. World population growth, the engine behind many factors contributing to global warming, continues to climb.

Pollution. In 1969, the air quality in Los Angeles became so poor that the city's inhabitants were warned against golfing, jogging, and most other outdoor activities. While strict regulations have since improved the quality of air in Los Angeles, it remains a concern. Air pollution causes acute respiratory illness, aggravates chronic heart and lung disease, and adversely affects the very old and very young.

Many different elements create air pollution, from car and industrial emissions and nuclear releases to paint, dry-cleaning fumes, and cigarette smoke. Among the worst are toxic trace elements, radioactivity, particulates, sulfur dioxide, and nitrogen oxide. The latter two combine with rain or snow to produce ACID RAIN. When that precipitation falls in areas with thin, alkaline soil, the chemical balance in streams and lakes is upset, damaging—in some cases seriously—the aquatic food chain, including fish, and then birds. Forests suffer as water carries nitrogen from acid rain into soils, upsetting the chemistry that gives trees life. Acid rain across Southern Canada and the Northern United States has brought tension to relations between the two countries. In 1977, the United States challenged the construction of a large coal-burning power plant in Ontario, across from Minnesota wilderness areas. In the end, construction of a smaller plant was allowed. Since then, the Canadian government has protested air pollution from the south blown north into its rivers and lakes.

In the early 1970's, public pressure resulted in the passage of the Clean Air Act and several later amendments mandating the addition of catalytic converters on cars and scrubbers on smokestacks of coal-burning utilities. By 1977, sulfur dioxide, particulate, and carbon monoxide levels improved. As leaded gasoline was phased out between 1983 and 1989, airborne lead fell 89 percent. Still, air quality remained poor, and many sources of air pollution had not been addressed. In 1990, the Clean Air Amendments Act was passed, aimed at reducing toxic emissions and sulfur dioxide even more. Activists applauded the bill, but feared that

Toxic dumps filled with hazardous wastes are a major environmental concern. (Archive Photos/Reuters/Petr Josek)

resistance by agencies and industry would prevent its total implementation, which proved to be the case.

Toxic chemicals, such as PESTICIDES AND HERBICIDES, have proved a problem where they are produced, used, and discarded, often carried into water bodies by rain. In the most famous instance of unregulated dumping, Love Canal, a disposal site for the Hooker Chemical Company in Niagara, New York, was discovered in 1977 to have caused a broad range of health problems in the local population.

The Toxic Substances Control Act was passed in 1976, requiring that chemicals suspected of causing cancer, birth deformities, or genetic problems be tested before they be put on the market. The legislation was a compromise between industry and those worried about the health effects of these chemicals. Issues such as how to determine acceptable levels of risk or how to weigh risks against benefits were by no means settled by it. Moreover, tests to determine the effects of

chemicals are expensive and time-consuming, while their results are not always clear. Meanwhile, some forty-six thousand pesticides are already in use, and two thousand new chemicals come into existence every year.

While the worst pesticides and herbicides have been banned in the United States and Canada, many are still sold to countries abroad that export food back. About 25 percent of all fruit and 98 percent of all coffee is imported, much of it from countries with few controls on chemicals, and the U.S. program for testing imports is inadequate. Chemicals and public sewage systems contribute to water pollution but are responsible for less than half of total volume of pollutants. The majority comes from "non-point sources": runoff from city streets, construction sites, and agriculture.

The 1972 Clean Water Act resulted in improvements in discharges from industry and sewage-treatment plants, but by the late 1980's, non-point sources remained unaddressed, primarily because of a lack of funds. According to a 1990 EPA report, the result was that at least one-third of U.S. rivers, half of the estuaries, and more than half of the lakes are not fully safe for swimming or fishing. Aquatic life forms are even more affected. Pollution is one factor contributing to the endangerment of 28 percent of amphibians, 34 percent of fish, and 65 percent of crayfish. Forty-five U.S. states reported almost one thousand fishing advisories and fifty bans in 1988-1989 as a result of pollutants such as pesticides, dioxin, mercury, and other metals.

Energy. No industrial society functions without consuming large amounts of energy, and all available forms of energy come with environmental price tags. Coal, an early energy source, led to black lung disease and other debilitating diseases in the people who mined it; to disruption of land in the digging of mines, particularly strip mines; and to air pollution when burnt. Coal burning emits particulate matter and sulfur dioxide, both of which harm human lungs.

The limits on emissions from coal imposed by the Clean Air Act have led to the use of low-sulfur, or "clean," coal and to the installation of gas scrubbers on utility stacks. The Surface Mine and Reclamation Act of 1977 mandated rehabilitation of old sites and the prevention of new massive scars, but enforcement of its provisions was lax and the problems remained largely unaddressed through the early 1990's.

Environmentalists have questioned society's undisputed reliance on petroleum because its extraction, transportation, and utilization have led to serious environmental problems. Ecological disruption from the extraction of oil particularly threatens fragile environments such as the Arctic Wildlife Refuge. Elsewhere, as along the coast of California, residents worry that drilling or transporting oil will result in spills. The EXXON VALDEZ OIL SPILL of 1989 highlighted the damage spills cause marine and bird life and the human communities dependent on them; however, the *Exxon Valdez* was only one instance of many. In 1991, 677 spills occurred in the Port of New Orleans alone, and 398 occurred in New York Harbor. The U.S. Congress passed the Oil Pollution Act in August, 1990, calling for improvements in transportation and storage of petroleum. The act was not all-inclusive, however, nor have all its provisions been acted upon.

The Cold War of the 1950's and 1960's led to the aggressive development of nuclear power, but by the 1970's, many questions had been raised about the industry's safety, health effects, and overall cost. In 1992, nuclear energy provided about 20 percent of U.S. electricity production, and about 8 percent of its total energy.

Fears about the safety of nuclear plants were fueled by the accident at Pennsylvania's THREE-MILE ISLAND, which cost an estimated $400 million to clean up. The daily operations of nuclear processing and power plants have caused widespread and long-term problems, chiefly that of how to dispose of radioactive waste. Its storage is made difficult by the extremely long lives—sometimes millions of years—of some radioisotopes. Many locations have been explored, in-

U.S. ENVIRONMENTAL PROTECTION AGENCY CRIMINAL ENFORCEMENT ACTIVITIES, 1984-1992

	1984	1985	1986	1987	1988	1989	1990	1991	1992
Enforcement activities									
Referrals to the U.S. Department of Justice	31	40	41	41	59	60	65	81	107
Cases successfully prosecuted	14	15	26	27	24	43	32	48	61
Defendants charged	36	40	98	66	97	95	100	104	150
Defendants convicted	26	40	66	58	50	72	55	82	99
Penalties for convicted defendants									
Months sentenced to prison	6	78	279	456	278	325	745	963	1,135
Months served in prison	6	44	203	100	185	208	222	610	744
Months sentenced to probation	552	882	828	1,410	1,284	1,045	1,176	1,713	2,478

Source: U.S. Department of Justice, Bureau of Justice Statistics, *Sourcebook of Criminal Justice Statistics—1993.* Washington, D.C.: U.S. Government Printing Office, 1994.

cluding burial in Antarctica, at sea, or in space, as well as in remote locations in the United States. The difficulty is to find locations that are not vulnerable to the movements of the earth's crust, that can be made secure from theft by terrorists, and where leakage will not occur, particularly into aquifers or other water sources. The problem is confounded by growing resistance by communities to housing such a repository.

These dilemmas led to the passage of the Nuclear Waste Policy Act of 1982, which required the development of two high-level repositories, one in the East, one in the West. So much resistance was met by proposed localities that by 1995 the only site identified for development was Yucca Mountain, Nevada. Nevada responded by passing a bill prohibiting the storage of any high-level waste at that site. The Department of Energy, however, continued to develop the site, although many conservationists doubt that it will ever be completed. Meanwhile, more than twenty-four thousand metric tons of commercial spent fuel waits to be stored.

Hydropower was initially thought to be less harmful to the environment than other energy forms, but the dams that make it possible have come under increasing criticism for their effects on the downstream rivers, and on fish, particularly the salmon that once were so abundant in the Northwest. The proposed James Bay hydropower project in northern Québec came under heavy criticism in the early 1990's for the disruption of the indigenous Cree people, wilderness, and wildlife.

Wind, geothermal, and solar power have been seen as the least destructive forms of harnessing nature's energy. Wind power, however, can be generated only in places where the force is frequent and strong enough, and then it requires many windmills, which to some are an eyesore on the landscape. Geothermal power can be generated only in those locations where hot water escapes from the earth's lower reaches. Solar is the method with the greatest potential, but technical problems remain in harnessing it.

Last, such environmentalists as Armory Lovins at the Rocky Mountain Institute claim that conservation is the best source of energy. They argued that the use of efficient appliances, compact fluorescent bulbs, and similar measures would cause significant savings.

Resource Depletion. Since life evolved on Earth, species, like the dinosaurs, have become extinct. What has changed is the rate at which extinctions occur. Experts estimate that before 1900, one species of bird or mammal was lost worldwide every four years; after 1900, the rate rose to one per year; and by the year 2000, one hundred species per day are likely to perish. In the United States, ninety-six species of vertebrates have disappeared since Europeans arrived.

The main cause of extinctions is the loss of habitat. Insects, animals, birds, reptiles, and amphibians are all adapted to live in specific kinds of locations, without which they die out. The history of the continent since the seventeenth century is one of increased settlement, the clearing of land, the damming of rivers, the harvesting of timber, the draining of wetlands, and mining. All of these activities disrupted places other organisms inhabited. In addition to the number of species already lost, many others are greatly diminished in number, some of which are in danger of being lost in the future. Many unique ecological communities have shared the same fate.

In 1973, concern over this issue led to the passage of the ENDANGERED SPECIES ACT, requiring the protection of threatened or endangered species. The act became controversial in the 1980's when environmental organizations such as the National Resources Defense Council and the Sierra Club used its provisions to challenge the logging of old-growth forests in the Northwest, home to the endangered Northern spotted owl, and to challenge logging and grazing practices and the management of hydroelectric dams contributing to the decline of the Pacific salmon. In each case, economic interests, whether of loggers, timber-mill workers, or consumers of electricity, were in opposition to saving species, leading to efforts by conservatives to weaken the act in the mid-1990's.

The Canadian-based organization Greenpeace has actively publicized the fact that many fish, along with marine animals, are significantly reduced in numbers. Overfishing, particularly by industrial trawlers, is one major cause. These boats, some longer than a football field, drag thousand-foot nets for miles across the bottom of the ocean, hauling in as much as 500,000 pounds of fish in a day.

Fish cannot reproduce fast enough to make up for these massive catches, which are turning what was a sustainable food resource into a rapidly declining one. Mammals that depend on fish for food are declining rapidly as well. The trawling industry is "managed" by a council of industry representatives and political appointees, and outside attempts to regulate the industry have achieved only small successes.

Development is also responsible for the decline of fish and sea mammals. Nearly 90 percent of all saltwater fish (the bulk of what humans consume) are caught

The fate of endangered species such as this snow leopard is a prime concern of many environmental activists. (Yasmine Cordoba)

along continental shelves, estuaries, and coastal rivers, where dredging, pollution discharges, and siltation have drastically affected the environment. Power plant draw-downs, dams, the diversion of water for irrigation, and human consumption also contribute.

With the future of the Pacific salmon in doubt, the role of dams in the Northwest United States is fiercely contested. Resistance to new dams is high; proposals to destroy several dams were gaining momentum until the Republicans gained control of Congress in the 1994 election. Agricultural interests and municipalities will continue to demand the diversion of water for their uses, and environmentalists will persist in attempting to claim the rights of the fish to the water.

Another rapidly diminishing resource is the continent's soil. The Dust Bowl era of the 1930's is the best-known example, but the problem has since become more acute. When farmers harvest grains, they rip the plants out, leaving soil bare and vulnerable to erosion until the next planting. The steady use of this system since European settlement has stripped the cropland of one-third of its topsoil.

The water supply, particularly groundwater, is being depleted by agriculture. The largest aquifer in the world is the Oglalla, stretching from South Dakota to Texas. Its water is being mined to support one-fifth of irrigated cropland in the United States at a rate fourteen-times faster than it can be replenished. A similar situation exists with smaller aquifers throughout the country. Surface water, too, has had heavy demands placed on it. Farmers and ranchers claim it for irrigation, municipalities for water supply, and conservationists for habitat and recreation. The Colorado River, one of the nation's major arteries, has had more of its water apportioned to the states it flows through than actually exists, and the once-mighty river no longer reaches the ocean. Future increases in population are expected to exacerbate this situation, leading to more intense conflicts between users.

The United States and Canada both have only remnants of their former forests—in the United States, only 5 percent of original forests remain. Forests were felled initially by settlers to clear land for agriculture and build homes. Since early in the twentieth century,

Demonstrators at the Portland Timber Summit call for the protection of old-growth forests. (Archive Photos/Reuters/ Steve DiPaola)

much remaining forest was managed by the U.S. Forest Service explicitly for the production of lumber, 12 billion board-feet per year by 1966. Only in 1960, with the Multiple Use Sustained Yield Act, were other uses given legitimate claim. In Canada, deforestation began later, but by the 1990's had picked up speed. In British Columbia alone, forests were being logged at a rate of 600,000 acres per year.

Population growth affects every area of resource depletion. Stanford University biologist Paul EHRLICH argued this case strongly—his detractors say sensationally—in his 1968 book *The Population Bomb*. Organizations such as Zero Population Growth (ZPG) have since worked to limit population growth. The U.S. population is growing at 2.6 million people per year, almost double the average for the developed world. By most indicators, the United States also has the highest level of consumption and waste in the world. With only 4.7 percent of the world's people, the United States produces more than 22 percent of its carbon dioxide and CFCs. More people means more strain on water supply, increased demand for energy, more clearing of forests for wood products and of land for settlement, more solid-waste generated, and more pressure on sensitive habitat, more of the activity that contributes to global warming and the loss of ozone.

Slowing growth would necessitate encouraging a lower birth rate and curbing immigration, which contributes more than nine-tenths of the annual increase—two highly controversial tasks. Lowering birth rates involves providing access to birth control and abortion, curbing poverty, and increasing access for women to education and training in the job market. The American people are far from a consensus on these issues. Without a reversal of current trends, the U.S. population is projected to grow by another 62 million by 2025.

—Maya Muir

SUGGESTED READINGS: Rice Odell's *Environmental Awakening: The New Revolution to Protect the Earth* (Cambridge, Mass.: Conservation Foundation, Ballinger, 1980) is an overview focusing on the growth of the environmental movement. Two classic early works are Rachel Carson's *Silent Spring* (Boston: Houghton-Mifflin, 1962) an exposé of the pesticide problem, and Paul Ehrlich's *The Population Bomb* (New York: Ballantine, 1968), a wide-ranging look at all the problems which stem from population pressure.

Sharon L. Roan's *Ozone Crisis: The Fifteen-Year Evolution of a Sudden Global Emergency* (New York: John Wiley and Sons, 1989) is an extensive report on

the science and politics of that issue, while Nicholas Lenssen's *Nuclear Waste: The Problem That Won't Go Away* (Worldwatch Institute, 1991) is a comprehensive summary in pamphlet form. Stephen H. Schneider's *Global Warming: Are We Entering the Greenhouse Century?* (San Francisco: Sierra Club Books, 1989) is thorough and scientific. Rocky Barker's *Saving All the Parts: Reconciling Economics and the Endangered Species Act* (Washington, D.C.: Island Press, 1993) is a balanced examination of the Northwest as a microcosm of the whole issue.

Environmental legislation: Laws governing the release of pollutants into the environment, setting air and water quality standards, regulating the use and disposal of hazardous chemicals, or in other ways acting to protect the environment.

History. The first U.S. laws concerning air quality were local ordinances passed in Chicago, Cincinnati, and other cities in the late nineteenth century to control the release of smoke from coal combustion. By the end of World War II, a large number of city, county, and state laws concerning air pollution were in effect. These laws, which usually focused on visible pollutants, were in some cases successful in controlling release of particulate matter but were often weak or not strictly enforced.

In the United States, the federal role in controlling AIR POLLUTION was initially limited to the areas of research and training. The first major federal legislation concerning air pollution was the 1963 CLEAN AIR ACT, which provided funds for state and local air-pollution programs, gave the government limited powers to control air pollution, and established a program to study the effects of pollutants from automobiles. In 1965, Congress passed the MOTOR VEHICLE AIR POLLUTION CONTROL ACT, which led to national standards for emissions from new automobiles similar to those previously set in the state of California. In 1970, the CLEAN AIR ACT AMENDMENTS resulted in national standards for air quality, along with a timetable for achieving the standards. The act also set new automobile emissions standards and created the Environmental Protection Agency (EPA).

Implementation of the air-quality and emission standards in the 1970 Clean Air Act Amendments was delayed in 1977, as the original standards proved more difficult to achieve than anticipated. No major federal air-pollution legislation was passed until the Clean Air

Environmental legislation

Act Amendments of 1990. These amendments set revised deadlines for meeting air quality standards, established a timetable for the reduction of emissions of sulfur dioxide and nitrogen oxides, and restricted the use and manufacture of CHLOROFLUOROCARBONS (CFCs) and related ozone-depleting substances.

As with air pollution, the regulation of WATER POLLUTION was for a long time left to state and local authorities. Early federal legislation, such as the 1948 Water Pollution Control Act and the 1956 amendments to the act, provided assistance to states for the construction of water treatment plants, but left primary responsibility for regulation and enforcement of water-pollution standards to the states. The 1965 Water Qual-

ity Act and 1966 Clean Water Restoration Act set federal water-quality standards, provided additional funds for improvement of water quality, and moved toward regional control of water pollution.

In 1972, the Federal Water Pollution Control Act (CLEAN WATER ACT) was passed. The act established a timetable for the improvement of municipal sewage treatment and provided $24.6 billion to assist cities and states in the construction of water-treatment plants and for water-quality research. Amendments to the act passed in 1977, 1981, 1987, and 1992 continued federal efforts to control pollution in the nation's surface waters. A 1990 report by the EPA indicated, however, that the sewer and wastewater treatment facilities in several

Major environmental disasters, such as the 1989 Alaskan oil spill by the tanker *Exxon Valdez* that prompted this cleanup effort, have often spurred calls for environmental legislation. (Reuters/Corbis-Bettmann)

Congressional Democrats celebrate a House of Representatives vote to override President Ronald Reagan's veto of clean-water legislation in 1987. (UPI/Corbis-Bettmann)

hundred cities still failed to meet federal standards.

The federal government also passed laws to control the use and release of hazardous and toxic substances. The 1960 HAZARDOUS SUBSTANCES ACT set labeling requirements for household chemicals and toys containing hazardous materials and provided a method for banning hazardous products in interstate commerce. In 1976, the Resource Conservation and Recovery Act required the EPA to identify hazardous-waste sites and regulated the disposal of hazardous wastes. Additional regulation of hazardous chemicals, including pretesting of industrial chemicals and a phaseout in the production of polychlorinated biphenyls (PCBs), was given by the Toxic Substances Control Act in 1976. In 1980, the Comprehensive Environmental Response, Compensation, and Liability Act established the Superfund program. SUPERFUND, amended in 1986 and 1990, provided money to identify and clean up waste sites and other sources of hazardous materials and established a procedure to determine liability and recover cleanup costs. While more than thirty-four thousand hazardous-waste sites, including approximately twelve hundred high-priority sites, were identified by the EPA, only sixty-four sites had been cleaned or stabilized by 1992.

Canadian environmental legislation in many ways paralleled that of the United States. For example, the 1971 Canadian Clean Air Act provided for the setting of national ambient air-quality objectives. Amendments to the act passed in 1980 further regulated sources of air pollutants, while automobile-emission standards were established by the 1985 Motor Vehicle Safety Act. Unlike the United States, the major responsibility for enactment and enforcement of pollution legislation in Canada has remained at the provincial level.

Arguments for Environmental Legislation. Proponents of strict environmental legislation claim that a cleaner environment will benefit human health and welfare. The WORLD HEALTH ORGANIZATION (WHO) estimates that from 1 percent to 10 percent of carcinogen exposure is from environmental pollutants. A 1984 study by the OFFICE OF TECHNOLOGY ASSESSMENT (OTA) claimed that as many as sixty thousand premature deaths per year in the United States may be associated with air pollution. The annual cost of exposure to air pollution in health-care expenses and loss of worker productivity is approximately $150 billion, according to a study by the American Lung Association. Reduction in pollution levels, particularly air pollution, should therefore lead to corresponding reductions in the health effects from exposure to pollutants and economic benefits associated with such reductions.

Those favoring environmental legislation can also point to specific successes stemming from antipollution laws. An 86 percent reduction in lead emissions occurred between 1975 and 1985; this was primarily the result of restrictions on the use of leaded gasoline. Within a few years of the 1979 ban on the production of PCBs, the concentration of PCBs in human body fat was found to have decreased by a factor of four. Annual releases of the major categories of air pollutants in all cases either remained constant or decreased between 1970 and 1990, despite the economic and population growth occurring during the period.

Finally, proponents of strict legislation note that a cleaner environment results in an improved quality of life. While it is difficult to give a specific dollar amount for the intrinsic value of clean air and water, the strong support for improving air and water quality by the general public indicates that most people value clean air and clean water independent of economic and health benefits.

Arguments Against Environmental Legislation. Those arguing for less stringent environmental legislation believe that a high cost is paid for a minimal improvement in environmental quality. A 1990 study by the EPA stated that total expenditures for pollution control by the private and public sector (in constant 1986 dollars) increased from $30 billion in 1972 to $100 billion in 1990. The Office of Technology Assessment estimated that the total bill for the cleanup of waste dumps mandated by the Superfund legislation would be $1 trillion. Several studies have shown that the costs of complying with pollution laws result in substantial decreases in worker productivity, affecting the competitiveness of American products in the world economy. Critics note that this could also lead to migration of industries to less-developed countries, where regulations tend to be less stringent, and therefore could result in a loss of jobs. The net result would be a weakened economy and a lower standard of living.

Those opposed to strict legislation feel that the large sums of money spent to control pollution have led to minimal benefits. Improvements in air quality were greater during the 1960's than the 1980's, despite increasing air-pollution regulation. Water quality during the same period showed little overall improvement. The health benefits associated with decreased levels of pollutants, critics claim, are often overstated; this was in part caused by the difficulty in separating the health effects of exposure to pollutants from those caused by voluntary lifestyle choices such as cigarette smoking, consumption of alcohol, and lack of exercise. Estimates on the costs of pollution and of deaths associated with exposure to pollutants are therefore unreliable.

Ongoing Controversies. During the 1980's, the focus of many environmentalists shifted to international controls to minimize the global effects of pollution. The 1990 MONTREAL PROTOCOL placed worldwide limits on the use and manufacture of CFCs and related chemicals because of their potential to reduce levels of ozone in the stratosphere. Fears that increases in atmospheric carbon dioxide and other greenhouse gases could lead to a general global warming led to discussions of ways to limit the release of such gases. Supporters of new legislation to attack global environmental problems pointed to the potential long-term damage that could result if no action were taken. Critics argued that there were uncertainties in the scientific evidence concerning ozone depletion and global warming and that new regulations would lead to large-scale economic disruption. It is clear that the debate concerning the costs and benefits of environmental legislation is one that will continue.   *—Jeffrey A. Joens*

SUGGESTED READINGS: A thorough discussion of early environmental legislation is given by J. Clarence Davies III in *The Politics of Pollution*, 2d ed. (Indianapolis, Ind.: Pegasus, 1975). *Environmental Politics and Policy: Theories and Evidence* (Durham, N.C.: Duke University Press, 1989), edited by James P. Lester, presents a series of essays on the factors involved in establishing environmental policy. Gary C. Bryner gives a detailed discussion of the 1990 Clean Air Act Amendments in the context of earlier federal air-pollution legislation in *Blue Skies, Green Politics: The Clean Air Act of 1990* (Washington, D.C.: CQ Press, 1993). A critical history of environmental legislation from an author skeptical of the utility of federal pollution regulations is provided by Bruce Yandle in *The Political Limits of Environmental Regulation: Tracking the Unicorn* (New York: Quorum Books, 1989).

Environmental racism: Perception that people of color shoulder a disproportionate burden of environmental hazards, especially in the siting of toxic-waste facilities. "Environmental justice," a related term, re-fers to the grassroots political movement to end such DISCRIMINATION.

History. Both terms were coined in 1982 by Benjamin Chavis, head of the United Church of Christ Commission on Racial Justice. Chavis was in rural Warren County, North Carolina, helping to organize a grassroots protest against the siting of a dump for soil contaminated with polychlorinated biphenyls (PCBs), which are believed to cause cancer. Many citizens of Warren County, the population of which was 60 percent African American and 4 percent Native American, felt that the decision by the Environmental Protection Agency (EPA) to site the dump closer to the water table than usual was racially motivated. The threatened minority community subsequently waged an unsuccessful nonviolent resistance campaign in which more than five hundred demonstrators were arrested.

Although the campaign was unsuccessful, the Warren County protest gave birth to the environmental justice movement. Minority communities can claim a

Residents of North Richmond, California, express anger over perceived environmental racism. (Impact Visuals, Mark Ludak)

long history of protest against unhealthy living conditions, particularly inadequate garbage service, unsafe drinking water, and lead poisoning, but until the Warren County protest, such problems were generally regarded as social issues. After Warren County, many health threats facing minority communities were seen as the result of either intentional or institutional (nonintentional) environmental racism. Chavis has defined environmental racism as racial discrimination in policy-making, in the enforcement of regulations and laws, in the deliberate targeting of nonwhite communities for toxic-waste disposal and polluting industries, and the official sanction of life-threatening environmental hazards in nonwhite communities. Some movement leaders would broaden this definition of environmental racism to include the absence of people of color from the membership rolls and staffs of mainstream environmental groups, decision-making boards, commissions, and regulatory boards.

The Warren County protest attracted national media attention to the environmental concerns of people of color and sparked efforts to examine the extent of hazardous conditions faced by other minority communities. Shortly after the protest, the U.S. General Accounting Office studied the racial and socioeconomic characteristics of four communities in the Southeast in which hazardous-waste disposal sites were located and discovered that the inhabitants of three of the four communities were predominantly African American and poor. In 1987, the United Church of Christ's Commission for Racial Justice published a much larger study, entitled "Toxic Wastes and Race in the United States," which examined the racial and socioeconomic characteristics of waste sites across the nation. The report concluded that race was the most significant variable in the location of commercial waste sites nationwide. Communities in which sites were located also tended to be poorer than surrounding communities in which no site was located. In all, the study found that three of every five African Americans and Hispanics and about half of all Asian/Pacific Islanders and Native Americans lived in communities that contained an uncontrolled toxic-waste site.

A wide range of hazardous activities in both rural and urban settings has been linked to environmental racism. For example, Chicago's South Side, which is predominantly African American and Hispanic, is host to what is probably the greatest concentration of hazardous-waste sites in the United States. In Washington State, the Puyallup Indian Tribe's reservation has served as a dump site for 300 million cubic yards of contaminated sediment containing more than a thousand different chemicals from more than three hundred polluters. The nation's largest hazardous-waste landfill is located in predominantly African American and poor Emelle, Alabama. Hispanic farmworkers in the Southwest face risks from handling dangerous pesticides. Other oft-cited examples are the petrochemical processing facilities along "Cancer Alley" in Louisiana and incinerator facilities in Hispanic neighborhoods in East Los Angeles.

Grassroots Movement. After Warren County, grassroots organizations led by people of color sprang up across the nation to protest environmental hazards they faced in their local communities. To achieve their goals, these groups employ a wide range of nonviolent protest strategies. Tactics can include demonstrations, letter-writing campaigns, lobbying legislators, and sponsoring public hearings and educational sessions, all of which are reminiscent of the confrontational strategies of the CIVIL RIGHTS MOVEMENT of the 1960's. As in the case of Warren County, demonstrators are often willing to risk arrest and jail sentences or the loss of their jobs. Leaders often come from local communities. In many cases, protests are led by women who are concerned about threats to their children's health. Journals and newsletters help to disseminate information and research on environmental justice issues.

The goals and personnel of the environmental justice movement differ from those of mainstream environmentalism. The mainstream environmental movement, which became popular during the 1960's, is represented by such groups as the Wilderness Society, the National Wildlife Federation, and the Sierra Club. These groups have been widely perceived as being led by and promoting the interests of white, middle-class suburbanites, who are mainly concerned about preserving wilderness areas, saving endangered species, and maintaining national forests and parks for recreation. Environmental justice leaders complain that these groups ignore the environmental concerns of people of color, who face health hazards every day in their own communities. Some have accused these organizations of failing to recruit and hire minorities for their administrative and professional staffs, thus excluding minorities from the process of setting agendas and defining issues for the environmental movement as a whole.

In October, 1991, more than six hundred observers, delegates, and representatives from groups throughout

Highland Park, Michigan, residents protest the siting of a hazardous-waste incinerator in their largely African American community. (Impact Visuals, Jim West)

the country came together in Washington, D.C., for the First National People of Color Environmental Leadership Summit. Conference delegates produced a statement that outlined seventeen Principles of Environmental Justice. In addition to calling for the elimination of the wasteful uses of natural resources and the production and disposal of toxic and radioactive substances, the statement demanded that minority groups participate in all levels, local and national, of the environmental decision-making process.

Critics. Criticism of the environmental justice movement has come from federal agencies, the hazardous waste and petrochemical industries, and the scientific community. In general, these groups are skeptical that racism has been a significant factor in the distribution of environmental hazards, even in the siting of waste facilities. A 1992 EPA report, *Environ-*

mental Equity: Reducing Risks for All Communities, acknowledged that minority communities have suffered a greater share of lead poisoning than other communities but emphasized the role of nonbiased, nonpolitical, scientific decisionmaking in authorizing waste facilities. Representatives of the hazardous-waste industry often point out that poor communities in search of a larger tax base and more jobs sometimes offer to host waste-disposal sites as a boost to the local economy. Some scientists have questioned the statistical methods used to show a strong relationship between environmental hazards and race. Other critics point out that poor white communities often face the same risks as poor minority communities.

Environmental justice advocates counter these criticisms by charging that the EPA is biased toward industry and the concerns of the predominantly white environmental groups. The advocates point out that in many cases in which business and political leaders have invited waste facilities to locate in their counties, the communities at risk have risen up in protest. Environmental justice supporters insist that their research methods are valid and that race is consistently shown to be more important than class as an indicator of degree of environmental risk.

Impact. The recognition that environmental racism is a pressing problem in American society has broadened the boundaries of the environmental movement to include the concerns of people of color. Perhaps the most important legacy of the environmental justice movement is that it has educated and empowered minority communities to protect themselves from environmental hazards. In 1992, the environmental racism concept entered the national political arena when Senator Al Gore, Jr., introduced into Congress the Environmental Justice Act. The purpose of this proposed legislation was to ensure that all Americans receive equal protection of health under the law.

—Robert E. McFarland

SUGGESTED READINGS: The philosophy of environmental justice, as well as statistical data on hazardous-waste siting, can be found in the Commission for Racial Justice's *Toxic Wastes and Race in the United States* (New York: Public Data Access, 1987). Robert D. Bullard examines hazardous wastes and minority protests in the Southeast in *Dumping in Dixie: Race, Class, and Environmental Quality* (Boulder, Colo.: Westview Press, 1990). A diverse collection of case studies can be found in *Confronting Environmental Racism: Voices from the Grassroots* (Boston: South End Press, 1993), edited by Robert D. Bullard. General accounts of environmental racism and justice can be found in Robert Gottlieb's *Forcing the Spring: The Transformation of the American Environmental Movement* (Washington, D.C.: Island Press, 1993) and Jim Schwab's *Deeper Shades of Green: The Rise of Blue-Collar and Minority Environmentalism in America* (San Francisco: Sierra Club Books, 1994).

Equal Credit Opportunity Act (1974): U.S. law mandating equal credit opportunity for women. This act made discrimination against women in credit transactions illegal by removing sex as an allowable classification in such transactions. Until 1974, it was legal for banks, stores, and credit companies to discriminate against women in giving credit. Married women were

often unable to get credit or take out loans in their own names but were required to rely on their husbands' credit. Such policies were particularly troublesome for divorcing women, who were often unable to establish credit histories prior to their divorces.

Equal Employment Opportunity Commission (EEOC): Created by Title VII of the CIVIL RIGHTS ACT OF 1964 to eliminate DISCRIMINATION based on race, color, religion, sex, national origin, disability, or age in hiring, promoting, firing, setting wages, testing, apprenticeship, and all other terms and conditions of employment. The commission, which began operations on July 2, 1965, is responsible for the oversight and compliance enforcement of equal-opportunity employment requirements among all federal employees and applicants.

Title VII was later amended by the Equal Employment Opportunity Act of 1972, the PREGNANCY DISCRIMINATION ACT of 1978, and the Civil Rights Act of 1991. In 1978, Executive Order 12067 abolished the Equal Employment Opportunity Coordinating Council and transferred its powers to the commission in an effort to consolidate antidiscrimination efforts. Included in this and subsequent transfers were duties under several acts and executive orders: Section 717 of Title VII of the Civil Rights Act of 1964, which outlaws discrimination in employment in the federal government on the basis of race, color, religion, sex, or national origin; Executive Order 11478, which set policy for AFFIRMATIVE ACTION programs in the federal government; the EQUAL PAY ACT of 1963, applying to the federal government; Section 15 of the AGE DISCRIMINATION IN EMPLOYMENT ACT of 1967 as amended in the federal sector; Section 501 of the REHABILITATION ACT of 1973 prohibiting discrimination against disabled individuals in the federal government; the Equal Pay Act of 1963 and the Age Discrimination Act of 1967, in state and local governments and the private sector; and the AMERICANS WITH DISABILITIES ACT of 1990 prohibiting employment discrimination against qualified disabled individuals and requiring employers to make reasonable accommodations for such individuals.

The commission operates through fifty field offices located throughout the country. Each office serves as a source of information for employers and employees or applicants. In addition, charges of discrimination under one of the commission's enforceable guidelines are filed with these field offices. Specific timelines and procedures vary according to the type of complaint filed. In general, the EEOC office, upon receiving a complaint of discrimination, will first investigate to determine the validity of the complaint. If the field office determines that there is reasonable cause to believe that a charge is valid, the office will first attempt to remedy the situation through informal means. If no acceptable agreement can be reached between the employer and the local or regional office, the case is submitted to the EEOC for further action, including possible litigation in the federal courts.

Other EEOC activities include promoting voluntary compliance with statutes through programs such as the Voluntary Assistance Program, which provides technical assistance and educational programs. The commission also implements the Expanded Presence Program, Educational Technical Assistance and Training Revolving Fund, an annual Federal Dispute Resolution Conference, and acts as a direct liaison between federal, state, and local governments, unions and employers, trade and civil-rights organizations, and other agencies involved in fair-employment opportunities.

Equal Pay Act (1963): U.S. law prohibiting unequal pay for equal work. The Equal Pay Act prohibits employers from paying women less than they pay men when both are performing equal work on an employer's premises, except when the difference in wages is justified by a widely recognized standard such as seniority, merit, or productivity. Although the prohibition is almost universally endorsed as equitable, its effectiveness is debated. Because the law applies only within a particular establishment, it does nothing to equalize wages among firms. That "equal work" is open to broad interpretation is another weakness of the law.

Equal protection: Constitutional guarantee. The Fourteenth Amendment requires all states to provide "equal treatment of the laws" to all citizens. This does not imply that all citizens must be treated exactly alike—certain persons and conduct can be singled out for special treatment—but all people within a classification must be treated the same. Behavior, state of mind, and occupation are categories that can be used for classification. Habitual felons can be treated more severely than first-time offenders; premeditated mur-

der is treated differently from negligent homicide. Classifications based on race or gender are almost always found to be unconstitutional.

Equal Rights Amendment (ERA): Proposed constitutional amendment. The Equal Rights Amendment, approved by Congress in 1972, was subjected to a contentious ratification debate in state legislatures between 1972 and 1982. The proposed amendment would have established grounds for eradicating discrimination in federal, state, or local laws.

History. Following the advent of woman's SUFFRAGE (approved by constitutional amendment in 1920), an Equal Rights Amendment was proposed. The amendment was initially introduced in Congress in 1923 on the urging of Alice Paul, leader of the National Women's Party (NWP), who was a central figure in the campaign for an ERA during its entire history. The original amendment held simply that: "Men and women shall have equal rights throughout the United States and in every place subject to its jurisdiction. Congress shall have the power to enforce this article by appropriate legislation."

While the proposed ERA seemed to stand simply for fairness and equality, controversy shrouded the amendment from its inception. The debate over the strengths and weaknesses of protective legislation split women's groups. Various women's groups were among early opposing forces, including the Women's Bureau of the U.S. government, the LEAGUE OF WOMEN VOTERS, and the Christian Temperance Union. The heart of the controversy concerned whether equality was really in women's best interests.

Progressive and labor organizations, which had fought for legislation favorable to women workers, also saw in the ERA a threat to hard-fought concessions for better working conditions for women, such as maximum-hours legislation, curbs on heavy lifting, required breaks, and limits on evening work.

Laws protecting employees from deplorable working conditions such as long hours, dangerous work environments, and low pay were overturned in the early 1900's by the Supreme Court, which ruled that such laws were contrary to freedom of contract. The Court accepted protection for women employees on the theory that women are more fragile, especially because of their reproductive function. In *Muller v. Oregon* (1908), the Court weighed sociological evidence about harms to women imposed by difficult working condi-

Supporters of the Equal Rights Amendment at the 1980 Democratic National Convention. (UPI/Corbis-Bettmann)

tions, upholding a ten-hour legal limit for women to work.

Alice Paul and the NWP supported equality promised by the Equal Rights Amendment, despite loss of protective legislation. Paul believed that treating women as equals provided greater promise for improving women's economic status than seeking laws protecting women. Protective legislation, while offering special privileges to women, also excluded them from employment opportunities. For their own protection, women were excluded from occupations that required intensive physical labor as well as occupations that posed a threat to women's morals.

At various times before final congressional approval in 1972, the ERA was debated or passed by one of the legislative branches. In the 1950's, the ERA passed the Senate with the stipulation that the amendment would

not be interpreted to reduce the special protections affecting women already in law. The amendment did not pass the House.

A turning point in ERA support occurred when Title VII of the CIVIL RIGHTS ACT OF 1964, which prohibits discrimination on account of sex in employment, was interpreted as invalidating protective legislation. Important projections for women, such as MINIMUM WAGE legislation, had meanwhile been extended to men. Union opposition to the ERA, therefore, also dissipated. By 1970, the United Auto Workers (UAW) pledged support, and other labor groups soon followed suit.

By the mid-1960's, women's groups solidified behind the ERA. In 1967, the NATIONAL ORGANIZATION FOR WOMEN (NOW) endorsed the ERA, citing passage as one of its major objectives. NOW became the primary sponsor of the ERA.

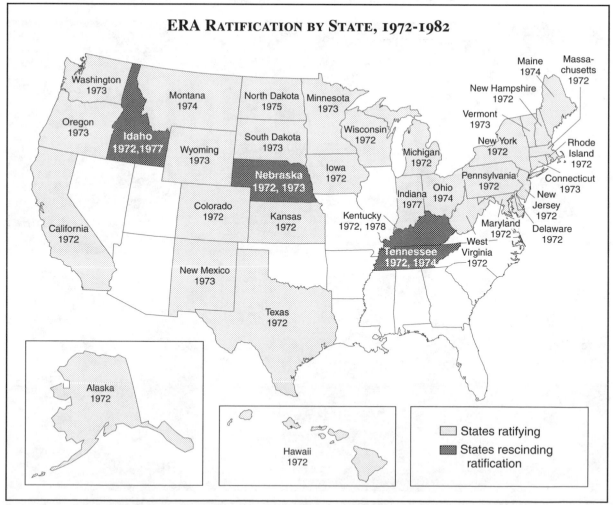

ERA RATIFICATION BY STATE, 1972-1982

Source: Data are from Janet K. Boles, *The Politics of the Equal Rights Amendment.* Pp. 2-3. New York: Longman, 1979.

Equal Rights Amendment

The ERA was easily passed in March, 1972, receiving the two-thirds vote by both houses of Congress required for passage of a constitutional amendment. The proposed amendment read, in principal part: "Equality of rights under the law shall not be denied or abridged by the United States or by any state on account of sex."

The next step to amending the Constitution was approval of the ERA by three-fourths of the state legislatures (thirty-eight of fifty needed). Almost immediately after the congressional vote, several state legislatures approved the ERA, many unanimously and without contentious hearings.

By 1977, thirty-five of the required thirty-eight states had ratified the amendment. Congress agreed to extend the original deadline for ratification from 1979 to 1982. During this time, no additional states ratified the amendment. Thus, in 1982, the amendment died despite considerable support for the principle of equality on which the amendment was based.

Perceived Need for the ERA. Supporters of the ERA were energized by the rights revolution precipitated by the Civil Rights movement, which raised expectations for fair, equal treatment. ERA supporters saw as outmoded and discriminatory sex-based distinctions that served to restrict women in a number of areas, such as education, family law, and the military.

One of the major hopes of ERA supporters was that the U.S. SUPREME COURT would reinterpret the Fourteenth Amendment's equal-protection clause (applying to state law) and the Fifth Amendment (applying to federal law) to render laws that make distinctions based upon sex "suspect." Placing sex distinctions into the "suspect" category, with race or national origin, would mean that laws that treat men and women differently would almost certainly be struck down.

First Lady Rosalyn Carter and former first lady Betty Ford lead a 1977 rally in support of the Equal Rights Amendment.
(UPI/Corbis-Bettmann)

Opponents of the Equal Rights Amendment demonstrate outside the White House. (Library of Congress)

Phyllis Schlafly leads a 1978 rally against ratification of the Equal Rights Amendment. (UPI/Corbis-Bettmann)

In a number of decisions, the Court struck down laws that made distinctions between men and women, such as laws that favored men as executors of estates, automatically granted dependent benefits to wives of military personnel but not to husbands, exempted women from jury duty because of their domestic role, and treated men and women differently with regard to alimony, marital property rights, and dependents' Social Security benefits.

The Court, however, had not consistently adopted the "strict scrutiny" classification standard, which would create the strongest assumption that laws distinguishing between males and females are inherently "suspect." Proponents of the Equal Rights Amendment touted it as a clear signal to the Supreme Court that sex classifications should be placed in the "suspect" category.

Why the ERA Failed. During the period of the ratification campaign between 1972 and 1982, polls showed support by a majority of U.S. citizens for the ERA. However, general public support was not a sufficient basis for approval.

First, constitutional amendments require extraordinary consensus. Not only must two-thirds of Congress assent, support by three-fourths of state legislatures is required. Campaigns must be waged not only on a national level but on a state-by-state basis. Lack of action by only thirteen state legislatures results in an amendment's defeat. Various patterns of opposition, for example, by states within a given region, may doom an amendment. In the case of the ERA, Southern states were among those that failed to provide support.

Second, while most people theoretically favored equal rights for women, opponents of the ERA raised doubts about the specific impact of the ERA. For example, opponents feared that the ERA would extend the military draft to women. Supporters of equality for women responded that if a draft were necessary, women should be subjected to it. Other opponents raised a variety of threatening scenarios such as prospects of unisex bathrooms (an unlikely result), extension of ABORTION rights, loss of protections for homemakers, and legalization of homosexual marriages.

The ERA prompted debate about the changing role of women. Opponents viewed ERA's staunchest supporters as advocates of substantial changes in sex roles and, especially, believed that supporters disparaged women's traditional roles as wife, mother, and homemaker. Opponents feared the impact of the ERA on "FAMILY VALUES" and further changes in the structure and functioning of the traditional family.

The ERA was also controversial because it would be left to the Supreme Court for interpretation. The Supreme Court had promulgated a number of controversial decisions in the 1960's and 1970's in cases involving abortion, civil rights, reapportionment, and school prayer. Conservative state legislators and others thus viewed with fear the prospect of vesting authority in the Supreme Court to interpret the ERA.

Impact. Through the mid-1990's, the possible impact of the ERA remained uncertain, since interpretation would have rested largely with the Supreme Court and, to a lesser extent, with other governmental institutions. One probable impact, supporters claimed, would have been to guide the Court to use the strongest possible standard in erasing inequality in law between men and women.

Yet debate about the meaning of legal equality between men and women continues. Some feminists argue that true equality between men and women would take into account some of the differences between men and women based upon socialization, biology (pregnancy), and past discrimination. This was necessary, they argued, to secure fair and comparable treatment. For example, *Personnel Administration of Massachusetts v. Feeney* (1979) upheld veterans' preference law in public-sector employment. Some feminists would view the outcomes as unfair because they had an adverse impact on women, who were less likely to have military experience and who faced exclusions in combat duty (combat service increased the preference given to veterans).

Many scholars believe that the ERA would not have had a major effect on the position of women in society. Perhaps the most compelling result of the ERA was that it would have embodied in the U.S. CONSTITUTION, a revered document expressing the nation's strongest values, the position that women have equal status in law.

—*Mary Hendrickson*

SUGGESTED READINGS: In Mary Frances Berry's *Why ERA Failed: Politics, Women's Rights, and the Amending Process of the Constitution* (Bloomington: Indiana University Press, 1986), the author examines the impact of the constitutional amendment process itself on the ERA's failure through comparison with other controversial amendments. *Rights of Passage: The Past and Future of the ERA* (Bloomington: Indiana University Press, 1986), edited by Joan Hoff-Wilson, discusses the origins and history of the ERA, the reasons for its defeat, and the significance of the defeat. In Jane J. Mansbridge's *Why We Lost the ERA* (Chicago:

University of Chicago Press, 1986), political and sociological theory is used to explain the ERA's defeat.

Equal time requirement: U.S. law codified in Section 315 of the Federal Communications Act. When broadcasters allow a candidate for office to broadcast campaign material, all other legally qualified candidates for that same office must be given the same opportunity. Broadcast time must be made available at the same rate and approximate time. Broadcasters are allowed to cover candidates as part of their news coverage without the rule applying; candidate press conferences and debates between candidates are also considered news events and are exempt. News interviews with candidates and documentaries in which a candidate's appearance is incidental to the subject of the documentary are also exempt.

Ergonomics: Science of finding the safest and most efficient way to perform a task. Ergonomics involves both the design of equipment and the education of the equipment operators. Ergonomics, also referred to as "human-factors engineering," by the 1990's had evolved into a wide-ranging interdisciplinary field, drawing upon knowledge developed by industrial engineers, psychologists, and physiologists.

The term "ergonomics" first gained wide usage during the 1970's, when the rise of the electronic office led to an increased general awareness of the connection between workplace design and occupational health. Growing numbers of data-entry operators complaining of CARPAL TUNNEL SYNDROME, eyestrain, and headaches drew the attention of researchers and regulatory agencies alike. In the United States, both the National Institute for Occupational Safety and Health (NIOSH) and the OFFICE OF TECHNOLOGY ASSESSMENT (OTA) conducted research into the problems associated with the use of COMPUTERS. To many observers in industry, the NIOSH and OTA recommendations regarding ergonomics appeared as references to totally new ideas. In fact, human-factors engineers, industrial hygienists, and industrial psychologists had been applying ergonomic principles in the workplace since the nineteenth century.

Credit for the first well-documented effort to design a work setting to achieve maximum efficiency must go to a mechanical engineer, Frederick Winslow Taylor. In the 1880's, Taylor analyzed specific tasks to determine both the best tools and what appeared to be the best methods of applying them. Industrial engineers later used many of Taylor's principles to develop factory assembly lines. Unfortunately, it was not until the mid-twentieth century that industrial hygienists recognized that some forms of efficiency carried hidden risks for the workers. In addition, development of new mechanized equipment often was accompanied or followed by the occurrence of new work-related injuries. For example, performing the same motion over and over while operating a machine could lead to problems with repetitive stress disorders.

By the 1960's, interest in occupational health issues had generated enough concern to lead to the creation of the Occupational Safety and Health Administration (OSHA) within the federal government. At the same time, advances in technology in a variety of industries led to a growing interest in human-factors engineering. Reliance on electronic control systems in aviation, electrical power plants, and other complex technologies meant that systems had to be designed that took into account human frailties—shortcomings or weaknesses in human physiology and psychology. By the 1990's, human-factors engineers and industrial hygienists were working together to design work settings and equipment that allowed workers to achieve maximum production at a minimum of risk to themselves and others.

As the notion of applying ergonomic principles gained wider acceptance in society, many common products ranging from stoves to computer keyboards were redesigned to make them safer and more efficient to use. Ergonomics, however, requires more than simply redesigning a work setting or a tool. For ergonomics to be truly effective, the users of a technology must also be educated in the proper operation or use of the work environment.

Esalen Institute: Alternative "NEW AGE" educational institution founded in 1962. Located in the Big Sur area south of Carmel, Calif., Esalen offers a range of experiential seminars and conferences promoting human potentials and values. Workshop leaders are frequently authors of books or originators of therapeutic ideas focusing on science and spirituality. Seminar topics explore YOGA, art, dance, body therapies, dreams, meditation, wilderness exploration, ecological awareness, and sensitivity. The campus overlooks the Pacific Ocean and features natural hot springs and a mainly vegetarian diet.